Michael Hu...

CHRISTIAN UNITY

An Ecumenical Second Spring?

VERITAS

First published 1998 by
Veritas Publications
7/8 Lower Abbey Street
Dublin 1

Copyright © Michael Hurley SJ 1998

ISBN 1 85390 354 X

British Library Cataloguing
in Publication Data.
A catalogue record for
this book is available
from the British Library.

The cover illustration is a detail from a woodcut by Hokusai entitled *The Hollow of the Deep Sea Wave off the Coast of Kanagawa*. This most famous of all Japanese prints conveys a strong sense of the unity of things, with the boats curving into the shape of the waves. The sailors' vulnerability is highlighted by the Shinto shrine in the stern of the boat to the right of the picture. Reproduced by kind permission of the V & A Picture Library, London.

Cover design by Bill Bolger
Printed in the Republic of Ireland by Betaprint Ltd, Dublin

Contents

Prefaces from Church Leaders

1. Seán Brady, *Archbishop of Armagh, Primate of All Ireland* ... ix
2. Robin Eames, *Archbishop of Armagh, Primate of All Ireland* ... xi
4. Samuel Hutchinson, *Moderator, Presbyterian Church in Ireland, 1997/8* ... xiii
3. Norman W. Taggart, *President, Methodist Church in Ireland, 1997/8* ... xv

Introduction ... 1

Part I Ecumenical Vision

1. Hoping against Hope ... 15
2. Christian Unity by 2000? ... 21
3. Reconciliation and Forgiveness ... 54
4. Ecumenical Tithing ... 78
5. George Otto Simms: Ecumenical Exemplar (1910-1991) ... 89

Part II Ecumenical Issues

6. Ecumenism, Ecumenical Theology and Ecumenics ... 103
7. Baptism in Ecumenical Perspective ... 115
8. Eucharist: Means and Expression of Unity ... 132
9. Catholicity: The Witness of Calvin's *Institutes* ... 146
10. Wesley Today and Evangelisation Today ... 169
11. The Church of Ireland: Challenges for the Future ... 182
12. Jesuits and Protestants Today ... 197
13. Reconciliation and The Churches in Northern Ireland ... 220

Part III Ecumenical Initiatives

14.	An Ecumenical Lecture Series: Milltown Park Public Lectures 1960-1969	239
15.	An Ecumenical Publication: *Irish Anglicanism 1869-1969*	250
16.	An Ecumenical Institute: The Origins of The Irish School of Ecumenics	265
17.	An Ecumenical Sabbatical: Mount Athos and China	292
18.	An Ecumenical Community: The Origins of The Columbanus Community of Reconciliation	317

Appendix:
  Milltown Park Public Lectures 1960-1969
  Topics, speakers and dates   341

Notes   348

Index   396

*To the Jesuit Community at Milltown Park
in gratitude for forty years of membership*

(1958-1998)

Prefaces from Church Leaders

1

Seán Brady
Archbishop of Armagh and Primate of All Ireland

The name of Father Michael Hurley will always be associated principally with the Irish School of Ecumenics, which he founded in 1970, and with the Columbanus Community of Reconciliation, which he founded in 1983. With extraordinary energy and enthusiasm he has dedicated most of his life to the planning, promotion, administration and fund-raising involved in both of these ventures. Yet he has somehow succeeded in keeping abreast of ecumenical scholarship and in fulfilling a formidable schedule of speaking and writing engagements, usually connected with big ecumenical occasions, for which his services were in constant demand.

Now busier than ever in retirement, he has put together a miscellany of those lectures and articles to form the chapters of this book. Updating and editing his material but, at the same time, retaining each chapter's original context, he succeeds in painting interesting developmental pictures of a number of themes, while giving, at the same time, a number of insights into his own psyche, as an ecumenist – a practical demonstration, incidentally, of one of his own theses, namely that ecumenism, as a science, should concentrate on describing what makes an ecumenist tick.

Father Hurley captures very powerfully the heady enthusiasm of the early days of ecumenism. To steer the ecumenical vessel between the rocks of complacency and frustration is not an easy one but in this work he has succeeded in doing so.

While giving understanding to those who feel that all ecumenical movement forward has ceased, he remains realistic in his expectations at international, national and domestic level.

Whereas the pessimism of those who had hoped for a more immediate and visible ecumenical success may be the mood of those who watched the seed sprout and fade on the stony ground, Michael is prepared to continue to try to prepare fertile soil.

At the same time he rightly sees no room for complacency. Even if we cannot dictate to the Spirit at what speed the vessel of ecumenism should move we certainly should all remain open to being moved.

Those of us who recall his early work *Praying for Unity* can only marvel at Michael Hurley's continued commitment to the ecumenical cause through times when it was internationally fashionable – and through times when it was in danger domestically of being suffocated by the weeds and thorns of bitterness and sectarianism.

We all know spiritually that our own individual journeys to Christ are not always smooth and traversed at even speed. If individuals find their closeness to God is a fitful one then we should not be surprised that our communal journeys suffer from the same difficulties.

Prophets of gloom remind us of limitations. Benign figures remind us of the possibilities that are allowed. True ecumenical figures keep before us insistently that these are not just allowed but required. To keep us aware of this requirement has been the life's work of Michael Hurley both in his academic research, in his spirituality and in his lifestyle. For this and for the sheer wealth of factual detail that this book contains many will be indebted to him.

2

Robin Eames
Archbishop of Armagh and Primate of All Ireland

Father Michael Hurley has made a unique contribution on a personal level to the ecumenical scene in Ireland. For years, when the major denominations were struggling to come to terms with the challenge of 'better understanding' and we were all passing through what many term 'the tea-cup ecumenism' era, he laboured with immense faith and courage to prompt responses which today are taken for granted. His vision and personal integrity compelled us all to ask questions of ourselves and of each other.

Today Irish ecumenism faces a period of reassessment as we approach the millennium. On the world scene there is a loss of momentum and particular problems between individual Churches have become restraints to genuine progress. In Ireland the problems of relationships between communities, years of distrust because of community tensions, and over a quarter of a century of violence which has highlighted the religious-political divisions, have resulted in ecumenism becoming for some a matter of grave suspicion. Yet, behind the smokescreen of all Ireland's divisions and suffering, understanding between the denominations has not always presented a totally negative picture. On a personal level friendships and reconciliation have flourished. The identity of the four Church leaders has its own symbolism. But reality compels us to understand and accept that the vision needs a new impetus. Sectarianism is the real cancer of our society. It continues to infect the attitude of Christians to each other. We need a new confidence in ourselves and in each other.

The publication of this book is timely. Do we see the first faltering signs of a new era of realism in Ireland, north and south? Do we see the first indications that the Churches are taking more seriously their corporate and individual responsibilities for the misunderstandings and divisions of the past? Do we see evidence that the 'doing' of practical ecumenism can lead to a new appraisal of the theories?

I commend Michael Hurley's book as one more contribution to our debate by a writer who was and is never afraid to face the hard questions – and suggest the Christ-like answers.

3

Samuel Hutchinson
Moderator, Presbyterian Church in Ireland 1997/8

Few in Ireland are better known in inter-Church relations circles or better qualified to write about the subject than Father Michael Hurley, who has long been working in this area, both as a scholarly writer and as an active participant in ecumenical bodies, as well as being the founder of the Irish School of Ecumenics and the Columbanus Community of Reconciliation. His publications and his practical experience combine to make him an eminent authority on this topic.

It is, however, particularly fitting that this latest publication should appear just now, near the end of the twentieth century. Some inter-Church contact and discussion did take place in earlier times, but it has been this century that has witnessed most activity. Countless councils of Churches and other ecumenical bodies have been set up at both national and international level, which have generally proved to be effective instruments for consultation and co-operation.

In more recent times there have been numerous theological conversations between different traditions, which in some instances have resulted in formal Agreements, such as the Leuenberg Agreement between the Lutheran and Reformed communions, and some Church unions in, for example, India and Australia. There have also been joint ventures on practical matters, such as Christian Aid or Youthlink.

Even more significant, however, is the fact that there has been a steady thaw in relationships. One hope expressed at the Second European Ecumenical Assembly at Graz in June 1997 was that relationships would continue to improve. We now realise that, whatever diversity there may be among Christians, anything other than a charitable approach is inappropriate.

All these developments have in turn produced a prodigious number of publications, so at the end of this significant century in Church history it is time to pause and take stock, and that Father Michael Hurley has now done. This is not just one more book on ecumenism but a wide-ranging and authoritative survey, looking not just to the past but to the future. Few would care to predict what the map of world Christianity will be like in the next century, but it is probable that it will be very different from this century.

In an introduction to *Praying for Unity* (ed. Michael Hurley, Dublin, Gill & Son, 1963) a previous Moderator, Dr W. A. Montgomery, wrote, 'We are growing increasingly tolerant towards others who differ from us, giving them credit for a sincerity at least equal to our own.... The state of the world calls for the fullest measure of Christian co-operation'. Those words are, if anything, even more true now than they were then. I reiterate them and wish this volume every success.

4

Norman W. Taggart
President, Methodist Church in Ireland, 1997/8

Your old men will dream dreams, your young men will see visions.

(Joel 2: 28)

Michael Hurley, it seems, has been seeing ecumenical visions and dreaming ecumenical dreams for a lifetime. By personal example, through conversation and in his writings, he has sought to share his visions with successive generations. It is a tribute to his persuasiveness and persistence that at least some of these visions have taken root. The Irish School of Ecumenics, based in Dublin, and the Columbanus Community of Reconciliation in Belfast, which features in these pages, are but two examples.

One consistent feature in Michael's approach to Christian traditions other than his own is his appreciation of wholesome elements in their distinctive emphases and the recognition that what the Churches hold in common is greater than what divides them. This was evident in one of our first public ventures together, when we shared with others in a radio broadcast to mark the two-hundredth anniversary in 1969 of the first Methodist conference in Ireland. On that occasion he spoke appreciatively of Methodism as 'a gift of God to the whole Church', and drew attention to its emphasis on personal renewal, outgoing love and social witness.

With a lifelong commitment to inter-Church co-operation in both parts of Ireland, his familiarity with ecumenical literature and trends, and his first-hand knowledge of many leading personalities within the world Church, Michael is especially well-placed to assess the ecumenical scene, particularly as it affects the mainline Churches. That he remains so deeply committed in this field, despite many disappointments and frustrations, is testimony to an abiding conviction that to work and pray for a more united Church, a more just society and a more peaceful world is to seek God's will and to bring him glory.

I conclude with words I wrote about Christian unity in one of a series of *Irish Ecumenical Pamphlets*, published by the Irish Council of Churches thirty years ago. Disunity among Christians distorts truth, wastes resources, hinders witness, impoverishes worship and discredits the gospel. 'The search for visible forms of unity', I claimed, 'is not a distraction from the task of proclaiming the gospel.... It is an essential part of our response to the gospel and unless we find ways of expressing our unity in Christ, we shall remain what we must now appear in the eyes of the world – insincere preachers proclaiming a gospel that does not work'. As this century draws to a close and a new millennium beckons, Michael Hurley's book reminds us of past achievements and points to present and future challenges in the quest for visible forms of unity, 'that the world may believe'.

Introduction

It was the millennium now coming to an end, the second Christian millennium, which saw disunity within the Christian family harden and set, take the form and shape of separate Churches and become a grave scandal. In the beginning of this millennium the Great Schism divided the West from the East; later, within the West, the Reformation divided Catholics from Protestants. Happily, the last century of the millennium has seen determined efforts by the Christian family to undo its scandalous divisions. But despite some remarkable success these ecumenical efforts have not only failed to achieve their goal but the whole movement has, it would seem, failed to maintain its momentum. It has lost its drive, its nerve, its sense of direction. It is now like a ship becalmed needing the mighty wind of the Spirit to get under way again.

Ecumenists have always been impatient and have regularly given expression to feelings of disappointment and frustration at the slow pace of the movement. In November of 1964 Catholics were rejoicing at the promulgation of the Decree on Ecumenism by Vatican II, but that August at a meeting at Aarhus in Denmark representatives of the World Council of Churches, established some twenty years previously in 1948, had been complaining that:

> We cannot go on for decades talking of meeting, dialogue, conversation and better understanding. Unless concrete results follow, joy in the ecumenical movement must turn to disappointment.[1]

Twenty years later in 1982 Cardinal Willebrands, President of what was then the Secretariat – but is now the Pontifical Council

– for Promoting Christian Unity, was urging that the time had come 'to pass from a time of research to a time of decision'; warning that otherwise 'there is a risk of going round in circles, of reducing the dynamism of the ecumenical movement and rendering it sterile'.[2] He seems to have been referring to the 1981 *Final Report* of the Anglican/Roman Catholic International Commission and the need to avoid any unnecessary delays in responding to it, but sadly the 'time of decision' was delayed for ten years; he himself had already retired and been succeeded by Cardinal Cassidy when the Vatican's Response eventually came in December 1991.

The crisis of ecumenism

As we now approach the end of the century and the end of the millennium negative feelings about the ecumenical movement not only continue but seem stronger and sharper and more general than ever. The movement is felt not only to have lost momentum but, in the words of an American commentator, 'there is serious concern whether it can recover its momentum'.[3] And in December 1996 a French theological periodical carried an article entitled 'L'Impossible Oecuménisme', which opened with the provocative statement:

> Dans le domaine religieux, un fait semble aujourd'hui acquis: l'oecuménisme aura été la grande illusion de ce siècle.[4]

More restrained language is more credible and convincing. The World Council of Churches (WCC) is probably the greatest achievement to date of the ecumenical movement but as it approaches its Golden Jubilee in 1998, one of its leading officials has acknowledged that

> [T]here has been a perceptible reduction of ecumenical *élan,* certainly at the international level. What was once

hailed as the 'great new fact' of twentieth-century Church history seems to excite fewer and fewer people. At best, ecumenism is taken for granted. This is true not only of the typical 'person-in-the-pew'; it is apparent in most churches that a whole generation of leadership has been formed with little awareness of what the ecumenical movement has accomplished and what remains to be done. While this may have the wholesome consequence of laying to rest certain fruitless old polemics, it does mean that the usefulness of the WCC and organisations like it needs to be re-argued in a convincing fashion.[5]

What is stated here in measured terms is unfortunately true at all levels and not only at the international. Even at this international level there is the ominous fact, noted by the same official, that soon the WCC may include only a minority of the world's non-Roman Catholic Christians: the majority will belong to Churches not wishing to be involved in ecumenism or in the WCC.[6]

And within the WCC itself the Orthodox, never entirely comfortable, have in recent years become much more uneasy and dissatisfied. In the words of a Bulgarian Orthodox theologian, formerly a staff member of the WCC:

> While still enduring the consequences of the decades of restriction and repression under atheistic regimes, the Orthodox and some other churches in Eastern Europe have been choked by a massive influx of sects and new religious movements. In this they have not felt a strongly and unanimously expressed solidarity on the part of the world ecumenical family. Nor have they heard unequivocal statements delimiting historical Protestant churches from sects. This combination of lack of knowledge and discernment on one side and the slowness of a concerted ecumenical approach on the other has opened the way to

additional confusion and a growing anti-ecumenical mood, worsened by deteriorating relations between Orthodox and Catholic churches, erroneously interpreted initiatives for large-scale evangelization and 're-evangelization', and inadequate preparation of the local Orthodox churches for renewal, religious education and dialogue with new religious movements.[7]

Though mild in its whole tenor this statement speaks openly of 'a growing anti-ecumenical mood'. In fact relations between the Roman Catholic Church and the Orthodox have, as the author acknowledges, greatly disimproved. And within the WCC the Orthodox, seeing themselves as 'a losing numerical minority' 'in the dialogue with arrogant and paternalistic partners', have become more insistent than ever in their demand to be treated 'as a real partner' and 'not to be pressured into any minimalistic conceptions of Christian unity'. They have not hesitated to state that unless this happens, 'unless this flexible method is put into practice, ecumenism in the twenty-first century will continue without the Orthodox'.[8]

The winter of ecumenism
There is certainly a difference of degree between the present crisis in the ecumenical movement and previous ones, so much so that it is tempting to suggest that the difference is one of kind rather than merely of degree. But the fact that the present crisis for all its gravity is commonly referred to as a 'winter' helps to keep this temptation at bay.[9] With its connotation of a spring to come and perhaps not too 'far behind', the image of winter guards against pessimism, allowing hope if not optimism to grow and develop.[10]

And there are grounds for hope. For its part the WCC is engaged on a radical, ambitious process of study and consultation

'Towards a Common Understanding and Vision of the WCC'. It plans to have the process completed for its Jubilee Assembly in 1998. This, it is hoped, will be 'an occasion not only for reassessment and recommitment, but also for lifting the ecumenical movement to a qualitatively new level, looking forward to the twenty-first century'.[11] The preparations for the WCC Assembly are big with promise; the reception and implementation of its results will certainly help to ensure that the new millennium will indeed bring an ecumenical second spring.

This very image of spring was used by Pope John Paul II on 8 September 1993 when addressing a mixed congregation of Catholics, Orthodox and Protestants in the Lutheran Cathedral in Riga: 'On the threshold of the third millennium of the Christian era, let us thank God for the new ecumenical springtime which engages all of us'. Since the very beginning of his pontificate the present Pope has put a particular emphasis on 'Unity by 2000'. It received special mention in 1994 in his apostolic letter on Preparation for the Jubilee of the Year 2000. The following year it was the subject of an encyclical letter, *Ut unum sint* and of an apostolic letter, *Orientale lumen*. The former, 'On Commitment to Ecumenism', considered relations between Rome and the other Churches in general and aroused a special interest because of its invitation to the other Churches 'to engage with me in a patient and fraternal dialogue on this subject [of papal primacy]'.[12] The latter was an appeal for closer relations between Rome and the Churches of the East in particular. The prospects, however, for improving relations between Rome and the Churches of the West may at present be better. 1998 brings with it the encouraging prospect of another Lambeth Conference when 'Christian Unity will be one of the most important themes that we shall explore',[13] and also of the acceptance by the Lutheran World Federation of a Consensus Statement on the Doctrine of Justification.[14]

A second spring of ecumenism?

This collection of essays appears as the second millennium draws to a close. Its aim is to make some modest contribution towards ensuring that the third millennium does in fact bring an ecumenical second spring, does inaugurate a new age of ecumenical zeal when the Churches will at last respond positively to the appeal made by the WCC three decades ago at Uppsala in 1968 and to be renewed at the 1998 Assembly that 'the ecumenical movement must become bolder, more representative and more binding upon the life of the churches'.

The central section of this book, 'Ecumenical Issues', is preceded by a section entitled 'Ecumenical Vision' and followed by one entitled 'Ecumenical Initiatives'. This order is intended to suggest that the present stalemate may be due in large part to lack of vision and lack of initiative; that a 're-visioning' and a re-vitalising programme is called for: that more vision and more initiative would bring the Churches more clarity and conviction in addressing the issues.

The vision adumbrated here in the chapters of the opening section is not, however, that of a united Church. This, however loosely envisaged, is as yet too remote, too far-fetched, too hypothetical, too improbable a prospect to liberate our energies and move us to take difficult, painful decisions and initiatives. The fact is that we do not as yet know – indeed we cannot know as yet – what we shall be, what we might be as a united Church in full and perfect communion with each other; and this ignorance only feeds our fears, immobilising us rather than encouraging us along the road. What we can know here and now and what deserves more exploration than it currently receives is what our present state of imperfect communion involves and permits and entails. The vision needed at present and developed in the opening chapters is that of 'uniting Churches', of Churches still separated but in process of uniting on the basis of our existing unity and 'feeling our way'[15] towards a more co-operative relationship with other religions.

A vision of ourselves as 'Churches in process of uniting' will see us as committed not so much to arriving at some unknown journey's end but to trudging together along the well-known pilgrim Christian way, not acting *as if* we were already one,[16] but accepting in deed and word the reality of the *status quo*, the existing separation, both its limitations and the ecumenical possibilities it allows and indeed requires. This vision will commit us more to 'the promotion of Christian unity', as the title of the Vatican 'dicastery' or agency for ecumenism puts it, than to the establishment of Church union. It will encourage and enable us to be, individually and corporately, people of hope, forgiveness and obedience, primarily in relation to other Churches but also in relation to other religions.

Churches committed to the promotion of Christian unity, Churches in process of uniting cannot be optimistic, carried along by success, 'hoping with hope',[17] as it were. Their experience will be characterised rather by much disappointment and failure; they will not, however, lose hope on that account but go on 'hoping against hope'. Newman's words when he delivered his famous sermon on 'The Second Spring' at the first synod of the new English Catholic hierarchy at Oscott on 13 July 1852 may be only too relevant. The second spring of the ecumenical movement may, like the second spring of the Catholic Church in England,

> turn out to be an English spring, an uncertain, anxious time of hope and fear, of joy and suffering, – of bright promise and budding hopes, yet withal, of keen blasts, and cold showers, and sudden storms.[18]

Because of our sad history the promotion of Christian unity cannot but include the promotion of mutual forgiveness culminating at times in acts and gestures of reconciliation. So Pope John Paul has emphasised in his Jubilee Letter. And because of the obedience which is part of our Christian faith the process must also include 'joint action'. Hope, forgiveness and obedience are the main characteristics of the ecumenical vision adumbrated in the opening section of this book.

Joint action
In all probability the space of time between partial and full communion must have something of the awkward, hobbledehoy, experimental character of adolescence, but the insights of the *Lund 1952 Faith and Order Report* surely provide a guiding light of immense significance and importance.

> We have now reached a crucial point in our ecumenical discussions…. The measure of unity which it has been given to the Churches to experience together must now find clearer manifestation. A faith in the one Church of Christ which is not implemented by *acts* of obedience is dead. There are truths about the nature of God and His Church which will remain for ever closed to us unless we act together in obedience to the unity which is already ours. We would, therefore, earnestly request our Churches to consider whether they are doing all they ought to do to manifest the oneness of the people of God. Should not our Churches ask themselves whether they… should not act together in all matters except those in which deep differences of conviction compel them to act separately?[19]

In its Decree on Ecumenism Vatican II not only endorsed this Lund principle but also indicated its wider relevance: it was to be applied not only in inter-Church but also in inter-faith relations; co-operation, at least as far as social matters were concerned, was desirable not only among all Christians but also among all who believe in God.[20] Appropriately, therefore, one of the events mooted for the celebration of the new millennium is a meeting on Mount Sinai of Christians, Jews and Muslims.[21]

Introduction

It is precisely obedience to the Lund principle of joint action according to conscience which will gradually lead the Churches to mutual understanding about ecumenical issues, to that clarity and conviction which continue to elude us. In 1981, some thirty years after Lund, the final resounding sentence of *The Final Report* of the Anglican/Roman Catholic International Commission read hopefully as follows:

> There are high expectations that significant initiatives will be boldly undertaken to deepen our reconciliation and lead us forward in the quest for the full communion to which we have been committed, in obedience to God, from the beginning of our dialogue.

A member of the Commission, Father Yarnold, has referred to these words as 'almost unbearably poignant' and revealed that they came from the able pen of Canon Bill Purdy, faithful co-secretary of the Anglican/Roman Catholic as well as the Methodist/Roman Catholic International Commission.[22] They are certainly words which put us all to shame. Joint action according to conscience, doing everything together unless deep differences of conviction compel us to act separately is, in principle, the essential mark of the uniting Churches, which our commitment to the ecumenical movement makes us, but it is far from being so in practice. Our vision is in a sense too grand: too focused on the distant scene, the great united Church of the future, leaving us no eyes to see and appreciate the profound, ultimate significance of simple steps in the here-and-now, the little simple acts of co-operation suggested here in the chapters on 'Ecumenical Tithing' and on 'Wesley Today and Evangelisation Today'.

The issues addressed in the central section of this book and the initiatives described in the concluding section form part of the writer's own ecumenical ministry. This autobiographical note may surprise some readers but the place of experience and of story-telling in theological and ecumenical discourse seems well enough established now to justify the inclusion of these matters as of more general interest in the field of inter-Church relations. What may cause readers somewhat more surprise is the fact that a greater emphasis is not given here to inter-religious dialogue, to the 'wider ecumenism' which is so emphasised in the Irish School of Ecumenics that it forms one of its three areas of study. Conventionally, however, it is agreed that ecumenism concerns itself mainly with inter-Church relations, with Christian unity.[23] And the celebration of the new millennium, especially as proposed and planned by Pope John Paul and the other leaders of the world Church, is essentially the celebration of the two-thousandth anniversary of the birth of Christ and therefore an 'acceptable time' for the promotion of Christian renewal and Christian unity.

It remains to express my thanks and in the first place to the Most Reverend Dr Seán Brady, Archbishop of Armagh, and the Most Reverend Dr Robin Eames, Archbishop of Armagh; also to the Very Reverend Dr Samuel Hutchinson and the Reverend Dr Norman Taggart who, though out of office at the time of publication, were respectively Moderator of the General Assembly of the Presbyterian Church in Ireland and President of the Methodist Church in Ireland when this book was in preparation; I am deeply grateful for the generous tributes which these Church leaders have contributed as Prefaces to this collection. My warmest thanks are owing as well to the staffs of the Irish School of Ecumenics Library, the Milltown Park Jesuit Library and the Representative Church Body Library of the Church of Ireland for their unfailing courtesy; to the Church of Ireland Priorities Fund, the Irish Jesuit Province and the Presbyterian Association for their encouragement in together providing a substantial grant-in-aid towards publication, and to the Columbanus Community of Reconciliation in Belfast for their kindness in applying on my behalf for this grant to the Church of Ireland Priorities Fund. Larry Allen of the Irish Messenger Office, Dublin, provided help with scanning; Maura Lynch, Honorah Phillips and Ann Lane of

Introduction

the Milltown Park reception office staff helped with word-processing, the Reverend Fergal Brennan SJ with computer problems and the Reverend Bill Callanan SJ kindly suggested Hokusai's woodcut as the cover illustration; I am most grateful to them for being so obliging. The Reverend Dr Dennis Cooke (Principal, Edgehill Theological College, Belfast), the Reverend Finbarr Clancy SJ (Milltown Institute), the Reverend William Kelly SJ (Milltown Institute), the Reverend Dr William Marshall (Vice-Principal, Church of Ireland Theological College), the Very Reverend Dr John Thompson (Professor Emeritus, Union Theological College, Belfast) and the Reverend Canon Edgar Turner (Registrar, Diocese of Connor) read parts of the manuscript and the Reverend Edward FitzGerald SJ (Milltown Park) read the whole of it; to all of them I am greatly indebted for their valuable comments. The publishers of the collections and the editors of the periodicals in which earlier versions of the text appeared have kindly given the required permissions: to them and to the staff of Veritas Publications, especially Fiona Biggs, for seeing the collection through press so expertly I express my deep appreciation and sincere thanks.

As it happens 1998 is the fortieth anniversary of my assignment to the Milltown Park Jesuit Community. It was in the summer of 1958 that I came here to teach systematic theology to the Jesuit and Carmelite (OCarm) ordinands in what was then the Milltown Park Jesuit Theological Faculty. Much has changed since then – the Milltown Institute and the Irish School of Ecumenics and the Columbanus Community of Reconciliation have come into existence – but in all these changes I have happily continued to remain a member of the Community here, to have my home here. To mark this auspicious occasion of my fortieth year as a member I gladly and gratefully dedicate this volume to the Jesuit Community at Milltown Park.

Part I
Ecumenical Vision

1

Hoping Against Hope*

'We had hoped'
In St Luke's splendid story of the journey from Jerusalem to Emmaus which the two disciples Cleopas and his friend made on the evening of the first Easter Sunday (Lk 24:13-35), the immortal words 'we had hoped' rarely fail to strike a chord in our hearts.

Too many of us today feel similarly disappointed, dejected and depressed. We all have our own stories of disappointed hopes: we had hoped for a more united Church, a more peaceful world, a more just society, but in vain. We had hoped that by now the spirit of the Second Vatican Council would have come to permeate all our people. We had hoped that the Council's insights on Religious Freedom and on Christian Unity – so critical for the work of reconciliation – would by now have won general acceptance. We had hoped that the task of the Anglican-Roman Catholic International Commission and of other similar bodies, which had begun so well with such exciting Agreed Statements, would by this time be nearing completion and that 'unity by 2000' might indeed be a viable proposition.

We had hoped that by now violence in Northern Ireland would have ceased altogether and that some satisfactory political settlement would have been reached. These hopes have not been realised and peace has not yet come. Indeed the segregation and

---

* The original version of this chapter was prepared for delivery as an address at morning service in Christ Church (Church of Ireland) Cathedral, Dublin, on 7 November 1993. This was Citizenship Sunday when every year representatives of all walks of life in the city, led by the Lord Mayor and with the President of Ireland in attendance, gather for the special purpose of praying for the welfare of Dublin and its citizens.

the sectarianism have perhaps only got worse and Northern Ireland is seen by some as having dragged the rest of the world in its dreadful wake, as similar conflicts erupted in Eastern Europe and the countries of the former Soviet Union.

We had also hoped for a more just society, but these hopes too begin to fade as we read, for instance, that the number of young homeless in the city of Dublin continues to increase, that the drug problem is worsening instead of improving and that 40 per cent of our children live in households below the poverty line.

Hope: other-worldly or this-worldly?
But are we right as Christians to have hopes that are so this-worldly? All three Scripture readings on which we are invited to reflect (Ezekiel 37:1-14; Romans 8:18-25; Luke 24:13-35) would certainly want us to distinguish more clearly than we often do between hope and optimism, but they still give every encouragement to the view that our Christian hope is not just for a remote future in another world but also for the immediate future in the here-and-now of this world.

It remains, of course, that the assurance of an after-life for our whole being and personality, as proclaimed in the last article of the Creed, is without any doubt the revolutionary tenet of our Christian faith. The risen Jesus is simply the first-born from the dead. We too enter into our glory. We now wait in hope for a new heaven and a new earth, a new universe where the former things have passed away, where death shall be no more, 'neither shall there be mourning nor crying nor pain'; where 'righteousness is at home', where all inequality is gone – 'no longer Jew or Greek, slave or free, male or female', where all principalities and powers, all structures have disappeared, where faith has given way to vision and the Church has given way to the Kingdom, where no eye has seen, nor ear heard nor human heart conceived what God has prepared for those who believe.

A foretaste here and now

But already we have a real foretaste of all this. The hereafter is not just postponed until some remote end-time. In a limited but real sense the new order, the new heaven and earth, have begun. The whole creation, as St Paul sees it in the Letter to the Romans, is in travail, pulsating with new life, struggling to be free of its bondage to decay. The Spirit has already been given and relationships have been transformed as a result. In the Trinity the Spirit is the Spirit of the Father and the Son, their bond of union. The role of the Spirit is to promote communication and communion within the bosom of the Trinity in the first place, then between God and creation, and finally within creation itself. The gifts of the Spirit, according to the Letter to the Galatians (5:22-23), are love, joy, peace, patience, kindness, goodness, faithfulness, gentleness and self-control. These gifts are meant to be distinguishing features of the Christian community, influencing not only our behaviour as individuals but also the structures of our society, so bringing heaven down to earth, ensuring a real anticipation here and now of the eternal happiness of the hereafter.

Unfortunately, as we all know only too well, the Spirit has to contend with the 'flesh', our lower nature. Humanity, indeed the whole of creation, has been subjected to futility, to frustration, becoming unable of itself to attain its true purpose. That inability we see in what St Paul calls the works of the flesh: fornication, idolatry, enmities, dissensions, drunkenness and other such evils. In the past this sinfulness of the human condition was too easily accepted. There was very little this-worldly hope. We hoped more for happiness in the next life than for happiness in this vale of tears. Our Christian conscience became too tolerant of the evil and injustice existing not alone at individual level but especially at structural level. The Christian religion came to be dismissed by many as the opium of the people.

Hope not optimism

Happily this is no longer the case. We live in a time of rising expectations, not only economically and politically but also spiritually. Much more is now expected, is now required, especially of believers, in particular of the institutional Church. There is now perhaps a danger of optimism. But St Luke shatters any this-worldly optimism of ours with his stark words: 'ought not Christ to have suffered and so enter into his glory?' The Christian religion is emphatically a religion of hope, of this-worldly and of other-worldly hope, but equally emphatically it is not a religion of optimism. It is signed with the sign of the Cross: pain and suffering and failure remain our unavoidable lot, especially perhaps the lot of those who work to change the structures of our society, both religious and secular.

So there is no cheap hope as there is no cheap grace. To hope is sadly to hope against hope (cf. Romans 4:18). But how do we hope against hope, yet with 'the hope that does not disappoint' (Rm 5:5)? How are we to persevere with patience and longanimity in seemingly fruitless efforts to change things for good in our world? How are we not to give in to pessimism and cry out: 'Our bones are dried up, our hope is lost' (Ezk 37:11)? How can we avoid sliding into individualism and pietism?

Inspiration and encouragement

We need inspiration and encouragement. We need to hear the reassuring words of the Prophet: 'I will put my Spirit within you and you shall live' (Ezk 37:14). We need the inspiration of the life of Jesus and, not least, perhaps, the story as recounted by St Luke. His Gospel is remarkable as a Gospel of the Spirit, as a Gospel of joy, of mercy and pardon, of universal salvation, of openness to all. St Luke shows favouritism towards minorities, segregated groups and the underprivileged. Samaritans, lepers, publicans, soldiers, public sinners in disgrace, unlettered shepherds, the poor – all these receive special encouragement in his Gospel'.[1]

Jesus, according to St Luke, certainly had this-worldly hopes; he entered into his glory not just at the end but continuously throughout his life as he went around doing good, giving his disciples and all of us glimpses of the Kingdom of Heaven.

But ongoing inspiration and encouragement from the life of Jesus as lived by his followers in our own time is also vital if we are to persevere in hope. The 1993 Report of the working party appointed by the Churches in Ireland to study sectarianism does, as might be expected, make for sombre reading, but at the end it declares:

> We first need hope. And if we look, we can certainly see enough to make us hope – from children's innocent friendships across the sectarian divide to costly acts of forgiveness by those who have the most reason to hate. We see politicians breaking old taboos, Church leaders admitting the Churches' failure to love enough and those people in areas of tension and danger who commit themselves to building bridges instead of walls.[2]

The Report then goes on to give examples. Happily all of us will have some of our own to offer. In the Irish context, one sign of hope is the fact that this address was originally given in the Anglican pulpit of Christ Church Cathedral, Dublin. Another is the existence in Northern Ireland of a number of centres of reconciliation, among them Corrymeela, Columbanus[3] and Cornerstone. A third is the 1988 document *For God and His Glory Alone*[4] and the ongoing ecumenical work of the Evangelical Protestants who produced it. A fourth sign of hope is the recent emergence in political circles of a new concern for peace in Northern Ireland and the resulting peace process which, since this was originally written, has given us the multi-party agreement of Good Friday 1998.

CONCLUSION

In conclusion, there are, in the Irish context, what seem to be particularly interesting and significant but less well-known signs of hope: the chains of office worn by the Lord Mayors of Belfast and of Dublin, the capitals of our two estranged political jurisdictions. The medallion of the Belfast chain displays the Arms of Belfast and its motto, surrounded by symbols of all four provinces of Ireland (a hand for Ulster, a round tower for Munster, a harp for Leinster, a wolfhound for Connaught) and not just by that of the one province of Ulster! And it carries the inscription on the front not in the English but in the Irish language: Éirinn go Brách ('Ireland for ever'), the language which many though not all Unionists disdain and reject! The medallion on the Great Chain of the Lord Mayor of Dublin is stamped with the bust of King William III, William of Orange, William of the Battle of the Boyne, William the Unionist hero who re-established the Royal Supremacy and the Protestant succession to the throne, who made secure from the tyranny of James and his 'Popish religion' the political and religious freedom won at the Reformation.

Ireland is certainly a country of paradoxes. This particular paradox gives me hope. In these days of social exclusion, politico-religious segregation and sectarian violence, these medallions gently invite us all to that generosity of spirit which would enable us to cherish equally all the people of our country, Protestants and Catholics, Unionists and Nationalists, and give them 'parity of esteem'. They help me to hope against hope with 'the hope that does not disappoint'.[5]

2
Christian Unity by 2000?

INTRODUCTION*

Pope John Paul II and 2000
It was Pope John Paul II who first raised the question of our title. In *Redemptor hominis*, the encyclical issued in March 1979 just six months after his election, he conveyed quite clearly that the approaching end of the second Christian millennium and the beginning of the third coloured his whole spiritual and missionary outlook: it was the subject of the opening paragraph of the encyclical. That his ecumenical outlook was also coloured by the closeness of the year 2000 was indicated when he visited Constantinople in November-December 1979.

> For nearly a whole millennium [he stated], the two sister Churches grew side by side, as two great vital complementary traditions of the same Church of Christ – keeping not only peaceful and fruitful relations, but also concern for the indispensable communion in faith, prayer and charity, which they did not at any cost want to question, despite their different sensitivity. The second millennium, on the contrary, was darkened, apart from some fleeting bright intervals, by the distance which the two Churches took in regard to each other, with all the fatal consequences thereof. The wound is not yet healed. But the Lord can cure it and he bids us do our best to help the

---

*The Introduction is followed by a second section (pp. 25-39) which suggests five general reasons for being ecumenically hopeful as we approach the new millennium. A third section is more specific and considers what in particular may be hoped for in Roman Catholic/Orthodox relations (pp. 39-44) and in relations between the Roman Catholic Church and the Churches of the Reformation (pp. 44-50).

> process. Here we are now at the end of the second millennium: is it not time to hasten towards perfect brotherly reconciliation, so that the dawn of the third millennium may find us standing side by side, in full communion, to bear witness together to salvation before the world, the evangelisation of which is waiting for this sign of unity?... It seems to me, in fact, that the question we must ask ourselves is whether we still have the right to remain separated. We must ask ourselves this question in the very name of our faithfulness to Christ's will for his Church.[1]

It is not only with the Orthodox but with all the Churches, West and East, that the Pope hopes to see the Roman Catholic Church more closely united by 2000. Addressing a mixed congregation of Catholics, Orthodox and Protestants on 8 September 1993 in Riga in the Lutheran Cathedral in which St Meinhard, 'the first apostle of your country', is buried, he said that

> [U]nity has become more and more a common aspiration and a challenge shared in a fraternal spirit by many Christians.... A common past challenges believers to work together fraternally in view of a common future.... On the threshold of the third millennium of the Christian era, let us thank God for the new ecumenical springtime which engages all of us.[2]

The following November he issued his Apostolic Letter for the Jubilee of the Year 2000 (*Tertio Millennio Adveniente*) in which he stated that 'preparing for the Year 2000 has become as it were a hermeneutical key of my pontificate', and went on to state:

> In the course of the thousand years now drawing to a close, even more than in the first millennium, ecclesial communion has been painfully wounded.... The sins of the past unfortunately still burden us and remain ever present temptations. It is necessary to make amends for them, and earnestly to beseech Christ's forgiveness.

> In these last years of the millennium, the Church should invoke the Holy Spirit with ever greater insistence, imploring from him the grace of Christian unity....
>
> This then is one of the tasks of Christians as we make our way to the Year 2000. The approaching end of the second millennium demands of everyone an examination of conscience, so that we can celebrate the Great Jubilee, if not completely united, at least much closer to overcoming the divisions of the second millennium.[3]

The next year, on 2 May 1995, Pope John Paul issued an Apostolic Letter about the Christian East, and on 29 June, on the occasion of the personal visit to Rome of Ecumenical Patriarch Bartholomew I of Constantinople, he concluded his homily at the Solemn Liturgy in the following moving terms:

> Christ is sending us out together, so that we may jointly bear witness to him. Thus we cannot remain separated! We must walk together, because this is Our Lord's will. The world must recover its faith at the end of the second millennium and at the start of the third! This is why we should redouble our efforts; we must commit ourselves actively to becoming truly one, just as he, Christ, is one with the Father (cf. John 17:22).[4]

The previous month (on 25 May) he had issued an Encyclical Letter 'On Commitment to Ecumenism', *Ut Unum Sint*. In this he addressed himself not only to the Catholic Church but also 'to you, my brothers and sisters of the other Churches and Ecclesial Communities', stressing that '[the new Millennium] will be an exceptional occasion, in view of which she [the Church] asks the Lord to increase the unity of all Christians until they reach full communion' and urging us *inter alia* 'to reject a half-hearted commitment to unity and, even more, a prejudicial opposition or a defeatism which tends to see everything in negative terms'.[5]

Nottingham 1964

Is this the first time in the history of the ecumenical movement since 1910 that a target date has been set for the achievement of full Christian unity? In the last decade of the nineteenth century 'the Evangelisation of the World in this Generation' was the watchword of the Student Volunteer Movement for Foreign Missions,[6] but it was not until the second half of this century that the ecumenical movement which grew out of the missionary movement gave itself a deadline. This was at the First British Conference on Faith and Order, held at Nottingham in England in September 1964, just a few months before the Vatican Council passed its Decree on Ecumenism. What happened at Nottingham may help us to understand what Pope John Paul has in his mind and heart. The following resolution was passed:

> United in our urgent desire for One Church Renewed for Mission, this conference invites the member Churches of the British Council of Churches, in appropriate groupings such as nations, to covenant together to work and pray for the inauguration of union by a date agreed among them.
>
> We dare to hope that this date should not be later than Easter Day, 1980. We believe that we should offer obedience to God in a commitment as decisive as this.
>
> We urge that negotiations between particular Churches already in hand be seen as steps towards this goal.
>
> Should any Church find itself unable to enter into such a covenant, we hope that it will state the conditions under which it might find it possible to do so.[7]

Only five of the 350 delegates voted against the first sentence of this resolution but forty-one voted against the second sentence with its specific date. Some felt that to set a date for Church union was dangerous and impractical because no agreed pattern of Church union had yet been found. Others felt that to set a date seemed like 'dictating to the Holy Spirit'. But the great majority felt, in the words of Dr Norman Goodall, that

> the issue before us in this resolution is not, I believe, whether the Holy Spirit may be offended by our daring hope and dated determination. It is whether the Spirit shall continue to be grieved by our tardiness in giving expression to a unity which we all affirm to have been given us already in Christ.

'Easter Day 1980' was accepted as a 'splendidly irrational symbol', but authentic because an attempt to speak 'in sharper accents of commitment and determination'. Easter Day 1980 has unfortunately now come and gone and Church union in Britain has not been realised. But the Nottingham resolution was not unrealistic because the aim was to galvanise the Churches into action, to give a fresh edge to their determination and to bring home to them that time is not on our side. The Conference Report quotes very appropriately from Bishop Leslie Newbigin:

> It is common to hear Christians speak as though they did not regard Christian unity as a serious question this side of the End.
>
> This is a disastrous illusion. Christians cannot behave as though time were unreal. God gives us time, but not an infinite amount of time.... His purpose looks to a real End and therefore requires of us real decisions.

The 1964 Nottingham debate would seem to suggest that Pope John Paul, in naming 2000 as a target date for a fuller if not full communion between Rome and the other Churches of both West and East, means primarily to galvanise us into action, to make us feel the urgency of our ecumenical vocation, to help us to renew our commitment to work for full and visible communion between all Christians, to 'redouble our efforts'. He wants 2000 to be for ecumenism the inauguration of a second spring after the winter for which he himself is often held to be mainly responsible.

GENERAL GROUNDS FOR ECUMENICAL HOPE

What then are the ecumenical prospects for the year 2000? What reasons could we have for being hopeful about Christian unity as we approach the new millennium? This next section considers five general reasons.

The base degrees by which we did ascend
We do well, perhaps, to begin by reminding ourselves of how bad things were, of 'the base degrees by which we did ascend': this will give us a first reason for being hopeful. In 1925 when the well-known historian of philosophy, Father Frederick Copleston SJ, became a Catholic, the Bishop of Clifton discouraged him from participating in the family prayers led by his Church of England father:

> When I had become a Catholic and asked the then Bishop of Clifton what I should do in the matter of family prayer, he replied that though I could put in a physical presence, if absence would cause trouble and distress, I must not join in. Being an obedient convert, I complied with this direction. [8]

When Cardinal Hinsley established the 'Sword of the Spirit' in 1940 in a letter to *The Times,* signed also by the Archbishops of Canterbury and York and by the Moderator of the Free Church Federal Council, and stated that 'Our unity must not be in sentiment and in word only, it must be carried into practical measures', the prospect of inter-Church joint action for peace was blocked by the problem which the common recital of the Lord's

Prayer in public was considered then to pose; the following year membership of the 'Sword' was restricted to Catholics and the other Churches set up a separate organisation entitled 'Religion and Life', linked to the 'Sword' by a Joint Commission. [9]

In Ireland, when Douglas Hyde, a member of the Church of Ireland and founder of the Gaelic League, became President in 1939, the Government enquired of Archbishop Byrne of Dublin 'whether it would be proper, from the point of view of the Catholic Church, that a Catholic Aide-de-Camp should be present in attendance on the President in a non-Catholic Church', and received the categorical answer: 'It would not be proper; particularly in this country where the danger of a grave scandal would be always present'.[10] And when President Hyde died in 1949 the Catholic members of the Cabinet sat in their cars outside St Patrick's (Church of Ireland) Cathedral in Dublin during the funeral service and joined the procession only when it left the Cathedral. [11]

And just before Vatican II opened, just after the first official conference organised by the (Catholic) Bishops' Committee for Christian Unity at Heythrop in August 1962, Archbishop Heenan created quite negative reactions among English Catholics by a remark he made in a sermon preached at the laying of the foundation stone of Portglenone Cistercian Abbey in County Antrim in Northern Ireland.

> In the course of my sermon of which every word was meticulously chosen, I said [he writes in his autobiography] that the friendship which had sprung up between the monks and the Protestant farmers did credit to them all: 'You are all brothers in Christ,' I said. 'Remember that being a Christian is more important than being Catholic or Protestant.' ... It did not occur to me that I had said anything startling yet I had scarcely reached home when letters of protest began to arrive from clergy and laity. Not one came from Ireland. All were from outraged English Catholics.[12]

The Decree on Ecumenism of Vatican II
Things have changed for the better since Vatican II, and the Decree on Ecumenism, *Unitatis redintegratio*, is the second reason for being hopeful. This Decree is immensely liberating. It is our *magna carta* for ecumenism in the Roman Catholic Church which, by this decree, to quote Pope John Paul in *Ut Unum Sint*, 'committed herself irrevocably to following the path of the ecumenical venture'.

> The movement promoting Christian unity [he went on to say] is not just some sort of 'appendix' which is added to the Church's traditional activity. Rather, ecumenism is an organic part of her life and work, and consequently must pervade all that she is and does; it must be like the fruit borne by a healthy and flourishing tree which grows to its full stature.[13]

Admittedly, despite many remarkable good effects, the Decree remains to a large extent a dead letter. Its very existence, however, already provides the responsible Catholic with considerable scope for personal ecumenical activity, and in order 'to motivate, enlighten and guide this activity' in March 1993 the Pope approved a new *Directory for the Application of Principles and Norms on Ecumenism*.[14] The publication of this document, with its welcome emphasis on the need for ecumenical formation and on the responsibility of each diocese to provide it, cannot but help to stimulate further ecumenical activity and so to ensure that the dawn of the new millennium will find the Christian world more united than ever before.

The economic factor
Ecumenics, that strange, Germanic, but invaluable word to designate the scientific study of ecumenism is often misspelt and written as 'economics'. This mistake serves as a salutary reminder,

if a reminder be needed, that what may be called an economic factor is indeed involved in the ecumenical movement: that a low level of Church life and work can lead to a high level of ecumenical activity. Tragically, in these last years of the second Christian millennium, Church life is, in too many places, in the Western world at least, at an all-time low, but paradoxically this 'economic factor' can be seen as a third reason for being hopeful about ecumenical progress.

In the ecumenically buoyant 1960s it seemed insulting to suggest that ecumenism was a symptom of Church decline, and the cynical spirit and mocking terms in which a sociologist like Bryan Wilson made the suggestion did nothing to commend it. Ours he saw as 'an age in which, from sheer weakness, ecumenicalism [what elsewhere he refers to as 'the ritual dance of ecumenism'] is sponsored on every side'.

> Although ecumenicalism has captured the imagination of the leaders of the Churches, this process has in part been a growing recognition of the essential weakness of religious life in the increasingly secularised society. The spirit has descended on the waters and brought peace between churchmen of different persuasions only as those churchmen have recognised their essential marginality in modern society.[15]

In the late 1990s it is easier to recognise the truth in Wilson's thesis. In 1996 the Roman Catholic Diocese of Lancaster produced a report arguing that 'the increasing priest shortage and other social trends should be seen as "opportunities", and as pointers towards a new church system', and it recommended 'that parishes group together in clusters, and share their buildings with Christians of other denominations'.[16] In 1995 an article in *The Observer*, entitled 'Profit in Unity', argued that

> Britain's Protestants, for centuries divided by history, doctrine and practice, are finally seeing the advantages of

working together. In the face of dwindling congregations, cash crises and underused church buildings, denominational leaders are now talking about formal unity.... Many churches recognise that they have more chance of surviving with other denominations than without them.... Few deny that harsh economic realities are playing a pivotal role.... Nowhere is the problem starker than in Wales.[17]

As a result there are in Wales 'eight hundred local ecumenical projects where members of different churches have pooled resources and are working together under one roof'.[18] In England the Methodists and Anglicans have re-opened discussions. In Scotland 'The Scottish Churches Initiative for Union' met on 19 April 1996 and hopes for a form of Church unity by 1998.[19]

The leaders interviewed for this *Observer* article all insisted that 'it is not economics alone that is driving us into talks.... Economics may be contributing to ecumenics but the main factor is a genuine desire for unity'. And a Roman Catholic ecumenist, commenting on moves towards closer unity in the USA, goes out of his way to emphasise that here

[W]e are not witnessing weak and dying churches coming together in a final act of desperation, but rather the much stronger encounter of living churches confident of what they have to offer to others and to a more fully shared Christian future.[20]

In our present-day circumstances ecumenism could, in some situations, easily appear to be no more than a face-saving device, a last-ditch attempt by the Churches to save something from the wreck, to retain some vestige of power in the world. That is how Bryan Wilson saw it. Ecumenism, however, is emphatically not a mere worldly expedient. It is what the Holy Spirit is saying to the Churches in our day. But why it takes crises and economic crises to make us listen and obey is ultimately a mystery. It seems to be the case, as St Paul suggests,[21] that we need to be humbled and reminded of our own insufficiency before we can hear and obey the Spirit, that divided Christians therefore have, in God's mysterious providence, to be humbled by crisis and failure before we can hear and obey the Spirit telling us of the disobedience of our divisions. It is in the crises, dwindling congregations for instance, that we see the scandal of ecclesiastical apartheid and feel drawn to inter-Church contact, conversation and co-operation.

Progress of theological dialogue
My fourth reason for hoping for a more united Church in the next millennium is the remarkable progress made during recent decades by the Roman Catholic Church in theological dialogue with the other Churches. This has been pursued multilaterally and bilaterally. In the multidenominational setting of the World Council of Churches one highly significant result is an agreed statement on Baptism, Eucharist and Ministry (known as BEM) from the Faith and Order Commission.

> The Eucharist [we read in BEM] is the sacrament of the unique sacrifice of Christ, who ever lives to make intercession for us. (§8)
>
> The words and acts of Christ at the institution of the Eucharist stand at the heart of the celebration; the eucharistic meal is the sacrament of the body and blood of Christ, the sacrament of his real presence ... Jesus said over the bread and wine of the Eucharist: 'This is my body ... this is my blood ...' What Christ declared is true, and this truth is fulfilled every time the Eucharist is celebrated. The Church confesses Christ's real, living and active presence in the Eucharist. (§13)
>
> It is in virtue of the living word of Christ and by the power of the Holy Spirit that the bread and wine become the sacramental signs of Christ's body and blood. They remain so for the purpose of communion. (§15)

It is quite clear that from these quotations that BEM, despite the wide denominational spectrum of the Faith and Order Commission (from Orthodox to Baptist), is far from being some lowest common denominator. Some of the more deep-seated differences (for instance the question of the ordination of women) still remain, but in the words of the former Director of Faith and Order, 'the text has helped to enrich and renew theological thinking, worship and practice in many churches'.... It may be seen as one example of how, again in the words of the former Director, 'the cooperation of Roman Catholic theologians has immensely expanded and enriched our work [in Faith and Order]'.[22]

The bilateral dialogue has taken place at national and international levels. At international level the Roman Catholic dialogue with Anglicans, with Lutherans and with Methodists had begun already in the late sixties. With the Presbyterians the dialogue was initiated in 1970, with the Pentecostals in 1972, with the Copts in 1973, with the Disciples of Christ in 1977, with the Orthodox in 1979 and with the Assyrian Church of the East in 1994.[23] All this work represents a quite remarkable commitment to the ecumenical ideal. It is astonishing both in its range and depth and also in the measure of agreement it registers on so many issues, especially on Eucharist and ministry. The search for unity in faith is well advanced, so much so, indeed, that already in 1978 Karl Rahner could state that 'today there are no theological opinions that with certainty can be pointed to as absolutely binding on Catholics or Protestants of such a nature as to require or to legitimate the separation of Churches'.[24] The findings of this dialogue still, however, remain to be assimilated and accepted by the Churches at large. Stiff resistance is to be expected – and is already being experienced – because the impression of convergence which is conveyed has a frightening rather than a comforting effect on too many people: it is a threat to their identity; it questions their right to remain separated. A considerable investment in education for ecumenism is, therefore, called for, but, if this is forthcoming, the task of assimilating the results of the dialogues should be well in hand early in the new millennium.

The use of a methodology associated mainly with the Anglican/Roman Catholic International Commission has been one key factor in facilitating ecumenical dialogue and in ensuring substantial agreements. It has been described as follows by Pope John Paul:

> Your method has been to go behind the habit of thought and expression born and nourished in enmity and controversy to scrutinise together the great common treasure, to clothe it in a language at once traditional and expressive of the insights of an age which no longer glories in strife but seeks to come together in listening to the quiet voice of the Spirit.[25]

It owes much to Pope John XXIII's statement at the opening of Vatican II that 'the substance of the ancient doctrine of the deposit of faith is one thing, and the way in which it is presented is another'. So far it is in dialogue between Rome and the East that this methodology has borne most fruit. As a result the Pope has been able to sign Common Christological Declarations with Patriarchs of Churches which rejected not only the Council of Chalcedon but also the Council of Ephesus and which therefore we have so far considered to be not only schismatic but also heretical.

In 451 Chalcedon, under the influence of Pope Leo I, defined that in Christ there are two natures and one person. This was rejected by the Copts of Egypt and others who, under the influence of Cyril of Alexandria, thought that the affirmation of two natures in Christ prejudiced the unity of his person. Rome now no longer insists on a 'two natures' terminology. The following formula was approved in 1988 by Pope John Paul and Pope Shenouda III:

> We believe that our Lord, God and Saviour Jesus Christ, the Incarnate Logos, is perfect in His Divinity and perfect in His Humanity. He made His Humanity One with His Divinity without Mixture nor Mingling nor Confusion. His Divinity was not separated from his Humanity even for a moment or twinkling of an eye.
>
> At the same time, we anathematise the Doctrines of both Nestorius [with whom is associated the doctrine that there were two separate Persons in the Incarnate Christ] and Eutyches [with whom is associated the formula 'two natures before, but only one after', the Union].[26]

More significant still is the Common Declaration signed more recently, on 11 November 1994, by Pope John Paul II and His Holiness Mar Dinkha IV, Catholicos-Patriarch of the Assyrian Church of the East. This Church venerates the Blessed Nestorius who disapproved of calling Our Lady *Theotokos* or 'God-bearer', because in his view it would prejudice the full humanity of her Son, and as a result its members have been considered to be the Protestants of the East.[27] In the past they have shown outstanding missionary zeal, bringing the Gospel as far as Xian in China, and nowadays they reject the designation 'Nestorian'. But the Common Declaration between Pope and Patriarch no longer insists that the term *Theotokos* be applied to Our Lady:

> The humanity to which the Blessed Virgin Mary gave birth always was that of the Son of God himself. That is the reason why the Assyrian Church of the East is praying to the Virgin Mary as 'the Mother of Christ our God and Saviour'. In the light of this same faith the Catholic tradition addresses the Virgin Mary as 'the Mother of God' and also as 'the Mother of Christ'. We both recognise the legitimacy and rightness of these expressions of the same faith and we both respect the preference of each Church in her liturgical life and piety.[28]

Many in both West and East would have thought that the terminology of 'theotokos', if not also the two natures of the Tome of Leo, were essentials of orthodoxy. The new comprehensiveness of these statements is big with promise for the future. At present the Vatican may see itself as unable to extend this generous comprehensiveness to the Churches of the West but, according to some, such an extension is no 'vague utopia'.[29]

Unity by stages

A renewed interest in schemes of unity by stages is the fifth reason I would offer for my hopes of a more ecumenical third millennium. On 27 September 1947, after many years of negotiations, most of the Churches in South India came together to form one united Church of South India. As a result, the preparation of plans to bring the Churches in other countries into union in some similar way, came to dominate the ecumenical scene at least in the Protestant world during the following two decades. In the seventies, however, the process of union became more important than the plan of union. Plans of union did not prosper in that decade. North India failed in the end to incorporate Episcopal Methodists. Church union in Ceylon, due to commence in Advent 1972, was blocked by action taken in the civil courts by Anglicans and others. In Australia, the Uniting Church was inaugurated in June 1977 but without the Anglicans and a sizeable minority of the Presbyterians. In England, the Anglican-Methodist scheme of union failed in 1972 to obtain the required 75 per cent majority in the Church of England Synod. In Ireland, tripartite conversations between Anglicans, Methodists and Presbyterians made little or no progress. This lack of success brought out the fact that plans of union were perhaps geared too much to the 'reconciliation' of systems of belief and structures of government, too little to the reconciliation of communities of believers. It led to the conclusion that union was likely to be achieved not so much by the once-and-for-all acceptance of the perfectly elaborated plan, but by stages, through an untidy process in which the divided communities co-operated at all possible levels, converged and came together by degrees, by 'a process of gradual rapprochement', through the achievement of 'intermediate goals'.

In so far as it involves a change of emphasis from plan to process this ecumenical methodology is new more for other Christians than for Roman Catholics. Being relatively recent arrivals on the ecumenical scene, we have had to date no part to play in any plans of union – except in that elaborated and consummated with the Orthodox at the Council of Florence in the fifteenth century, and this was a far greater failure than anything in modern times. However, considerable support for an ecumenical strategy of unity by process has been forthcoming from the Roman Catholic Church since Vatican II. Collaboration between the divided Churches is the subject of a long paragraph in the Decree on Ecumenism (§12). 'Through such co-operation', it says, 'all believers in Christ are able to learn easily how they can understand each other better and esteem each other more, and how the road to the unity of Christians may be made smooth'.

Unity by process or stages was also the subject in 1968 of *The Malta Report* of the Anglican Roman Catholic Joint Preparatory Commission, the publication of which the Congregation for the Doctrine of the Faith attempted to block.[30] In 1975 the Vatican Secretariat for Promoting Christian Unity published its own document entitled *Ecumenical Collaboration at the Regional, National and Local Levels*. This developed the paragraph in the Decree on Ecumenism, proposing various forms of co-operation in a very imaginative and positive way with the hope of encouraging local bodies to discover what may be best in their particular situation.

Special importance still attaches to the section in this document on 'Councils of Churches and Christian Councils'. Whether the Roman Catholic Church should join the World Council of

Churches and National Councils of Churches was a subject much discussed in the late sixties and early seventies.[31] The official stance seemed to be negative. The 1975 document, however, revealed that the Roman Catholic Church was already a member of nineteen (out of a total of some eighty) National Councils of Churches. What was highly significant about the 1975 document in its attitude to Roman Catholic membership of Councils of Churches was its calm approach and positive stance. As a result, Roman Catholic membership in National Councils of Churches was likely to grow during the following years. And grow it did. The 120 participants at the Third International Consultation on National Councils of Churches in February 1993 in Hong Kong included seventeen Roman Catholics who brought with them a special message from Cardinal Cassidy, President of the Pontifical Council for Promoting Christian Unity. It emerges that the Roman Catholic Church is now a member of 'close to fifty' out of a total of some ninety NCCs or their equivalents. The number therefore has more than doubled since 1975 and Cardinal Cassidy indicated that the Council is interested in increasing that number.[32] The Irish Inter-Church Meeting, the Council of Churches for Britain and Ireland, Churches Together in England, Churches Together in Wales and Action of Churches Together in Scotland happily account for some of that increase.

With regard to the World Council, it would now be generally agreed, I stated in 1980, that Roman Catholic membership of this will come as the climax to developments by country and region and I boldly or rather with temerity went on to add: 'the date can hardly be much later than the mid-nineties.[33] Unfortunately, the mid-nineties have now, like Easter Day 1980, come and gone, and the Roman Catholic Church is not yet a member of the WCC. What deserves special emphasis, however, is the highly significant fact which I failed even to mention in 1980, that the Roman Catholic Church is since 1968 a member of the WCC's Faith and Order Commission which has Church unity issues as its particular concern: of the Commission's 107 members thirteen are Roman Catholics. Faith and Order's BEM statement shows, as we have seen, clear signs of Catholic influence. When Faith and Order held its Fifth World Conference in 1993 it chose Santiago de Compostela in Spain, an 'exclusively Roman Catholic' city, as its venue. This was seen as 'a powerful sign of a changed ecumenical situation, reflecting a growth of closer relationships also with the worldwide Roman Catholic Church'.[34] A number of individual Roman Catholics are on the staff of the WCC. Roman Catholic membership of the Council will certainly 'come as a climax to developments by country and region'. These developments are proceedings apace, but when the climax is likely to come is now more difficult to estimate. Its coming will certainly be accelerated by the proceedings of the 1998 General Assembly of the WCC and its adoption of the new 'Common Understanding and Vision' which is at present in preparation and which speaks very positively of closer relationships between the Roman Catholic Church and WCC.[35]

The strategy of unity by stages received a fresh fillip in 1980 from the International Lutheran/Roman Catholic Joint Commission which issued a report entitled *Ways to Community*. The thesis is that the final goal of 'full spiritual and ecclesial fellowship' will be a unity in diversity, a 'reconciled diversity'; that it can be reached 'only by means of' what are termed 'intermediate goals', which bring us gradually 'from an incomplete to a more and more complete communion', and that there is 'an astonishing number of important practical steps which we can take together to achieve this [final] goal'. Father John Hotchkin calls this process 'phased reconciliation' and sees it as 'the ecumenical movement's third stage'. In the USA the Consultation on Church Union, established in 1970, had originally planned to unite all its nine member churches into a single ecclesiastical body. That plan having failed, it now proposes the inauguration on the first Sunday of Advent 2000 of a Church of Christ Uniting which will be a communion of communions instead of a single ecclesiastical body. John Hotchkin sees this as the most ambitious but not the only example of what he calls proposals for 'phased reconciliation'.

> It is these proposals [he emphasises] which characterise the ecumenical movement today and indicate its overall direction. The most notable difference between these proposals and corporate union or merger plans is that none of these new proposals envisage [sic] the disappearance of the present churches as we know them or the emergence of newly identified churches, successor bodies different from and replacing them.[36]

In a 1996 interview with the Rome correspondent of *The Tablet* Cardinal Cassidy agreed that the Churches should maximise the opportunities for partial unity. 'The Catholic Church is fully in agreement with such an approach', he said. 'The attitude of the Catholic Church in this regard is not one of insisting on full communion or nothing. Rather we want all concerned to enjoy and live to the full this communion that we share – while at the same time seeking to deepen that same communion and bring it to perfection....' He added: 'We should keep constantly in mind the question posed by the participants in the Faith and Order Conference at Lund, Sweden, in 1952, who asked the member Churches "whether they should not act together in all matters except those in which differences of conviction compel them to act separately". There is much room in all Christian communities for this principle to find greater application.'[37]

There are of course many other reasons for being hopeful about an improved ecumenical climate in the new millennium. It would, however, be historically shortsighted as well as politically incorrect if, before concluding this section, I made no mention whatever of the greatly increased influence of women in the ecumenical movement in recent years. At the Fourth World Conference on Faith and Order in 1963 only *three* of the 310 participants were women: they formed just 1 per cent. At the Fifth Conference in 1993 the Moderator and 'over 30 per cent' of the four hundred participants were women.[38] Whether you are Anglo/American or French/European in your gender theory[39] this fact is surely big with promise, especially if a focus on relationships and a capacity for perseverance – both badly needed in the ecumenical movement – may be associated more with women than with men.

HOPES FOR UNITY BETWEEN ROME AND ORTHODOX

In the first part of this third section we look at Roman Catholic/Orthodox relations in particular and ask ourselves what we may hope for by the next millennium. According to Vatican II the eastern Churches are united to Rome 'in a very close relationship' which Pope Paul VI did not hesitate to describe as one of 'almost full communion'. The Decree on Ecumenism emphasises that 'These Churches, although separated from us, yet possess true sacraments, above all – by apostolic succession – the priesthood and the Eucharist, whereby they are still joined to us in closest intimacy'.[40] In his recent apostolic letter *Orientale lumen* Pope John Paul develops more fully the Vatican II paragraphs which describe the common heritage of East and West and states very clearly: 'A particularly close link already binds us. We have almost everything in common.'[41] He has a 'passionate longing' that the Church once again 'breathe with her two lungs'.[42]

On 7 December 1965 Pope Paul VI and Patriarch Athenagoras I of Constantinople abrogated the reciprocal excommunications of 1054. But subsequently it took no less than fifteen years to prepare the official dialogue which began eventually in 1979. Between East and West there is fixed a great chaos of lovelessness and lack of trust. So much so that Vatican

II's invitation to eucharistic sharing has not been accepted. The Decree on Eastern Catholic Churches stated:

> Eastern Christians who are separated in good faith from the Catholic Church, if they ask of their own accord and have the right dispositions, may be granted the sacraments of penance, the Eucharist, and the anointing of the sick. Furthermore, Catholics may ask for these same sacraments from non-Catholic ministers whose Churches possess valid sacraments, as often as necessity or a genuine spiritual benefit recommends such a course of action, and when access to a Catholic priest is physically or morally impossible.[43]

This invitation has in fact been firmly declined. Indeed in some parts of the Orthodox world, notably in some of the Mount Athos monasteries,[44] Roman Catholics are not allowed to join the monks in church for the offices but must stay outside in the porch, nor are they allowed to join the monks for community meals which include prayers and readings. This is a sad experience; all the more so as it is a feature not of a monasticism which is decadent but of one which is flourishing. It can, however, be a salutary experience: it can appropriately be considered part of the penance which the Churches of the West must do for their past treatment of the Christian East. It can also help to give a more realistic character to our ecumenical policy and programme.

Unfortunately the fall of Communism has only aggravated the antipathy between East and West. It led to the re-emergence, especially in the Ukraine and Romania, of Byzantine Rite Catholic Churches in communion with Rome ('Uniates') which had been outlawed by the Communists after World War II. The Orthodox deeply resented and resisted this development and were unwilling to return the relevant ecclesiastical properties. The fall of Communism also led to the arrival in Russia of thousands of foreign missionaries of all sorts and in particular to the appointment by the Pope of Bishops for Latin Catholics in Russia and elsewhere. In recent years the Catholic presence in Russia has, according to Archbishop Tadeusz Kondrusiewicz, Apostolic Administrator of Russia in Europe, grown from two parishes to eighty-six.[45] All this has happened without reference to the Orthodox authorities who have been infuriated as a result and who have attempted – without success – to get the Russian Government to ban the missionary work of foreigners.[46] For the Orthodox it has been no simple reminder of the infamous Crusades which are an ever-present reality in their psyche. It has been more a re-enactment of those medieval invasions which, in the view at least of Steven Runciman,[47] so aggravated ancient animosities as to lead to the establishment of schism. Recent events, these 'new moments of difficulty'[48] (as Pope John Paul euphemistically calls them) have seen a recrudescence of some of the worst features characteristic of East-West inter-Church relations.

One particular result has been that the Orthodox/Catholic Joint International Commission decided in June 1990 to suspend its strictly theological work and to address instead the emerging crisis. Three years later the Commission produced 'The Balamand Statement' entitled *Uniatism, Method of Union of the Past, and the Present Search for Full Communion*.[49] This admits that 'these partial unions with the See of Rome' have been counterproductive: have 'resulted in fact in tensions and oppositions' (§10) and led to proselytism; that they can 'no longer be accepted either as a method to be followed nor as a model of the unity our Churches are seeking' (§12); that the already established Eastern Catholic Churches 'have the right to exist and to act in response to the spiritual needs of their faithful' (§3) but in accordance with the spirit of Vatican II.

The Statement recommends a 'will to pardon', mutual respect, the condemnation of violence, the avoidance of 'everything that can foment division, contempt, and hatred between the

Churches', the rejection of proselytism, and the sharing of church buildings. Paragraph 22 states:

> Pastoral activity in the Catholic Church, Latin as well as Eastern, no longer aims at having the faithful of one Church pass over to the other; that is to say, it no longer aims at proselytising among the Orthodox. It aims at answering the spiritual needs of its own faithful and it has no desire for expansion at the expense of the Orthodox Church. Within these perspectives, so that there will no longer be room for mistrust and suspicion, it is necessary that there be reciprocal exchanges of information about various pastoral projects and that thus cooperation between bishops and those with responsibilities in our Churches can be set in motion and develop.

Paragraph 29 goes further, adding that

> it is necessary that Catholic and Orthodox bishops of the same territory consult with each other before establishing Catholic pastoral projects which imply the creation of new structures in regions which traditionally form part of the jurisdiction of the Orthodox Church, in view to avoid parallel pastoral activities which would risk rapidly degenerating into rivalry or even conflicts.

'I think it would be difficult', Father Frank Sullivan has written, 'to find comparable examples of so explicit a *mea culpa* and purpose of amendment expressed by official representatives of the Catholic Church.'[50]

Another commentator suggests that Balamand implies a repudiation of the new Code of Canons of the Eastern Churches.[51] The implementation of the Balamand Statement is far from proceeding smoothly because of divisions within Orthodoxy (e.g. in the Ukraine and between Moscow and Constantinople), because of the pre-Vatican II formation and attitudes of many of the Eastern Catholic clergy and because the Orthodox have understood the Statement to give the Eastern Catholic Churches no more than 'a pastoral tolerance ... to enable them to find the path made easier for their natural return to the mother Churches of the East'.[52] On the occasion of his visit to Rome in June 1995, Ecumenical Patriarch Bartholomew I of Constantinople made a speech, not intended perhaps for publication, which was extremely negative. He referred not to 'new moments of difficulty', but to 'massive difficulties', stressed that the 'tolerance' of Balamand had 'not been properly understood and appreciated by the Church of Rome', criticised *Orientale lumen* for treating 'the Uniate Communities of the East as if they were on an equal footing with the Ancient Orthodox Churches', adding that 'this is something which we assuredly will never *consent or agree to*'. In June 1996 a meeting at Pannonhalma in Hungary between Pope John Paul and the Russian Orthodox Patriarch Alexis was cancelled and the meeting of the Joint International Commission scheduled for June was postponed.[53] Plans for meetings in the summer of 1997 also fell through and for the first time in twenty-one years the Ecumenical Patriarch was not represented at the celebrations in Rome for the feast of Saints Peter and Paul on 29 June.[54]

When in 1980 I looked forward to AD 2000 and asked myself what to expect of Catholic-Orthodox relations by then, 'the most', I suggested, 'that we can expect is that the Orthodox and other Eastern Churches not in communion with Rome will accept and reciprocate the invitation to common worship given to them by Vatican II'. That, I'm afraid, I cannot now see happening in any near future.[55] My present hope is that the first decade of the new millennium will see some substantial progress in the implementation of the Balamand Statement. But for this to happen there must be more contact.[56] If there is one thing that the history of relations between the Christian East and the Christian West has taught us, it is this: that theology alone will not reconcile and unite us. Theology, of course, has its contribution to make: a contribution which is necessary and of primordial importance. But by itself alone theology is insufficient. This has been stressed again by Pope John Paul in *Orientale lumen*.[57] Contacts of all sorts at all levels are necessary in order to create the climate of trust which will enable Balamand to be implemented. In the aftermath of Vatican II many Roman Catholics followed courses of theology in Anglican and Protestant seminaries and universities and undertook summer projects of study or fieldwork with their Anglican and Protestant counterparts. Perhaps something comparable has to be promoted now if we are to acquire some appreciation of each other's Church life and create an atmosphere of confidence. Can we, for instance, afford to leave Mount Athos in its isolation? It must surely be part of the ecumenical apostolate of our Western Latin Rite monks to attempt to make some contact with their Mount Athos counterparts, especially as St Benedict is held in honour there. The difficulties are enormous, but a real improvement in Roman Catholic/Orthodox relations seems to depend on initiatives such as this. The task is far beyond the minuscule resources of the Latin Rite Catholic Church in Greece which numbers only about forty-five thousand. Unless these resources are supplemented, no significant improvement in Catholic-Orthodox relations can be seriously envisaged.

HOPES FOR UNITY BETWEEN ROME AND CHURCHES OF THE REFORMATION

The first time Pope John Paul expressed his hopes for unity by the end of this millennium, he was speaking in a Roman Catholic/Orthodox context and not thinking of Roman Catholic relations with the separated Churches of the West. Subsequently however, as we have seen, he expressed his hopes in more general terms to include the Anglican and Protestant Churches as well.

Can we share his hope that, as he put it at Riga, the dawn of a new millennium will bring 'a new ecumenical springtime' or, as he put it in his apostolic letter on the year 2000, that we may be able to celebrate the Jubilee 'if not completely united, at least much closer to overcoming the divisions'?

Writing in 1980 and making a general observation I saw the relationship with the Anglican and Protestant Churches to be, by the year 2000,

> one of peaceful co-existence in the negative sense that such a major irritant as the present Roman Catholic regulations on mixed marriage will have been removed and in the positive sense that our regulations on eucharistic sharing will have been further developed and envisage further possibilities than at present. On the issue of mixed marriage, two international interdenominational commissions have been at work and their findings will surely have won acceptance even before the end of the present decade. Eucharistic sharing is a much more delicate matter. According to the Decree on Ecumenism of Vatican II, common worship, though it must generally be ruled out insofar as it should signify the unity of the Church, yet is sometimes to be commended for the sake of gaining a needed grace. The application of this principle in subsequent documents since Vatican II could be wider and it is hard to see how recent developments in inter-Church dialogue on the subjects of Eucharist and ministry can leave our present Roman Catholic regulations untouched. By the year 2000 the occasional admission of other Christians to communion at a Eucharist presided over by a Roman Catholic will certainly be less restrictive and Roman Catholics will also be allowed to participate on occasion in a Eucharist presided over by an accredited member of another Church.

These hopes, I added, 'may appear to be minimalist and unduly cautious. I only hope they may prove to be such. I should be very happy to be proved wrong.'[58]

With regard to mixed marriages, the findings of the two interdenominational commissions have not been accepted; the Roman Catholic regulations have not been 'removed' but they are no longer 'a major irritant'. A dispensation is still required but in general it seems to be readily granted. The requirement of a promise by the Roman Catholic to seek the 'conversion' of her/his partner has been dropped. The only promise still required concerns the upbringing of the children as Roman Catholics but this promise is now understood in a more sophisticated, flexible way, as a conditional rather than an absolute promise. Moreover, in Ireland at least, it is now required of Roman Catholics in all marriage situations. Special permission is still needed to have the wedding celebrated in the Anglican or Protestant church but this too is readily granted. Further simplification of these regulations is of course possible and desirable but the serious, social character of marriage will always require religious as well as civil society to surround it with some rules and regulations. What matters above all is the spirit in which the officials of Church and society approach their task, do their duty. The ecumenical formation of clergy and laity is an indispensable pre-requisite. But generally speaking it does seem to be true that, as we approach the new millennium, mixed marriages have ceased to be 'a major irritant'.

But this is putting it too negatively. Mixed marriages have not only ceased in general to be an irritant, they have ceased to be a problem at all and have become rather an opportunity, at least for some if not yet for enough couples. The suggestion that inter-Church couples, i.e. those committed to their own Churches and also to the ecumenical ideal 'ought not to be perceived as a problem for the churches, but as a gift for the restoration of the unity of the

Church' was put forward some thirty years ago in an editorial in *One in Christ*,[59] and is now at last receiving some official if limited acceptance. A special section on mixed marriages in the 1993 *Directory for the Application of Principles and Norms of Ecumenism* quotes Pope John Paul's positive statement in *Familiaris consortio*:

> These marriages, even if they have their own particular difficulties, 'contain numerous elements that could well be made good use of and develop[ed] both for their intrinsic value and for the contribution they can make to the ecumenical movement. This is particularly true when both parties are faithful to their religious duties'.[60]

Such couples can experience themselves as belonging to both the Churches which are represented in their persons and wish their children like themselves to come to belong to both these Churches. Their ideals include joint celebration of the wedding, joint celebration of baptisms, joint catechesis and occasional eucharistic sharing. Despite the restrictions of canon law these ideals are not altogether beyond realisation. The Association for Interchurch Families which now exists in many countries has given inspiring and judicious leadership. Their faith has moved mountains. As a result many inter-Church families are in the vanguard of the ecumenical movement. As Pope John Paul said to them in York in 1982: 'You live in your marriage the hopes and difficulties of the path of Christian unity.'

A new flexibility and generosity has also come to mark Roman Catholic attitudes to eucharistic sharing, not least in the case of inter-Church families. The ancient truth that the Eucharist is not only a sign of unity but also a means of realising it is receiving a welcome and liberating emphasis. *The Directory on Ecumenism* declares that

> The Eucharist is, for the baptised, a spiritual food which enables them to overcome sin and to live the very life of Christ, to be incorporated more profoundly in him and

share more intensely in the whole economy of the Mystery of Christ.[61]

It is a source of joy [Pope John Paul declares in *Ut unum sint*] to note that Catholic ministers are able, in certain particular cases, to administer the sacraments of the Eucharist, Penance and Anointing of the Sick to Christians who are not in full communion with the Catholic Church but who greatly desire to receive these sacraments, freely request them and manifest the faith which the Catholic Church professes with regard to these sacraments. Conversely, in specific cases and in particular circumstances, Catholics too can request these same sacraments from ministers of Churches in which these sacraments are valid.[62]

Commentators have noted that no reference is made here to the inaccessibility of the non-Roman Catholic minister (which is a fourth condition in canon law), that the *Directory ... on Ecumenism* recognises mixed marriages as 'a particular case' and that, especially in the absence of episcopal guidelines, it is left to a priest's own discretion to judge if the three requirements mentioned are fulfilled.[63] Both in law and in practice 'the occasional admission of other Christians to communion at a Eucharist presided over by a Roman Catholic priest' is already 'less restrictive'. Participation by Roman Catholics in Eucharists presided over by Anglicans and Protestants does continue to be restricted in law: the presiding ministers must be validly ordained. In practice, however, such participation seems to be a more frequent occurrence but it happens for the most part among committed ecumenists who will always have due regard for paragraph 8 of the Decree on Ecumenism which states that 'worship in common [*communicatio in sacris*] is not to be considered as a means to be used indiscriminately for the restoration of unity among Christians'. There is no longer therefore much danger that what the French called 'l'oecuménisme sauvage', an undisciplined, casual practice of eucharistic sharing will return.

> If [I wrote in 1980] the Roman Catholic Church is to be involved by the year 2000 in Church union with another Church, the most likely partner, probably the only likely partner, is the Anglican Communion. Here the theological ground is already well prepared and the alienation to be overcome on non-theological grounds is not so deep. No Church responded to the overtures of Vatican II with such alacrity as the Anglican Communion. It was not for nothing that successive Lambeth Conferences had for almost a century been repeating their conviction that 'there can be no fulfilment of the divine purpose in any scheme of union which does not include the great Latin Church of the West with which we are bound by so many ties of faith and tradition'. Vatican II was the answer. But if it be too much to hope for full communion by 2000 between Anglicanism and Roman Catholicism, we can without doubt look forward to a mutual recognition of ministries and, therefore, to a pulpit and table fellowship which is quite unrestricted.[64]

That, it now sadly appears, was premature. But if decisions about the ordination of women have unfortunately postponed the date of organic union between Rome and Canterbury they have not dampened either the desire for it or the determination to continue to pursue it by ecumenical dialogue and other appropriate means.[65] And if I were to rephrase the original question and ask with which of the other Churches has Rome the closest unity and the best prospects of eventual union, I would still have to answer: 'the Anglicans'. To the reasons already adduced I would add the statement of the Decree on Ecumenism of Vatican II that 'among those [separated communions] in which Catholic traditions and institutions in part continue to exist, the Anglican

Communion occupies a special place'.[66] The fact that when Church of England clergy are being ordained as Roman Catholic priests the liturgy may give explicit recognition to and thanks for 'the value', 'the fruitfulness for salvation' of their 'faithful ministry in the Church of England' is also encouraging.[67]

I am not unaware of the fact that in a 1996 interview with the Rome correspondent of *The Tablet*, Cardinal Cassidy stated 'that most progress in unity talks has been made with the Lutherans'.[68] In a world context and especially in a European and North American context, Lutherans are more numerous than Anglicans (80 million compared to 70 million), more highly organised and recently more active in promoting relations with the Roman Catholic Church. In their dialogue with Rome they also pay more particular attention to the controversial documents of the past than Anglicans seem to do. Some thirty years' intense work in the USA, in Germany and at international level on the crucial doctrine of justification seems to be reaching a climax at last. There are solid hopes that the emerging consensus can be officially declared in 1998.[69]

In either case, however, and indeed in the case of each and every bilateral dialogue, reception and receptivity are critical factors. The Council of Florence proved that long ago. So it is, that in the words of Father Edward Yarnold,

> [T]he focus of importance is shifting from centralised discussions to local activity. A multitude of small actions can combine to establish a climate of mutual trust and affection which might eventually justify the Churches in putting a favourable interpretation on one another's teachings and practices, and create the readiness to do all possible to satisfy the demands of one another's consciences. The responsibility for pursuing this process of reunion by stealth falls above all not on Rome and Canterbury [and Geneva] but on dioceses, parishes and neighbourhoods.[70]

CONCLUSION

Because of the more relaxed, more encouraging attitude to ecumenism prevailing in the post-Vatican II era, it belongs to each of us to ensure that the new millennium ushers in a new era in inter-Church relations, a second spring to replace our present winter. We must all apply to ourselves what the Pope said in an address to the Roman Clergy on 2 March 1995: 'It is now necessary to continue tirelessly to place the commitment to ecumenism among the Diocese's pastoral priorities and to help mature the seeds of hope that have already been sown.'[71] It will be reunion by stages rather than 'reunion by stealth', as clergy decide how to do everything together with their neighbouring Churches as far as conscience permits and so avoid overlapping as well as competition;[72] as families and individuals discern the appropriate way to share out their time, their talents, their energies, all their resources between their own and the other Churches in their neighbourhood. It is not however easy, it is not possible to be optimistic. In a recently published volume of sociological findings about the Republic of Ireland, it was revealed that there was no less than a 23 per cent drop over the last twenty years or so in support for the view that Christian unity was desirable and, more alarmingly, that 'young respondents' were 'substantially less supportive than those of the older subsample'.[73] This is a disturbing but not altogether surprising finding which, I fear, is likely to be replicated elsewhere. Cardinal König has remarked that 'In Europe ... the People of God at the local level in parishes and dioceses have become somewhat sceptical .... The commitment at the base remains feeble'.[74]

In conclusion, may I say that I share Pope John Paul's impatient hope for closer unity by the year 2000, not only with the Orthodox Church but also with the other Churches of both East and West. He chose a target date for the same reason that the Nottingham Faith and Order Conference chose one: to capture our imaginations and energies in the service of ecumenism, to make us become 'inventive and courageous'[75] in the cause of Christian unity. If I have been too unimaginative and literal in my approach and as a result too niggardly in my expectations, I still hope against hope with the hope that does not confound.[76]

3
Reconciliation and Forgiveness*

INTRODUCTION: THE PROBLEM

'Reconciliation' is now a familiar term in both secular and religious modern discourse. Vatican II used it to give a new meaning and, according to some, a new name to the sacrament of penance.[1] In ecumenical theology it suggests the new approaches in the Christian unity movement which emphasise the importance of 'reconciling memories' and of 'reconciled diversity'.[2] In ecumenical praxis the word immediately calls to mind the great inter-Church monastery at Taizé in France and the other 'communities of reconciliation' which have been inspired by it and tried to follow in its footsteps. In liturgy since 1975 we have the splendid Preface of the Second Eucharistic Prayer for Reconciliation.

But 'reconciliation' has also become a familiar word in non-religious discourse. The Republic of South Africa passed a Bill 'for the promotion of national unity and reconciliation', which set up a 'Truth and Reconciliation Commission' to investigate gross violations of human rights and to facilitate the granting of amnesty.[3] The Dublin Government for its part set up a Forum for Peace and Reconciliation 'to consult on and examine ways in which lasting peace, stability and reconciliation can be established by agreement among all the people of Ireland'.[4] The Northern Ireland Community Relations Council includes a 'Reconciliation Committee' as well as, for instance, a 'Cultural Relations Committee'. And the Victim Offender Mediation Programmes which have recently come into existence in many countries have in some places been given the title Victim Offender Reconciliation Programmes (VORP).[5]

---

* The original version of this chapter appeared in *The Jurist*, 56/1 (1996), pp. 465-486, as part of the Ladislas Örsy SJ *Festschrift*.

However, in Christian circles which have a special interest in socio-political issues and situations of conflict, the term 'reconciliation' has not yet won general approval or acceptance. The *Kairos* document drawn up first in 1985 by an interdenominational group of South African theologians provides what is probably the best known instance of this negative stance.[6] *Kairos* associates 'reconciliation' with a 'Church theology' which would condone injustice instead of confronting it, which would try 'to persuade those of us who are oppressed to accept our oppression and to become reconciled to the intolerable crimes that are committed against us'. *Kairos* rightly stresses justice. But this emphasis on justice and the need for structural change seems to become in the *Kairos* document an overemphasis, reminiscent of the *sola justitia* stress in some liberation theology. It remains unbalanced by any corresponding stress on the mutual forgiveness without which people, groups or individuals, cannot hope to live together in peace.

The *Kairos* document has been widely influential. Its thinking, its mistrust of reconciliation as soft and unreliable on justice issues, is widespread. In Ireland, according to one unsympathetic commentator, 'the main efforts of the Churches have been directed at the more anodyne and less fearsome project of reconciliation'.[7] Even someone who is sympathetic to an emphasis on reconciliation can still feel it necessary to use both words, e.g. 'reconciliation and justice', 'neither reconciling nor just'.[8] Clearly the image if not the reality of the Church's ministry of reconciliation stands in need of correction. To some extent at least 'reconciliation' is a word in search of a more precise meaning. In this connection it may not be irrelevant to note that there is no entry for 'reconciliation' in the quite detailed index of the Dehoniane Latin-Italian edition of the documents of Vatican II; that Deretz and Nocent do have an entry but with only six references (five in the English translation!): two from the Constitution on the Church, three from the Decree on Ecumenism, one from the Liturgy Constitution and none from the Pastoral Constitution on the Church in the Modern World;[9] and that Alberigo's Indices merely add one further reference: an allusion to 2 Corinthians 5:19 in the Decree on the Church's Missionary Activity.[10]

A research project which I had the opportunity of directing a few years ago on behalf of the Irish School of Ecumenics in Belfast gave me a new appreciation of the rich, complex reality of reconciliation. This chapter aims to deepen and develop the reflections which arose out of that project.[11] Arguing for the essential place and priority of forgiveness I shall be emphasising in a first part that reconciliation at the social as well as the personal level does indeed require justice from the offenders but also forgiveness from the victims. In a second part I shall go on to suggest that, for Christians if not for Jews, the offering of forgiveness by the victims comes first, facilitating the making of amends by the oppressors. In a third part I shall focus more particularly on some of the problematic aspects of reconciliation in the socio-political sphere.

BOTH FORGIVENESS AND REPENTANCE

Koinonia

It will be generally agreed that reconciliation means the ending of an estrangement, the restoration of *shalom*, of communication and communion, of *koinonia* between individuals or groups who are no longer talking to each other, who have broken off relations and are at odds with each other. According to the 1984 Post-Synodal Apostolic Exhortation of John Paul II on *Reconciliatio et paenitentia*,[12] it is the overcoming of the 'many deep and painful divisions' that exist in the world and in the Church, the 'desire among people of good will and true Christians to mend the divisions, to heal the wounds and to re-establish, at all levels, an essential unity'.

Such a state of estrangement is considered to be unacceptable, intolerable, unChristian. But any unilateral imposition of a solution to the quarrel, in particular any escalation of the quarrel into violence, is also considered to be unacceptable as a means of at-one-ment, of restoring communion. Problems, of course, are involved as the cause of the estrangement, and the usage therefore is well established, especially in secular contexts, by which such problems, difficulties and differences are said to be reconciled. It is, I would suggest, an unhelpful and indeed misleading usage. We do well, I think, especially in the Christian context, always to emphasise the personal character of reconciliation. It is people *primarily*, groups or individuals, who are reconciled, not problems.

And similarly – to anticipate somewhat – with 'forgiveness'. I now find it more helpful, at least in religious (as distinct from economic or legal) discourse, to limit to personal contexts my usage of this term also. In the world of economics, debts are forgiven.[13] In the world of politics pardons are bestowed, penalties are remitted. For me in the world of religion it is always people who are forgiven; it is always the sinners and wrongdoers, they themselves and the communities involved in their wrongdoing, who are forgiveable and forgiven; never, I prefer to think, their sins or misdeeds: these have to be repented of by the wrongdoer, not forgiven by the victim. Forgiveness for me is supremely and essentially personal. The remission of sins in the Christian context I understand as the forgiveness of sinners and the remission of the penalties resulting from their sins.

Metanoia

But if reconciliation is the overcoming of estrangement, the problems which are the cause of this estrangement cannot of course be ignored. So, for example, in the particular context of Christian unity, Vatican II stresses renewal, the Groupe des

Dombes stresses conversion, and others stress *kenosis*.[14] So in the South African socio-political context the *Kairos* document stresses justice. 'No reconciliation', it states, 'is possible in South Africa [or anywhere else, it may be added] without justice.... What this means in practice is that no reconciliation, no forgiveness and no negotiations are possible *without repentance*'.[15] So Pope John Paul II says in *Reconciliatio et paenitentia*, reconciliation requires confession, acknowledging like David my offence; contrition, expressing my sorrow; and conversion or penance 'to re-establish the balance and harmony broken by sin, to change direction even at the cost of sacrifice'. Even though 'contemporary man seems to find it harder than ever to recognise his own mistakes and to decide to retrace his steps and begin again after changing course', this precisely is what reconciliation requires from individuals and from communities: the *metanoia* which acknowledges wrongs, makes amends and restores justice, which leads to a change of mind and heart, a change of behaviour and of structure.[16]

Forgiveness

But 'is justice enough?' That is the very title of paragraph 12 in Pope John Paul II's Encyclical Letter *Dives in misericordia: On The Mercy of God*. This paragraph recalls for me the fundamental moral theology taught by René Carpentier at Eegenhoven-Louvain in the 1950s and expounded by Gérard Gilleman SJ in his *The Primacy of Charity in Moral Theology*. Virtues as such are mediations of love and charity. Without love justice divides: it concentrates on 'mine' and 'thine'. With love, however, justice unites. It is 'the specific form of love that must rectify the instinct of self-defence and of the opposition of self to others and its prolongation in exterior possessions'.[17]

So the Pope answers his own question in the negative:
> The experience of the past [he writes] and of our own time demonstrates that justice alone is not enough, that it can

even lead to the negation and destruction of itself, if *that deeper power, which is love,* is not allowed to shape human life in its various dimensions. It has been precisely historical experience that, among other things, has led to the formulation of the saying: *summum ius, summa iniuria.*[18]

Significantly, therefore, the next section of the encyclical is entitled 'The Mercy of God in the Mission of the Church', and emphasises that justice requires mercy and forgiveness as the expressions of a love which perseveres in spite of infidelity and sin:

Society can become 'ever more human' only when we introduce into all the mutual relationships which form its moral aspect the moment of forgiveness, which is so much of the essence of the Gospel. Forgiveness demonstrates the presence in the world of *the love which is more powerful than sin.* Forgiveness is also the fundamental condition for reconciliation, not only in the relationship of God with man, but also in relationships between people. A world from which forgiveness was eliminated would be nothing but a world of cold and unfeeling justice, in the name of which each person would claim his or her own rights *vis-à-vis* others.[19]

The forgiveness of the renewed relationship required by reconciliation envisages offenders more than offences. It means, as I understand it, not wanting to harbour any animosity or ill will towards offenders, any desire for revenge or retribution against them; forgoing all rights to recompense arising from the offence, seeking no remedy or redress. Forgiveness is the willingness, the desire to rehabilitate and reinstate the offender, to re-establish a relationship of friendship broken by another, to re-admit offenders to the community which they have rejected, to re-incorporate them. Forgiveness is persevering in love for the offenders but, paradoxical though it may appear, without in the least condoning the offence. To forgive is to reject the deed, the offence, not, however, the doer, not the offender. To forgive is to continue to wish the offender well, despite the offence; it is to return good for evil, instead of evil for evil – as, for example, St Patrick did to his Irish captors, coming back to them after his escape to bring them the light of the Gospel.[20]

Forgiveness and repentance
The co-relative of this forgiveness is of course the *paenitentia* of Pope John Paul II's Post-Synodal Exhortation, the justice of the *Kairos* document: repentance. By contrast with forgiveness this envisages the offence more than the offender. The offence is admitted, sorrow is expressed, amends are made. But it is surely worthy of note that the reparation which the victim forgoes as a right in the spirit of forgiveness is undertaken as a duty by the wrongdoer in a spirit of repentance. Reconciliation takes place when the forgiving victim and the repentant offender meet. It requires both forgiveness and repentance: 'it is only through forgiveness and repentance that we can restore communication and recreate community'.[21]

Repentance and forgiveness, it has been well said, 'fulfil their final purpose as the dynamic components of reconciliation'.[22] But forgiveness and repentance, however closely related both may be to reconciliation and geared to it as their end, can fail in their reconciling objective. Each can exist on its own. It is, unfortunately, possible to have forgiveness without reconciliation and repentance without reconciliation. It can certainly happen that the persevering, forgiving love of the victim, of the injured party, may be unrequited, may not be returned or reciprocated, may not lead to the repentance of the offender, the oppressor and so to the reconciliation of both. But even in that case the forgiveness remains authentic, though incomplete, and indeed God's own love for sinners is seen as such in the devotion to the Sacred Heart.

In this connection the question arises whether, in the words of the *Kairos* document, 'there is a difference between the willingness to forgive, on the one hand, and the reality of forgiveness or the experience of being forgiven with all its healing consequences, on the other hand'. *Kairos* suggests that there is and adds:

> Human beings must ... be *willing to forgive* one another at all times, even seventy times seven times. But forgiveness will not become a reality with all its healing effects until the offender repents. Thus in South Africa forgiveness will not become an experienced reality until the apartheid regime shows signs of genuine repentance. Our willingness to forgive must not be taken to mean a willingness to allow sin to continue .... What is required at this stage above all else is repentance and conversion.[23]

Here the radical distinction between the offering of forgiveness by the victim and the receiving of forgiveness by the repentant oppressor ('being forgiven') is left unclear. A one-sided 'willingness to forgive' seems too lightly dismissed as somehow unreal. Its certain demands (on the victim) and its possible effects (on the offender) seem insufficiently appreciated. Above all, what the passage refers to as the reality of forgiveness with all its healing effects seems to be identical with what is now ordinarily referred to as 'reconciliation'. And forgiveness can be and is an authentic reality with healing effects at least for the victim, even when it is not accompanied or followed by the repentance of the oppressor.[24]

Just as the forgiveness of the victim can exist on its own, so too the repentance of the oppressor. Being repentant, apologising, begging pardon, asking for forgiveness, making amends, undoing a wrong, doing justice, can also be one-sided actions on the part of the offender, the oppressor, and may also fail to evoke a response: to lead to the forgiveness of the oppressed and so to the reconciliation of both. But the repentance is none the less authentic for that, though incomplete. It does remain, however, that the logic, the dynamic of both forgiveness and repentance is the restoration of communion between the estranged parties, their reconciliation. Personal relationships are mysterious; all the more so the workings of grace.

Forgiving and forgetting

Does forgiveness involve forgetting? Is to forgive also to forget? In former times the British Crown did use 'Acts of Oblivion' to re-integrate resurgents into the body politic. By such an Act those who by rebelling had forfeited both life and lands were offered amnesty and so had both restored on condition that they renewed their oaths of loyalty, i.e. that they repented. So, for example, James VI and I in 1603 *vis-à-vis* the Irish rebels led by Hugh O'Neill and Rory O'Donnell.[25] So also at the Restoration of Charles II, Parliament passed a general Act of Indemnity and Oblivion.[26] It will also be remembered that in 1965 in order to improve relations between the Roman Catholic and Orthodox Churches Pope Paul VI and Patriarch Athenagoras I together solemnly consigned to oblivion the excommunications of 1054, 'the memory of which has been right down to our time an obstacle to a coming together in charity'.[27] And in the Old Testament God is said to forgive our sins by remembering them no more (Jr 31:34), by casting them behind his back (Is 38:17).

On the other hand the Judaeo-Christian tradition is all about memory and remembering; the Eucharist is precisely a memorial. Recent commemorations of the fiftieth anniversary of the ending of World War II have served to remind us and very tellingly that for everyone – and not only for the Jews – it is crucially important to remember the past so that it never recurs. It is also a fact that in recent times truth commissions have been established in a number of countries as a way of ensuring that the past is not forgotten and glossed over. The influence of the human rights movement is evident here, but in general and in principle the main aim has been twofold: not only justice but also forgiveness, not only the past but also the future; not only remembering the past but healing its wounds.

The most recent instance at the time of writing is in South Africa.[28] Here a Constitution has been adopted which states that the wrongs of the past 'can now be addressed on the basis that there is a need for understanding but not for vengeance, a need for reparation but not for retaliation', and which has provided that 'amnesty shall be granted in respect of acts, omissions and offences associated with political objectives and committed in the course of the conflicts of the past'. Since 17 May 1995 a Bill for the Promotion of National Unity and Reconciliation has become law in South Africa. The Act provides for the setting up of a Truth and Reconciliation Commission with three committees to deal with 1) Human Rights Violations; 2) Amnesty and Indemnity; 3) Reparation and Rehabilitation.

The task facing this and all such commissions is almost impossible. The ideal of reconciliation does not mean forgetting in the sense of glossing over, much less condoning wrongs either past or present. But what it does mean is that justice alone cannot reunite the estranged, that by itself the repentance of the wrongdoer is not enough; that forgiveness is also required and that forgiveness involves forgetting in the sense that the victims for their part, despite feeling righteously angry, focus less on the offence and more on the offenders, less on the past and more on the future; that they want to exorcise their feelings and forgo their rights in the hope and assurance of a renewed personal or group relationship. Forgiveness is an act of faith in the spirit of Paul's words to the Philippians: 'forgetting what lies behind and straining forward to what lies ahead, I press on towards the goal for the prize...', which in this case is *koinonia*, communion, *shalom*.

Christian Unity

FORGIVENESS: FIRST OR FINAL?

What then is the precise connection between forgiveness and repentance? Does one have any logical priority over the other? And, if so, which follows which? In the aftermath of the ceasefires in October 1994 here in Ireland I suggested in a letter to Church leaders and some of the religious press in this country that 'we in the Church should be more zealous than ever and more imaginative than ever in exercising our ministry of forgiveness'. I put forward the view that 'forgiveness is surely the heart and soul of reconciliation', that 'the ministry of forgiveness is quintessentially our "business" as Christians and as Churches' and that 'the reconciliation now so widely and so hopefully sought may be at risk, to say the least, unless the Church puts a new emphasis on its ministry of forgiveness'. 'There is of course', I went on, 'no cheap forgiveness. It is costly to receive. It is costly to give. Forgiveness also involves change: it facilitates change but demands change; and change often goes against the grain, it can hurt.'

There was one letter in reply which I particularly appreciated. 'Forgiveness', my correspondent agreed, 'is the key to that process [of peace and reconciliation], but perhaps', the reply continued, 'it is the final rather than the first step.' These were not words I had myself actually used but they sum up very well one of the points at issue: does forgiveness come before repentance or repentance before forgiveness in the process of reconciliation? Is forgiveness first or final?

Judaism

It may be helpful and instructive to begin by noting the Jewish response to this question. The words spoken at the recent Auschwitz commemoration by the winner of the Nobel Prize, Elie

Wiesel, are not untypical: 'God of forgiveness', he prayed, 'do not forgive those murderers of Jewish children here.' 'I bring no forgiveness or forgetting', the former president of Israel, Chaim Herzog, stated bluntly at Belsen.[29] According to the French Jewish philosopher, Emmanuel Levinas (at least as interpreted by Huub van Beeck in his *Loving the Torah More than God?*[30]), Christianity is inferior to Judaism because it gives 'a message of tolerant forgiveness from God who acts towards us as an indulgent parent-figure ... it is all too ready to excuse and tolerate wrongdoing, to indulge a sense of helplessness and to evade the demands of justice and right living'. The Jewish emphasis, it seems clear, falls heavily, if not exclusively, on repentance. And it does so irrespective of the Shoah and the whole question of the possibility of offering and accepting forgiveness in a representative as distinct from a personal capacity. Judaism abhors any attitude or action which might suggest the condoning of an offence. Forgiveness before repentance is therefore anathema. As Carmel Niland writes:

> It is clear that a blanket unconditional forgiveness of the unrepentant wrongdoer is not advocated in Judaism. Such forgiveness is of itself productive of evil and condones evil.[31]

For Jews repentance is all-important; it clearly comes first. To repent is to undo as far as possible the wrong done, to undergo the consequent penalties. There is no place therefore for a forgiveness which in its willingness to remit the penalties seems to condone the offence and to preclude repentance altogether. The personal dimension of forgiveness seems entirely lacking.

The Churches

Turning in the second place to Christian sources, there can be no doubt that the emphasis again falls on repentance. My first example is from the Irish Presbyterian General Assembly of 1965 which urged its people:

> humbly and frankly to acknowledge and to ask forgiveness for any attitudes and actions towards our Roman Catholic fellow-countrymen which have been unworthy of our calling as followers of Jesus Christ ....
>
> We submit this resolution [the joint-convener of the Committee on Inter-Church Relations, Rev. Carlisle Patterson, stated] because we believe that humility is the foundation of reconciliation, and penitence the essential pre-condition of forgiveness and peace.[32]

My other examples are more recent.

> Now is the time for the churches [Bishop Mehaffey of the Church of Ireland diocese of Derry said to his synod after the 1994 ceasefires] to openly acknowledge their responsibility for this situation [of division in Northern Ireland] and to show penitence, which is the only adequate Christian response.[33]

Preaching in Christ Church, Dublin, in November 1994, Archbishop Carey of Canterbury did not hesitate to say:

> As an English churchman, I am aware of just how much we English need to ask forgiveness for our often brutal domination and crass insensitivity in the eight hundred years of history of our relationships with Ireland.[34]

Responding to this when preaching in Canterbury the following January, Cardinal Daly stated:

> I wish to ask forgiveness from the people of this island for the many hurts and wrongs inflicted by Irish people upon the people of this country during that shared history and particularly the past twenty-five years.[35]

These are not untypical Church responses to our Irish situation. Quite clearly the emphasis is on repentance, on the need for the offender to confess and ask for forgiveness. The reaction, it may be worth noting, was not all positive: some nationalist people resented Cardinal Daly's words.[36] Some English papers omitted Archbishop Carey's words. The passage quoted above, which an *Irish Times* journalist referred to as 'a historic act of generosity',[37] was conspicuous by its absence from the account of the Archbishop's visit given in the English Catholic weekly *The Tablet*. In the *Church Times*, the Church of England weekly, the whole visit merited no more than two column inches. Political developments in this country took pride of place instead and the readers were treated to an editorial entitled 'The slow wane of Roman Catholic influence in Ireland'.

Neither was the reaction all positive when Bishop Walsh of Killaloe stated in an ecumenical address during the 1997 Unity Week:

> To our eyes today the Roman Catholic *Ne temere* decree was indeed contrary to the spirit of Christian generosity and love. I feel many of us would want to apologise and to ask forgiveness from our non-Roman brethren for that pain and hurt [caused by *Ne temere* and mixed marriages in the past].[38]

When this address was later published, *The Catholic Herald* (London) replied with a negative editorial,[39] and *The Irish Catholic* (Dublin) with two negative articles which dismissed Bishop Walsh's gesture as 'cultural cringe' and 'misleading digression'.[40]

These reactions may serve as a reminder that in the horizontal context of a human quarrel we all tend to be less conscious of ourselves as the offenders. We need, therefore, as these Church leaders realised, to be brought to a sense of our own responsibility for the estrangement, to say 'sorry', to repent. But to acknowledge our own fault and to ask for forgiveness, do we not need to be assured of the other's readiness to forgive? In personal relations, among family and friends for instance, this readiness can often be presumed: the fault will have been on one side only or mainly; there will have been no complete break. In situations of group conflict, however, this readiness can rarely be presumed: there will be faults and wrongs on both sides and we can be so conscious of the speck in the others' eyes, so full of negative feelings of bitterness, resentment and vengefulness that often we cannot bring ourselves to ask for forgiveness; our prior need is to be helped to exorcise these feelings, to be helped to forgive those whom we see as the chief offenders. If that be so, Archbishop Carey and Cardinal Daly and Bishop Walsh might well have been more helpful and effective if what they had suggested was: 'Let us try to begin to forgive each other for the ways we have wronged each other down the ages, to share with each other the forgiveness we have both received from God.'

Is it the case that 'either repentance or forgiveness can take the initiative and inspire the other'?[41] It is of course true that personal relations defy all logic and all regulation, but patterns do seem to exist although theologians seem unable to agree about them. The systematic theology of classical Lutheranism held that repentance preceded faith, that faith was the completion of true repentance, while the systematic theology of classical Calvinism held the opposite: that faith preceded repentance, that repentance was the fruit of faith.[42] My hypothesis would be that Christian forgiveness logically precedes repentance, that forgiveness is first rather than final in the process of reconciliation; such is certainly my own spiritual experience in the past and such is my hope for the future. The forgiveness before repentance which is, it seems, so repugnant to Judaism is the very essence of my Christianity.

The Scriptures
But what do the Scriptures say? It must be recognised in the first place that, according to the Bible, God for the most part forgives us if and when we repent. But perhaps this emphasis indicates the

necessity of repentance rather than its priority? There is certainly no suggestion, least of all in the prophetic literature, that because of our sin God ceases to be God: 'merciful and gracious, slow to anger, and abounding in steadfast love and faithfulness'.[43] We do suffer as a result of our sin and this suffering is represented as divine punishment, but it is not suggested that, until we repent and return, God is unforgiving and vengeful. On the contrary the whole motivation for our return, for our repentance, is precisely the ongoing, forgiving love of God, his readiness to welcome us back and reinstate us, the fact that, in Jeremiah's words,[44] his heart yearns for us. It would seem to follow that any transference of the prophetic ministry of repentance from the vertical to the horizontal, any urging of an offender to apologise and make amends to a fellow human being must also be able to count on an analogous yearning in the heart of this human victim; otherwise it may run the risk of being more counterproductive than helpful. Such a yearning, however, such a spirit of forgiveness is still tragically lacking in many a human heart, especially in the context of a group conflict, as the reaction to Archbishop Carey's and Cardinal Daly's remarks seems to indicate.

In the second place it must be recognised that certain biblical passages do quite explicitly give priority to forgiveness. These occur in Paul and Luke. In 2 Corinthians 5:19 Paul says that 'God was in Christ reconciling the world to himself, not counting their trespasses against them'. In Romans 5:8 he says that 'God shows his love for us in that while we were yet sinners, Christ died for us'. In Luke we have the prayer of Jesus on the Cross: 'Father forgive them for they know not what they do' (Lk 23:34), and Stephen's imitation of that prayer when being stoned to death (Ac 7:60). Above all, Luke gives us the parable of the Prodigal Son (15:11-32) and the story of Zacchaeus (19:1-10). The Prodigal is moved to repent and return by the memory of his home and his father's persevering love. Zacchaeus changes his sinful life as a result of the hospitality and table fellowship offered to him by Jesus.

Forgiveness as essential

My main concern here, however, is not so much the priority of forgiveness over repentance as the essential place of forgiveness in the whole process of reconciliation as a Church ministry; not so much the emphasis given to repentance/justice as the almost exclusive nature of this emphasis which tends to ignore the place of forgiveness.[45] My concern is the imbalance I perceive in the current understanding of the ministry of reconciliation: I read and hear far more about repentance than about forgiveness, far more about the necessity of apologies and amends on the part of the oppressor than about the necessity of pardon and absolution on the part of the victim, far more about helping the victims to obtain justice than about helping them to exorcise their negative feelings and become forgiving, far more about asking for forgiveness in a spirit of repentance than about about offering forgiveness in a spirit of love. Vatican II emphasised both aspects in its Decree on Ecumenism (§7) as did Pope John Paul II at the canonisation of Jan Sarkander in the Czech Republic in May 1995:

> In the name of all Catholics [he stated] I, the Pope of the Church of Rome, ask forgiveness for the wrongs inflicted on non-Catholics during the turbulent history of these peoples [of Bohemia and Moravia]. At the same time, I pledge the Catholic Church's forgiveness for whatever harm her sons and daughters suffered.[46]

In this connection more than one commentator on the Irish situation has pointed out with regret the sad contrast between the Irish Churches and the Black Churches in the USA.[47] Thanks to the work of Donald Shriver we know how much the Afro-American struggle for justice and for civil rights was accompanied, influenced and transformed by a religious emphasis on forgiveness: this led to the rejection of revenge, the promotion of pacifism and the adoption of the togetherness of Black and White in a new integrated society as the ideal and aim of the movement.[48]

Despite outstanding exceptions this emphasis on forgiveness has been and still is too often missing in justice and peace circles. In Ireland there is a long and strong tradition of physical force, but this, although a factor, cannot be the main, much less the sole explanation. Even where there is no commitment to violence the emphasis among Irish nationalists has been more on justice than on forgiveness. 'How much', Father Brian Lennon asks, 'was forgiveness a central demand of the type of faith that was practised in the Catholic Church at the time [in 1969]?'

> What their faith did [he replies] was to console them as victims – which was important; it gave them a sense of unity and of perseverance; and it may have helped many of them to renounce violence. But it did not help them to forgive their enemies in advance of any repentance. It did not help them to bring their faith to bear on politics. And it did not help them to link justice with reconciliation. Similar criticisms could also be made of Protestants.... It is extraordinary that in a situation of such prolonged conflict Irish Christians have not developed a spirituality as rich as that of Gandhi or of Martin Luther King, arising out of our own context.[49]

In all this nothing less than Christian identity and distinctiveness seem to be at stake. For me the Church is *par excellence* the place, the community where forgiveness is preached and practised, where we sinners find God's forgiveness mediated to us in Word and Sacrament, and where we share this forgiveness with others. We are first and foremost a forgiving people because we are a forgiven people. We can share with others the Spirit of forgiveness – and that is our essential vocation – precisely because we have first received this Spirit ourselves.

The Christian community of forgiveness remains of course a mystery of faith; it is indeed an article of the Creed. When recounting the cure of the paralytic and the forgiveness of his sins Mark highlights the mystery: 'Who', he writes, 'can forgive sins but God alone?' (2:7). Matthew, however, in his treatment of the same incident, omits this particular remark and adds at the end: 'the crowds ... praised God who had granted such power to mortals' (9:8). Matthew, it seems, is reflecting the Church life of his time, glorifying and praising God for the mysterious fact that a community of mere men and women can exist, reborn of water and the Spirit of forgiveness and empowered in that same Spirit to share God's forgiveness with others, indeed with all nations.

Paradoxical though it may appear, it is, at least in a Lukan perspective, this ministry of forgiveness which inspires repentance. In the Christian scheme of things – as adumbrated certainly in the stories of Zacchaeus and the Prodigal Son – forgiveness is the cause of repentance, not its reward. Forgiveness, *pace* my correspondent of autumn 1994, is 'first, not final'. And, *pace* the resolution of the 1965 Irish Presbyterian General Assembly, it is forgiveness which is 'the essential pre-condition' of penitence rather than *vice versa*. Christians do not offer forgiveness on condition that the person who has offended us repents. Christians do not withhold forgiveness until there is an expression of repentance, until wrongs are righted, until justice is done. Reconciliation of course, being mutual of its very nature, does require both the repentance of the offender and the forgiveness of the offended, but it is by taking the initiative and magnanimously forgiving a still unrepentant offender that we inspire and enable the offender to repent so that we can both be reconciled. Paradoxical though it may seem, it is the unconditional offer of forgiveness, the dropping of any pre-requirement of repentance that encourages the spirit of repentance, prompts the making of amends and brings about reconciliation. The repentance of my oppressor, my offender, begins at home with my forgiveness, just as the repentance of the prodigal son began at home with his father's forgiveness, just as my repentance began in heaven with God's forgiveness.

SOCIO-POLITICAL RECONCILIATION

Corporate repentance

The idea that a measure of co-responsibility and a degree of complicity can attach to a whole group or community because of the misdeeds of one or some of its members and that consequently a communal form of repentance is appropriate has now won wide but not yet general acceptance.[50]

> The idea of corporate repentance [Dr Liechty explains] derives from the fact that we are social beings who find our identity in historically rooted communities .... To the extent that we identify with a particular community, we must be involved in repentance for its sins .... Authentic repentance for corporate sins requires finding terms of reference that accurately reflect our degree of complicity.... In general, moral maturity is likely to involve increasing awareness of our complicity in sins that we could plausibly deny or hold at a distance.[51]

As we have seen earlier, the need for such corporate repentance by the Churches in Ireland and elsewhere, their need to ask for forgiveness in deed as well as word and to make amends is now widely but not yet generally admitted as a result of the work of Peace and Justice groups. In Ireland, for instance, 'An Inter-Church Group on Faith and Politics' has not hesitated to write:

> The paramilitaries, both Loyalist and Republican, are deeply rooted in their respective communities. They have acted out the aspirations, fears, angers, hatred and hurts of us all.... They cannot be written off as having total responsibility for the violence of the last twenty-five years. We all have our particular responsibilities.[52]

Pope John Paul's Apostolic Letter for the Jubilee Year 2000, *Tertio millennio adveniente*, has given considerable emphasis to the idea of corporate repentance:

> [The Church] cannot cross the threshold of the new millennium without encouraging her children to purify themselves, through repentance, of past errors and instances of infidelity, inconsistency, and slowness to act.[53]

Echoing these words, the Roman Catholic Bishops of Ireland declared in a Letter on the Millennium issued in Advent 1996:

> We remember with sadness that the divisions between Christians occurred during this Millennium (we are particularly conscious of the divisions in our own country). We must all respond generously to the Pope's call to the whole Church for a collective examination of conscience regarding the mistakes and sins of this Millennium, especially sins against Christian Unity.[54]

In Church circles at least, the celebration of the new millennium should give new credibility and authority to the idea of corporate repentance and help to make it more of a reality.

Corporate forgiveness

The idea of corporate forgiveness creates greater difficulties than that of corporate repentance. It is sometimes stated by way of objection that 'we can never forgive someone on behalf of someone else'.[55] Of course forgiveness is possible only if we ourselves really feel hurt or wronged: 'internal participation is... a necessary feature of forgiveness in its deepest and characteristically Christian sense'.[56] But the very word 'sympathy' and St Paul's statement in 1 Corinthians 12:26 that 'if one member suffers, all suffer together', together with our own personal experience of suffering with fellow members of our family or some other grouping, make it abundantly clear that suffering will rarely be merely individual but involve others to some extent or other.

Besides, in the sphere of religion if not of politics, we all have organs of leadership which can speak on our behalf. It remains for us of course to appropriate their words and sentiments in due course – those already mentioned, for instance, of the Archbishop of Canterbury in Dublin and of the Cardinal-Archbishop of Armagh in Canterbury and of Pope John Paul in various places – but in this regard our leaders surely have an inspiring and facilitating role. If clergy are ministers of an essentially forgiving community, is it not their vocation and responsibility to speak words of forgiveness and make gestures of forgiveness on behalf of a parish or congregation which has been injured by, for example, the murder of one of its members? Such words and deeds I would see as means of grace, encouraging and enabling the members 'to produce the inner disposition which is the heart of unfeigned forgiveness'.[57] All who then forgive do so of course on their own behalf as members of an injured and offended community rather than just on behalf of the individual member through whom the whole community has been injured and offended.

'Where there is forgiveness', it has been well said, 'there is God'. If forgiveness has a transcendental dimension, if it is 'a mark of the inbreaking of the Kingdom of God',[58] its transference from the spiritual to the secular and in particular to the political sphere does raise problems. The very religious connotations of the idea and the all too common but mistaken impression that it implies the condoning of offences tend to make it unacceptable and unwelcome.

> It is not implausible to argue [Father Gabriel Daly writes] that the idea of forgiveness spontaneously suggests a religious context; and this fact may paradoxically militate against a recognition of its social and political implications. The introduction of forgiveness as an ideal into a political context may actually appear to rob that context of its secular autonomy; which in turn may lead the politically minded theologian to play down its transcendent reference. Forgiveness is not, in point of fact, a prominent feature in

much political theology, presumably because it can seem to act as a brake upon revolutionary ardour. It is extremely difficult for a politician to speak of forgiveness, and sometimes even of reconciliation, without sounding like a preacher.[59]

But deeds are more important than words, not least for politicians. It remains, as was seen in the case of the Israeli and Palestinian leaders and in other recent cases too, that the ancient, simple gestures, the handshake and kiss of peace exchanged between former opponents and enemies, still retain their deep meaning: their power to move hearts and minds and, in due course, to change structures. Happily the capacity to forgive is not confined to the members of any one church or any one religion. The Northern Ireland poet, Michael Longley, has reminded us of the rich, heroic humanity which breaks through in the relationship between Priam and Achilles in Homer's *Iliad*:

I get down on my knees and do what must be done
And kiss Achilles' hand, the killer of my son.[60]

Commenting on these lines an *Irish Times* journalist has written:

But if we are to achieve the transformation from the absence of war to a true inclusive peace, it will take more than political ingenuity and courage, rare and desirable though those qualities may be. It will require the capacity for forgiveness which continues to elude most of us, and the imagination to understand and seize the opportunities for making the peace.[61]

The deeds and words of political leaders do, of course, labour under at least the same limitations as those of their religious counterparts. It remains that their vocation is similar, that they enjoy a similar power to change people and situations, in particular to encourage a climate and culture of forgiveness by the gestures which they perform, the example which they give, the legislation which they sponsor.

CONCLUSION

The Gospel of forgiveness is always hard to hear, to obey. To hear it is to accept that, if we want eventual reconciliation whether in South Africa or Bosnia or Northern Ireland or wherever, then there must be mutual forgiveness: we need to forgive and to be forgiven. We cannot just wait till the others, till those who we feel have offended and injured us, say they are sorry and ask for forgiveness and make amends. We must accept that according to the Gospel we, the very injured and offended, are invited and enabled to take the initiative and offer forgiveness to the offenders and so help them to make amends. In this process, however, we come to discover and admit that we too are at fault, that we are offenders as well as offended; that we also need to be forgiven, that we also must apologise and change our ways. A ministry of forgiveness facilitating the offering and asking of forgiveness is quintessentially the role of the Church in conflict situations where reconciliation is the ultimate objective. As Pope John Paul said in Prague in April 1997:

> In charity we can together ask God for forgiveness and find the courage to pardon one another for the injustices and mistakes of the past, no matter how serious and offensive they were.[62]

4
Ecumenical Tithing*

Reference was made in an earlier chapter to the disturbing new fact of our day which is the ecumenical recession: the decline in interest in the movement for promoting Christian unity, a decline all the more alarming because it seems more pronounced among the young than the old.[1] Why the buoyancy has gone out of the ecumenical movement is of course a complex question to which there can be no single, certainly no simple answer. But one part of the answer must surely be the sad fact that too little attention has been given too late to the need for ecumenical formation.

The ecumenical spirit
In the awkward space of time between separation and union when the Churches are meant to be moving closer together but have not yet in fact been reconciled and entered into full communion, the accepted ideal is that we all have the ecumenical spirit and give it appropriate expression all the time; that ecumenism be a dimension of our whole life and work.

This ecumenical spirit excludes killing and hating other Christians but it means much more than that. It includes being kind and charitable and forgiving to them but it means even more than that. It means acquiring a number of new and quite radical

---

* In 1997 'ecumenical tithing' was the third of three suggestions put forward as an agenda for the Church in Ireland by the Department of Theological Questions of the Irish Inter-Church Meeting (cf. *Freedom, Justice & Responsibility in Ireland Today*, published by Veritas, Dublin, 1997, p. 94).

insights and convictions: for example, that Christian disunity is a scandal, that it is a structural obstacle to the preaching of the Gospel, so that an ecumenical approach is one of the conditions of the very possibility of an effective evangelisation. It means agreeing that divided Christians, although they do differ, share nevertheless the one faith and are in communion with each other, although not yet perfectly. It means accepting that we must think positively not only of other Christians as individuals but also of their Churches; that we must recognise and accept these as means of salvation and that, for the sake of the unity which is God's will, the Churches should do everything together as far as conscience permits.

These are hard sayings – hard to hear and to accept – so hard that for the most part the ecumenical spirit, the ecumenical dimension is conspicuous by its absence in the life of the Churches. This absence is evident not only in the ugly sectarianism which has raised its head in some parts of the world but also in the countless opportunities for inter-Church contact and co-operation which occur in so many places but are missed. It is perhaps these sins of omission which most clearly betray the lack of an ecumenical spirit.

Ecumenical formation

The fact seems to be that, for historical and theological reasons, the ecumenical spirit is something acquired. Our souls are not naturally ecumenical. Ecumenists are made, not born. And ecumenical formation is the making of ecumenists, the acquiring of the ecumenical spirit. The precise question raised by the topic of ecumenical formation is not how to practise ecumenism or how to understand it, but how in the first place to get people interested in ecumenism so that they want to practise and understand it.

Two documents now exist on the subject of ecumenical formation, both issued in the same year, 1993. The first is the

Directory for the Application of Principles and Norms on Ecumenism (DIR) prepared by the Pontifical Council for the Promotion of Christian Unity and approved for publication by the Pope on 25 March 1993.[2] The second is *Ecumenical Formation: Ecumenical Reflections and Suggestions,* A Study Document of the Joint Working Group [JWG] between the Roman Catholic Church and the World Council of Churches (EF).[3] It is dated 20 May 1993.

Both documents took many long years to prepare. Work on the first began in 1987, work on the second in 1983! It was sobering in 1983, almost two decades after Vatican II, to hear the JWG insist on 'the present urgency' of 'this basic task of ecumenical formation'. It was also exciting, but the report issued by the JWG ten years later still fails to live up to expectations. Labouring under the disadvantage of having to address many constituencies, many Churches rather than just a single one, it lacks the vitality and challenge of the particular and the practical. It does 'insist on the strategic importance of giving priority to the ecumenical formation of those who have special responsibility for ministry and leadership in the Churches'. But for the most part and especially in the section entitled 'Ecumenical Formation: How to Realise it?', it confines itself to generalities. And the reference in the second section, entitled 'Ecumenical Formation: What is meant by it?', to the 'spirit of ecumenism' needing '*nurturing*' has a disquieting effect. The basic task of ecumenical formation is surely not so much how to nurture the spirit of ecumenism where it already exists but to create it where it is missing and especially where there is resistance to its development, as is the case to a greater or lesser extent in most parishes and congregations in all the Churches.

By comparison with the JWG report the Vatican *Directory* is fuller, more comprehensive and concrete. It had a rough passage with the Congregation for the Doctrine of the Faith, who kept it under scrutiny for three years, but despite the revisions imposed it emerges as a progressive and inspiring document. The critique by

Diane C. Kessler, the executive director of the Massachusetts Council of Churches, provides an encouraging introduction.[4]

> We can [she writes] read this *Directory* in two ways. We can focus on the negatives ... or we can concentrate on the positives .... I prefer the latter approach. In fact, if every diocese around the world took fully to heart all that is now possible ecumenically, other Churches would be scrambling to catch up with the Roman Catholic Church, and we would be ahead of where we are now.
>
> I approach this document with holy envy. Would that many of the Protestant Churches took their ecumenical life seriously enough to produce such comprehensive guidelines. I am especially pleased to see that the *Directory* takes seriously the importance of ecumenical formation in seminary education, and I hope Protestant seminaries will take a leaf from this book. I wanted to dance in the aisles when I read that a course in ecumenism 'should be compulsory'.... We have been educating generations of ecumenically illiterate clergy and the ecumenical movement is paying the price ...

Kessler singles out for special mention the *Directory's* approach to ecumenism in parish life:

> *The parish,* as an ecclesial unity gathered around the Eucharist, should be, and proclaim itself to be the place of authentic ecumenical witness. Thus a great task for the parish is to educate its members in the ecumenical spirit. This calls for care with the content and form of preaching, especially of the homily, and with catechesis. It calls too for a pastoral programme which involves someone charged with promoting and planning ecumenical activity, working in close harmony with the parish priest; this will help in the various forms of collaboration with the corresponding parishes of other Christians. (§67)

She adds: 'If this actually were implemented in parishes, Roman Catholics would be light years ahead of most Protestant congregations.' This paragraph on parish life is certainly impressive. So also is the paragraph on 'The Diocesan Ecumenical Officer' whom the bishop 'should appoint', 'even in areas where Catholics are in majority, or in those dioceses with limited personnel or resources', and who 'will work to see that ecumenical attitudes influence the activities of the diocese, identify special needs and keep the diocese informed about these'(§ 41).

Ecumenical tithing

'If this were actually implemented...'. Unfortunately, up to the present the provisions of the *Directory* remain for the most part a dead letter. So it is that for many if not most parishes and people ecumenism is not yet a dimension of their whole life and work. Ecumenical activity is extraordinary and additional and therefore marginal. It consists for the most part in participating in events which are out of the ordinary or special, such as the annual services for Unity Week in January, or in some occasional celebration to commemorate, for instance, the fifth centenary of Luther's birth in 1983 or the tercentenary of the Lutheran Church in Dublin in 1997, or to inaugurate the third Christian millennium in 2000. Almost of their very nature these activities tend to be additional, extras which are done over and above the normal round of religious duties and observances. They are not enough by themselves to nurture, to deepen and develop the ecumenical spirit of those already interested or to enable others to acquire the ecumenical spirit and become really interested and involved. To cease therefore being marginal, to move from the wings to centre stage, ecumenical activity would have to become ordinary instead of extraordinary. And instead of being additional, a work of supererogation, it would have to become part of the normal round of religious duties. Is this possible? In what follows I explore an idea which I call 'ecumenical tithing'.

Tithing

In an Irish context tithing can still evoke unhappy memories. Irish Presbyterians and Roman Catholics deeply resented being obliged to contribute to the support of the Established (Anglican) Church. The result was the Tithe War of the nineteenth century in the days before Disestablishment. Tithing, however, has a long if not always honourable history going right back to Old Testament times. 'You shall tithe', we read in Deuteronomy 14:22, 'all the yield of your seed, which comes forth from the field year by year'. Nowadays, however, the practice seems to have mostly disappeared. But in some Christian traditions and in some modern Christian communities it does continue to exist: membership can still involve tithing one's income. And outside these circles the word is now becoming current again but with a somewhat new meaning: to denote a voluntary instead of an obligatory contribution to a good cause. For example, people speak of tithing their time to the poor. It is in this spirit and in this general sense that I wish to explore the possibility of ecumenical tithing.

Each of us devotes a certain amount of our time, our energies, our resources, our services, our money to our own Church – to its worship and its other various religious activities. The question is: could we withdraw a tenth of that time and energy and money from our own and devote it to another Church? Is it possible that, however we view our responsibilities as Christians, we might exercise them in more than one Church: partly in one, partly in another; mostly in our own, of course, but also, to some extent, to the extent of a tithe, in another? For most of us these responsibilities as Christians include worship, engaging in some form of social work and giving financial support to the Church at home and overseas.

But could Presbyterians tithe their Sundays to the Church of Ireland, i.e. go to Church with the Anglicans rather than with their fellow-Presbyterians some five times a year? Could a member of the Church of Ireland reciprocate this ecumenical gesture or do likewise with the Methodists, worshipping with them on the occasional Sunday and also transferring a tithe of their support for the Church Missionary Society to the Methodist Missionary Society? Could Roman Catholics transfer a tithe of their support for Trócaire to Christian Aid? And sometimes buy and read the *Church of Ireland Gazette* instead of the *Irish Catholic* or *Catholic Herald*? Could Roman Catholic ordinands tithe their theological studies to another Church? In other words, could they study and live with Anglican, Orthodox or Presbyterian ordinands for a part of their course?

On the face of it all this seems possible with good will. But could Roman Catholics tithe their Sundays to other Christians? Could they, on occasional Sundays throughout the year, go to an Anglican, Orthodox or Protestant service instead of to Mass? Here we meet a real difficulty which deserves careful consideration. It is, however, worth recalling that there seems to be no comparable difficulty on the non-Roman Catholic side and that the ecumenical tithing being explored here is for all of us and not just for Roman Catholics. The ecumenical recession is a general phenomenon. It is not only among Roman Catholics but in all the Churches that ecumenism has declined and become marginalised and needs to be reinvigorated.

Missing Mass?
In the Roman Catholic Church eucharistic sharing is governed at present by strict rules.[5] We are, for instance, not allowed to communicate at Eucharists celebrated by non-Roman Catholic ministers unless their orders are considered to be valid, unless, for example, they are priests of one of the Eastern Churches. And special permission of the bishop is required to invite Western Christians to receive communion at a Roman Catholic Mass. As I see it, however, ecumenical tithing need not involve any infidelity to this discipline. I am not suggesting that a Roman Catholic

going to a Church of Ireland, Methodist or Presbyterian service on a given Sunday also go to communion at that service, if it be a Eucharist. Even if it excludes going to communion, participation in a eucharistic service celebrated by a Protestant or by any other non-Roman Catholic minister can still be a deeply meaningful and moving experience.[6]

But if the service is not a Eucharist, such Roman Catholics will miss Mass and communion, will indeed be deliberately absenting themselves from Mass and communion. Is this not an obvious breach of Roman Catholic discipline? There is, however, no rule obliging Roman Catholics to receive communion every Sunday. Missing communion on certain Sundays would be a great spiritual loss but no breach of rule. Some would be able to see it as the making of a personal sacrifice perfectly in keeping with the ecumenical principle that, so long as no essential of the faith is endangered, the Church must be ready to make every sacrifice to promote Christian unity so that the world may believe.

But if there is no rule about receiving communion every Sunday, there is a rule obliging Roman Catholics to attend Mass every Sunday and this obligation has not been mitigated but rather confirmed by the 1983 code of canon law. This is true, but the question of Roman Catholics tithing their Sundays to other Churches still seems open to exploration.

In the first place it would be agreed that to attend the Divine Liturgy of the Orthodox Church is equivalent to attending Mass. Roman Catholics therefore could tithe their Sundays to the Orthodox, with whom in particular Pope John Paul II hopes us to be reunited by AD 2000. It must be noted, however, that the Orthodox in general, while allowing Roman Catholics to attend the Divine Liturgy, would not welcome us to communion. It must also be noted that there is now some doubt as to whether such attendance would satisfy our *canonical* Sunday obligation.[7]

The main difficulty arises, however, in relation to the Western Churches not in communion with Rome because, according to

Vatican II, 'they have not preserved the proper reality of the eucharistic mystery in its fullness'.[8] Thus, to tithe our Sundays to Anglicans or Protestants would indeed result in our missing Mass.

Canonists, however, and moral theologians have always been less strict than the faithful in assessing the nature of this obligation to attend Mass every Sunday. Whereas traditionally many of the faithful would see missing Mass as ordinarily a matter for confession, canonists and moral theologians would be more careful and lenient: granted certain dispositions or circumstances, they would not view the occasional absence as of itself gravely sinful. They would now argue that what is required as a matter of grave obligation is the 'substantial observance' of the Sunday obligation.

Substantial observance

'Substantial observance' is a concept which was formally introduced into Roman Catholic canon law and moral theology by Pope Paul VI on 17 February 1966 in his Constitution on Fast and Abstinence, *Paenitemini*, which stated that 'the substantial observance of these days [of penance] is a grave obligation'. Three days later the *Osservatore Romano* published a commentary which declared:

> We think that the word 'substantial' was chosen designedly, especially in order the better to show the personal responsibility of each one before God, so that every one may practise penance in spirit and in truth .... Consequently a single violation could not be considered a grave sin, but the repeated and habitual violation would certainly be grave.
>
> Hence the more serious and sincere is the will to practise penance on the days and in the manner prescribed by the Church, the less inclined one should be to consider a partial violation as grave.

One year later the Sacred Congregation of the Council replied as follows to a formal query about the matter:
> One sins gravely against the law who, without an excusing cause, omits a notable part, quantitative or qualitative, of the penitential observance which is prescribed as a whole.[9]

Since 1967 canonists and moral theologians have extended the application of this concept of 'substantial observance'. They have applied it also to the Sunday obligation to attend Mass and to the priest's obligation to say the breviary. On that view 'the repeated and habitual violation' of the Sunday obligation would certainly be grave, but a 'partial violation' would not. What is of grave obligation is 'substantial observance', regular attendance. The obligation to attend on each and every Sunday is not grave and therefore a grave reason is not required in order to absent oneself occasionally. An occasional absence can be excused on any reasonable ground and ecumenists would certainly see the promotion of Christian unity as such a reasonable ground.

Pastoral care
On the other hand those engaged in ecumenical tithing of this and every other sort would need special pastoral care. The aim is to halt the marginalisation of ecumenism in the life of the Churches, to help those whose ecumenical spirit has already come alive to give it due expression and so to survive the present ecumenical winter. Ecumenical tithing would, of course, also bring a deepening of the ecumenical spirit, a growing realisation that Christians of all traditions have almost everything that matters in common, that we belong not only to our own Church but also to the other Churches, that we are in communion with them too, although as yet less than perfectly. This is an exhilarating discovery but it could also be confusing and disturbing. As a result ecumenical tithing is best done in pairs or

small groups with an opportunity for sharing with a soul-friend who is more experienced. Such pastoral care of those engaged in ecumenical tithing would be part of the role of the diocesan ecumenical officers envisaged by the Vatican *Directory*. The ecumenical spirit nurtured by ecumenical tithing cannot but spread to others. In this way ecumenical tithing becomes a significant agent of ecumenical formation.[10]

5
George Otto Simms: Ecumenical Exemplar (1910-1991)

George Otto Simms, the former Archbishop of Armagh who died on 15 November 1991, will long be remembered – and with great affection – for the remarkable way he showed himself to be an exemplary ecumenist as well as a man of God, a devoted Irishman, a devout churchman.[1]

Spirituality

As a man of God, George Simms' spirituality was Church-centred and also Celtic. He loved the psalms, collects and offices of the Prayer Book; he greatly appreciated liturgical worship, especially all that St Bartholomew's and St John's, Sandymount, had to offer in Dublin.[2] As a churchman he was Anglican, Catholic as well as evangelical, but devotion was his *métier* more than doctrine; he was more a Father in God than a doctor of divinity. And his Anglicanism also had what he liked to call 'a slight brogue', a phrase he seems to have borrowed from his friend Michael Ferrar.[3] He himself was steeped in the lore of the island of saints and scholars, an expert in particular on the Book of Kells. He was, however, as European and international in his Irishness as he was catholic in his churchmanship and comprehensive in his Anglicanism. It is surely because he was such an all-round, outstanding, ecumenical Irish Christian that George Simms endeared himself to such a wide circle of friends at home and abroad.

Ecumenical spirit

During the lifetime of the future Primate many changes, many revolutionary changes, occurred for good or ill in communications, in politics – in almost everything. Of them all, the ecumenical revolution touched and affected him most intimately, most profoundly. In 1908, two years before he was born, the Lambeth Conference of Anglican Bishops made its historic statement to the effect that 'there can be no fulfilment of the Divine purpose in any scheme of reunion which does not ultimately include the great Latin Church of the West, with whom our history has been so closely associated in the past, and to which we are still bound by very many ties of common faith and tradition'. But that year also the notorious *Ne temere* decree came into effect.

In 1910 a happier coincidence occurred. That year, that very summer, saw not only his own birth but that also – at an international conference in Edinburgh – of the whole modern ecumenical movement. When he was ten the 1920 Lambeth Conference, following the example of the Ecumenical Patriarchate of Constantinople, issued its passionate Appeal to all Christian People 'to think of the reunion of Christendom, not as a laudable ambition or a beautiful dream, but as an imperative necessity'. One result was the Malines Conversations (1921-26) begun by Cardinal Mercier and Lord Halifax. It was not, however, until 1948 that the World Council of Churches was finally inaugurated. And it was not until the 1960s that the Roman Catholic Church as a whole became officially involved. On 21 November 1964 the Second Vatican Council issued the 'Decree on Ecumenism', with its reference (which always reminds me of the Lambeth statement of 1908) to the 'special place' of the Anglican communion among the separate Churches of the West. The first international conference between Anglicans and Roman Catholics took place at Gazzada in Italy in January 1967.

This whole ecumenical revolution was not just something George Simms lived through. He took an active, leading part in it.

He believed in Church renewal and Church unity and promoted both. One of his teachers at Trinity College, Dublin, Professor J. E. L. Oulton, said of him (so I was told by Archdeacon Jenkins[4]) that he had an *anima naturaliter Christiana*, a naturally Christian soul, a naturally ecumenical soul. In either case, of course, the phrase is a paradox, indeed a contradiction in terms. Ecumenists, like Christians, are made, not born, and it is a very costly, painful process. There can be no doubt, however, that, whether by nature or grace, George Simms possessed many of the gifts which are a special help in reconciling the divided Christian family, in renewing and reuniting the Church. He was patient and gentle, with a deep interest in and concern for others and a phenomenal memory for their names: he had a preference for listening over arguing and a humility which was unable to take umbrage or offence. He combined a high intellectual calibre with a deep interior life and a great personal charm.

Prayer for Vatican Council II

To give just one example of George Simms' ecumenical spirit, I recall that on 24 August 1962, shortly before Vatican II opened, the *Church of Ireland Gazette* carried the text of a prayer for the Council, generous and judicious in its wording, 'approved by the Archbishops of Armagh and Dublin and commended for use in churches'. The text was as follows:

> O Lord Jesus Christ, who hast promised to be with thy Universal Church to the end of the world; hear our prayer for our brethren, members of the Roman Catholic Church, who are about to assemble in Council to consult for the good governing and unity of thy Church: and vouchsafe to pour out a new measure of the Holy Spirit on them, and also on us; so that the whole Church may be renewed in the unity of the Spirit, in the bond of peace, and in righteousness of life; and that the world may see and believe

that thou alone art the Way, the Truth and the Life; who livest and reignest with the Father and Holy Ghost, world without end. Amen.

It is hard to believe that this initiative did not come from Dublin where George Simms was Archbishop at the time. Archbishop McCann, then Primate, was more cautious. In 1966 he had at first been less than enthusiastic about an ecumenical conference at Greenhills in his diocese and took some persuasion before finally allowing it.[5] And that same year he seems to have objected to the inclusion of Bishop McAdoo's name in the initial list of members of the Anglican-Roman Catholic Joint Preparatory Commission.[6] I recall this ecumenical gesture of an official Church of Ireland prayer for Vatican II because there is no mention of it in the Simms biography by Lesley Whiteside and so it is in danger of being forgotten. I recall it also because to me it reveals something of the man's ecumenical genius: his imaginative ability to see and to seize a simple opportunity; his sensitivity to the unifying power of intercessory prayer for others.

Devout and loyal churchman
According to the cynics, ecumenists are people who love all the Churches – except their own. This was certainly not true of George Simms who dearly loved the Church of Ireland, brogue and all. What he wrote of his friend Michael Ferrar can, I think, be applied to himself:

> A strictly loyal son of the Church of Ireland, he kept her rules and valued the uniformity of her discipline.... The task for one of his generous sympathies with, and understanding of, the world-wide mission of the Church never proved easy. In the tricky setting of a minority Church in a deeply religious country, he managed to be loyal, though he longed to see changes.[7]

The main changes George Simms longed for, and indeed managed to achieve, in the Church of Ireland were a renewal of its liturgy and of its Irishness. And Church renewal, as Vatican II emphasised, has profound ecumenical significance.

Liturgical renewal

The pre-Disestablishment, early nineteenth-century Church of Ireland had been, as he saw it, 'reluctant to be caught praying'; an 'arid officialdom stifled its inner life'.[8] Then in the decade that followed Disestablishment the Catholic features of the Prayer Book had been at risk. They had survived, but a price had to be paid. In George Simms' own words the anti-ritualism of the end of the century had introduced 'a quality of rigidity and conservatism',[9] and lent 'a negativity to faith and devotion'[10]. For this reason in particular there was a need, as he put it at the Anglican Congress in Toronto in 1963, 'to find more flexibility in the expression of our corporate life and worship'.[11] The need was felt not only in the Church of Ireland but, for a variety of reasons, throughout the Anglican communion and in the Church as a whole. He himself had been chairman, at the 1958 Lambeth Conference, of the sub-committee on The Book of Common Prayer. It was on his proposal that the General Synod in 1962 – the year Vatican II opened – set up a Liturgical Advisory Committee. He was appointed its chairman and even during his years as Primate, he retained this office. *The Alternative Prayer Book* was not finally published until 1984, four years after he had retired, but, without any doubt, it is a monument to him, to his vision and inspiration as well as to his tact and patience. The Book was no less than twenty-two years in the making, but a thorough revision had been undertaken and, despite much opposition and many other difficulties, successfully completed. Probably nobody was more conscious of its limitations than he himself but he knew, in the immortal words of the Preface to the 1870 edition of the *Prayer Book*, that 'what is imperfect with peace is often better than what is otherwise more excellent without it'.

A secure Irish identity

A secure Irish identity was one of George Simms' great gifts. Despite the important part played in the cultural and political life of the country by such individual Church of Ireland members as Isaac Butt, Charles Stewart Parnell, Douglas Hyde, Lady Gregory, W. B. Yeats, Sir Horace Plunkett, Robert Barton and Erskine Childers, the eventual settlement caused a serious identity crisis in the Church of Ireland as a whole, especially in the South. Its members for the most part were unionist in background; they couldn't easily accept or be accepted by the new regime. It took time and much painful experience for both sides to adapt to the new situation.

In these circumstances the confidence in their Irish identity of such men as George Simms was a great blessing. He had a German mother and went to school in England,[12] was Anglican in his understanding and practice of Christianity, but he felt – and was – none the less Irish for that. A native of Donegal, Lifford was home for him, Portnoo his favourite holiday resort, and Irish a language he loved and could speak. He took seriously 'the ancientness and the catholicity'[13] of the Church of Ireland and became an expert on the early Irish Church, the Book of Kells in particular, but he was no antiquitarian: he knew too well that 'continuity for our Church must spell out something continuing and living, a continuous expression of truths for present needs'.[14] So he was comprehensive and inclusive in his Christianity and his Irishness. He was far from seeing Roman Catholics as 'a schismatic and intruding mission from Italy' – a phrase of Archbishop Gregg's when Dean of Cork. And he was far from seeing his fellow Protestants with all their political ambiguity as alien non-Irish.

Responsible citizenship

Like W. B. Stanford[15] George Simms always insisted that citizenship had its responsibilities. Addressing a youth conference in Dublin in 1943 he stated:

> The Church of Ireland which guards and expresses our Faith does not at her best expound middle-class morality or reflect a West-British ethos. Republican, Imperialist, West African, Pacifist, Socialist, may all belong to the Church of Ireland. If the Church has a reputation for snobbery and exclusiveness, there is cause for penitence and amendment of life. For, at her best, she bears witness to a world-wide faith which makes war on political and social distinctions, seeing in such distinctions the breeding ground of pride, and an obstacle of spiritual growth.[16]

In 1969, while still Archbishop of Dublin, he contributed, with the political leaders Jack Lynch and Terence O'Neill, among others, to a symposium on 'Ireland Tomorrow' which appeared in the pages of *Everyman*, a review edited by the Servites of Benburb, County Tyrone. He wrote on 'The Role of Protestants'[17] and took Margaret Cunningham, Warden of Trinity Hall in Dublin for many years, as an example. He praised her, in words which seem to give us a pen-picture of himself, as:

> a thinker and friendly personality whose allegiance was firmly given to a religious minority. Yet her whole life, so far from being cooped up in the traditions and beliefs that inspired it, was freely and generously dedicated to the service of the country where she lived and worked.

He ended by speaking feelingly of

> [T]he sense of fulfilment experienced by those who choose a career in Ireland and decide to have a stake in the country rather than to emigrate.

Here, of course, he was speaking from personal experience as one who had himself declined positions in England, in the Church of England.[18] In this as in everything else, George Simms led by example, and Donald Caird, former Archbishop of Dublin, was surely right to say in his appreciation:

> It was he perhaps more than anyone else who encouraged the Protestant population in the Republic of Ireland to take a more active part in national and social life.[19]

This change too has made a noteworthy contribution to inter-Church relations: the Church of Ireland can no longer be dismissed as an alien, English intrusion.

Mixed marriages
At international level George Simms made his most significant contribution to the ecumenical movement in his capacity as Anglican co-Chairman of the Anglican-Roman Catholic International Commission on the Theology of Marriage and its Application to Mixed Marriages. This was established in 1968 and issued a unanimous report in 1975. With regard to mixed marriages it made two recommendations for alterations to canon law, neither of which has so far been accepted. It also reiterated what Pope Paul VI had written in 1970 about pastoral care and joint pastoral care. This it saw as 'the main hope for the future', helping 'to determine whether mixed marriages are to be an occasion of spiritual growth or decay, an ecumenical opportunity or an ecumenical menace'.[20]

In the last few decades a sea change has come about not only in the general area of inter-Church relations but even in the particular and peculiarly difficult area of mixed marriages. We do not yet fully understand how such change occurs but there is now a greater appreciation than before of its complex nature. We have come to see more clearly that it requires a process as well as a plan, a re-education of hearts as well as of minds. The work and reports of this Anglican-Roman Catholic Commission, and not least the gentle chairmanship of Archbishop Simms, have been an indispensable part of the gradual process by which mixed marriages are now ceasing to be a bone of contention and becoming the 'ecumenical opportunity' which the Commission had envisaged and hoped for. He has himself described for us in his own inimitable style the ethos and environment of the dialogue:

> Five aside in an encounter soon became a fellowship of ten or so round a table, not confronting but sharing their thinking, their residential life, worship, in a spirit of friendliness, disagreeing at times without being disagreeable, always frank and always charitable, and often penitent.
>
> This was the atmosphere which prevailed – and the experience defies description in words. I am only anxious to assure you that it was far from being merely another committee – but much more like a colloquy in which conferring brought increasing understanding and a growing readiness which produced something of that respect and tolerance which had been hoped for when the 1966 Declaration was made by His Holiness and His Grace [of Canterbury].[21]

Northern Ireland 1969-80

The summer of 1969 when Archbishop Simms went to Armagh as Church of Ireland Primate saw the Battle of the Bogside in Derry, rioting, shooting and killing in the Falls and Ardoyne in Belfast, the deployment of troops in the streets, the arrival of James Callaghan, British Home Secretary, the setting up of field hospitals near the border by the Dublin Government and the appearance together on television for the first time of the four Church leaders. When he retired as Primate in February 1980 the violence had not stopped, the Troubles had not come to an end, the Northern Ireland problem had not yet been solved but the Standing Committee of the General Synod wished to put it on record that:

> The Church of Ireland must ever be grateful for his Grace's reconciling influence and his tireless efforts in the cause of Church and community relations during a difficult and troubled decade.[22]

In the preamble to its 1870 Constitution the Church of Ireland committed itself to 'set forward, as far as in it lieth, quietness, peace and love among all Christian people'. All his life George Simms honoured this commitment, heroically so in the years of his primacy. According to historians of the period, 'during the 1970s the organised Churches achieved considerable innovations and development in their relationships'.[23] A Joint Group was set up in 1970. The first Ballymascanlon inter-Church meeting took place in September 1973. Joint meetings of the four Church leaders became a regular feature. 'During those nine years the ecclesiastical scene at that level was transformed. Joint statements, meetings, and television appearances became commonplace.'[24] In all this the Church of Ireland Primate played a full part, helping perhaps especially to encourage the Roman Catholic Church which was still a relative newcomer to the whole ecumenical scene. Whereas the Methodist President and the Presbyterian Moderator changed every year, George Simms remained Archbishop and Primate and thus had the time as well as the personality to build up a good relationship with Cardinal Conway and, after him, with Cardinal Ó Fiaich. This must have been an important factor in the 'greatly enhanced collaboration' which was the main thrust of the Churches' contribution to peace in the 1970s.[25]

It was, of course, too little too late, in so far as finding solutions to religious and political issues was concerned. Recent happenings in Yugoslavia and elsewhere, what someone has called 'the

Ulsterisation of Europe',[26] only go to confirm what a chimera any quick solution was or still is. Chaos, however, was avoided, substantial progress towards solutions was made; 'far more had been achieved ... than many could have thought possible in 1969';[27] above all, hope was kept alive.

In his presidential address to the General Synod in 1974 Archbishop Simms said: 'I would like to pay tribute to the courage and faith of the many who have had to endure what is unimaginable unless it is being personally endured.'[28] Few in the Church of Ireland can have suffered more than its Primate but none of us can even imagine how much and how deeply he did suffer. The strain and hardship must at times have been almost intolerable, especially as he had no chauffeur and little secretarial assistance. Somehow, however, he managed to remain in good health and in good spirits, to keep what in 1980 Archbishop Armstrong, his successor, could still refer to as his 'boyish figure'.[29] His courage and faith were truly remarkable.

Jesuit connections
The Jesuit community at Milltown Park in Dublin enjoyed numerous contacts with George Simms. In April 1970 he formally received on behalf of the Church of Ireland the volume of essays *Irish Anglicanism* which I edited for the centenary of Disestablishment,[30] and in a gracious speech at the dinner afterwards in the community refectory he thanked 'the members of the Society of Jesus for their munificent entertainment'.[31] He encouraged the subsequent establishment of the Irish School of Ecumenics and, on the occasion of the International Consultation on Mixed Marriage in September 1974, he celebrated the Eucharist for the participants in the domestic chapel at Milltown Park.

The medieval historian Father Aubrey Gwynn, a cousin of Mercy Simms, was also a Jesuit and a member of the Milltown

Park Community; and in his later years when he was unwell George frequently came to visit him, and attended his funeral Mass and burial in 1983. George also on one occasion gave what, in Jesuit jargon, is called a 'domestic exhortation', a devotional talk to the assembled brethren usually given by a member of the community. On another occasion he gave one of our Milltown Park public lectures, on the Lambeth Conference of 1968, the text of which was published in the pages of *Studies*.[32] Indeed, in the 1960s he seemed to be present quite often at these Milltown Park lectures because Mercy, his *alter ego*, attended frequently, and whenever Archbishop McQuaid was criticised she always stood up to defend him: both Archbishops enjoyed in private a very good relationship. George Simms was undoubtedly a man of God, a devoted Irishman, a devout churchman and an exemplary ecumenist.[33]

Part II
Ecumenical Issues

6
Ecumenism, Ecumenical Theology and Ecumenics

In this chapter an attempt is made to clarify the meaning of the terms in its title. Are they synonyms to be used interchangeably or are they different, though related in meaning, and, therefore, not interchangeable in usage? The chapter falls into three, unequal parts, according to the terms of the title.

WHAT IS ECUMENISM?

My approach to this first question is to concentrate on the subject rather than the object and to attempt a description of the ecumenist. It may sound contradictory but in the first place I would see ecumenists as in a very real sense intolerant persons. They will be wholly in favour of pluralism but firmly opposed to a plurality of Churches: they exist to put an end to this plurality. If this sounds paradoxical it is because ecumenism has mistakenly, however understandably, been identified with tolerance.

Recognition of and respect for other Christian traditions and institutions (as distinct from other Christian individuals) is still so new that many have not yet been able to see beyond it and to grasp that this may be only a stage on the road towards some form of Church union in which the hitherto separated denominations die. Others, from a very understandable fear of dying, as well as for other reasons, lay considerable emphasis on respect for, and maintenance and promotion of our different traditions. And, as a previous chapter has indicated,[1] this position has come to acquire a new status in recent times. The classical ecumenist, however, is a person who holds that there are limits to pluralism and to 'reconciled diversity'. The unity which the ecumenist seeks is indeed a unity in diversity but not a unity in many diverse Churches. The existence of many Churches is the precise problem which ecumenists exist to solve.

The scandal of disunity
Ecumenists are intolerant of many Churches for a very particular reason. They are intolerant because they are convinced that the present situation is intolerable. They experience it as something which 'openly contradicts the will of Christ, provides a stumbling-block to the world, and inflicts damage on the most holy cause of proclaiming the good news to every creature'.[2] And the situation they find so intolerable is not only that existing in Belfast or Bosnia, where disunity can erupt into violence, but also that in Dublin or London or Minneapolis, where Church disunity mostly takes the form of peaceful coexistence. In their view even this form, in the words of the World Council of Churches, 'distorts the witness of the Church, frustrates its mission and contradicts its own nature'.[3]

Ecumenists, in the second place, are those Christians who have come to realise how much they have in common with the members of other Churches. They have discovered the many close bonds of unity existing between themselves and other Christian believers. The remaining differences are not denied but take very much second place. They see the way forward, therefore, as that of theological dialogue in the name of the Spirit, who alone can lead our partially united Churches into the fullness of truth and unity.

In the third place, however, ecumenists hold that theology alone will not end the plurality of Churches and create the one Church which is in accordance with God's will. Of theology, they are agreed, we cannot have enough; but we need more than theology. The Council of Florence, which succeeded so well at the level of theology and truth, but failed so badly at the level of psychology and trust, is seen by the ecumenist as a monument to this conviction, but it is a forgotten monument because, if it were remembered, so many Roman Catholics would not have gone on for so long thinking and saying that their prospects for unity and union with the Orthodox were the best of all. The ecumenist is convinced that it is groups of people, not sets of doctrinal or theological propositions, communities of belief, not systems of belief, which primarily need to be reconciled; and that this is a task which theologians alone cannot accomplish. It is love more than truth that makes us free and enables us to overcome our estrangements. Theology alone, the ecumenist is adamant, cannot hope to cope with the host of social, cultural, historical, political and psychological factors involved in the disunity of the Churches.

A threefold, trinitarian approach

The way forward, therefore, according to the ecumenist, is not only the way of theological dialogue in the name of the Spirit. It is threefold or trinitarian. It is also the way of co-operation and the way of Church renewal. Christians must 'do everything together as far as conscience permits' in the name of the Father, who creates and sustains. The ecumenist sees such co-operation as liberating the Churches from their ancestral prejudices and antipathies, and as deepening and developing their existing unity. The Churches must also engage in the mortifying work of Church renewal and reform in the name of the Son, who died and rose. Ecumenists see this as necessary because they accept that, in the words of the New Delhi Assembly of the World Council of Churches, 'the achievement of unity will involve nothing less than a death and rebirth of many forms of Church life as we have known them'.

In the fourth place, and finally, the ecumenist is someone who is painfully wondering whether and to what extent ecumenism is applicable to religions as well as to Christian traditions. In the summer of 1975 the first Asian Congress of Jesuit Ecumenists declared:

> We believe that concern for ecumenism has wider connotations in Asia than in Europe. Here it extends beyond Christian denominations with their theological and organisational (faith and order) preoccupations, and reaches out to all the religious traditions of Asia. Dialogue with men of these religious and spiritual traditions is the central area of ecumenism in Asia. This conviction is based on the awareness of difference in Asian historical experience. The divisions within Christianity have neither roots nor context in the history of Asian peoples. They are imported realities and have little meaning for the believing peoples, especially with the disappearance of ancient hostilities between the Churches in which the divisions originated. Asian ecumenism therefore consists primarily in dialogue with the millions of men and women of faith in the various traditions of Asia, among whom we live.[4]

Not only in Asia, however, but all over the world, although still very tentatively, inter-faith dialogue is now considered to be a necessary part of ecumenism.[5] Its place and nature, however, are even yet not clear. Can we hold the primacy and Lordship of Christ and engage in inter-faith dialogue? Can we engage in this dialogue and, at the same time, hold a policy of individual conversions? Would it be possible to elaborate a new Toronto Statement[6] on relations between the many religions and the one Kingdom? But it is hoped to solve these unresolved questions *ambulando*.

WHAT IS ECUMENICAL THEOLOGY?

This second part falls into three short sections, with the following sub-headings: a) ecumenical theology in a general sense; b) ecumenical theology in the strict sense; and c) denominational or confessional theology.

Ecumenical theology in a general sense

For some, theology is ecumenical if there is no *odium theologicum*, if the old polemical approach has disappeared; if we no longer make *a priori* assumptions about the falsehood of the positions held by members of other denominations, but seek to understand these positions even though we may eventually have to disagree with them. To be 'ecumenical' according to this usage is in one sense to be no more than irenic, reasonable and fair. In another sense, however, it is much more: it is to recognise the existence and validity or salvific value of other Churches and other beliefs.

According to a second, and quite common usage, 'ecumenical theology' is the study of a tradition other than one's own. At a Consultation of European Ecumenical Institutes in October 1976 representatives were present from, for instance, the Konfessionskundliches Institut of Bensheim (Lutheran), the Konfessionskundliches Institut of Budapest (Reformed) and the Ostkirchliches Institut of Würzburg (Roman Catholic – Augustinian), which are denominational establishments devoted to the study of traditions other than their own. Also represented was the Katholisch-Oekumenisches Institut of Münster (Roman Catholic), the speciality of which has been nineteenth-century Protestant theology. In the past the aims of such institutions as these were controversial and not ecumenical. In 1925, 'moved by a wish to reconcile the East to the One Church',[7] Pius XI enlarged the Oriental Institute which had been established by Pope

Benedict XV. Their work, however, is now rightly termed ecumenical, because of 'a greater hope and a more irenic and understanding approach'[8] and because a certain element of comparative Christianity and comparative religion can be used even after Lund[9] to prepare the ground for inter-Church and inter-faith dialogue.

There is a third usage which deserves mention: it adds the idea of inter-denominational collaboration. A piece of theological work by a member of one tradition is said to be ecumenical if it takes into serious consideration the corresponding contributions by members of other traditions, above all, if the work is carried out in collaboration with these latter in, for instance, the setting of an inter-denominational institute. Scholars engaged in such co-operative theological ventures are not always concerned with the issues of unity and union and, to that extent, their work might be more clearly described as interdenominational rather than ecumenical. The use of this latter adjective cannot, however, be deprecated and is richly deserved because these joint projects are in such glaring contrast with the unecumenical isolationism of the past, when, instead of doing everything together as far as conscience permitted, the Churches did everything separately as far as possible.

To sum up then, theology, it would seem, is ecumenical in a general sense when ecumenism under one or other of its aspects is a *dimension* of the exercise, when theology is pursued ecumenically. And, by contrast, I now wish to suggest, theology is ecumenical in the strict sense when religious unity or union 'so that the world may believe' is the whole object of the exercise, when ecumenical theology is a *special discipline*.

Ecumenical theology in the strict sense

The ecumenical movement has by this stage developed a whole history and literature of its own. To concentrate on this corpus, to excavate in this quarry, to study this material in particular is to engage in ecumenical theology in the strict sense. We must be prepared, however, for the eventuality that this ecumenical theology in the strict sense of a positive kind may not be ecumenical theology in the general sense insofar as the study is conducted unecumenically, in a way, for instance, that is not 'irenic, reasonable and fair'. An unsympathetic exposé and evaluation of the work of the Anglican-Roman Catholic International Commission would, for instance, fall into this category.

Ecumenical theology in the strict sense of a more speculative kind can be described as reflection according to certain specific principles on a shared faith. An experience of shared faith is fundamental and in 1952 at the Lund Faith and Order Conference this point was stressed in a highly significant, new way. Up to then the method or style adopted in ecumenical theology and Church union negotiations was to state as clearly as possible the existing different positions, to compare and contrast them, to delimit the precise areas of agreement and disagreement, and then to search for ways and means of surmounting the disagreements. Since Lund this comparative approach has in principle been abandoned. The post-Lund approach in ecumenical theology is

> to go together straight to some of the great themes of the Christian faith, to study them together on a soundly biblical basis and then, working outwards from the centre, to challenge each other to justify the things that divide us, as they begin to appear in the light of our previous agreement on fundamentals.[10]

The comparative character of the early pre-Lund ecumenical theology reflects the fact that, in general, prior to the ecumenical movement, the Churches existed in isolation from each other and understood themselves over and against each other as mutually exclusive expressions of the Christian faith. The only reality, therefore, which could be the subject of theological reflection was the Christian faith as experienced in the narrowly denominational context of separated and separatist Churches. The ecumenical movement changes all that. The result is believers of a new sort, believers who come to feel and see and, however confusedly, know themselves as belonging not just to one Church, but really and truly, if inexplicably and only partially, to the two or more Churches in whom they have discovered a common faith, and with whom they have together sounded its depths in joint worship and witness.

This experience of shared faith is of primordial importance: ecumenical theology in the strict sense and of the more speculative kind is constituted by reflection on that experience. Because of the nature of the experience it is relatively easy to see that its verbalisation, as for instance in the modern Agreed Statements on the Eucharist, will begin to depend less and less on the phrases and formulas hammered out in the controversial confrontations of the pre-ecumenical past. More difficult, perhaps, to appreciate are the principles or criteria adopted in the process of reflection.

The general principle is that religious unity, according to God's will, so that the world may believe, is the specific aim and object of the exercise. Theology becomes ecumenical theology in the strict sense and of the speculative kind only when it adopts unity as its overriding concern, only when unity becomes its be-all and end-all.

Some particular conclusions follow from this general principle and leave their mark on the work of reflection. Two which are closely related deserve special mention. Firstly, the existing disunity is to be ended only insofar as it is scandalous, 'blocking the way to the faith'.[11] Otherwise differences and diversity are to be lived with and indeed rejoiced in as signs of the richness of God's revelation. Secondly, religious unity so that the world may believe is a unity in essentials only, a unity in faith, but not a unity in theology, because the one same faith is patient of different approaches, emphases, explanations and formulations. In the words of Vatican II:

> While preserving unity in essentials, let everyone in the Church, according to the office entrusted to each, preserve a proper freedom in the various forms of spiritual life and discipline, in the variety of liturgical rites, and even in the theological elaborations of revealed truth. In all things let charity prevail.[12]

The main effect of these principles is to impose severe limitations on the theological enterprise. Ordinary theology, however, cannot accept these limitations. Theology can never say 'it is enough'. Ecumenical theology in the strict sense must do precisely that and so it becomes a special discipline.

Denominational or confessional theology

It remains in this section to add some remarks about denominational or confessional theology. From the point of view of positive theology, this is the study of denominational sources, of the Council of Trent, for instance, or Karl Rahner or the Westminster Confession. The critique included in such study must, for scientific reasons, be conducted, in the first instance, from the same denominational standpoint, but not necessarily by a member of the same denomination. Excellent studies in Orthodoxy and in all the traditions have been produced by scholars not belonging to these traditions.

From the point of view, however, of a speculative theology or dogmatics, denominational theology must, it would seem, be described as the study of any theological topic by a committed member of a particular tradition. A chair of Roman Catholic theology or a Roman Catholic chair of theology can presumably be held only by a committed Roman Catholic. In their study of, for instance, christology, Roman Catholic lecturers will, of course, exploit all the available resources. They will read everything worthwhile, no matter what the denomination of the author. In their life and lectures they will have a viewpoint which they will endeavour to expose and to commend. But, because they are serious scholars and because of the development of ecumenical theology in general, this viewpoint will nowadays for the most part and increasingly, be tenable by scholars of other denominations and, if not in fact shared by them, this will be for reasons of scholarship rather than for denominational reasons.

WHAT IS ECUMENICS?

The word 'ecumenics' is German in origin and has no equivalent in any other language except English, but even in Germany it is not too much used in ecumenical circles. Ecumenics is not just another word for ecumenical theology. Neither is it just another word for ecumenism. Ecumenics is the scientific study of ecumenism, of the movement to promote inter-Church and inter-faith unity. This movement, we have seen, has many aspects. The disunity it seeks to overcome is not just theological, but also involves cultural and other factors. The unity it seeks to promote is not just a unity of beliefs, but a unity of believing peoples in all their diversity. To do justice, therefore, to the ecumenical movement historians, sociologists, social-psychologists and others are needed as well as theologians. Ecumenics as the scientific study of ecumenism is necessarily multi-disciplinary and inter-disciplinary. It is a whole of which ecumenical theology in the strict sense is indeed a part, and an important part, but only a part.

By way of conclusion I wish to rehearse briefly the arguments for ecumenics as a single obligatory discipline in theological education.[13] The content of the discipline will of course vary somewhat, according to the time available and according to the place. The aim, however, will always be twofold: firstly, to create a familiarity, at once critical and intimate, not so much with other Churches and other religions, but rather with the ecumenical movement itself: its people, developments and methods; and secondly, to provide some in-depth treatment of the chief ecumenical issues of the day, so that students can learn, not only how to deal with these particular issues, but also how to begin to cope with the different ecumenical issues which may face them later and elsewhere.

The argument for such a discipline as obligatory will, I think, best begin from the theoretical recognition of the need for an ecumenical dimension in the whole of theology as in the whole of life. This need is now granted and is formally accepted in the two recent documents on 'ecumenical formation' mentioned above in chapter four.[14] The need for an ecumenical dimension to theology had however been accepted in earlier documents. Following the publication in 1970 of Part II of the Vatican's *Ecumenical Directory, The Norms for Priestly Training in Ireland* and the *Directory on Ecumenism in Ireland*,[15] both called for 'an ecumenical dimension in the various branches of theology'. *The Programme of Priestly Formation* issued by the National Conference of US Catholic Bishops also included an eight-page chapter entitled 'Ecumenical Dimension in Theological Education'.

It seems only too clear from the lack of response to these documents of the 1970s that to give theology its due ecumenical dimension is easier said than done. We do well to remember that:

> If ecumenism is to carry into theological education its benefits of correction, wideness, wholeness, and hence nearer approach to the truth, it is in the very first place those who teach or in any way lead and direct theological education that must be its agents, and this means that they be themselves both knowledgeable about ecumenism and

> concerned with and for it. It cannot be too plainly said: no system of education can at this point (or perhaps at any other) be a substitute for interested men.[16]

In other words, if theological education is to have an ecumenical dimension, it must ordinarily include the discipline of ecumenics by which students and future teachers begin to become 'knowledgeable about ecumenism and concerned with and for it'.

An example from another area of theological education will make this abundantly clear. Vatican II invited Roman Catholics to make the 'sacred page' the soul of sacred theology, to ensure, in other words, that all theology included a strong biblical flavour, emphasis, dimension. This happened and continues to happen. It can happen, however, only because Scripture is and has long been a subject, a discipline in its own right. It would not be happening, not at least, so soon and so successfully, if the study of the Old and New Testaments had not already been included in the syllabus. To teach theology with a proper scriptural dimension calls for a knowledge of and a familiarity with Scripture, which only a special study of Scripture itself can begin to provide. Similarly, to teach theology with a proper ecumenical dimension calls for a knowledge of and a familiarity with ecumenism, which only a special study of ecumenism itself can begin to provide. If, therefore, the 'ecumenical dimension in the various branches of theology' called for in the 1970s is weak or altogether lacking, if theological education in all our Churches has not so far succeeded in filling the ranks of the clergy with committed ecumenists, we do not have to look too far for one reason. As a matter of fact, Episcopal Conferences in Ireland and other countries have also called for 'special courses in ecumenism' or ecumenics. It is here surely that a beginning should be made. Happily, in its 1993 *Directory ... on Ecumenism* the Roman Catholic Church has made such a course *obligatory* for all students to be awarded its own 'pontifical' degree of BD.[17]

7
Baptism in Ecumenical Perspective

In the pages which follow I propose to deal with some of the main questions which now arise about baptism, firstly in the context of Church renewal (pp. 115-122), secondly in the context of inter-Church relations (pp. 123-127) and, thirdly, in the context of Church union (pp. 127-131).

BAPTISM IN THE CONTEXT OF CHURCH RENEWAL

At Lima in Peru in January 1982, after some fifty years of study, the Faith and Order Commission of the World Council of Churches issued its agreed text on 'Baptism, Eucharist and Ministry' (BEM). This document, already referred to here in chapter 2, has been widely welcomed. According to the Bishops' Conference of England and Wales it 'represents one of the most significant milestones of the ecumenical movement in this century…. It would be hard to praise too highly the painstaking scholarship and the deep commitment to Christian unity which lie behind this statement.'[1] Because of this wide welcome it will not, I hope, be thought ungracious or lacking in due appreciation to avert to the fact that neither in the document itself nor in any of the Church responses to it has any reference been made to the catechumenate.

Baptist perspectives

The catechumenate is an institution deserving to be better known in ecumenical circles and especially perhaps in the secularised Western world. According to the distinguished Baptist scholar, Dr G. R. Beasley-Murray:

> There is everything to be said in favour of the Church's providing for children a solemn rite of entry into its midst .... Baptists are aware that there are needs which infant baptism seeks to meet and which ought to be met by some means or other. Their own service of infant blessing or dedication has been instituted in recognition of this fact, and I have little doubt that other Churches could improve on it .... The need for initiation into the Christian society, or the catechumenate, or call it what you will, is to be granted.[2]

The author is not alone in these views. The service of infant dedication just referred to above is now, in fact, quite common among Baptists, at least in England. The Winward order for this service falls into three parts: (1) Thanksgiving; (2) Promises; and (3) Blessing. The responsibility of both parents and congregation for the Christian education of the child is clearly emphasised. The minister addresses the latter as follows:

> Do you, as members of the Church, acknowledge and accept the responsibility, together with the parents, of teaching and training this child that, being brought up in the discipline and instruction of the Lord, he may be led in due time to trust Christ as Saviour, and confessing him as Lord in baptism, be made a member of his Church?[3]

The minister's concluding prayer of blessing for the child includes an epiclesis and looks forward to the child's conversion and final perseverance:

> O God, our heavenly Father, we pray that thy Spirit may rest upon this child and dwell in him for ever. Keep him, we

entreat thee, under thy fatherly care and protection; guide him and sanctify him both in body and in soul. Grant that he may grow in wisdom as in stature, and in favour with God and man. Abundantly enrich him with thy heavenly grace; bring him safely through the perils of childhood, deliver him from the temptations of youth, and lead him in due time to witness a good confession, and to persevere therein to the end; through Jesus Christ our Lord. Amen.[4]

This order has been criticised by other Baptist theologians on the grounds that the parents envisaged seem to be committed Christians only and that 'it is too much concerned with us and our children and what we do for them, and too little concerned with a child as a child of God and what God has done for him'.[5] Those who emphasise this latter point and who would keep the service more open suggest that the children of parents who are not Church members be adopted by a family that is Christian in order that their 'new relationship with God, declared in dedication, may become realised in a relationship with God's people'.[6] But, however this Baptist service is conceived and ordered, the intended effect, although quite clearly not 'full membership of the Church', nor 'initiation into Christ and his body in the full sense', is indeed 'initiation into the Christian society', entry 'within the sphere of the Church', 'into its midst', its 'outer circle'.[7] It is in reality a service for the making of a catechumen.

Anglican perspectives

What of Anglicanism? Dr Beasley-Murray, writing in 1966, saw the Church of England as possibly 'in the van of baptismal reform within the Church of Christ in Europe, with unforeseeable consequences for the Church in the rest of the world'.[8] This baptismal reform movement dates mainly from the end of World

War II. One of the principal motives was pastoral and one of the principal issues was how to cope with the continuing demand for baptism coming from non-practising parents. Could 'indiscriminate baptism' or 'open baptism' – the description now preferred[9] – be justified? Ought not the font to be fenced as well as the table?

In 1948 an official report entitled *The Theology of Christian Initiation* suggested that the establishment of a catechumenate should be considered. In 1955 this was done in a minority report submitted to the Canterbury Convocation. The authors saw two advantages in the restoration of a catechumenate. Firstly, it would, in certain cases, prevent 'a profanation or misuse' of the sacrament of baptism and, at the same time, 'satisfy the proper desire of the parents that their child should be immediately associated in some objective way with the life of the Church'. Secondly, 'it would make possible in the case of children come to "years of discretion" the reuniting of the entire Rite of Initiation, by, once again, bringing the sundered parts together, if possible, on a single occasion'.[10]

During the 1960s it was being proposed rather widely that the Church should institute a 'rite of Naming and Blessing, together with Admission to the Catechumenate', which would be offered to non-practising parents.[11] This proposal was formally considered by a commission appointed in 1969. Its report, the Ely Report, recommended in 1971 that:

1. A new Service of Thanksgiving for the birth of a child be prepared by the Liturgical Commission of the Church of England for general use throughout the Church.
2. Such a Service of Thanksgiving be available to all who ask for it, but is not to be regarded as a substitute for baptism.[12]

'All who ask' includes, according to the Report, those 'who are unwilling to bind themselves or their children into an organic relationship with the institutional Church', those who hold that baptism is a matter for adult decision and also those who intend to have their child baptised in infancy.[13]

In 1971 the Doctrine Commission also issued a report entitled *Baptism, Thanksgiving and Blessing,* which wished to emphasise more than the Ely Commission had done the element of Blessing in the Thanksgiving Service. It also contained the following Appendix note: 'The Catechumenate':

> It should not be forgotten that during long periods of Church history and at present in the Churches of many developing countries, the catechumenate has proved a valuable tool for holding and teaching people within the ambit of the Church whilst retaining baptism until the candidate is willing and ready to take the step of personal commitment. Despite difficulties the Commission saw no decisive objections to the idea that – under whatever name – this possibility should be made available. Such a view would have the effect of defining more clearly the Church over against society at large. It might well appeal to many sensitive and intelligent Christian parents as well as to well-disposed agnostics who, while not believing themselves, might want their children to be committed to learning at first hand about the Christian faith before coming to an informed decision for or against it. Liturgically speaking, it would be simple to add an appropriate section to any proposed service if parents wished to promise that the child would receive regular Christian instruction.[14]

According to the theology of the Ely Report, Baptism is 'the full and complete rite of Christian initiation'.[15] In other words, Christian initiation begins and ends with Baptism. It ends with Baptism because Confirmation is not to be regarded as in any way a prerequisite for Holy Communion. It is to be regarded primarily 'as a service of commitment and commissioning' to be administered 'at a suitable stage in adult life'. It is not to be administered to a person baptised in adult life because 'commitment and commissioning for responsible Christian life and service are adequately declared in the Rite of Baptism of adults'.[16]

And Christian initiation begins with baptism because no rite of thanksgiving or blessing or admission to the catechumenate is a rite of entry into the Christian society, into the Christian Church. There is one such rite of entry, which is baptism, and 'there can be no other'.[17] The child for whom thanksgiving has been offered is not a 'member of Christ' but should be assured of the continuing pastoral care and concern of the Church.[18] The Report has the following paragraph with reference to the catechumenate:

> The fact that reception [into Church membership] and baptism are identical has also been obscured by the development at various times in Church history of a long catechumenate with its own ceremonies of admission. But these have admitted to a course of preparation for Church membership and not to membership itself. The catechumen is not within the fellowship of the Church, or he may be reckoned to be so only by virtue of a 'baptism of desire' which it would be difficult to attribute to infants. We cannot therefore acknowledge any 'reception' into the Church of unbaptised infants. No rite of thanksgiving can do duty for baptism, or be regarded as in any way an equivalent to it.[19]

It needs to be stressed that the Church of England has not endorsed this entire theology. On the contrary, General Synod decided in 1976 that there should be no change in the traditional order of Baptism, Confirmation and Eucharist. A number of individual dioceses are however experimenting with the practice of Communion before Confirmation but 'this is a practice now questioned by the House of Bishops, and not encouraged'.[20] The service of Thanksgiving for the Birth of a Child, incorporated in the 1980 Alternative Service Book, did follow the theology of the Ely Report rather closely; it could hardly be thought of as an order for the making of a catechumen. But a motion suggesting a revision of this service has been accepted by General Synod: 'we need something with a much stronger ecclesiological dimension, with a much stronger statement that the candidates are being accepted by the Church'.[21]

Roman Catholic perspectives

The restoration of the catechumenate for adults was one of the historic achievements of Vatican II,[22] and the *Ordo Initiationis Christianae Adultorum*, which appeared in 1972, was greeted as 'the most mature piece of liturgical reform to have issued from the Second Vatican Council, and the most portentous by far for both theological reflection and pastoral practice in the future'.[23]

This Rite of Christian Initiation of Adults sees the catechumenate preceded by a period of evangelisation, the fruits of which are: the initial faith and initial conversion by which each one feels himself or herself called away from sin and drawn toward the mystery of God's love; a true desire of following Christ and of seeking baptism; a beginning of the practice of prayer and a first taste of the life and spirit of Christians.[24] The catechumenate proper is to begin only when these basics are ensured,[25] and there is a special rite for the making of catechumens. Because they still await their baptism, the catechumens attend only the Liturgy of the Word. Already, however, they 'are joined to the Church and are part of the household of Christ',[26] and, with the exception of the Eucharist, they participate fully in the life and work of the Christian community to which they belong.[27]

This first stage of initiation is a noviciate which can last many years. The second stage ordinarily coincides with the period of Lent. The candidates are now known as *electi* or *competentes* or *illuminandi* and various ceremonies mark the course of this final period of preparation. The climax comes on the night of Holy Saturday when they are baptised, confirmed and admitted to Holy Communion. This latter is seen as 'the culminating point of their initiation'.[28] A further stage follows during Eastertide when the neophytes, through the experience of sharing in the mysteries, acquire a new sense of the faith, the Church and the world and bring to their community 'renewed vision and a new impetus'.[29]

The introduction of the catechumenate could help the process of Church renewal and baptismal renewal in various ways. For Catholics it would give new emphasis to the unity of the three sacraments of Christian initiation and, therefore, to the anomalousness of First Communion before Confirmation. It is noteworthy that the new Rite of Christian Initiation of Adults includes, despite its title, a chapter devoted to a 'Rite of Initiation for Children of Catechetical Age', i.e. of those 'who have reached the age of reason and are able to be taught'. This suggests a way in which the Christian school could renew itself by taking as its aim and object the Christian initiation of the pupils. For Baptists and other Protestants the introduction of the catechumenate would underline the radical implications of Christian initiation by adult baptism and could not but lead to a reduction in the number of those individuals calling for 'rebaptism'. For all those involved in 'local ecumenical partnerships' the introduction of the catechumenate could be a help in addressing not only the problem of 'rebaptism' but also the problems which have arisen from 'multiple membership' in the participating Churches. In fact a Working Party appointed in 1994 by Churches Together in England has recommended

> that the churches explore these issues related to 'extended membership' together, and in particular look at the ancient tradition of the catechumenate in the Church. The catechumenate allowed for a step-by-step approach to membership of the Church.[30]

BAPTISM IN THE CONTEXT OF INTER-CHURCH RELATIONS

The questions raised today about baptism in the context of inter-Church relations are chiefly two: (1) how to conceive and order the baptism of the children of an inter-Church marriage? and (2) how to cope with the continuing problem of 'rebaptism'.

Inter-Church marriage
In the inter-Church marriage situation the questions being asked are: 'Cannot our children be baptised into the One Church of Christ as it exists in our two Churches and not exclusively into one or other Church?' and 'Cannot our children be baptised jointly by ministers of both our Churches?'

According to Vatican II the Church 'subsists in the Catholic Church which is governed by the successor of Peter and by the bishops in communion with him'. Vatican II also states that 'some, even very many, of the most significant elements and endowments which together go to build up and give life to the Church itself, can exist outside the visible boundaries of the [Roman] Catholic Church'.[31] It seems possible, therefore, to suggest that the Church subsists in, is incarnated, embodied in all the Churches, but that this is so in some to a greater extent and degree, in others to a lesser extent and degree, according to the ecclesial endowments of each. If so, it would seem that we could go on to say of baptism, which begins our initiation into the Church, that it makes us belong to the Church in that particular communion which is present at the baptism and forms part of the sacramental sign, but that, radically and potentially, it makes us belong to all the Churches in which the Church is embodied. In that case, it would be our Christian upbringing which decides whether, in actual fact, we shall also come to belong to some extent to some other Church.[32]

The sacramental sign

But, it may be asked, could the sacramental sign not be so ordered that the baptism itself from the beginning signifies and effects incorporation into the Church in the two traditions of the parents of an inter-Church marriage? Could such a baptism not be registered in the parishes of both in the same way as the marriage itself has been registered? Pope Paul's 1970 Apostolic Letter on Mixed Marriages did indeed recommend the dual registration of such a marriage, but it said nothing about dual registration of the baptism of the children. It did, however, emphasise that 'both husband and wife are bound by that responsibility [for the religious education of the children] and may by no means ignore it or any of the obligations connected with it'.[33] The Catholic-Protestant Working Group in France develops this emphasis and states:

> Dual inscription would underline the fellowship and the joint responsibility of the two parishes in the Christian upbringing of the child, and the willingness of them both to welcome him in a definitive way, without his becoming a 'refugee'. The child is thus in a position to benefit from the riches of both traditions, in the first place through the ministry of his parents.

The French statement adds that 'this dual responsibility for the child is in practice much more important than the dual inscription itself'. It 'sees nothing objectionable' in dual inscription, but 'would not want to encourage this in every case'.[34]

But can baptism itself be so ordered that it signifies and effects incorporation into the two Church traditions of the parents? Can the objective intention of the rite be made to coincide with the subjective intention of some parents? The French statement insists that the child must be 'linked in a preferential way' with one of the parents and, therefore, will have the baptism performed not jointly but by the minister of the Church which is to be mainly responsible. On the other hand, it does consider the child as belonging to both Churches and as entitled to the ministrations of both, and, indeed, as belonging to the Church tradition presiding at its baptism only 'in a way which is provisional and open to the future'. It encourages, therefore, the presence and active participation at the baptism of the minister and congregation of the Church which is not presiding:

> The minister of the other Church can participate actively, especially in the Liturgy of the Word, the intercessions and prayer of praise, similarly to what is done in the celebration of mixed marriages. Where possible, it would be good to invite lay people of the other Church to take part.[35]

There is, therefore, a real, if limited, sense in which, with this French statement, we can reply in the affirmative to the questions: 'Cannot our children be baptised into the One Church of Christ as it exists in our two Churches and not exclusively into one or other Church?'; 'Cannot our children be baptised jointly by ministers of both our Churches?'

'Rebaptism'

In the context of inter-Church relations so-called 'rebaptism' has largely ceased to be an issue, at least between the Churches which practice infant baptism. Ecumenical contacts have served to promote mutual understanding and trust and to remove suspicion and doubt about the administration of baptism as about many other matters. The 1967 Ecumenical Directory, with its important section on baptism, was particularly helpful on the Catholic side. 'Rebaptism', however, continues to be a problem in the context of relations between, on the one hand, the Churches which practise infant baptism and, on the other, those which reject this in favour of believer's baptism.

If the problem of 'rebaptism' is indeed a growing one, if there is in our day a new threat to the 'once-for-all' character of baptism, it comes, I think, from the heightened importance of religious experience in modern spirituality. In the context of the charismatic renewal the danger may not, however, be so great. Not all Pentecostal Churches reject infant baptism and baptism by pouring or sprinkling. Besides, the importance Pentecostals in general attach to water baptism, whenever and however administered, is not easy to gauge. It certainly pales into insignificance by comparison with baptism in the Holy Spirit. We cannot, however, overlook the following paragraph in the Final Report of the Roman Catholic-Pentecostal Dialogue:

> Attention was drawn to the pastoral problem of persons baptised in infancy seeking a new experience of baptism by immersion later in life. It was stated that in a few traditions rites have been devised, involving immersion in water in order to afford such an experience. The Roman Catholics felt there were already sufficient opportunities within the existing liturgy for reaffirming one's baptism. Rebaptism in the strict sense of the word is unacceptable to all. Those participants who reject paedobaptism, however, explained that they do not consider as rebaptism the baptism of a believing adult who has received infant baptism. This serious ecumenical problem requires future study.[36]

Paradoxical though it may appear to some, it is in the Baptist Churches, who inherit the Anabaptist tradition, that we may find our best help in attempting to cope with the modern problem of 'rebaptism'. Some of these also fear that, because of the charismatic movement, 'it may only be one step before the baptism in water is denigrated and baptism in the Spirit exalted and made the touchstone of a person's real Christian faith'.[37] Some too are traditionally less rigid in their attitude to infant baptism. In the case of a change of Church allegiance, they would not require believer's baptism from someone baptised in infancy who had made profession of faith and been received into membership of the Church by confirmation and communion. Indeed, in an important Baptist symposium on baptism the following significant passage occurs:

> The rebaptism as believers of those who have received baptism in infancy constitutes a blow at the heart of the Christian faith. As there is one Lord, and one faith, so there is but one baptism .... Baptism stands under the ephapax of redemption. The whole meaning of the rite hinges on its once-for-allness, its unrepeatability. The assertion of the partial nature of infant Baptism and the serious theological distortion it involves does not carry with it the unqualified dismissal of it as 'no Baptism', rather does the eschatological nature of the rite forbid so negative a verdict. For no baptism can lack its proleptic element, and every baptism points forward for its completion and fulfilment.[38]

Positive thinking such as this helps to remove any grounds for 'rebaptism' on the Baptist side. Sacramental rituals which provided an affective experience and integrated faith and feeling and (as has been seen above) the establishment of the catechumenate would help on all sides.

BAPTISM IN THE CONTEXT OF CHURCH UNION

In the context of Church union there would seem to be only one baptismal question of any major significance to be faced: 'Can infant baptism and believer's baptism co-exist within a united Church?' Among Anglicans and Protestants the answer is now in the affirmative. Catholics, however, have as yet hardly begun to ask themselves the question. I shall attempt to suggest here that, other things being equal, Catholics can also give a positive answer.[39]

Church of North India

Pioneering work on this question was done by the Churches which united finally in 1970 to form the Church of North India. They included three Churches which practised believer's baptism and the Plan of Union proposed that both infant and believer's baptism be adopted as alternative practices in the united Church. An Appendix to the Plan in its first three editions addressed itself to some of the issues arising from this original proposal. On the one hand, it affirmed that 'there is one baptism which is unrepeatable in the lifetime of any person', and urged ministers to refrain from encouraging a second baptism. But, on the other hand, it did seem to leave the door, not open, but ajar for this latter possibility in the case of a person baptised in infancy and afterwards desiring believer's baptism. In the event the Baptist demand for freedom of conscience disappeared in the fourth and final edition of the Plan. 'Baptists', it has been said, 'were reluctant to press the matter because they knew the abuses that could follow from allowing rebaptism'.[40] But, unfortunately, the affirmation of the unrepeatability of baptism also disappeared and what now remains of the famous Appendix B is contained in the following Clauses of the *Constitution of the Church of North India:*

> The Church of North India is keenly aware of the fact that divergence of conviction on certain other matters of faith and practice is something which can only be borne within one fellowship by the exercise of much mutual forbearance and charity. Nevertheless, it believes that it is called to make this act of faith in the conviction that it is not the will of the Lord of the Church that they who are one in him should be divided even for such causes as these. It further believes itself to be called to this venture in the confidence that in brotherly converse within one Church those of

diverse convictions will be led together in the unity of the Spirit to learn what is his will in these matters of difference.[41]

Subsequent Church union negotiations have benefited enormously from the labours of the Churches involved in the North India scheme. The ecumenical principle just quoted which was discovered in the discussions on baptism has now come to be widely accepted. There is also general acceptance of infant and believer's baptism as alternative practices in a united Church. It only remains to note that the affirmation of the unrepeatability of baptism which was omitted in the case of North India now finds emphatic expression in the recent World Council of Churches Agreed Statement on Baptism (BEM):

> Confessing, as they do, that there is 'one baptism', all Churches are convinced that in the life of any one individual baptism is a unique and unrepeatable act. In order to safeguard this uniqueness, it is clearly necessary that Churches should be able to recognise each other's baptism and avoid any practice which could be interpreted as 'rebaptism'. Where means can be found to express publicly such mutual recognition this should be done.[42]

A Roman Catholic perspective

The Roman Catholic Church has not yet been involved in any schemes of Church union. It is not surprising, therefore, that Catholics have so far not addressed themselves to the question: 'Can infant baptism and believer's baptism co-exist within a united Church?' There would seem to be two considerations suggesting a negative answer. The first is methodological and appeals to the ecumenical principle that Church renewal is a necessary means to Church union, that 'the achievement of unity will involve nothing less than a death and rebirth of many forms of Church life as we have known them'.[43] To allow the co-existence of different baptismal disciplines in a united Church can easily be seen as nothing less than a lazy rejection of this principle.

This first consideration is not, however, conclusive. The ecumenical principle invoked is sound, but the conclusion follows only when existing differences are essential ones demanding to be resolved. In the present instance this might be true if the adherents of believer's baptism in the united Church were of such a mind as to want to unchurch their paedobaptist brethren. However, in the context of a united Church, this is impossible.

The second consideration is theological and appeals to the doctrine of original sin. It arises because an unconcerned postponement of baptism can seem to call into question the universality of original sin and the necessity of baptism for salvation. Anglicans and Protestants have, in general, been less moved by this consideration than Roman Catholics. They have found a reverent agnosticism more acceptable and have not, therefore, agonised as much as we did over the fate of infants dying without baptism. Vatican II, however, has now assured us that 'since Christ died for all, and since all men are in fact called to one and the same destiny, which is divine, we must hold that the Holy Spirit offers to all the possibility of being made partners, in a way known to God, in the paschal mystery'.[44] More significantly, the restoration of the catechumenate has given us to understand that the baptism which remits original sin can be a process lasting for many years and beginning long before water is poured on a person's head with the invocation of the threefold name. Still more significantly, perhaps, those who practise believer's baptism are coming more and more to use a service of infant dedication, the intent of which is to bring the child within the sphere of the Church and the Spirit and so to put it in the way of salvation from the corruption of sin. In which case, there are no longer any grounds for interpreting the rejection of infant baptism as implying a disregard for the doctrine of original sin.

The water that divides?

The Water That Divides is the title of a volume on baptism published some twenty years ago.[45] It is true that differences continue to exist between the Churches on the subject of baptism. However, it seems appropriate that I should end this chapter by reiterating my conviction that these differences are not major obstacles. The water of baptism unites rather than divides. In the words of Vatican II:[46]

> By the sacrament of baptism, whenever it is properly conferred in the way the Lord determined and received with the proper dispositions of soul, a person becomes truly incorporated into the crucified and glorified Christ and is reborn to a sharing of the divine life …. Baptism, therefore, constitutes the sacramental bond of unity existing among all who through it are reborn. But Baptism, of itself, is only a beginning, a point of departure, for it is wholly directed towards the acquiring of fullness of life in Christ.[47]

8
Eucharist: Means and Expression of Unity

Is the Eucharist a means of restoring unity between Christians of different traditions? Or is it rather the expression of unity already restored between Christians of different traditions – and in this latter case also a means of deepening and developing the restored unity?

Formerly the Catholic tradition (as represented among others by Anglicans, Orthodox and Roman Catholics) tended to answer this question in the negative. The reply was 'No, the Eucharist is not a means of restoring unity between Christians of different traditions; it is the expression of this unity already restored'. The Protestant tradition on the other hand tended to answer the question in the affirmative. The Protestant reply was 'Yes, the Eucharist is a means of restoring unity between Christians of different traditions'. In recent years, however, the Catholic tradition (as represented by Anglicans, many Roman Catholics but no Orthodox) tends to say: 'Yes, the Eucharist can be a means of restoring unity between Christians of different traditions but not a means to be used indiscriminately'. And this new 'yes' is increasingly finding expression in practice as well as in theory, in deed as well as in word. The aim of this chapter is twofold: firstly to attempt some explanation of the change in the Catholic position, to indicate the reasons why Roman Catholic theologians can now consider the Eucharist as a means of promoting Christian unity; and secondly to indicate very briefly some ways in which the Eucharist does deepen and develop the unity of Christians.[1]

What I wish to suggest in the following pages is that both of the

Catholic positions (the classical and the modern) can perhaps be best understood not so much in the light of a doctrine of the Eucharist or a doctrine of the ministry but rather in the light of a doctrine of reconciliation, penance, conversion; and that the change is one of application more than of principle.

Excommunciation

The statement which in Roman Catholic theology denies the Eucharist to be a means of restoring, of regaining unity, and considers it to be instead an expression of unity restored, unity regained, refers only by extension to Christians of other denominations. Traditionally it refers in the first instance to a particular class of Roman Catholics. It refers to those who have excommunicated themselves; to those who have so lapsed that they have no place at the Eucharist. They have been disobedient to their missionary calling, they have offended their brothers and sisters in the Christian community and their Father in heaven, they have alienated and estranged themselves from the Church and from God. They have done so to such an extent that they are completely out of place when the members of the community foregather to express and to strengthen their unity with one another and with God and their common dedication to the service and salvation of God's world. In such extreme cases lapsed Roman Catholics may not offer their gift at the altar and receive in return God's gift, the bread of life, until they are first reconciled with the Church and with God in the sacrament of Penance.

Reconciliation

In pre-ecumenical days the Roman Catholic Church held, in the words of Pius XI's encyclical *Mortalium animos*, that 'there is but one way in which the unity of Christians may be fostered, and that is by furthering the return to the one true Church of Christ of those who are separated from it; for from that one true Church they have in the past fallen away'.[2] It was entirely logical, therefore, for Roman Catholics to apply their doctrine of reconciliation to these other Christians and to hold that the Eucharist could not for them be a means of regaining unity with the Roman Catholic Church, but only the expression of this unity regained. Because they were considered to be outside the fold, other Christians could not be admitted to the Eucharist celebrated by Roman Catholics without first being reconciled to the Church. And Roman Catholics could not participate in Eucharists celebrated by these other Christians, or indeed in any of their church services, not, however, because their orders were held to be invalid (this would have been untrue at least of the Orthodox) but for the more obvious reason that heretics and schismatics and excommunicated persons were to be altogether avoided.

It seems relevant to note here that the Protestant traditions have not generally maintained any special ritual for the reconciliation of their own lapsed members. They would see the Eucharist itself as a converting, reconciling ordinance. This seems true of Methodists in particular.[3] If not actually related to these developments, the Protestant discipline of Open Communion is at least entirely consistent with them.

Traditional doctrine

The doctrine of reconciliation which I have sketched in outline is traditionally Catholic. It has deep roots in the past. It was well known and very dear to Calvin, whose ecclesiology is distinctive in that, for him, the ministry of the Church is not only a ministry of Word and sacrament but also a ministry of discipline. This latter consists chiefly in excommunicating and reconciling public sinners. The Eucharist, according to Calvin, is emphatically not a means of regaining unity for those who 'are divided and separated by hatred and ill-will from their brethren, that is, from the members of Christ, and thus have no part in Christ'.[4] Roman Catholics today still hold this doctrine of reconciliation. Our problem is when and how to apply it and the problem is perhaps just as acute in regard to our own members as it is in regard to other Christians.

Sacrament of Penance

We have deepened our understanding of mortal sin. Because it excludes us from the Eucharist, because it requires prior reconciliation with the Church in the sacrament of Penance, we know it must be something which puts us outside the pale of the Church. For this reason mainly, and only secondarily because of our deepened appreciation of the distinction between subjective and objective guilt, we are finding it more difficult than before to identify mortal sin and to discern the role of the sacrament of Penance in the life of the ordinary churchgoing Roman Catholic.

We have always held, in theory at least, that there were other means, besides the sacrament of Penance, of reconciling baptised sinners and re-uniting them with the Church and with God. Penance, we have held, and hold, to be a special means for the special case of those persons who, by mortal sin, have excommunicated themselves. All baptised persons, however, who fall into sin, do, to some extent at least, disobey their missionary calling, injure and offend the Church and God, become alienated and estranged from the Church and from God. In the measure therefore in which they have sinned, they stand in need of being reconciled and re-united. In the case of those who have not sinned to the extent of excommunicating themselves, the Church exercises its ministry of reconciliation by its whole life, by the preaching of the Word and by the sacrament of the Eucharist. Since the Reformation, however, we have for polemical reasons so emphasised the sacrament of Penance as the Church's reconciling ordinance that the reconciling role of the Church's other means of grace was largely forgotten and the sacrament of Penance became in practice our sole means of reconciling sinners. We are now trying to restore the balance. In particular we are coming to realise once again that the Eucharist itself holds a very important place in the Church's ministry of reconciliation, though without prejudice to the sacrament of Penance. We are coming to see that the Eucharist can be a means of regaining unity, of restoring unity, at least for our own members.

The Eucharist and reconciliation
To describe the relationship between the Eucharist and post-baptismal sin, Roman Catholics would in the past have had recourse to the words of the thirteenth session of the Council of Trent: it is 'an antidote by which we are freed from daily faults and preserved from mortal sins'.[5] We have now discovered that at a subsequent session, the twenty-second, the same Council of Trent stated: 'If we approach God with a sincere heart and right faith, with fear and reverence, contrite and repentant, we obtain mercy and grace [through the sacrifice of the Mass]. Placated by this oblation, the Lord grants grace and repentance, and remits crimes and even the greatest sins (*crimina et peccata etiam ingentia dimittit*).'[6]

This is a hard saying for most Roman Catholic theologians and we still await a satisfactory synthesis of the theology of Penance and Eucharist.[7] No explanation, however, can be allowed to explain away the latter statement of Trent. It reminds us that when we maintain that Christians communicating together are proclaiming that they are one Church, when we maintain the Eucharist to be a manifestation of the unity of the Church, we must also recognise the limitations of this position. Because the Eucharist is, at least for members of our own Church, a reconciling and re-uniting ordinance, because the eucharistic Church can sincerely pray for 'that peace and unity which are agreeable to thy will', it follows that the unity which the Eucharist manifests and pre-requires cannot be as complete and perfect as it might and ought to be here below. The unity manifested and pre-required by the Eucharist is the unity of a pilgrim people needing reconciliation and a perfecting of its unity. The statement quoted from the twenty-second session of Trent also confirms that the sacrament of Penance is a very special, indeed exceptional means of reconciling and re-uniting the baptised sinner; that, in the ordinary life of committed, practising Roman Catholics, the Eucharist is meant to be their ordinary means of regaining any unity which they may lose by sin.

Conversion

The application within our own Church of the traditional Roman Catholic doctrine of reconciliation is further complicated by the fact that, for theological as well as psychological reasons, we are coming to appreciate more and more the place of conversion in the reconciling of sinners. The *ex opere operato* doctrine in the case of the sacraments of Penance and Eucharist and the efficacy we attribute to the ministry of the Word will not, we know, automatically ensure the reconciliation of sinners. To be reconciled sinners must have a change of heart; they must repent and be converted. Their baptismal faith must be revivified, their baptismal promises must be renewed. There must be a rupture with godless ways and worldly desires, a turning away in detestation from the follies and idols of the past. There must be a reversal of the process of the fall, of the lapse, of the sin. And this reversal cannot now but be laborious and penitential. Instead of being instantaneous it will ordinarily take time, a considerable time, perhaps. The place, therefore, of such a reconciling ordinance as the sacrament of Penance will be towards the end of a long road of conversion.[8]

Conversion to ecumenism

We may now go on to consider how the Roman Catholic doctrine of reconciliation might be applied to Christians of other Churches in the very changed circumstances of the modern ecumenical movement. The conversion aspect of the doctrine seems immediately relevant. There are still some Christian Churches who will have nothing to do with ecumenism. In addition, there are very many Christians in all the Churches whose attitude to other denominations and their members is either one of bitterness and bigotry, of pride and prejudice, of arrogance and antipathy, or, on the other hand, one of coldness and indifference, of apathy and unconcern. Is the Eucharist in these cases a means of regaining, of restoring unity? The answer I suggest is quite clearly in the negative. Their conversion has not even begun. They are in no way, to no extent, committed to the ecumenical movement. All other considerations apart, this, in the light of the doctrine of reconciliation, seems a sufficient reason for not inviting or admitting them to share the Eucharist. But what of those Christians whose ecumenical conversion has already begun but as yet has not advanced very far? Here I would refer to those whose contribution to the ecumenical movement is made in words rather than in deeds, to those who only sporadically (on such occasions as the annual Unity Week) engage in some interdenominational activity. For these too, and on the basis of our theology of conversion and reconciliation, I would maintain that the Eucharist is not a means of regaining unity with other Christians. It follows that the Eucharist is, to say the least, not a means to be used indiscriminately to promote unity between Christians of different traditions and that the Open Table position of Protestants as commonly understood gives rise to serious difficulties.

But what of those Christians whose ecumenical conversion has advanced a considerable distance? What of those who are painfully concerned about the scandal of Christian disunity, who make a sustained effort in joint action for mission, who have plenty of experience in working together and in praying together, though without sharing the Eucharist? Because in this case the situation obtaining is not one of total alienation and estrangement, because the process of conversion is well advanced, a shared Eucharist can, it seems to me, be considered justifiable, desirable and necessary as a means of furthering ecumenical conversion, of deepening the unity already achieved, with a view to the eventual re-establishment of some form of Church union. This position is no longer new in Roman Catholic circles. What is new, to my knowledge, is the approach, the argument. I am submitting that the Eucharist can be a means of promoting Christian unity on the basis of the traditional Catholic doctrine of reconciliation, penance, conversion.

Imperfect communion

But someone may say, and quite rightly, that the progress made in the way of conversion has never been the only relevant factor in deciding whether to readmit a person to eucharistic communion. According to the traditional, still valid, doctrine of reconciliation there are certain cases where the original situation involved such a degree of alienation and estrangement that at a certain stage in the process of conversion the persons concerned must be formally reconciled before being readmitted to the Eucharist. This is indeed true, but is it relevant in the context of the ecumenical movement? However imperfect, a very real ecclesial communion in baptismal faith, hope and charity does exist between the separated Churches, and one of the fundamental features of a commitment to ecumenism is a recognition and acceptance of this communion. The ecumenically-committed Christian of another denomination is, in Roman Catholic theology, neither juridically nor spiritually excommunicated. To be an ecumenically-minded Christian is to experience and to know oneself growing in communion with other Churches and with their spiritual leaders and authorities as well as with their ordinary members. This growth, indeed, can reach such a point that dual membership of some sort becomes a theoretical and practical possibility if no more.

Precisely because of the existence of an ecclesial though imperfect communion between members of separated Churches, the analogy, it may be urged, is not with the persons who have excommunicated themselves by mortal sin but rather with those in the state of venial sin. But just as these latter may be admitted immediately to the Eucharist as their means of regaining such unity with their sisters and brothers in the Christian community and with their Father in heaven as they have lost, why not therefore admit to the Eucharist in the Roman Catholic Church any members of another Church, even though they are in no way committed to ecumenism, in order precisely to draw them into, to convert them to the ecumenical movement? This is a fallacy because those who are opposed or apathetic to or only faintly interested in ecumenism differ from the venial sinner in that they will not want to engage in eucharistic sharing. The unity subsisting between persons in the state of venial sin and their own communion goes very much deeper than that existing between Christians of different Churches whose commitment to the ecumenical movement is non-existent or negligible. To be opposed or indifferent to the ecumenical movement means to reject the ecclesial communion subsisting in fact between the separated Churches. *It is only where a very real ecclesial communion still subsists and is recognised and accepted, welcomed and obeyed that the Eucharist can be a means of regaining, of restoring unity.* The Eucharist, because it is a sacrament, is 'primarily' an expression, a sign and 'only secondarily' a means. It is basic to sacramental theology that the sacraments are effectual because and insofar as they are signs: *significando causant*.

Emerging consensus on the Eucharist

It remains to consider briefly some ways in which the Eucharist does deepen and develop the unity of Christians who are ecumenically committed. We need to remind ourselves that, for many other reasons besides ecumenism, theology in the main Churches is ceasing, if it has not altogether ceased, to be polemical; that Roman Catholics, therefore, for the most part no longer see and understand themselves as non-Protestants or as anti-Protestant; that in like manner other Christians no longer see and understand themselves as non-Romans or anti-Romans. This now means, if it did not already mean it in the past, that the prevailing intention of non-Roman Catholics celebrating the Eucharist or assisting at its celebration consists in fidelity to the Lord's command to 'do this in memory of me'. The positive exclusion of doing whatever it is that the Roman Catholics do has no place or at least no significant place in their aim and intention. The same holds, too, in relation to ministers ordaining others to the ministry of Word and sacrament. Their overriding concern is to enable the Lord's command to be fulfilled in the ecclesial communities which are their spiritual responsibility.

Another related result of the current non-polemical character of theology in our different Christian traditions is the emergence of a consensus on the Eucharist which would be unbelievable were it not true. The Eucharist, we would all now tend to agree, is not to be understood merely as a means of personal, spiritual growth. As a 1972 Roman Catholic document on admission to the Eucharist stated: 'simultaneously and inseparably it concerns our entering more deeply into Christ's Church, 'which is his body, the fullness of him who fills all in all' (Ep 1:23).[9] In theory, if not yet in practice, the centrality of the Eucharist is now a generally accepted truth. The Eucharist, we would agree, is the means *par excellence* by which the Church becomes the Church: a more committed, believing, worshipping and witnessing community; the means *par excellence* by which the people of God grow in love, in faith, in hope, in their dedication to the Lord and his world, and so become, more really and truly and effectively, the sign and sacrament and instrument of universal, cosmic salvation. It is the

Eucharist above all which builds up the body which is the Church, until all 'attain to the unity of the faith and of the knowledge of the Son of God, to maturity, to the measure of the full stature of Christ' (Ep 4:13).

Anamnesis

There are two ways worthy of special mention in which this now generally accepted truth is verified for ecumenically-minded Christians in regard not only to the members of their own Church but also to the members of other Churches. The first way worthy of mention here in which the Eucharist builds up the Church, builds up the Churches into the one Church, involves its nature as the mystery of faith, as the sacrament of the Christian faith. The faith which the Eucharist develops and also requires is baptismal faith, the faith of the creeds, faith in the principal mysteries of Christianity, faith as the believing hope aroused by salvation history. The Eucharist builds up this faith (which is common to all Christians) because it is the anamnesis of this salvation history. Nothing perhaps is more characteristic of modern eucharistic theology than its emphasis on the real meaning of the biblical notion of anamnesis as 'the making effective in the present of an event in the past'.[10] This has made it possible to understand the Eucharist as an effectual proclamation of salvation history, to see how it increases as well as manifests our faith and, in consequence, to appreciate how sharing the Eucharist can help to build up our separated Churches into the one Church united in faith which we are meant to be. It should be noted in addition that a shared Eucharist is a vital element of the common experience necessary if the agreed statements on the Eucharist are to be generally received. Such agreed statements will not of course impose complete uniformity in the analysis and verbalisation of the common faith experience. Roman Catholics already know this from their own history which has enriched us with many differing theologies of the Eucharist itself and of every other area of the faith which is expressed in the eucharistic mystery.

The second way which seems worthy of mention here in which the Eucharist builds up the Church involves its essential missionary nature. The Eucharist is missionary. It manifests and builds up the Church as an institution for others, as an agent of God's salvation, as an instrument of the Kingdom. This is a point which the Constitution on the Sacred Liturgy of the Second Vatican Council did not sufficiently stress. As one Roman Catholic liturgist put it:

> That Christ's Body and Blood is the source of strength for our human task of social love and justice, that God's gift becomes our personal and communal obligation to the world in which we live, is, most regrettably, not an evident major concern of the Constitution on the Sacred Liturgy. Despite conscious efforts to strike a better balance, the cult motif still predominates at the expense of mission to men, to all men, to the world. The worship of the transcendent God continues to obscure to some extent our recognizing his immanence in the world and among the men he redeemed.[11]

No doctrine of Vatican II can, however, be derived from the exclusive study of any one of its documents. The Eucharist is missionary of its very nature because, as the Council states explicitly elsewhere, the Church is 'by its very nature missionary'.[12] Through the Holy Spirit in the Eucharist Christ – so we read in the Anglican/Roman Catholic Agreed Statement – 'builds up the life of the Church, strengthens its fellowship and furthers its mission'.[13] The Faith and Order BEM statement of the World Council of Churches is fuller and stronger.[14]

Basically the Eucharist builds up the Church as missionary, builds up the separated Churches in their efforts towards joint action for mission, builds them up into the one Church united for mission, which is their vocation and God's will because it is the anamnesis, the Church's effectual proclamation of God's mighty deeds of salvation, because it is a foretaste of the *Parousia* when Christ shall appear in the fullness of his Kingdom (cf. 1 Corinthians 15:28), and because in the Eucharist we partake of the Body and Blood of the Lord which was given and shed for the world and, by so partaking, express and renew our dedication to the service and salvation of the world in the manner and in the power of Christ.

Conclusion

There are, of course, degrees of eucharistic sharing, as there are degrees of ecclesial communion. Active participation in the Eucharist is not to be identified with, does not require 'going to communion', 'receiving the elements'. Catholic practice in pre-Vatican II days and Orthodox practice today clearly demonstrate this. There is real if imperfect eucharistic sharing when those present at a celebration of the Eucharist take part fully in the Liturgy of the Word, but at communion time present themselves to receive a blessing rather than the eucharistic elements. This practice shows very clearly that unfortunately our Churches are not yet in full communion, but that, nevertheless, though our communion is still imperfect, it is none the less real. The sharing is, of course, enhanced, if the actual reading of the Word, if not the preaching, is done by someone of a Church other than that of the presiding celebrant. In any case the practice can be a very painful experience but still very positive, moving and salutary.[15]

Finally, it must be remembered that all our problems as disunited Christian believers, and not only the problem of eucharistic sharing, pale into almost complete insignificance when we see them in perspective: when we view them against the backdrop of our problems as disunited religious believers, some of whom are followers of Christ, most of whom are not, but all of whom are servants of the one Kingdom of God and yet have hardly begun to enter into dialogue; and when we view them as well against the backdrop of our problems as disunited human beings, some of whom can indeed live according to human standards, but most of whom are condemned to a subhuman existence in poverty, hunger, illiteracy and various other forms of injustice. Without the stimulus of this perspective we cannot but shy away from the risks which our Christian faith imposes on us. But, if we continue to refuse (as the WCC put it at Uppsala in 1968) to 'anticipate God's Kingdom in joyful worship and daring acts', we run the other risk of ending up, as the British sociologist Bryan Wilson claims we are already: relatively tiny and totally insignificant sects.[16]

9
Catholicity: The Witness of Calvin's *Institutes*

INTRODUCTION[*]

The terms 'Catholic' and 'Evangelical' describe two contrasting if not opposing styles or emphases in churchmanship. Traditionally Catholics are not Evangelical and Evangelicals are not Catholic; Protestants in general are Evangelical and not Catholic – Anglicans an uneasy combination of both – and in German there is even still no common wording of the creed: 'Some confess that the church is "catholic", others that it is "christian", others again that it is "general" or "universal".'[1]

Liberal Protestantism and Evangelicalism
According to Liberal Protestantism 'the whole outward and visible institution of a Church claiming divine dignity has no foundation whatever in the Gospel... Let anyone who has such a Church have it as though he had it not'.[2] Evangelicalism, by contrast, does not reject but puts less emphasis on the visible institutional Church as indwelt and empowered by the Spirit of Jesus. It does not reject but neither does it give pride of place to the sacraments as saving encounters with Christ. Evangelicalism tends to emphasise the cross more than the incarnation, Word more than sacrament, faith and conversion more than baptism, devotion more than doctrine, the individual more than the body.

---

[*] This chapter falls into four parts: I 'Introduction' (pp. 145-147); II 'The Problem: Evangelical or Catholic?' (pp. 147-151); III 'The Institution: Mother Church' (pp. 151-159); IV 'Church as Mystery' (pp. 159-167). It is of course presumed throughout that 'Catholicity' is not exclusive to Roman Catholicism.

Clearly the whole tenor of the work of the Faith and Order Commission of the World Council of Churches is a far cry from any form of Protestantism which might be thought to have 'an inherited inability to take the visible Church with due seriousness'.[3] It is certainly far removed not only from the Liberal Protestantism of Harnack but also from much of the Evangelical Protestantism of the Anglo-Saxon world. The World Council of Churches' BEM Report makes it abundantly clear how much the Churches of the WCC have agreed in principle to take Catholicity 'into their system'.[4] And Vatican II shows how much Catholicism has taken Evangelicalism into its system by becoming, for instance, more Bible-centred in its life and thought. Ecumenical progress involves a convergence of the Evangelical and Catholic traditions.

On the other hand the less than unanimous welcome given so far to Faith and Order Reports, the slow reception of its insights goes to show that within the WCC the Evangelical spirit still remains strong, resistant to change and to the challenges of Catholicity. More significantly, however, the WCC may soon include only a minority of the world's non-Roman Catholic Christians.[5] The majority will belong to Churches which are Evangelical in ethos and untouched by the influence of the ecumenical movement.

That is the context which helps to highlight the relevance of this chapter's study of Calvin's *Institutes*. It may help reluctant Evangelicals to take Catholicity into their system when they find how profoundly Catholic Calvin himself was and is and how true it is that 'a good deal of "Calvinism" does ill justice to Calvin'.[6] And it may help reluctant Catholics to be more sympathetic to Evangelicalism when they discover the depths of Calvin's religious experience and the mystical strain[7] in his theology.

According to the American Presbyterian scholar J. T. McNeill, *The Institutes of the Christian Religion* is 'one of the few books that have profoundly affected the course of history'.[8] According to the

English Methodist scholar, Gordon Rupp, it 'ranks alongside St Benedict's *Rule* and Marx's *Das Kapital* as a normative document of European history .... Here was a coherent, superbly lucid theology .... Not least important was its display of the majestic place of the visible Church within this divine order, and of the dignity and importance of the pastoral office'.[9]

THE PROBLEM: EVANGELICAL OR CATHOLIC?

In its final form, published in Latin in 1559,[10] Calvin's *Institutes* is composed of four books entitled as follows:

- The Knowledge of God the Creator
- The Knowledge of God the Redeemer in Christ, First disclosed to the Fathers under the Law, and then to us in the Gospel
- The Way in which we Receive the Grace of Christ: what Benefits come to us from it, and what Effects Follow
- The External Means or Aids by which God invites us into the Society of Christ and holds us Therein

As the latter title indicates, the fourth book deals with the Church (including the sacraments) and in the Barth-Niesel Latin edition it is a separate volume of some five hundred pages constituting one-third of the whole work. Quantitative considerations cannot, of course, by themselves be decisive, but with all due reserve we can agree already with the editor of the modern English translation that 'the space accorded by Calvin to the doctrine of the Church in the *Institutes* is evidence of the high importance it assumed for him'.[11] Against this, however, it may be argued at once that the position if not the length of the fourth book shows that Calvin lacked a true sense of the Church's centrality in the Christian dispensation. Does he not in the third book 'put his whole teaching on the Christian life before a single word on the Church'?

It may be admitted that Calvin's order of exposition does seem to support this conclusion but the whole history of the development of ecclesiology reminds us that we must be slow in arguing to the churchmanship of theologians from the place they give the Church in their theological exposition. St Thomas Aquinas also presents his teaching on the Christian life before treating the sacraments, indeed even before treating of Christ and of redemption. Calvin in the *Institutes* is in fact broadly following the order of the Apostles' Creed: Father, Son, Holy Spirit, Church.

Sanctification

It can be further argued, however, that the content, if not the position, of the third book shows Calvin to be very much an Evangelical Protestant. This argument is worthy of more lengthy consideration and I now propose to outline in summary form and in his own words to a large extent Calvin's ideas on sanctification as found chiefly in the third but also in the fourth book of the *Institutes*.

For Calvin sanctification means union with Christ himself. It is our growing, our being ingrafted into one body with Christ and becoming his members. Salvation is this 'joining together of Head and members', this 'indwelling of Christ in our hearts', this 'mystical union',[12] because Christ is our only saviour and our mediator. It is by being in Christ, by being united to him that God's promise of grace becomes ours effectively and that we are saved. Salvation is faith by the operation, 'the secret energy' of the Holy Spirit. It is not faith deprived of charity. It is not the faith which is a bare and simple assent arising out of knowledge without confidence and assurance of heart. 'Faith is a singular gift of God both in that the mind of man is purged so as to be able to taste the truth of God and in that his heart is established therein.'[13] Faith makes the promises ours. 'Faith properly begins with the promise, rests in it, and ends in it.'[14]

This saving faith by which we possess Christ and God's mercy, by which we participate in Christ's death and resurrection, includes as its formal effect repentance and forgiveness of sins. And the fruits of this repentance are 'the duties of piety toward God, of charity toward men, and in the whole of life, holiness and purity'.[15] But if we are to remain in Christ and retain this saving faith, he alone should rule and reign. He is the only food of our soul. He is our sole teacher and only lawgiver. 'They should acknowledge one King, their deliverer Christ, and should be governed by one law of freedom, the holy Word of the gospel, if they would retain the grace they once obtained in Christ.'[16]

The third book of Calvin's *Institutes* ought perhaps to be regarded as largely a *summa pietatis* rather than a *summa theologiae*.[17] It is certainly the fruit of deep spiritual experience but none the less certainly, as we can now see, it raises a serious problem. Does the book not imply the typically Protestant idea that 'the real Church is invisible', that 'the negation and condemnation of intermediaries' is 'the Gospel within the Gospel',[18] that faith in Christ rather than any institution is the real essence of Christianity? And this in the past was the answer of some commentators:

> When Calvin put his whole teaching on the Christian life before a single word on the Church and made the Church simply an external aid to the individual he rightly stressed the need of personal faith but he failed to give that picture of the Church as the Body of Christ which is so prominent in the Apostle's thought. He did, however, produce this picture in the last book of the *Institutes* after a more individualistic one. But it was the former [*sic*] which came to dominate the seventeenth century.[19]

This 'individualistic' interpretation of the third book is hardly sustainable. It is possible only in the light of a preconception which posits a dichotomy between mystical body and visible Church and which is unable to understand how a deep Catholic sense of the Church could underlie Calvin's religious experience.[20] In any case his *Institutes* must surely be read steadily and read whole; the fourth book is essential to his thought. Despite appearances to the contrary his awareness of a close relationship between *in Christo* and *in Ecclesia* is already apparent in the third book. It is there notably if paradoxically in his long anti-Roman discussion of repentance and sacramental confession and his remarkably positive outlook on the latter. This awareness, however, of an intimate relationship between Christ and the Church is a special feature of Book IV and it now remains for us to consider it. An introductory word, however, on the background of the *Institutes* and the variety of its polemical trends will, I think, be of some help.

Background

Anti-Romanism is a prominent feature of Calvin's work. It is there with all the sixteenth-century's power of invective and the author's own magnificent power of language, in French as well as Latin. But anti-Romanism is something we all expect to find in Calvin. Roman Catholics may indeed be pleasantly surprised to find that, like Luther, he does not altogether unchurch us – a compliment we have taken four centuries to return – and that he explicitly recognises our baptism and other *vestigia ecclesiae*.[21] We will certainly be surprised to find that his theology is far from being monochrome; that besides being anti-Roman it is also anti-Anabaptist, anti-Zwinglianist and anti-Lutheran. The greatest surprise of all, however, will be to find that these three latter trends have profoundly influenced his thinking; more so, it might be argued, than his anti-Romanism. The reason for our surprise at this may well be our own ignorance but it does seem more than a coincidence that the popular idea of Calvinism as understressing sacraments and liturgy and visibility coincides precisely with the anti-Roman trend of his thought as uncorrected by the other three. It is in these at any rate that Calvin's Catholicity shows forth most clearly. His stress on visible structures and visible unity, on sacraments and liturgy, on the real eucharistic presence is closely associated with the anti-Anabaptist, anti-Zwinglianist and anti-Lutheran trends in his theology. Hence, to take these away, to put an exclusive or unbalanced emphasis on Calvin's anti-Romanism, cannot but endanger the more positive, more orthodox, more Catholic aspects of his teaching. But whatever the real explanation of the popular image of Calvinism, it is the three non-anti-Roman trends in the fourth book of the *Institutes* which must receive special attention in what follows.

THE INSTITUTION: MOTHER CHURCH

In the title of the first chapter of the fourth book of the *Institutes* the Church is referred to as 'the mother of all the faithful' (*piorum omnium mater*)[22] and this idea of the Church as mother is almost immediately expanded in two remarkable passages which deserve to be quoted here in full:

> I shall start, then, with the Church, into whose bosom God is pleased to gather his sons, not only that they may be nourished by her help and ministry as long as they are infants and children, but also that they may be guided by her motherly care until they mature and at last reach the goal of faith. 'For what God has joined together, it is not lawful to put asunder', so that for those to whom he is Father the Church may also be Mother ....
>
> But because it is now our intention to discuss the visible Church, let us learn even from the simple title 'mother' how useful, indeed how necessary, it is that we should know her.

> For there is no other way to enter into life unless this mother conceive us in her womb, give us birth, nourish us at her breast, and lastly, unless she keep us under her care and government until, putting off mortal flesh, we become like the angels. Our weakness does not allow us to be dismissed from her school until we have been pupils all our lives. Furthermore, away from her bosom one cannot hope for any forgiveness of sins or any salvation, as Isaiah and Joel testify. Ezekiel agrees with them when he declares that those whom God rejects from heavenly life will not be enrolled among God's people.... By these words God's fatherly favour and the especial witness of spiritual life are limited to his flock, so that it is always disastrous to leave the Church.[23]

Calvin the man and Calvin the theologian emerge from these quotations in a rather unexpected light. This is authentic Catholic piety and Catholic insight without any trace of Protestantism, either evangelical or liberal. Calvin is re-echoing a venerable tradition: showing his indebtedness to and continuity with the Church of the Fathers, Cyprian and Augustine in particular. So much so indeed that in the past some of his commentators have found this Catholic insight or Roman conceit an embarrassing puzzle. 'In spite of the combined approval of Cyprian and Calvin, these words, in their plain meaning, are [I believe] untrue.'[24] On the contrary I wish to suggest in the rest of this chapter that they are not only true in themselves but vital to Calvin's thinking; that they are no mere purple passages but integral to his doctrine of the Church; that they provide a happy summary of his whole ecclesiology. For Calvin (I hope to show) the Church is a visible, functional, structured community born as such not of 'the will of man but of God'. It is the sphere and place in which the divine event of salvation in Christ is continually 'exhibited', made visible and available, because the Holy Spirit has come upon it and the power of the Most High overshadows it.

The Church's ministry

From the passages just quoted it is clear that for Calvin the Church is a mother in and through her ministry. This he chiefly understands as a special ministry, reserved to some, and whatever his views on the collegiality of Church structures and on the 'priesthood' of all believers, they were certainly not such as to abolish all distinctions. Calvin, in fact, has as little scruple in dividing the Church into clergy and people as he has in speaking of the popularly un-Protestant notion of 'ecclesiastical power'.[25] And he is emphatic that a layman cannot administer even baptism, let alone the Eucharist.[26] Now one notable feature of the fourth book of the *Institutes* is that Church and ministry (in this sense) are closely associated and almost identified. 'The majestic place of the visible Church' is largely the majestic place of the Church's authoritative ministry. It is mainly in his doctrine of the ministry that Calvin presents his doctrine of the Church as an institution and it is above all, therefore, in his vindication of the divine origin of the ministry that we find his doctrine of the Church as itself an institution which is divine. All this strangely recalls the post-Tridentine tendencies of the Roman Catholic Church and it has of course its explanation to a large extent in somewhat similar circumstances: the menace of schismatic spiritualism and individualism present in the contemporary Anabaptist movement. 'Satan', Calvin says explicitly, 'is now striving to overthrow the ministry.'[27]

Ministry of 'discipline'

According to the *Institutes* the ministry of the Church is not only a ministry of Word and sacrament but also a ministry of discipline, i.e. of jurisdiction or spiritual government. Besides the preaching of the gospel and the celebration of the sacred mysteries, it includes the exercise of discipline which consists chiefly in excommunicating and reconciling public sinners; and this inclusion is a distinctive feature of Calvin's ecclesiology. In all its three aspects the ministry is presented in the fourth book of the *Institutes* as of divine origin and therefore essential. The ministers are those 'who take the place of the apostles'.[28] Already in the first chapter (the whole burden of which is unity) Calvin speaks of God as 'the author of this order' and of 'this ministry ... Christ so ordained in the Church that, if destroyed, the upbuilding of the Church would fail'. He recognises that 'God's power is not bound to outward means' but adds, in a passage referring to preaching, that 'he [God] has nonetheless bound us to this ordinary manner of teaching'. Calvin therefore has no hesitation in saying that it is always disastrous to leave the Church:[29]

> Where the preaching of the gospel is reverently heard and the sacraments are not neglected, there for the time being no deceitful or ambiguous form of the Church is seen; and no one is permitted to spurn its authority, flout its warnings, resist its counsels, or make light of its chastisements – much less to desert it and break its unity.[30]

Calvin and schism

By way of digression it may be noted that this is only one of many similar passages which puzzle outsiders even when they appreciate the Anabaptist background. How, we wonder, can this founder of the Reformed, Presbyterian family of Churches speak in such earnest, indeed passionate terms of the evils of disunity and the 'sacrilege of schism'? At first sight the qualifications added do not seem to solve the puzzle if only because Calvin himself proceeds to modify them. 'Some fault', he says, 'may creep into the administration of either doctrine or sacraments, but this ought not to estrange us from communion with the Church'.[31] And of itself, he notes with particular emphasis, scandal in the Church ('even if it otherwise swarms with many faults') does not justify separation. 'For a godly conscience is not wounded by the unworthiness of another, whether pastor or laymen; nor are the sacraments less pure and salutary for a holy and upright man because they are handled by unclean persons.' The perfectionist Anabaptists are 'vainly seeking a Church besmirched with no blemish'.[32] On second thoughts, however, we are forced to admit that in intention and in conscience Calvin was in no sense a schismatic, much less the founder of a new Church. For him it was Rome (because of its essential corruption of Word and sacrament) which had seceded and largely unchurched itself.[33] Calvin considered himself a reforming member of the one, holy, Catholic Church of the Creed. He says explicitly that 'there could not be two or three Churches unless Christ be torn asunder – which cannot happen'.[34]

A Pauline argument
Returning to our subject of the Church's ministry and proceeding to chapter 3 of the fourth book we now find Calvin formally treating 'of the order by which the Lord willed his Church to be governed', 'as it has been handed down to us from God's pure Word'.[35] Leaving aside his discussion of the forms of the ministry we may note in particular his commentary on a passage from the fourth chapter of Ephesians:

> Paul shows by these words [Ep 4:8, 10-16] that this human ministry which God uses to govern the Church is the chief sinew by which believers are held together in one body. He then also shows that the Church can be kept intact only if it be upheld by the safeguards in which it pleased the Lord to place its salvation …. Whoever, therefore, either is trying to abolish this order of which we speak and this kind of

government, or discounts it as not necessary, is striving for the undoing or rather the ruin and destruction of the Church. For neither the light and heat of the sun, nor food and drink, are so necessary to nourish and sustain the present life as the apostolic and pastoral office is necessary to preserve the Church on earth.

I have accordingly pointed out above that God often commended the dignity of the ministry by all possible marks of approval in order that it might be held among us in highest honour and esteem, even as the most excellent of all things .... He [Paul] therefore contends that there is nothing more notable or glorious in the Church than the ministry of the gospel .... The purport of these [2 Co 4:6; 3:9] and like passages is that the mode of governing and keeping the Church through ministers (a mode established by the Lord forever) may not be ill esteemed among us and through contempt fall out of use.[36]

The superlatives here are rather remarkable for Calvin but, to leave us in no possible doubt about the majestic place of the authoritative ministry in God's own design for the Church, he returns to the subject again and again throughout the entire book and especially in chapters 8 to 12. Here in particular the emphasis is all apparently anti-Roman but the underlying stress on the ministry, on visible structures, on the power of the Church which 'is to be not grudgingly manifested',[37] above all the stress on discipline as 'the Church's sinews through which the members of the body hold together, each in his own place',[38] is as a result only all the more significant. This stress, it may be noted, is the main distinguishing feature of the second and later editions of the *Institutes* as compared with the first. Mere anti-Romanism combined with Lutheranism and its lack of emphasis on the ministry of discipline could easily lead to a docetic, 'invisibilist' stress in ecclesiology. And this in fact is what happened in the first edition of the *Institutes* written before

Calvin himself assumed the grave responsibilities of a ministry being undermined by Anabaptists.[39]

Collegiality

Before closing this section on the Church as institution, a special word ought to be added on the collegiality of Church structures according to Calvin. Peter, he says, did excel the others in fervour of zeal, in doctrine and in courage, but he had no primacy of power.[40] Still:

> Nature bears this, man's natural constitution demands it, that in an assembly, even though all are equal in power, one should be the moderator, as it were, to whom the others look. There is no meeting of the Senate without a consul, no session of judges without a praetor or prosecutor, no committee without a chairman [*collegium nullum sine praefecto*], no association without a president. Thus there would be nothing absurd in our confessing that the apostles yielded primacy of this sort to Peter.[41]

Christ himself, however, gave nothing to Peter 'which was not also common to his colleagues'.[42] Christ's intention was 'not to prefer one man to the others but that he might so commend unity to the Church'. In the words of Augustine, 'as Peter spoke for all so he received this [the power of the keys] with all as the personification of unity, '*tamquam personam gerens ipsius unitatis*'.[43]

In the early Church too collegiality was the mark of Church government at all levels and unity was its purpose. Calvin does not reject in principle a collegial primacy,[44] and Gregory the Great (who in his opinion was the last true bishop of Rome) is quoted with approval as saying:

> I do not through ambition deprive anyone of what is his right but I desire to honour my brothers in all things …. I

know of no bishop who would not be subject to the apostolic see where he is found at fault. When there is no fault all are equal according to the order of humility.[45]

With regard to the episcopate and the clergy Calvin again finds a delicate balance of power to have existed, the presbyters being subject to the presiding bishop and the latter subject to the assembly of his brethren. Jerome is quoted with approval and Calvin writes as follows:

> And the ancients themselves admit that this was introduced by human agreement to meet the need of the times .... Just as the presbyters, therefore, know that they are, according to the custom of the Church, subject to him who presides, so bishops recognise that they are superior to the presbyters more according to the custom of the Church than by the Lord's actual arrangement, and that they ought to govern the Church in co-operation with them .... Each college was under one bishop merely for the preservation of its organisation and peace. While he surpassed the others in dignity, he was subject to the assembly of his brethren.[46]

Finally, with regard to the laity, Calvin also shows that they too co-operated in the government of the Church. Cyprian is now quoted with approval: 'From the beginning of my episcopate I determined not to do anything without the advice of the clergy and the consent of the people.'[47] In the calling of ministers, therefore, the people's approval is necessary but, Calvin adds characteristically, 'other pastors ought to preside over the election in order that the multitude may not go wrong either through fickleness, through evil intentions or through disorder'.[48] There are also to be 'elders chosen from the people ... charged with the censure of morals and the exercise of discipline along with the bishops'. In incorporating the laity into the Church's structures Calvin does show a certain reserve which in expression at least seems to owe something to his legal studies and love of Plato as well as to the Anabaptist movement.[49]

CHURCH AS MYSTERY

From the foregoing there can hardly be any doubt about 'the majestic place of the visible Church' in Calvin's *Institutes*. The work lends no support whatever to anti-institutionalist tendencies either of liberalism or of evangelicalism. But our task is not as yet complete. We have now to see how for Calvin the mystery of salvation gives its whole meaning and *raison d'être* to the institution.

The very title of the fourth book makes it clear that according to Calvin the institutional Church is related and as 'external means' to the end which is faith and salvation in Christ. We soon realise, however, that the Church in her visible ministry is much more than this. It is not only a necessary means but such a most mysterious means that, in a passage on schism, Calvin can write as follows:

> The Lord esteems the communion of his Church so highly that he counts as a traitor and apostate from Christianity anyone who arrogantly leaves any Christian society, provided it cherishes the true ministry of Word and sacraments. He so esteems the authority of the Church that when it is violated he believes his own diminished.
>
> It is also no common praise to say that Christ has chosen and set apart the Church as his bride, 'without spot or wrinkle' …. From this it follows that separation from the Church is the denial of God and Christ. Hence we must even more avoid so wicked a separation. For when with all our might we are attempting the overthrow of God's truth, we deserve to have him hurl the whole thunderbolt of his

wrath to crush us. Nor can any more atrocious crime be conceived than for us by sacrilegious disloyalty to violate the marriage that the only-begotten Son of God deigned to contract with us.[50]

We have here in this passage not only 'the majestic place of the visible Church' but its mystical identity with Christ. But is Calvin here to be taken seriously? Does the general trend of the fourth book fall into line with this? Or does Calvin's thought lend support rather to the view that 'there is in Protestantism an inherited inability to take the visible Church with due seriousness'?

The Lordship of Christ
In many contexts the *Institutes* certainly emphasises that the visible Church is an unprofitable servant. This emphasis appears chiefly in anti-Roman contexts, in the treatment, for example, of the sacraments in general. The sacraments in themselves, i.e. the visible signs merely, 'can accomplish nothing'. They are 'empty trifles', we are told, and 'profit not a whit'. We are not to think that 'there is some secret force or other perpetually seated in them … by which they of themselves confer the graces of the holy Spirit upon us, as wine is given in a cup'.[51] This would be 'to repose in the appearance of a physical thing rather than in God himself'.[52] It would amount to denying the Lordship of Christ. And because in him alone is faith and salvation 'he alone should rule and reign in the Church as well as have authority or pre-eminence in it'.[53]

In passing we may note that this emphasis is not (as might be thought) altogether at variance with Calvin's maternal approach to the Church but, on the contrary, in harmony with it. The patristic idea of the Church as mother contains a pronounced anti-Pelagian stress which is mostly missed because modern physiology has obscured it. The simple fact is that in antiquity and in medieval times the woman was not (as she now is) considered to be active in conception. And this fact is surely relevant in understanding the patristic idea of motherhood as applied to the Church.[54] Similarly we may note that this same idea is particularly apt – though for other, more biblical reasons – to express the Lordship of Christ, the Church's subjection in love to her Spouse.

For all his anti-Romanism Calvin was no Zwinglianist and he makes it abundantly clear that in his view the Church's visible structures are not obstacles to faith and salvation in union with Christ himself, are not intermediaries coming between our only Saviour and us, are not denials of the Lordship of Christ. On the contrary and paradoxically, or rather mysteriously, it is in and through these visible structures that Christ reigns supreme. The Church's ministry of word and sacrament and discipline, being precisely a *diakonia* and not a *dominium*, is a mediation of Christ's own very word and life and authority. 'The ministry ... is the administration of the Spirit and of righteousness and of eternal life'.[55]

Faith comes by hearing. In the preaching of the Gospel 'by a puny man' it is Christ himself who teaches his own. 'He deigns to consecrate to himself the mouths and tongues of men in order that his voice may resound in them.' 'He who hears you hears me, and he who rejects you rejects me.' 'God himself appears in our midst, and, as Author of this order, would have men recognize him as present in his institution.'[56] And again in the sacraments of faith: it is Christ the Saviour himself who is shown forth and met in these earthly elements and who deepens our saving union with him:

> It is he who speaks to us through the sign .... It is he who purifies and washes away sins .... It is he who comes into a unity with us so that, having put on Christ, we may be acknowledged God's children. These things, I say, he performs for our soul within as truly and surely as we see our body outwardly cleansed, submerged, and surrounded with water .... And he does not feed our eyes with a mere appearance only, but leads us to the present reality and effectively performs what it symbolises.[57]

Similarly, in the exercise of discipline, the tribunal of the Church is the tribunal of Christ and the judgment of the Church may not be despised 'as a trivial thing: the Lord has testified that this is nothing but the publication of his own sentence, and what they have done on earth is ratified in heaven'.[58] Calvin therefore urges that 'the whole sequence of the action, besides the calling on God's name, ought to have that gravity which bespeaks the presence of Christ in order that there may be no doubt that he himself presides at his own tribunal'.[59]

Finally it must be mentioned that the collegial character of the ministry has for Calvin its true meaning ultimately in this whole doctrinal context of the Church as Christ's own Kingdom, as at once Event and Institution.[60] This relationship between collegiality and the Lordship of Christ is most clearly expressed in Calvin's Commentary on Ephesians but it is also found in the *Institutes* with Cyprian's *de unitate* quoted in support. It is because Christ himself is her sole head and only bishop that all authority in the Church is essentially ministerial, essentially corporate; a sharing together in Christ's own authority, 'a common ministry with a particular mode to each' participant.[61]

Why the visible Church?

But how will Calvin answer if we ask why this institutional Church and her complicated ministry is needed at all? He will insist first of all that God 'could indeed do it [rule and save us] either by himself without any sort of aid or instrument, or even by the angels', but then go on to indicate reasons 'why he [God] prefers to do it by means of humankind'. The institutional Church provides for our ignorance, sloth and fickleness of disposition, for our weakness. She also fosters humility, piety and obedience towards God, and unity among humankind. In her visible structures God accommodates himself to us. He addresses us 'in human fashion'.[62] He 'so tempers himself to our capacity that, since we are creatures who always creep on the ground, cleave to the flesh and do not think about or even conceive of anything spiritual, he condescends to lead us to himself even by these earthly elements, and to set before us in the flesh a mirror of spiritual blessings. For if we were incorporeal (as Chrysostom says), he would give us these very things naked and incorporeal. Now, because we have souls engrafted in bodies, he imparts spiritual things under visible ones'.[63]

The most significant, however, of all these considerations offered by Calvin seems to be that based on Christ's ascension :

> Because he does not dwell among us in visible presence, we have said that he uses the ministry of men to declare openly his will to us by mouth, as a sort of delegated work, not by transferring to them his right and honour, but only that through their mouths he may do his own work – just as a workman uses a tool to do his work.
>
> By his ascension Christ took away from us his visible presence; yet he ascended to fill all things. Now, therefore, the Church still has, and always will have, him present. When Paul wishes to show the way in which he manifests himself [*se exhibit*], he calls us back to the ministries which he uses.[64]

For Calvin, therefore, it might be said, the Church and its ministry and the sacraments in particular are the ascended Christ himself made visible as Saviour, 'exhibited' in signs understood by faith.

Role of the Spirit

This consideration prepares us for Calvin's answer to another question. How, if it is so impotent and he by his ascension so far off, can the institutional Church succeed in uniting us to Christ our Saviour? His answer to this question is always the same and repeated again and again: in the power of the Spirit. 'God himself is present in his institution by the very-present power of his Spirit (*praesentissima Spiritus sui virtute*)'.[65] 'He in a certain manner exhibits himself as present by manifesting the power of his Spirit in this his institution so as to prevent it from being vain or idle.'[66] Remembering therefore Calvin's idea of the Church as a mother we might express his thought as follows: Just as the mother of Jesus conceived and brought forth only when the Holy Spirit came upon her and the power of the Most High overshadowed her, so the Church and her ministers receive from the ascended Christ the gift of the Holy Spirit and in him become an effectual exhibition of Christ: his visible, efficacious presence on earth till the Lord comes.[67]

The place of the Eucharist

It remains to see, by way of conclusion, how for Calvin the Church in her threefold ministry of word, sacrament and discipline is essentially eucharistic.[68] Baptism he calls our 'entry', our 'initiation', our 'engrafting', 'into the society of the Church, in order that, engrafted in Christ, we may be numbered among God's children'. Including Word and sacrament it is at once our initiation into faith in Christ and into the Church his Body.[69] It is administered only by a minister who, before baptising the candidate, ought first 'to present him to the assembly of believers and, with the whole Church looking on as witness and praying over him, offer him to God'.[70] Once initiated into the Church we have 'no greater help than public worship for by it God gradually raises his own to heaven'.[71] Baptism is never to be repeated but in apostolic times 'it became the unvarying rule that no meeting of the Church should take place without the Word, prayers, partaking of the Supper, and almsgiving'. And this rule 'remained in use for many centuries after'.[72] The Eucharist, therefore, Calvin says, ought to be celebrated by the minister 'very often and at least once a week for the assembly of Christians to recognize the mystery of their unity'.[73] Not, therefore, as the Roman 'priestlings' *(sacrificuli)* do. For 'after that custom of offering without communion once crept in, they gradually began to make innumerable masses in every corner of the Churches and to drag the people hither and thither, when they should have come together in one assembly to recognise the mystery of their unity'.[74] And 'is this not openly to mock God when one person privately seizes for himself what ought to have been done only among many?'[75]

At the Eucharist, the word of God is preached. Unfortunately, Calvin laments,

> [M]any are led either by pride, dislike, or rivalry to the conviction that they can profit enough from private reading and meditation; hence they despise public assemblies and deem preaching superfluous. But, since they do their utmost to sever or break the sacred bond of unity, no one escapes the just penalty of this unholy separation without bewitching himself with pestilent errors and foulest delusions.[76]

Here too at the Eucharist the ministry of discipline is exercised. The minister 'should excommunicate all who are debarred from it [the Supper] by the Lord's prohibition', since by their sins 'they are divided and separated by hatred and ill will from their brethren, that is, from the members of Christ, and thus have no part in Christ'.[77] According to Calvin the ultimate purpose of Church discipline in all its various stages from admonition to excommunication is to ensure the worthy celebration of the Eucharist: 'that the Supper of our Lord may not be polluted by people of scandalous lives'.[78]

Besides the ministry of word and discipline, that of sacrament is also exercised at the Eucharist. 'Through the symbols of bread and wine Christ is truly exhibited to us, his very body and blood … in order that we may be united into one body with him'.[79] The Lord so communicates his body to us that here he is made completely one with us and we with him. Now, since he has only one body, of which he makes us all partakers, it is necessary that all of us also be made one body by such participation.[80] It is indeed the secret power of the Spirit which effects all this,[81] but in the Eucharist, Calvin emphasises, we are not made 'partakers of the Spirit only'.[82] 'It would be extreme madness', he says, 'to recognise no communion of believers with the flesh and blood of the Lord'. We cannot be the body of Christ and his members 'otherwise than by his cleaving to us wholly [*totus*] in spirit and body' and our being 'joined with his flesh' in the Eucharist.[83] Calvin rejected the Eucharist as sacrifice.[84] He also rejected transubstantiation, but he says explicitly that this doctrine was 'more tolerable or at least more modest' than the Lutheran,[85] and there can hardly be any doubt, such is his patent eucharistic realism, that he found it much more tolerable if not more modest than Zwinglianism.

Catholic and evangelical

The rich Catholicity of Calvin's ecclesiology – and of his mystical piety[86] – nowhere emerges more clearly than in his treatment of the Eucharist. He shows a profound sympathy with the venerable tradition which sees the Church as essentially eucharistic. This, only among other things of course, helps us to understand how the Protestant Churches of the WCC were able to accept the high sacramental doctrine of the BEM Report of the Faith and Order Commission. There was a time when the fourth book of Calvin's *Institutes* 'attracted little attention from his interpreters'.[87] That time is long past and BEM is one proof of its passing. It still remains, however, to stress the cruciality of the Church as well as of the Cross. The hesitations on the part of some WCC member Churches revealed in the volumes *Churches Respond to BEM,*[88] the prospect of a majority of Evangelical Protestants being outside the 'fold' of the WCC and the ecumenical inertia which is widespread on all sides, are factors underlining the urgency of a theological education which will be sympathetic to both Evangelical and Catholic traditions and so help to soften any lingering antipathies and redress any existing imbalances for the sake of the 'wholeness' of the gospel 'so that the world may believe'.[89]

10
Wesley Today and Evangelisation Today

John Wesley, the man whose overriding concern was 'to reform the nation by spreading Scriptural holiness over the Land', distributed pills as well as tracts. He established clinics and schools and facilities for interest-free loans. He joined in condemning slavery as well as smuggling, bribery and corruption. He could pen and publish 'Thoughts on the Present Scarcity of Provisions', and even seem to suggest that only Government control over some aspects of the economy could remedy poverty. He did, of course, forbid 'meddling in politics', but his followers had been taken as Papists in disguise in the pay of the Pretender. Clearly this eighteenth-century Church of England clergyman was no radical. His outlook was to a large extent time-conditioned, with the result that, though he protested, for instance, against prison conditions, he issued no 'Thoughts on Prison Reform'. It may be true that his most enlightened social attitudes owed much to Moravian and Quaker influence and that he was more concerned with alleviating the social evils of his day than with eradicating them by pioneering reform of the underlying structures which were their root cause, but what matters most is that the man who told his Helpers they had 'nothing to do but to save souls' was concerned with people's physical, mental and economic welfare as well as with their spiritual welfare, that he was also intent on saving society.[1]

Spiritual or social gospel?

As a result of John Wesley's words and example, the Methodist Church which he founded has been outstanding in witnessing to both the vertical and horizontal dimensions of the gospel, in promoting both piety and social concern, in proclaiming and spreading a faith that does justice; and in encouraging other Christians and their Churches to do likewise. Theologians still struggle to understand and make clear how and why the two are related and belong together in the work of evangelisation but no one doubts that if the Church is to be the Church, evangelisation today must include both. A 1982 WCC statement on 'Mission and Evangelism' speaks of 'the old dichotomies between evangelism and social action' being overcome, adding:

> The 'spiritual gospel' and 'material gospel' were in Jesus one Gospel. There is no evangelism without solidarity... Proclamation that does not hold forth the promises of the justice of the kingdom to the poor of the earth is a caricature of the Gospel.[2]

The salvific role of other religions?[3]

The dichotomy which still remains to be overcome, however, is that between proclamation and dialogue. What continues to be particularly problematic in the context of evangelisation today is the attitude Christians should have towards people of other living faiths – are Hindus and Muslims potential or anonymous Christians? – and towards their religions – is it possible that Hinduism and Islam have a salvific role in God's providence? Can John Wesley also be of help to us as we struggle with this aspect of the 'evangelisation today' problem? In what follows I wish to suggest that he can indeed help us, that his distinctive theology of prevenient grace[4] provides a very positive orientation. He himself would, of course, want to insist in the words of his brother's hymn, 'And Can It Be?' that 'tis Mystery All'.

Original sin

I begin with a quotation from one of Wesley's letters. The words are actually those of a Quaker but they are followed immediately by the statement: 'in these points there is no difference between Quakerism and Christianity'.

> All mankind is fallen and dead, deprived of the sensation of this inward testimony of God, and subject to the power and nature of the devil, while they abide in their natural state. And hence not only their words and deeds, but all their imaginations, are evil perpetually in the sight of God.
>
> God out of his infinite love hath so loved the world that he gave his only Son, to the end that whosoever believeth on him might have everlasting life. And he enlighteneth every man that cometh into the world, as he tasted death for every man.
>
> The benefit of the death of Christ is not only extended to such as have the distinct knowledge of his death and sufferings, but even unto those who are inevitably excluded from this knowledge. Even these may be partakers of the benefit of his death, though ignorant of the history, if they suffer his grace to take place in their hearts, so as of wicked men to become holy.[5]

This passage does not contain the term 'prevenient grace', nor what I take to be its equivalent, 'preventing grace'. Neither does it indicate what the reality of prevenient or preventing grace might be. It does, however, point to the context, the basis and the evangelistic/missionary implications of this Wesleyan notion.

The Atonement

The context – partly at least – is the doctrine of original sin. John Wesley yields to no one in his acceptance of the total depravity of fallen human nature.[6] The first paragraph of the passage just quoted is a relatively mild description. Fallen humanity is 'indeed all sin, a mere lump of ungodliness',[7] 'altogether corrupt and abominable, more than it is possible for tongue to express'.[8] But the worst that can be said of fallen human nature is, for Wesley, only half the truth. Besides the Fall there is the fact of the Atonement: there is Christ, 'the true light that enlightens everyone'.

According to Wesley the Atonement of Christ means that there is and since the fall of Adam always has been grace for all and in all 'to balance the corruption of nature'.[9] In his sermon 'On Working Out Our Own Salvation' he writes:

> For allowing that all the souls of men are dead in sin by *nature*, this excuses none, seeing there is no man that is in a state of mere nature; there is no man, unless he has quenched the Spirit, that is wholly void of the grace of God. No man living is entirely destitute of what is vulgarly called *natural conscience*. But this is not natural: it is more properly termed *preventing grace*. Every man has a greater or less measure of this, which waiteth not for the call of man. Every one has, sooner or later, good desires; although the generality of men stifle them before they can strike deep root, or produce any considerable fruit. Every one has some measure of that light, some faint glimmering ray, which, sooner or later, more or less, enlightens every man that cometh into the world. And every one, unless he be one of the small number whose conscience is seared as with a hot iron, feels more or less uneasy when he acts contrary to the light of his own conscience. So that no man sins because he has not grace, but because he does not use the grace which he hath.[10]

Prologue of St John's Gospel

Here again, as so often, we hear an echo of the Prologue of St John's Gospel. Here too we find that the reality corresponding to Wesley's prevenient grace is closely associated with conscience.

The frequent allusions to the ninth verse of St John's Prologue can leave us in no doubt that this verse provides John Wesley with the immediate basis for his theology of prevenient grace. We may also remember that this verse influenced Vatican II's 'Declaration on the Relationship of the Church to Non-Christian Religions', where it is stated that these religions 'often reflect a ray of that truth which enlightens all people'.[11] It is not yet clear, however, what the connection is for Wesley between prevenient grace and conscience, or, more importantly, what the connection is for him between prevenient grace and salvation.

Stages of salvation

This latter connection becomes clearer if we turn again to his sermon 'On Working Out Our Own Salvation' and read the following passage on the stages of salvation:

> Salvation begins with what is usually termed (and very properly) *preventing grace*, including the first wish to please God, the first dawn of light concerning his will, and the first slight transient conviction of having sinned against him. All these imply some tendency towards life; some degree of salvation; the beginning of a deliverance from a blind, unfeeling heart, quite insensible of God and the things of God. Salvation is carried on by *convincing grace*, usually in Scripture termed *repentance*, which brings a larger measure of self-knowledge, and a farther deliverance from the heart of stone. Afterwards we experience the proper Christian salvation; whereby, 'through grace', we 'are saved by faith'; consisting of those two grand branches, justification and sanctification.[12]

Here we find no mention of conscience, but another sermon on 'The Scripture Way of Salvation' does link the three (salvation, prevenient grace and conscience) as follows:

> The salvation which is here spoken of [Ep 2:8: 'Ye are saved through faith'] might be extended to the entire work of God, from the first dawning of grace in the soul, till it is consummated in glory. If we take this in its utmost extent, it will include all that is wrought in the soul by what is frequently termed 'natural conscience', but more properly, 'preventing grace'; all the drawings of the Father – the desires after God, which, if we yield to them, increase more and more; all that light wherewith the Son of God 'enlighteneth every one that cometh into the world' – showing every man 'to do justly, to love mercy, and to walk humbly with his God'; all the convictions which his Spirit, from time to time, works in every child of man – although it is true, the generality of men stifle them as soon as possible, and after a while forget, or at least deny, that they ever had them at all.[13]

'Reaction'

It would seem to follow from these passages that the reality corresponding to prevenient grace is not so much conscience *simpliciter* but conscience insofar as it is drawn by the Father of our Lord Jesus Christ, illuminated by the Word Incarnate, stirred by the Spirit of Jesus and thus enabled, in the same Spirit, to 'react' in repentance and faith leading to justification and sanctification. Prevenient grace, so interpreted, has much in common with the fifth and sixth chapters of the Tridentine Decree on Justification.

Between the various stages of salvation sketched in outline above there is a certain continuity and, for Wesley, the individual's 'reaction' is vital. Today we would say 'response', but the term 'reaction' is typically Wesleyan. (The editor of the *Standard Sermons* tells us that the *Oxford English Dictionary* quotes Wesley as the earliest example of the use of 'reaction' in the sense of 'the influence which a thing, acted upon by another, exercises in return upon the agent', as distinct from the older meaning: 'repulsion exerted in opposition to impact of pressure'.[14])

By faith

What Wesley says of the believer we may, I suggest, apply to sinners co-operating in the process of their salvation:

> [He] continually receives into his soul the breath of life from God, the gracious influence of his Spirit, and continually renders it back;... by faith [he] perceives the continual actings of God upon his spirit, and, by a kind of spiritual reaction returns the grace he receives .... For it plainly appears, God does not continue to act upon the soul, unless the soul reacts upon God. He prevents us indeed with the blessings of his goodness ... [But] he will not continue to breathe into our soul, unless our soul breathes toward him again.[15]

But in what sense, if any, may we say of repenting sinners as of believing Christians that it is by faith that they 'react' to God's grace? Wesley, himself, states that faith is already operative in the early stages of the sinner's salvation, but it is, in his own words, 'a low species of faith, i.e. a supernatural sense of an offended God'.[16] It is not yet faith in Christ and in the gospel. It is not yet the saving fiducial faith which must be preceded by repentance. This saving faith, he tells us, is:

> A sure trust in the mercy of God, through Christ Jesus. It is a confidence in a pardoning God. It is a divine evidence or conviction that 'God was in Christ, reconciling the world to himself, not imputing to them their former trespasses' and, in particular, that the Son of God hath loved *me* and given himself for me; and that I, even I, am now reconciled to God by the Blood of the cross.[17]

The initial faith of repentance in reaction to prevenient and convincing grace is not however such a 'low species' of faith that it cannot provide what Wesley calls 'foretastes of joy, of peace, of love and those not delusive, but really from God ... [and] may be a [degree] of long-suffering, of gentleness, of fidelity, meekness, temperance (not a shadow thereof, but a real degree, by the preventing grace of God)'.[18] It would seem that Wesley does not wish us to distinguish too sharply his various stages of salvation, nor, indeed, to exclude fiducial faith entirely even from repentance.

Salvation possible for all
Whether or not this interpretation be valid, Wesley holds in general (as we saw in the passage quoted at the beginning) that:
> the benefit of the death of Christ [everlasting life] is not only extended to such as have the distinct knowledge of his death and sufferings, but even unto those who are inevitably excluded from this knowledge. Even these may be partakers of the benefit of his death, though ignorant of the history, if they suffer his grace to take place in their hearts, so as of wicked men to become holy.[19]

Many of the ancient heathens, especially in the civilised nations were, he wrote, 'taught of God, by his inward voice, all essentials of true religion'.[20] In particular Wesley has no doubt but that Marcus Aurelius, whose *Meditations* he had been reading, 'is one of those "many" who "shall come from the east and the west, and sit down with Abraham, Isaac and Jacob", while "the children of the Kingdom", nominal Christians, are "shut out" '.[21] He is quite definite in stating (what the fifth and sixth chapters of the Tridentine 'Decree on Justification' do not state) that 'no man living is without some preventing grace, and every degree of grace is a degree of life'.[22]

But prevenient grace alone hardly provides us with an adequate explanation of his conviction about the possibility of salvation for those who do not know Christ. The Conference of 1748 considered the problem. It stressed the concept of 'sincerity' which was defined as 'willingness to know and do the will of God'. And to the question, 'But can it be received that God has any regard to the sincerity of an unbeliever?' it answered: 'Yes, so much that if he persevere therein, God will infallibly give him faith.'[23] The following year the Conference also wrestled with the problem:

> Men may have many good tempers and a blameless life (speaking in a loose sense) by nature and habit, with preventing grace, and yet be utterly void of faith and the love of God. 'Tis scarce possible for us to know all the circumstances relating to such persons, so as to judge certainly concerning them.
>
> But this we know, that [if] Christ is not revealed in them, they are not yet Christian believers.
>
> But what becomes of them then, suppose they die in this state? That is a supposition not to be made. They *cannot* die in this state. They must go backward or forward. If they continue to seek, they will surely find righteousness, peace and joy in the Holy Ghost.[24]

These answers surely imply that prevenient grace can flow into saving grace. Indeed, only insofar as it can do so, does it seem possible to envisage with John Wesley the salvation of those who do not hear of Christ. But does this possibility not also suppose (what Wesley accepts) that God was revealed to be, but did not become, our Saviour in the life, death and glorification of Jesus? Is this supposition not required in order to be able to consider that those without knowledge of Christ can have that 'confidence in a pardoning God' which is of the essence of saving faith?

Are all in fact saved?

It seems to follow that Wesley's theology of prevenient grace does imply the possibility of salvation for non-Christian individuals, for the adherents of other living faiths. Before passing on, however, we must ask: did Wesley's 'optimism of grace' allow him to envisage the universality or majority of humankind as in fact saved? The answer here must be negative. 'Every one', we have already found him stating, 'has, sooner or later, good desires; although the generality of men stifle them before they can strike deep root, or produce any considerable fruit.'[25] This same pessimistic view finds frequent expression, notably perhaps in his sermons 'Upon Our Lord's Sermon on the Mount' and, very strikingly, in his 'short, plain, infallible rule' for Methodists: 'be singular, or be damned'.[26] Before going to Georgia he entertained high hopes of 'the heathen' as 'fit to receive the gospel in its simplicity ... as humble, willing to learn, and eager to do the will of God'.[27] In the event, however, he was disillusioned and wrote in his journal that 'they show no inclination to learn anything, but least of all Christianity; being full as opinionated of their own parts and wisdom, as either modern Chinese, or ancient Romans'.[28] Wesley's standards of holiness were, of course, high, and he is aware that 'the more we grow in grace, the more do we see of the desperate wickedness of our heart';[29] that, indeed, 'all that are convinced of sin undervalue themselves in every respect'.[30] But does the saints' undervaluing of themselves involve an undervaluing of others also? Even allowing for the evangeliser's need to exaggerate, Wesley's firm views on the general corruption of humankind seem at odds with his 'optimism of grace'.

A salvific role for other religions?
With regard to the salvific role of other religions, we do have a letter written by Wesley before he left for Georgia in 1735, which shows him hoping 'to learn the true sense of the gospel of Christ by preaching it to the heathen'.[31] But no one who knows Wesley will expect what follows to anticipate in any way the inclusivist views prominent in modern inter-religious dialogue. There are, however,

aspects of his theology which would seem to make possible a positive approach to the other religions themselves as well as to their individual adherents. Wesley recognises many means of grace and a previous chapter has recalled how he considers the Eucharist as 'a converting ordinance', as 'ordained by God to be a means of conveying to men either preventing, or justifying, or sanctifying grace, according to their several necessities'.[32] For Wesley, however, the law – the moral law – is a means of fundamental importance. Without the law there is 'no proper means either of bringing us to faith, or of stirring up that gift of God in our soul'.[33] He has to emphasise that the law is not abolished for the believer, that it is 'the grand means whereby the blessed Spirit prepares the believer for larger communications of the life of God'.[34] But the first use of the law is to bring sinners to repentance: 'It is the ordinary method of the Spirit of God to convict sinners by the law. It is this which, being set home on the conscience, generally breaketh the rocks in pieces'.[35] The pertinent question, therefore, for our present purpose is: what, if anything, may be found in John Wesley's theology which would enable us to consider other religions as, to some extent, embodiments of the law?

Religion as social not solitary

Of relevance here is the fact that Wesley holds the universality of prevenient grace and also the related fact that he considers all humankind since the Fall to be under the covenant of grace established by God in Christ. More immediately relevant, perhaps, is Wesley's emphasis on religion as social and not solitary. This is a point he makes about Christianity in particular. For Wesley, however, the social character of Christianity is not one of its distinctive features.

> Men who did fear God, and desire the happiness of their fellow creatures, have, in every age, found it needful to join together, in order to oppose the works of darkness, to

spread the knowledge of God their Saviour, and to promote his kingdom upon earth. Indeed he himself has instructed them so to do. From the time that men were upon the earth, he hath taught them to join together in his service and has united them in one body by one Spirit.[36]

Wesley's attitude to the observances and structures of the other religions will, of course, be similar to his attitude to those of the Christian religion: 'They are good in their place; just so far as they are, in fact, subservient to true religion'.[37] On his own principles we today can see much in the other religions which is in fact 'subservient to true religion'. We can, with Vatican II, see them as often reflecting 'a ray of that truth which enlightens all people'.[38]

Hand in hand

In any case we must apply not only to individuals but also to communities, and not only to Christian communities but also to those of the other living faiths, the spirit at least of Wesley's sermons entitled 'A Caution against Bigotry' and 'Catholic Spirit':

Everyone is either on God's side, or on Satan's. Are you on God's side? Then you will not only not forbid any man that casts out devils, but you will labour, to the uttermost of your power, to forward him in the work…. What if I were to see a Papist, an Arian, a Socinian, casting out devils? If I did, I could not forbid even him, without convicting myself of bigotry. Yea, if it could be supposed that I should see a Jew, a Deist, or a Turk, doing the same, were I to forbid him either directly or indirectly, I should be no better than a bigot still…. Encourage whomsoever God is pleased to employ, to give himself wholly up thereto [and say to him], so far as in conscience thou canst (retaining still thy own opinions, and thy own manner of worshipping God), join with me in the work of God; and let us go on hand in hand.[39]

Surely it is only in so far as we do in fact begin to co-operate in this spirit with other religions and go hand in hand with them that we can be in a position to discern how much 'God is pleased to employ them' for his saving purpose and in what ways and to what extent we can continue to work together with them for the glory of God and the salvation of the world. John Wesley invites and helps all of us involved in evangelisation today to transcend the dichotomy between proclamation and the dialogue of co-operation as well as that between the 'spiritual gospel' and the 'social gospel'.[40]

11
The Church of Ireland: Challenges for the Future

TO DISAPPEAR?

> The vocation of Anglicanism is, ultimately, to disappear. That is its vocation precisely because Anglicanism does not believe in itself but it believes only in the Catholic Church of Christ; therefore it is for ever restless until it finds its place in that one Body.[1]

So in 1954 wrote Stephen Bayne who was to become a bishop of the Episcopal Church in the USA and first General Secretary of the Anglican Consultative Council. And in 1966 something similar was stated by the Church of Ireland Primate, Archbishop McCann, in his presidential address to General Synod:

> Denominationalism is outmoded. Sectarianism is no longer relevant. The major issues of evangelisation in a secular and largely non-Christian world completely eclipse the relatively minor subjects debated by our forefathers.[2]

Encouraged by these statements as well as by other ecumenical considerations and writing in the anxious summer of 1969 I made bold to open the original version of this chapter with the following uncompromising paragraph:

> The Church of Ireland has no future except as united with all its non-Anglican sister Churches – Rome included – in that visible unity which is God's will and his gift to his people so that the world may believe.... [This] statement is in no way based on the findings of demography or of the sociology of religion but on the findings of theology which

are at once more reliable as well as more sombre .... It is the considered unanimous view of all the Churches involved in the ecumenical movement that Christian disunity is a contradiction of the Church's very nature, preventing the Church from being the Church, reducing it steadily to the position in which it is more an obstacle than an instrument of the Spirit, more an enemy than an ally of the Gospel. The statement besides is true of all the Churches and not only of the Church of Ireland and indeed it is more true of majority than of minority Churches insofar as the latter can be less prone to the deadening temptations of complacency and triumphalism and more open to the energising stimuli of pain and dissatisfaction. The statement moreover simply recalls and applies to the home scene what Bishop Bayne of the Anglican Consultative Council and others have said of Anglicanism as a whole.

Reconciled diversity

Since then, as the Introduction to this volume and chapter 2 have attempted to convey, much water has flowed under the bridges of the Church and the world. For a whole variety of reasons the worldwide ecumenical movement finds itself in a state of crisis.[3] The euphoria, the *élan* and enthusiasm of the 1960s has gone. A deep winter has followed that high summer. For the present at least the movement for Christian unity has lowered its sights and prefers to speak of 'reconciled diversity' or 'phased reconciliation' or 'a communion of communions'. As a goal this would not involve 'the disappearance of the present Churches as we know them or the emergence of newly identified Churches, successor bodies different from and replacing them'.[4] But whether this is envisaged as an ultimate or intermediate goal remains unclear.

Despite these current ecumenical trends the language of 'disappearance' does not go away. In the 1980s the Hanson brothers did not hesitate to write that 'to Anglicanism surely can be appropriately applied that sentence that is the motto of the Irish School of Ecumenics: *floreat ut pereat* (may it flourish in order to perish).[5] The Stephen Bayne statement quoted at the beginning of this chapter has recently been endorsed in a General Synod report of the Church of England.[6] The closely related idea of the 'provisionality' of Anglicanism found expression in Archbishop Runcie's opening address to the 1988 Lambeth Conference. 'Anglicanism', he stated, 'has a radically provisional character which we must never allow to be obscured.'[7] And full communion, however remote a possibility it has now become, can hardly be envisaged without some measure of disappearance. It will of course depend, among other things, on each local situation: either both Churches are already present locally or only one. In the latter case, whichever is already present remains, and in many places, in England at least, this will be the Anglican Church. In the former case, however, one or other of the Churches may well have to disappear in order to avoid a scandalous squandering of resources. But which one disappears will depend on regional as well as local circumstances and will, of course, be a matter for consultation and agreement.

Both 'disappearance' and 'provisionality' have however been subjected to severe criticism and, among others, the former Anglican Chairman of the Anglican-Roman Catholic International Commission has felt it necessary to protest:

> I deprecate the suggestion current in some circles ever since Lambeth 1930 that the vocation of Anglicanism is to disappear once unity has been achieved .... The notion is invalid and untrue not only because it appears to imply a concealed identification of unity with uniformity but because it misses the point that any unity worth having will be rich with all the treasures of the uniting Churches.[8]

What Archbishop McAdoo deprecates[9] is the suggestion that Church union requires a 'submerging of ecclesial identities', the 'disappearance of our distinctive traditions into the anonymity of some sort of ecclesial amalgam'. 'No doubt', he agrees, '*some* aspects of *all* our traditions must indeed go but the best, *each tradition at its best*, must remain.' The ideal is that expressed at Malines long ago: 'united not absorbed'. 'True unity must involve a pooling of spiritual resources.' 'The coming Great Church', as he would envisage it, 'will embody *the best of ourselves* as the gift which each tradition can bring to Christ who prayed that they may be one in Him'; it will be 'a communion of Communions' which have preserved 'their proper patrimony, themselves at their best', and the Anglican 'best' he would identify as its threefold appeal to Scripture, Tradition and Reason which he sees as 'a necessary ecumenical methodology'. The way forward is to implement the strategy of 'unity by stages', which he himself proposed at Malta in 1968.

Renewal and reform
But if Church unity does not involve 'disappearance', it does involve renewal and reform. A union of what Bishop Oliver Tomkins at Nottingham in 1964 called 'unrepentant, unrenewed, self-regarding denominations' would not greatly help the world to believe. There is no cheap unity as there is no cheap grace. Unity requires sacrifice. The famous 1920 Lambeth Conference Appeal to All Christian People called on all 'to make sacrifices for the sake of a common fellowship, a common ministry and a common service to the world'.[10] The Church of Ireland Bishop of Meath and Kildare was recently urging 'sacrifice' instead of 'woolly good will'.[11] And the New Delhi statement of the World Council of Churches still remains only too true:

> The achievement of unity will involve nothing less than a death and rebirth of many forms of Church life as we have known them. We believe that nothing less costly can finally suffice.

There is, however, an element of disappearance in renewal and reform. Many Roman Catholics feel that liturgical changes, for example the use of the vernacular and the distribution of communion by women, have caused their pre-Vatican II Church to disappear. For them and many others the papacy itself would disappear if it began to operate according to a collegial instead of a monarchical model, as adumbrated in the *Final Report* of the Anglican/Roman Catholic International Commission.

Looking to the future, therefore, is it the 'vocation' (Stephen Bayne's term) of the Church of Ireland to disappear? Certainly not if the ideal is 'a pooling of spiritual resources', if the Malines phrase 'united not absorbed' is really accepted as the ecumenical commonplace which it has now become, if it is 'the best' which 'must remain', and if the Anglican best is the threefold appeal to Scripture, Tradition and Reason which many non-Anglicans as well as Archbishop McAdoo would see as 'a necessary ecumenical methodology'; and certainly not in any even remotely discernible future. But if to disappear means to renew and reform itself, to be more serious, for instance, about addressing the problem of sectarianism and about implementing the World Council of Churches' guideline which suggests that already we should all do everything together with other Churches as far as conscience permits, then a positive answer can hardly be avoided.

TO CUT LINKS WITH THE ORANGE ORDER?

Does 'addressing the problem of sectarianism' mean that the Church of Ireland should sever its links with the Orange Order? Because of the Order's bad name it is only fair to begin consideration of this question by recalling that the Order is a religious society with some high ideals:

An Orangeman should have a sincere veneration for his Heavenly Father; a humble and steadfast faith in Jesus Christ, the Saviour of mankind.... He should cultivate truth and justice, brotherly kindness and charity, devotion and piety, concord and unity and obedience to the laws; his deportment should be gentle and compassionate, kind and courteous ... he should honour and diligently study the Holy Scriptures, and make them the rule of his faith and practice; he should love, uphold and defend the Protestant religion and sincerely desire and endeavour to propagate its doctrines and principles.... The Glory of God and the welfare of man, the honour of his Sovereign and the good of his country, should be the motive of his actions.[12]

It is true that the Order is opposed to the ecumenical movement but it is also true that 'no organisation has done more to encourage interdenominational services and mutual exchanges of pulpits between the Protestant denominations'. Again it is true that its members are required to abstain 'from all uncharitable words, actions, or sentiments towards his Roman Catholic brethren'. Furthermore, in the words of the Methodist authors of *Christians in Ulster 1968-1980*, Dr Gallagher and Dr Worrall:

If any are tempted to poke fun at Orange ritual, regalia, and insignia, they would do well also to recall that Irish Protestantism is otherwise sadly lacking in the colour and ceremonial that make Catholicism (whether Roman or Anglo) so appealing to its rank and file. The Order answers the need for celebration, hierarchy, and public display. 'In [Belfast] working class communities like Sandy Row and the Shankill', as Frank Wright points out, 'it has become a central fact of social life: it is not merely a political institution but a community institution with social and religious significance.' Again, if the critic is concerned at Orange reactionary attitudes and conservatism, he does well also to recognise that often, where there is no constitutional issue at stake, where the Faith or the Crown is not being called into question, working-class Orangeism can be as radical and as critical of the Establishment as anyone. The 1980 resolution denouncing the government's policy on unemployment may have been unusual: it is not unprecedented. Politicians should never presume to count on the Orange vote.

Anti-Romanism
It remains, however, that the Order's aims and ideals are also clearly and unashamedly anti-Roman:
> An Orangeman should strenuously oppose the fatal errors and doctrines of the Church of Rome; and scrupulously avoid countenancing (by his presence or otherwise) any act or ceremony of Popish worship; he should by all lawful means, resist the ascendancy of that church, its encroachments and the extension of its powers.

In the summer of 1969 when I was preparing the original version of this chapter, 'the Troubles', as we euphemistically call them, had once more broken out in Northern Ireland. The Orangemen were no innocent bystanders. In 1967 their threats had led to the cancellation of a visit to St Anne's (Church of Ireland) Cathedral in Belfast by the prominent Church of England ecumenist, the Bishop of Ripon, who had been an observer at the Vatican Council and become Anglican Chairman of the recently appointed Anglican/Roman Catholic Joint Preparatory Commission.[13] Encouraged by this success the Order was becoming more aggressive and it provoked the *Church of Ireland Gazette* to publish forthright editorials such as the following on 29 August:
> Our cardinal sin, as a Church, has been that of capitulation to the forces that work to keep alive in parish and diocese the fears and hatreds that have now erupted in violence,

forces that have even made their presence felt in the General Synod of the Church of Ireland. Is the Church so bankrupt of moral courage that it must bow, as so notably and tragically it did in the case of the cancelled visit of the Bishop of Ripon to Belfast, to those whose ignorance is as vast as their uncharitableness is terrifying ? What is the wisdom and learning of our bishops for if it is not for leadership and admonition ? Are we to be led, in the things that really matter, by the opponents of what we know to be right?

The Orange Order 1969

Taking my cue from these broadsides and betraying my own authoritarian Church background, I took the liberty of stating in 1969 that

> the handwriting is now on the walls for Irish Anglicanism unless some courageous, charismatic leadership emerges which, among other things, will not hesitate to declare whether membership of the Orange Order in its present form is possible for an Irish Christian worthy of the name in the second half of the twentieth century.

And I went on:

> The extinction or reform of the Orange Order in its present state is absolutely crucial to the promotion of the ecumenical movement in Ireland and so to the credibility and survival of Irish Christianity as an effective sign of love, justice, peace and reconciliation. Nothing less is at stake and it will be no consolation for any of us if, when the handwriting does appear on the walls, it reads not just 'no popery' or 'no prelacy' but simply 'no Church: to hell with the Churches and all their works and pomps'. There is no cheap ecumenism as there is no cheap grace or Christianity.

The phrase 'in its present state' was an addition to allow for the possibility of change and reform within the Order; it was suggested by some Church of Ireland friends who had very kindly read an early draft. It was influenced also by a recent Quaker study which had seen such reform as possible but gone on rather discouragingly to add:

> Some believe, however, that to imagine this is to misconceive utterly the true nature of the structure and purposes of the Orange Order which, they say, already looks out-dated and old-fashioned, and which can become only more cantankerous and evil while it loses evolutionary purpose and effectiveness, and finishes up as a Brontosaurus-like relic of an incredible past.[14]

The Orange Order 1997

Over a quarter of a century has now gone by. Meantime all the Churches have been active in promoting reconciliation.[15] The present Church of Ireland Primate, Archbishop Robin Eames, has, *inter alia,* put a particular emphasis on the problem of sectarianism; he it was who took the initiative in getting the Irish Inter-Church Meeting to set up a Working Party to do an in-depth study of the subject.[16] But 'the Troubles' go on, the Northern Ireland conflict still remains unresolved and the Orange Order, as feared by the Quaker study just quoted, still remains unchanged in its basic tenets and, therefore, a large part of the problem. Indeed, the Order is perhaps a larger part of the problem than ever before. It provides succour and support for a Protestant/Unionist population which is declining in political power (because it has to share this much more than before with Catholics/Nationalists), and which, as a result, is suffering from a severe identity crisis and profound insecurity. The rule obliging the Orangeman to abstain from all 'uncharitable words, actions, or sentiments towards his Roman Catholic brethren' is often more honoured in the breach than the observance. Ceasefires did take place in 1994; for one almost miraculous period of seventeen months all was relatively quiet and the Dublin Government set up a 'Forum for Peace and Reconciliation, which was chaired by a distinguished Church of Ireland lay member, Judge Catherine McGuinness.

Drumcree
Unfortunately those halcyon days of the 1994 ceasefires were only an interlude. Violence broke out once again and things went from bad to worse, reaching their nadir in the summer of 1996 in circumstances which tragically involved both the Orange Order and the Church of Ireland, in particular the parish of Drumcree near Portadown and its Church of the Ascension. After morning service there on the Sunday before 12 July the Portadown Orangemen used the church grounds and the church hall of the parish for a stand-off with the security forces, refusing to re-route their march back from church away from the Catholic/Nationalist neighbourhood of the Garvaghy Road. Feelings always run high in Northern Ireland around 12 July when Unionists commemorate the Battle of the Boyne where Protestant William beat Catholic James in 1690. In July 1996 the Orange stand-off at Drumcree lasted several days; Orangemen from all over Northern Ireland converged there in support; the mood became more and more ugly and dangerous; and the security forces, sadly unprepared for a crisis of this scale, finally reversed their original decision and allowed the Orange march through the nationalist neighbourhood. This meant forcing the march along the Garvaghy Road: the violence escalated and spread throughout the whole of Northern Ireland. News and pictures of it were broadcast throughout the whole world: Drumcree had become a synonym for Orange sectarianism.

General Synod 1997

The apparent complicity of the Church of Ireland in the events of Drumcree 1996 caused consternation and revulsion among many of its own people, especially but not at all exclusively in the Republic of Ireland. The powerlessness of its bishops to intervene in such extreme situations, the alarming fact that 'under the present Constitution any Select Vestry may allow its Church halls to be used by any organisation or group, and a Bishop has no authority to intervene even if he wished to',[17] was for many particularly galling and unpalatable. One of the Church of Ireland members who had expressed their disquiet in forceful terms was the former General Secretary of the Irish Council of Churches, the Reverend William Arlow.[18] It was thus a very chastened Church of Ireland which gathered for General Synod in Dublin in May 1997.

Meantime, however, the Orange Order had given itself a new Grand Master who had been remarkably tolerant and a moderating influence in deed as well as word at moments and in situations of sectarian confrontation.[19] Meantime, too, influential figures in both the Order and the Ulster Unionist Party had again openly questioned the appropriateness of their present relationship which gives the Order, among other organisations, official representation on the Ulster Unionist Council. Members of the party like Dr Christopher McGimpsey would like to see it as 'a particular political ideology, not exclusive but general so that anyone of any religious persuasion could join it'.[20] Members of the Order such as the Reverend Brian Kennaway, Presbyterian Convenor of its Education Committee, would also like to see the link with the Party broken so that the Order's religious nature could become clearer and its religious tenets become 'more pro-Protestant than anti-Catholic'.[21]

Presidential address

At General Synod Archbishop Eames seemed to be referring to these developments when, in a powerful and moving presidential address which received a standing ovation, he stated that:

> The Order is currently engaged in a profound debate about its ethos and future. What is needed is encouragement for those who are honestly seeking to influence its life in a realistic and Christian manner.

Condemnation in these circumstances would, in his view, not be 'right, helpful or justified'. He went on to stress that there was not and never had been any official link between the Order and the Church of Ireland and to express regret at the Order's 'prohibitions' *vis-à-vis* Roman Catholicism which, in subsequent media interviews, he agreed were unecumenical and out-of-date.[22] Before it closed the Synod passed a motion requesting its Standing Committee

> to initiate an examination of Church life at all levels to identify ways in which the Church may be deemed to be accommodating to sectarianism, and as a means of combating sectarianism to promote at all levels of Church life tolerance, dialogue, co-operation and mutual respect between the Churches and in society, to identify and recommend specific actions towards this end and then to report progress in the matter to the meeting of General Synod in 1998.[23]

A Sectarianism Sub-Committee was duly established.

The future

Is the future of the Church of Ireland then to sever its links with the Orange Order? There is, as the Primate stressed, no official link to be severed and there can be advantages in the indirect, unofficial links which membership of the Order by individual

Church of Ireland people does provide. In the summer of 1997 the Orange march from Drumcree Church on the Sunday before 12 July was unfortunately again forced through the Garvaghy Road neighbourhood by the security forces and this again led to an outbreak of considerable violence. But the main marches on the Twelfth itself were re-routed away from contentious areas by the Order's own decision, and the person chiefly responsible for this 'momentous'[24] decision was none other than James Molyneaux who, besides being a former Ulster Unionist Party Leader and former Imperial Grand Master of the Orange Order, is a devoted member of the Church of Ireland.[25]

In his presidential address at General Synod the Primate, according to some commentators, 'distanced the Church of Ireland from the Orange Order'.[26] Not being an authoritarian institution, however, the Church of Ireland is unlikely to forbid its laity to join the Order. On the other hand those responsible for the education of its clergy can hardly remain indifferent to the Order's open anti-Romanism. This must surely become a matter of more concern to bishops sending clerical aspirants forward to 'Selection Conferences', to Selection Conferences when accepting these aspirants as candidates, and to bishops when eventually ordaining them as curates. For the sake of that improvement in inter-Church and cross-community relations which peace requires, it is very much to be hoped that clerical membership of the Order will soon decline and before too long cease altogether – as episcopal membership has done already.[27]

The Primate did urge the Order 'to look again at the parts of its constitution that are offensive to Roman Catholics'[28] and, it may be added, that are scarcely compatible with the Church of Ireland's own official ecumenical stance. Any members of the Church, whether clerical or lay, who do join the Order will therefore be encouraged to use their influence to get its unecumenical anti-Roman prohibitions changed and in the meantime to be flexible in observing them. And measures will surely be taken to protect the integrity and good name of the Church by preventing the use of its property 'as an opportunity to oppose the law of the land or to confront the forces of law and order'. The general aim of the Sectarianism Sub-Committee's recommendations will be to take the anti-Romanism out of Protestantism and out of Unionism. Support for the work at the international level of The Evangelical Roman Catholic Dialogue[29] and at the local level of ECONI (Evangelical Contribution to Northern Ireland)[30] would greatly help towards this end: the example of both is inspiring and enlightening.

CONCLUSION

According to the Preamble to its 1870 Constitution the Church of Ireland is determined to 'set forward, so far as in it lieth, quietness, peace, and love among all Christian people'. It no longer dismisses the Roman Catholic Church, as Archbishop Gregg once did when Dean of Cork in a sermon of 1909, as a 'schismatic and intruding mission from Italy'.[31] Neither is it dismissed itself as a heretical and intruding sect from England. Both Anglicans and Roman Catholics treasure the sentence which in his own hand Pope Paul VI added to his allocution on the occasion of the canonisation of the English Martyrs in 1970:

> There will be no seeking to lessen the legitimate prestige and the worthy patrimony of piety and usage proper to the Anglican Church when the Roman Church – this humble 'Servant of the servants of God' – is able to embrace her ever beloved Sister in the one authentic communion of the family of Christ.[32]

Our common vocation is to hasten this day by exorcising the demon of sectarianism in the ways suggested by the Inter-Church

Report of 1993 and 'to promote at all levels of Church life tolerance, dialogue, co-operation and mutual respect' in the ways to be recommended by General Synod in 1999.[33]

POSTSCRIPT

As this book goes through press it is the July marching season once again in Northern Ireland and, for the fourth year in succession, Drumcree has been a focus of particular attention. The violence this time has included the murder of three young children in an arson attack on their family home in Ballymoney. The public anxiously awaits the recommendations which the Church of Ireland's Sectarianism Sub-Committee will be presenting to General Synod in May 1999.

12
Jesuits and Protestants Today

Unhappy memories

In the past Jesuits and Protestants have had bad memories of each other. Protestants could remember Jesuits as dedicated to the undoing of the good work of the Reformation, as the leaders of the Counter-Reformation which, for instance, kept southern Germany Catholic, in communion with Rome. And Jesuits for their part could remember Protestants as their persecutors and oppressors, as their opponents who, for instance, saw to it that even the Catholic Emancipation Act of 1829 banned them from the United Kingdom. In the past too Jesuits and their fellow Roman Catholics have also had bad memories of each other. Roman Catholic authorities could remember Jesuits as difficult and troublesome. And Jesuits could remember how, for instance, they were suppressed in 1773 by Pope Clement XIV.

Our concern here, however, is with Jesuits and Protestants and their relationship at the present day: do we still have bad memories of each other? Do we still think negatively of each other? Do Protestants still see Jesuits as the archenemies of a reformed faith and a reformed Church? Do Jesuits still see Protestants as heretics on the way to hell? For some on either side this sadly is still the case. Some Jesuits are less than enthusiastic about ecumenism: I think of the English periodical *Christian Order* and its Jesuit editor. So are some Protestants: I think of a leaflet being distributed from Omagh in the early 1970s which referred to me as 'this blasphemous, hypocritical Jesuit emissary of the Church of Rome' and which alleged that Jesuit priests take an oath as follows:

> I do declare that I will do my utmost to exterpate [*sic*] the heretical Protestant or Liberal doctrines, to destroy all their

pretended powers, legal or otherwise, I do further promise and declare, that I will, when opportunity presents, make and wage relentless war, secretly and openly, against all heretics, Protestants and Masons, as I am directed to do, to exterpate [*sic*] them from the face of the whole earth: and that I will spare neither age, sex or condition, and that I will hang, waste, boil, flay, strangle and bury alive these infamous heretics; rip up the stomachs and the wombs of their women, and crush their infants' heads against the walls in order to annihilate their execrable race. Then, when the same can not be done openly, I will secretly use the poisonous cup, the strangulation cord, the steel of the poniard, or the leaden bullet, regardless of the honour, rank, dignity or authority of the persons, whatever may be their condition in life, either public or private, as I at any time may be directed to do by any agents of the Pope or superior of the Brotherhood of the Holy Father of the Society of Jesus.[1]

A new ecumenical relationship

These, however, are the exceptions which simply prove the rule that the ecumenical movement in general and Vatican II in particular have, in principle at least, healed the relationship between Catholics and Protestants and between Jesuits and Protestants.

After Vatican II the Jesuit Order for its part, at its Thirty-First General Congregation (1965-66), formally accepted the new relationship, 'humbly acknowledging the sins against unity committed by members of the Society [of Jesus], whether in the past or in more recent times'. In what follows however I propose to concentrate not so much on how Jesuits have accepted the new relationship but on how they have been active and influential in developing and promoting it. I shall dwell on three aspects of the new relationship: its acceptance of ecumenism and consequent exclusion of proselytism and the work of individual conversions; its emphasis on the Bible and common Bible work; its approval of of the principle of religious liberty. I shall refer to the contribution of three Jesuits in particular: Cardinal Augustin Bea, Father Walter Abbott and Father John Courtney Murray. My references to Jesuits are of course neither exclusive nor comparative. I am not suggesting – far from it – that only Jesuits have made significant contributions or that the contributions of Jesuits are more significant than those of others.

YES TO ECUMENISM/NO TO PROSELYTISM

The new ecumenical relationship between Catholics and Protestants is a rich, complex reality. As such it includes aspects which, except in general terms, still remain unclear, uncertain. One aspect however is altogether clear and quite certain and nothing must be allowed to obscure it in any way, to any extent: the new relationship excludes all initiatives aiming to persuade any of us to change our Church allegiance.

Though negative in expression, this principle indicates the most original and, for some, most disturbing feature of the new relationship between Christians. It represents our most obvious departure from traditional attitudes and principles and practices. It is the great test of the sincerity of the new relationship and the clarity of the thinking behind it. All of us reject in advance any attitudes and overtures, any dialogue which is aimed at our conversion to another Church. Evangelical Protestants in particular are extremely allergic to the idea of conversion to Rome. Many of them still suspect that our ecumenism is nothing more than a cloak for our Roman malice, a new jesuitical tactic in the old, unchanged strategy of conversion. For Dr Paisley ecumenism is nothing else but 'Rome's takeover movement of the main Protestant denominations', and the movement, he thinks, is spearheaded by the Jesuits.[2] A crucial importance attaches therefore to the principle that the main road to full Christian unity according to God's will is not the way of individual conversions. It is a condition of the very possibility of a new ecumenical relationship; on it ecumenism stands or falls; it is an *articulus stantis vel cadentis ecumenismi*.

Cardinal Bea

Acceptance of this principle in the Roman Catholic Church came on 21 November 1964 when the Second Vatican Council formally promulgated the Decree on Ecumenism which, it is generally agreed, is the great achievement of Cardinal Augustin Bea. Bea was a German Jesuit, an Old Testament scholar and Rector of the Biblical Institute in Rome. As such he had many close contacts with his Protestant counterparts and, when the Secretariat for Promoting Christian Unity was created in 1960, he was appointed its first President, although nearly eighty at the time. The role of the Secretariat was to involve the other Churches as much as possible in the preparations for and in the work of the Council and in general to hold a watching brief for the interests of ecumenism. This it did chiefly by piloting through the Council with consummate skill, under the guidance of Bea who was an ecclesiastical diplomat of the highest calibre, a document which in its whole tenor far surpassed the expectations of everyone.

Unity by return

Right up to the 1960s general conviction and official policy in the Roman Catholic Church still maintained that the only road to

Christian unity was that of individual conversions.[3] According to the 1928 encyclical *Mortalium animos* of Pius XI, the apostolate of individual conversions was not only permissible; it was essential for the achievement of Christian unity:

> There is but one way in which the unity of Christians may be fostered, and that is by furthering the return to the one true Church of Christ of those who are separated from it; for from that one true Church they have in the past fallen away.

As late as 1949 an Instruction of the Holy Office was laying it down that:

> Bishops will see to it that facilities are provided for non-Catholics seeking knowledge of the Faith, and that there are centres where specially appointed persons may be visited and consulted by non-Catholics.

Indeed, in the early days of the Second Session of Vatican II Archbishop Heenan of Westminster delivered a speech which provoked the *Church Times* (11 October 1963) to criticise him sharply for seeming to imply that 'ecumenical dialogue is simply a drive for converts' and to remind him that, if so, 'the only result will be to put an end to any expectations of progress to better relations with Roman Catholicism in this country'.

Individual conversions

Earlier drafts of the Decree on Ecumenism contained no reference to the apostolate of individual conversions. This omission was clearly deliberate and an implicit statement that the ecumenical relationship was considered to be a new and very different form of approach to other Christians. The final draft did, however, contain such a reference but ninety-six of the bishops found it unsatisfactory and asked for the following addition to the text:

Besides, the Catholic Church is strictly bound to fulfil the Lord's command (Mk 16:15) to preach the gospel to every creature or to all men.

This proposed emendation was not accepted on the grounds that it would be 'false and fatal' to apply Mark 16:15 to those already baptised. Thus the Decree as promulgated makes it clear that ecumenism is not a new way of making converts. Ecumenical action 'is of its nature distinct' from 'the work of preparing and reconciling those individuals who wish for full Catholic communion'. This latter, it is subsequently agreed, should, as an organised institution, be confined to the uncommitted, non-practising members of other Churches, to those who have 'no living relationship with any Christian Church'.

Partners – not opponents or competitors

For Cardinal Bea and his Secretariat, and for the Decree on Ecumenism, it is clear that Protestants are no longer heretics on the way to hell, needing to be rescued or converted from their Churches; their own Churches, despite their perceived limitations, are used by the Spirit as means of salvation. But the new relationship envisaged between Catholics and Protestants is not therefore thought of as some sort of non-intervention pact for the sake of peaceful co-existence. It is rather a dynamic commitment to co-operation as far as conscience permits in the work of renewal and reform, of mission and evangelism, so that the Church may be one and the world may believe and be at peace. The basic insight is this: that our Churches may be good enough as they are to get their members to heaven after death but that they are not good enough as they are to convert the world; that they may be able as they are to cope with the personal needs of their believing members but that they are unable as they are to cope with the unbelief of the world; that our Churches, as they are, are obstacles rather than aids to faith, examples and agents of disunity rather than the sign and cause of unity which they are meant to be. Thus the new ecumenical relationship to which we are called is thoroughly evangelical, profoundly missionary; it is for mission as well as for unity. It is Cardinal Bea we have to thank for the Decree on Ecumenism which describes this relationship. His Jesuit spirituality, I like to think, will have helped him in his laborious efforts to get it through the Council. There is a traditional Jesuit emphasis on finding God in all things, in all people, a traditional Jesuit concern for Church renewal and reform, a traditional Jesuit interest in missionary work so that the world may believe. This whole Jesuit spirituality seems to require a commitment to ecumenism.

YES TO THE BIBLE

From Vatican II's Decree on Ecumenism we now pass on to its Constitution on Divine Revelation, from the apostolate of individual conversions to the apostolate of the Bible, from Cardinal Augustin Bea SJ to Father Walter Abbott SJ.

Traditionally, 'the Bible', in the famous phrase of Chillingworth, the seventeenth-century Anglican, 'is the religion of Protestants'.[4] But another of the sea changes happening in our time is that the Bible is becoming not only the religion of Protestants but also the religion of Roman Catholics. It always was so, some apologists will insist – and not without reason. Certainly, in the age of reform and of printing, a Jesuit like Salmeron (the same original companion of Ignatius who came to Ireland as Papal Legate in 1542) could bring out in 1597 his *Commentaries on the New Testament* in no fewer than sixteen volumes; the fruit, we are told, of some forty years of expounding the Bible, book by book, in the pulpit. And Ignatius himself laid down in his Constitutions that in Jesuit universities there should be lectures on Old Testament and New Testament and professors of Greek and Hebrew. But when all is said that can and ought to be said, the fact remains that, up to the present, nervousness, defensiveness and fear have been very characteristic of Roman Catholic attitudes to the Bible.

The Church and the Bible

And not without reason it will be said. On the one hand, the Church had to contend with the intrinsic obscurity of the Bible which, in the words of a Spanish bishop at Trent, made vernacular versions 'mothers of heresy'.[5] On the other hand, it had also to contend with the fact that for Protestants the Bible was the great instrument of evangelism and that for all of us evangelism of whatever sort was aimed largely at making converts, i.e. at persuading people to change their Church allegiance. In the nineteenth century scientific developments, Darwinism, the Modernist crisis, the higher criticism with their challenges to biblical historicity, inspiration and truth made the Roman Catholic Church particularly cautious about any use of the Bible and extremely allergic to the way Protestants understood and used it. Even Leo XIII, in an otherwise positive enough encyclical, *Providentissimus Deus,* in 1893, could write:

> The sense of Holy Scripture can nowhere be found incorrupt outside the Church [i.e. outside the Roman Catholic Church] and cannot be expected to be found in writers who, being without the true faith, only gnaw the bark of Sacred Scripture and never attain its pith.

Already in 1713 Pope Clement XI had condemned the following, among other, propositions attributed to the Jansenist Quesnel:

> The reading of Scripture is useful for everyone. The holy obscurity of God's word is no reason why the laity may dispense themselves from reading it. Christians should

sanctify the Lord's Day by pious reading, above all of the holy Scriptures. It is damnable to want to restrain a Christian from such reading.

Vatican II and the Bible

It is some measure of the distance travelled since then that the Roman Catholic Church no longer says 'no' to these views but a 'yes' and a confident, whole-hearted, enthusiastic 'yes'. According to Paul Blanchard, the anti-Catholic controversialist, whom no one will accuse of pro-Roman sympathies:

> At Vatican II all that was changed. An illuminated copy of the scriptures, a kind of Holy Golden Book, was enthroned every morning by a bishop at the beginning of each session in St Peter's. Almost every declaration about divine authority appealed to the Bible; almost every speech, if there was any excuse for it, brought in biblical sources. From the Protestant point of view the greatest single theological advance of the Council was this new and reverent emphasis on the Bible. If the Church still claimed exclusive right to interpret the Bible correctly, it also demonstrated that it regarded biblical treasures with the same worshipful esteem that had characterised Protestantism for so many centuries. Thus, while the scripture-tradition conflict ended in a draw, ecumenism triumphed in a new and common veneration for the Bible. The Church demonstrated a new loyalty to the scriptures and a new willingness to co-operate with Protestants in biblical promotion.
>
> Vatican II also produced a new and powerful movement toward a Common Bible, a modern translation of the whole Bible that would be acceptable to both Catholics and Protestants. Indeed, the accomplishment of this purpose may be one of the few quick and specific achievements of the Council.[6]

United Bible Societies (UBS)

The changes recognised by Blanchard had of course begun long before Vatican II but they were given a great fillip by the Council's deliberations and not least by the sixth chapter of *Dei Verbum*, its Constitution on Divine Revelation. Here it is stated in brief but very forthright fashion:

> Access to sacred Scripture ought to be open wide to the Christian faithful.... The word of God must be readily available at all times.... 'Ignorance of the Scriptures is ignorance of Christ'.

In retrospect we can see that the close co-operation which exists today between the Roman Catholic Church and the United Bible Societies, once anathema, ought to have been expected but it remains one of the most extraordinary and in our part of the world too little known and appreciated phenomena of the post-Vatican II religious scene, and much of our thanks for it are due to the pioneering work of Walter Abbott, SJ.

The United Bible Societies (UBS)[7] is an association of national Bible societies established in the 1940s, with its headquarters now in Reading. The history of UBS goes back, however, to 1804 when the British and Foreign Bible Society was started in London, to be followed two years later by the Hibernian Bible Society in Dublin. The national Bible societies, of which there are at present about one hundred at work in some 180 countries, have as their aim the translation and distribution of biblical texts and audio-visual materials at affordable prices. They are almost all non-denominational and exclusively Protestant. One of the few exceptions, as it happens, is the Dublin-based society which, since May 1989, is inter-denominational, with the Roman Catholic Archbishop of Dublin as one of its patrons and other Roman Catholics on its committee. This development cannot, however, be unreservedly welcomed because it has involved a formal partitioning of the old Hibernian Bible Society into the Bible

Society in Northern Ireland and The National Bible Society of Ireland in the Republic.

UBS and the Roman Catholic Church

Seeing themselves as agencies at the service of the Churches, the Bible societies have not in principle ruled out co-operation with the Roman Catholic Church. Indeed, in the words of one of their officials speaking at the Vatican in 1967:

> The British and Foreign Bible Society in London was from the beginning in frequent communication with Roman Catholic leaders and at a very early stage had sanctioned and circulated as many as eight Roman Catholic translations of the Scriptures in the principal languages of Europe. Similarly, Roman Catholic churchmen were invited to participate in the formation of the American Bible Society in New York a few years later. However, the bright promises of those early days were eclipsed by a long period of mutual misunderstanding and mistrust, an eclipse that has now, praise God, given way to a bright new dawn.[8]

It was in fact from the United Bible Societies, through their General Secretary, Dr Oliver Beguin, that the initiative came for the inauguration of a new relationship between them and the Vatican. It came as early as February 1963, more than two years before the promulgation of the Constitution on Divine Revelation in November 1965, but in response to a number of local uncoordinated approaches and requests for help from Roman Catholic sources.

Common Bible work

When Vatican II was over it was Walter Abbott SJ who was appointed to pursue and develop contacts with the UBS. Abbott, who is still alive, is an American Jesuit, A New Englander, a New Testament scholar who was Religion Editor of the Jesuit magazine *America* for eight years before being invited to join the Vatican Secretariat for Promoting Christian Unity to act as Executive Secretary for common Bible work. As such he travelled widely, attending and addressing, for instance, the Council meeting of the UBS in New York in 1966 and subsequently its Africa, Europe and Asia regional conferences in Ghana, Switzerland and Bangkok and its first world assembly at Addis Ababa in 1972.

Roman Catholic authorities were also contacted on the occasion of these travels and also by means of a questionnaire to episcopal conferences. In these and other ways it became clear that there was general approval on both sides for common Bible work but also that there was a felt need in the Roman Catholic Church for what came to be called biblical associations which would help the faithful to study and understand the Bible. Eventually in April 1969 a World Catholic Federation (of these associations) for the biblical apostolate was established to be a partner with UBS in the ministry of the Word and Walter Abbott became its first General Secretary.[9] Ireland, it appears, is one of the few countries not a member as yet of this Federation.

Guiding principles

Meantime on Whit Sunday 1968 a document entitled *Guiding Principles for Interconfessional Cooperation in Translating the Bible* was published jointly by the UBS and the Vatican Secretariat for Promoting Christian Unity. A 'new revised edition' came out in 1987. Two difficulties among others were resolved in principle by this document. The Churches disagree on what books belong to the canon of the Old Testament because there is a Greek version, the Septuagint, which has seven more books that the Hebrew version. Protestants for the most part follow the Hebrew canon and so have the Bible Societies. But the Roman Catholic Church on the contrary follows the larger Greek canon. It is suggested as a solution that in editions published by a Bible Society with a Roman Catholic *imprimatur* the additional books appear in a separate section before the New Testament. The new edition states clearly: 'It is the aim of the Bible Societies to provide the Scriptures in the canon desired by the Churches.'

'Without note or comment'

A more difficult problem was how to reconcile the Bible Societies' rule to publish 'without note or comment' with the Roman Catholic rule that notes were obligatory. According to Father Abbot:

> The solution to the problem was found in the fact that the rule of the Bible Societies actually means that they should publish Bibles without dogmatic, doctrinal or interpretative material that would be controversial among their various constituencies, and in the fact that Catholic law does not call for doctrinal or dogmatic notes, although in some places traditional practice has included use of such material in the notes. The document of guiding principles, therefore, can say that 'both the needs of the reader and the traditional requirements of the Church' can be satisfied with annotations that give alternative readings, alternative renderings, explanations of proper names, explanations of plays on words, historical and cultural background material, and cross-references.[10]

The *Guiding Principles* themselves raise the question whether different sets of beliefs should be explained 'by noting that certain interpretations are held by Roman Catholics and others by other Christian constituencies' and suggest that such a procedure is neither wise, because it tends to accentuate differences, nor necessary. According to the new edition most exegetical differences are not denominational but are to be found within our various denominations:

> Most of the real differences of interpretation are rarely to be understood from a simplistic view of their being distinctively of one tradition or another since the differences in exegetical approach vary as much within one particular constituency as across confessional lines. Accordingly, it seems far wiser to identify various positions within the history of interpretation without labelling them as belonging to one or another Christian constituency. Where the differences are not of great consequence, it is better to simply omit reference in the interest of joint undertakings.[11]

Against the backdrop of history the new working relationship between Catholics and Protestants with regard to the Bible is altogether extraordinary and a most encouraging example of Christian faith and missionary zeal casting out denominational fear and prejudice and bigotry. But, it may be asked, to what effect? With what results? The Bible is now much more widely available and much more widely used. In the last twenty years some 160 inter-confessional Bibles have been published and many more are being prepared in various languages. But what are these among so many? There are over six thousand languages and dialects in the world but only 310 have the complete Bible, and only 1,900 have a part in translation. The harvest is great but the labourers are few. If the whole wide world is our parish, if we do believe that 'ignorance of the Scriptures is ignorance of Christ' then – but only then – our hearts will rejoice at the progress which co-operation has made possible in making the Bible more widely available and more widely used. And we shall thank God and all those who under God have helped to bring this about, among them Walter Abbott SJ.

YES TO RELIGIOUS LIBERTY

The third aspect of the new relationship between Protestants and Roman Catholics which this chapter proposes to consider is its acceptance of the principle of religious liberty. The Second Vatican Council document in which for its part the Roman Catholic Church formally accepted this principle, the Declaration on Religious Liberty, was promulgated on 7 December 1965 on the last working day of the Fourth Session of the Council. And one of the people who helped to get the document and the doctrine accepted was the Jesuit, Father John Courtney Murray.

John Courtney Murray

John Courtney Murray was an American theologian of considerable repute who in his lifetime was featured in *Time*, appearing on its cover (12 December 1960), and on his death on 16 August 1967 was the subject of a long appreciative obituary in *The New York Times*. According to this notice he was 'generally credited with having been the major author of the decree favouring religious liberty passed by the Ecumenical Council, Vatican II'... 'one of the most liberal spokesmen of the Roman Catholic Church in America'... who had 'made a lifelong study of the interaction between his country and his religion' and 'contended that the Vatican should give its formal blessing to the pluralist system in the United States as a new, permanent kind of relationship between religion and government'...; 'he was known', it said, 'to be the principal architect of the council's declaration on religious liberty'.

This assessment by *The New York Times* would not be disputed. According to the Introduction to a 1975 symposium on the Declaration held in the USA,

> [I]t was John Courtney Murray who not only prepared the way for the Declaration by his brilliant rethinking of the

development of Catholic doctrine on religious freedom, but also, in the short run, distinguished himself as one of the master draughtsmen of the final Declaration....

Moreover, when the inside story of the Council is finally written, the record will show that he drafted many, if not most, of the major interventions made by the leading members of the American hierarchy in support of the Declaration (and certainly they were among the best and most effective of all the interventions on this subject) and was consulted on the drafting of several others.[12]

Religious freedom and the Roman Catholic Church
A belief in religious freedom for all, heretics included, has not, unfortunately, been a traditional tenet of any of our Churches, but happily, in recent decades it has come to be generally accepted by the members of the World Council of Churches which in 1948 issued its Amsterdam Declaration on Religious Liberty. Until Vatican II, however, the theoretical position of the Roman Catholic Church towards those who differed from it continued to be one of toleration based on expediency. Error, it was held, had no rights but it was not always practical or possible to suppress error, so it could and might be tolerated as the lesser of two evils. What Vatican II did was to change this position. It didn't happen easily. It took time and patience and skill. The debates were tense and dramatic. Ecclesiastical politics of the best but also of the worst kind seems to have been involved.

Vatican II
Eventually, on 7 December 1965, the Roman Catholic Church formally recognised that religious freedom was not something to be grudgingly conceded but an intrinsic universal right.

> The Vatican Council declares that the human person has a right to religious freedom. Freedom of this kind means that all men should be immune from coercion on the part of individuals, social groups and every human power so that, within due limits, nobody is forced to act against his convictions in religious matters in private or in public, alone or in association with others.(§2)

Here the Declaration describes the content or object of the right. It is a moral claim to immunity; it is a 'freedom from' rather than a 'freedom for'. In this regard the Declaration is very much in line with the First Amendment to the American Constitution.

What is the foundation of this right? Two approaches are possible here, one more theological, the other more philosophical. The former would base the moral claim on the freedom of the act of faith which must be freely made; the latter would base it on the dignity of the human person. An earlier draft did emphasise the more theological line of what is sometimes called the French school of thought, which the World Council of Churches in fact follows in its statements on religious liberty. But the final text gives first place to the more philosophical line preferred by John Courtney Murray.

> The Council further declares that the right to religious freedom is based on the very dignity of the human person as known through the revealed word of God and by reason itself. (§2)

In a commentary on the Declaration Father Murray notes that there was no intention 'to affirm that the argument, as made in the text, is final and decisive'. 'Complete and systematic study of the arguments for religious freedom is a task left to the scholars of the Church.' Since Vatican II, therefore, the strengths and weaknesses of the Courtney Murray approach have been the subject of discussion, notably in the pages of *Theological Studies*. Its great strength is, in Murray's own words, that 'the objective foundation of the right to religious freedom is presented in terms that should be intelligible and acceptable to all men, including non-believers'. Its weaknesses are described as follows by a fellow-Jesuit, John A. Coleman:

> The first relates to the bias toward liberty at the expense of justice in the American public-philosophy tradition and its concomitant individualistic tone .... A second weakness ... is his failure to admit that his own theory of natural law rests on particularistic Catholic theological principles .... The final weakness in Murray's strategy for public discourse lies in the nature of the symbols he uses. There is a sense in which 'secular' language, especially when governed by the Enlightenment ideals of conceptual clarity and analytic rigor is exceedingly 'thin' as a symbol system. It is unable to evoke the rich, polyvalent power of religious symbolism, a power which can command commitments of emotional depth. The very necessity of seeking a universality which transcends our rootedness and loyalties to particular communities makes secular language chaste, sober, and thin. I wonder if a genuine sense of vivid *communitas*... is possible on the basis of a nonreligious symbol system....
>
> The tradition of biblical religion seems the most potent symbolic resource we possess to address the sense of drift in American identity and purpose.[13]

Universality of right to religious freedom

While the foundations of the right to religious freedom are very much open to argument and discussion, this is not so with regard to its universality. In the past it did often seem that religious freedom was something the Roman Catholic Church claimed for itself but refused to others, thus denying its universality. The Declaration, however, makes it abundantly clear that the Roman Catholic Church is claiming nothing for itself here which it does not also claim for the other Churches and religious bodies:

The freedom or immunity from coercion in religious matters which is the right of individuals must also be accorded to men when they act in community. Religious communities are a requirement of the nature of man and of religion itself.

Therefore, provided the just requirements of public order are not violated, these groups have a right to immunity so that they may organise themselves according to their own principles. They must be allowed to honour the supreme Godhead with public worship, help their members to practise their religion and strengthen them with religious instruction, and promote institutions in which members may work together to organise their own lives according to their religious principles ....

Religious communities have the further right not to be prevented from publicly teaching and bearing witness to their beliefs by the spoken or written word. However, in spreading religious belief and in introducing religious practices everybody must at all times avoid any action which seems to suggest coercion or dishonest or unworthy persuasion, especially when dealing with the uneducated or the poor. Such a manner of acting must be considered an abuse of one's own right and an infringement of the rights of others.

Also included in the right to religious freedom is the right of religious groups not to be prevented from freely demonstrating the special value of their teaching for the organisation of society and the inspiration of all human activity. Finally, rooted in the social nature of man and in the very nature of religion is the right of men, prompted by their own religious sense, freely to hold meetings or establish educational, cultural, charitable and social organisations. (§4)

This formal, unequivocal recognition by the Roman Catholic Church of the universality of the right to religious freedom may not, it is true, be a milestone in human history but it certainly is so in ecclesiastical history. According to Paul Blanchard 'it marked a great advance in Catholic policy, perhaps the greatest single advance in principle during all four sessions of the Council'; it was 'a glorious victory in the history of an institution that had fathered the Inquisition'.[14]

Religious freedom and Christian unity
The critical importance of Vatican II's Declaration on Religious Liberty was well expressed by the Lutheran theologian and professor at Yale, Dr George Lindbeck, in his contribution to the 1975 symposium already mentioned:

> Most of us remember the preconciliar situation in which ecumenical discussions revolved around the issue of religious liberty. Non-Catholics, perhaps especially in America, were obsessed with the question of what would happen to civil and religious liberties if Catholics became a majority. They constantly asked if the Church approved of the disabilities under which non-Catholics suffered in places like Spain. This was the end-all and the be-all of most inter-Church exchanges. Ecumenism could not advance under these circumstances. It was only because of the Declaration on Religious Freedom ... that the way was opened for the Decree on Ecumenism. Thus any suggestion that there is something reversible about the Declaration would be extremely shocking, indeed traumatic, for Protestant sensibilities. This is paradoxical. By and large Protestants resist the notion that there is anything irreversible or infallible in the pronouncements of the Church – except in the case of this Declaration.[15]

The preoccupation referred to here by George Lindbeck – the 'obsession', to use his own word – remains, as is only too well known, a prominent feature of Protestantism in Ireland, especially in Northern Ireland. Protestants here have still a very real fear of living in a society with a majority Roman Catholic population. They are afraid because they think that nothing has changed in the Roman Catholic Church and because what they know of life in the South seems to confirm them in their worst fears. The 1986 referendum about the constitutional ban on divorce did nothing to allay these fears. According to one commentator, Father Patrick Riordan SJ, who lectures at the Milltown Institute of Theology and Philosophy in Dublin, the Roman Catholic Bishops had carefully distinguished between private and public morality, between Catholic teaching on divorce as a practical option for individuals and Catholic teaching on divorce as a practical option for the State. These two, however, had been greatly confused by priests and people who had voted against a divorce jurisdiction, as the bishops had indeed advised, but not for the reasons given by the bishops. In its members if not in its hierarchy the Roman Catholic Church in Ireland had seen it to be the function of the State to embody traditional Catholic teaching in its laws. 'What is needed', he concludes, 'is a serious programme of re-education for both laity and clergy which will allow dearly-held [pre-Vatican II] notions to be challenged and reformed'.[16] This conclusion would be widely endorsed. It is stressed, for example, by Dr Stanley Worrall who, of course, adds that 'The Protestant Churches have to ensure that their members are well-informed about Roman Catholic doctrine and practice, as they are seen in today's post-Vatican II situation'.[17] It is thanks in large part to John Courtney Murray SJ that there is a new, a radically new post-Vatican II position on religious freedom. It comes as no surprise that in a *Christianity and Crisis* obituary notice John C. Bennett of Union Theological referred to Murray as 'one of the most significant thinkers belonging to and honoured by the whole ecumenical community'.

CONCLUSION

Why, it may be asked in conclusion, has this chapter concentrated on the basics of the new relationship between Roman Catholics and Protestants which Vatican II inaugurated? Why has it omitted all mention of the exciting developments which we owe to the bilateral ecumenical commissions which have been hard at work in the years since Vatican II. There are quite a number of these and most of them do seem to have a Jesuit member. These Commissions have indeed produced many exciting agreements, in the area, for instance, of eucharistic theology. This chapter has not considered them because they have not as yet been ratified by the Church authorities and because the Jesuit contribution in each case is not so easy to identify. I have concentrated instead on certain basics because they are achievements in the fullest sense of the word and because the Jesuit contribution can be clearly enough identified.

But there is a third and perhaps more important reason. It is, it seems to me, becoming increasingly clear that, if the movement for Christian unity is to renew its youth, to come alive again and gather momentum, at every level of our Churches here and elsewhere, but perhaps especially here, then we cannot afford to take the basics for granted, least of all in this decade of evangelism when unchurched and unbelievers were probably never more numerous and certainly never more accessible. Ecumenism and evangelism – we do well to remind ourselves – have both the one same, basic aim, the one same motto: so that the world may believe; both are about helping the world to believe. We can, of course, go about this evangelism either separately or together. In fact, much of it is being done by groups in isolation and one result, we are told, is that Latin Americans are converting to Protestantism at a rate of five hundred per hour but not, I suspect, for the most part to a form of Protestantism that any of the so-called 'main-line' Churches would wish to endorse. Whether in any case we go it alone in our evangelism or do it together, the Bible must be our chief means of facilitating faith, of introducing the gospel. And respect for the other must be the hallmark of all such activity: respect for the freedom of the individual, respect – despite possible reservations – for the authenticity of her or his Church as means of salvation. But so many of us have still so much to unlearn, not just about the others but paradoxically perhaps about ourselves, about our own tradition and not least with regard to the Bible and with regard to freedom, both individual and corporate. The views prevalent in United Bible Society circles are not yet shared by enough Protestants or Roman Catholics. The views about religious freedom taught by Vatican II are not yet shared by enough Roman Catholics or Protestants. If, therefore, the work of evangelism and the work of ecumenism are to prosper – and they can prosper only if they go together – then the Churches, all of us, may need to concentrate more on the basic principles which Augustin Bea, Walter Abbott and John Courtney Murray helped to get established.[18]

13
Reconciliation and the Churches in Northern Ireland

'The Churches are very much part of the solution – rather than part of the problem – in Ireland today': so ran an editorial in *The Irish News*, a Belfast nationalist/Catholic daily newspaper on Friday, 24 March 1995.

The occasion for this editorial was a visit by a delegation from the Presbyterian Church in Ireland to the Forum for Peace and Reconciliation in Dublin to make a submission on behalf of their Church and Government Committee. The visit was highly significant. The Forum, which held its inaugural meeting on 28 October 1994,[1] was established by the Dublin Government 'to consult on and examine ways in which lasting peace, stability and reconciliation can be established by agreement among all the people of Ireland'. It was 'especially anxious that the voices of members of both the unionist and nationalist traditions as well as of others, be heard'. Unionists, however, especially the main unionist political parties, had been conspicuous more by their absence than their presence.

The Presbyterian Church in Ireland is not to be confused with Dr Paisley's Free Presbyterian Church, which is Presbyterian in name only. On the other hand, although it does include a large number of members who are outstanding in every way – in particular The Very Reverend John Dunlop, a former Moderator – and although it is in no sense 'the unionist party at prayer', its membership is in fact mostly Northern, mostly unionist and mostly un- and anti-ecumenical: in 1979 it suspended and in 1980 it terminated its membership of the World Council of Churches; in 1990 it declined to join the new Council of Churches for Great Britain and Ireland of which the Roman Catholic Church in England and Wales did become a member. An *official* submission from this Church is, therefore, in the words of *The Irish News*, 'an important groundbreaking development', all the more so as (according to this newspaper) it urged a 'growing togetherness' among all the people of Ireland, Catholic and Protestant, North and South, and stated:

> We yearn for a new kind of society in Ireland, marked by co-operation, mutual affirmation, honour and respect, in which all are winners .... We must work with models of co-operation, and not with models of domination or assimilation.[2]

Many other facts, as this chapter hopes to indicate, go to corroborate the judgement of *The Irish News* that 'the Churches are very much part of the solution – rather than part of the problem – in Ireland today'. But was it always so and what is the problem? According to the editorial of *The Irish News* already quoted:

> It has often been wrongly suggested that tensions between the two communities in Northern Ireland stem from religion rather than politics.

This is a re-statement of what has been a traditional nationalist, Catholic viewpoint and, though it plunges us *in medias res*, some consideration of it will be of help to begin with.

The problem
Nobody denies that Northern Ireland is a political and also an economic and cultural problem.[3] The island is territorially, politically divided. According to the unionist story the twenty-six counties of the South seceded from the United Kingdom some seventy-five years ago. According to the nationalist story the

Northern unionists refused to be included in the Home Rule Bill passed at Westminster in 1913 and succeeded eventually in securing a separate existence for the six counties in the north-east of the country.

So Ireland is 'partitioned': there are two political jurisdictions. One with its headquarters in Dublin comprises twenty-six of the thirty-two counties; it is a Republic and largely (91%) Roman Catholic in population. The other with its headquarters in Belfast comprises the remaining six counties where some 60% of the population is Protestant. It is part of the United Kingdom of Great Britain and Northern Ireland. Until 1972 it had its own parliament at Stormont, but since then has been governed by direct rule from Westminster.

In its Constitution the Dublin jurisdiction lays claim to the six counties of the North; it looks forward to a united Ireland, to the abolition of the border dividing the country politically. The vast majority of the people in the South are now nationalists but, with the growing apart of the two jurisdictions, especially since World War II, their nationalism has become more notional than real, more a patriotic aspiration than a political goal. The North rejects the constitutional claim of the South. The Northern majority are determined to maintain the union with Britain: they are unionists and they are mostly Protestants. But in the North there is also a large minority, some 40%, who are nationalists, most of them being Roman Catholic.[4]

As recent decades, indeed as the whole history of Northern Ireland has shown, some nationalists and unionists do not hesitate to resort to violence and bloodshed to further their ends. Between 1968 and 1994 nearly 3,500 people were killed. But happily the violence is now over. The IRA (Irish Republican Army), the nationalist paramilitaries, declared a ceasefire which began on 1 September 1994 and their unionist counterparts, the CLMC (Combined Loyalist Military Command), followed suit on 14 October. The Dublin and Westminster governments have published *A New Framework for Agreement: A Shared Understanding between the British and Irish Governments to assist discussion and negotiation involving the Northern Ireland parties.* The question at issue is: How is Northern Ireland to be governed and how, in consequence, are its economic, social and cultural problems to be solved? An answer satisfactory or acceptable to all interests will take years rather than months to emerge. In the words of our former Prime Minister, architect of the Anglo-Irish Agreement of 1985, Dr Garret FitzGerald, the way forward will be 'long, tortuous and thorny'.[5] A multi-party agreement was, however, reached on Good Friday, 10 April 1998.

A religious problem?
But is Northern Ireland not also a religious problem? *Pace The Irish News* is it wrong to suggest that the tensions between the two communities stem, if not 'from religion rather than politics', at least from religion as well as politics?

Unbelievable as it always sounds to outsiders, the Church in Ireland is *not* partitioned. There may be two political jurisdictions but there are not two ecclesiastical jurisdictions. The Church in Ireland is not territorially divided. Each of the main Churches is a united, all-Ireland, thirty-two county organisation, as was the whole country up to some seventy years ago, and the primatial see for both Anglicans and Catholics is in Armagh in Northern Ireland. The history of the Churches goes back centuries and bears witness to the way things were before the political border was created earlier this century. So it is that there are Anglican and Roman Catholic dioceses, Methodist districts and Presbyterian presbyteries which are partly in the South, partly in the North, which straddle the political border because they pre-date it. So it is that in ecclesiastical affairs and circles there is no controversy as to whether a certain city is to be called 'Derry' (as in nationalist parlance) or 'Londonderry' (as in unionist parlance). For both

Anglicans and Roman Catholics it is now, as always, the diocese of Derry, and for Presbyterians too it is now, as always, the Presbytery and Synod of Derry. It may be noted, however, that, unlike the Church, the Jewish Community in Ireland did reorganise itself and become 'partitioned' in 1919. An Irish Chief Rabbinate was set up in Dublin whereas Belfast and the North continued to be under the jurisdiction of London. The traditional contacts between Southern and Northern Jews have, however, been maintained; in the main all would be Orthodox.

Precisely because it is not itself partitioned, the Church in Ireland has been a unifying factor, if not within Northern Ireland, at least between North and South, and to that extent it has always been part of the solution to the conflict. It remains, however, that the coincidence in the North of political and religious loyalties gives the conflict a religious dimension. This is especially true in the unionist experience and has been put beyond question by the work of, among others, the sociologists John Hickey and Steve Bruce, both of whom lived and taught in Northern Ireland.

Unionism and religion
In his *Religion and the Northern Ireland Problem* Hickey, one-time Senior Lecturer in Sociology at the University of Ulster in Coleraine, underlined the 'deep core of fear, suspicion and hostility' prevalent among Northern unionists and concluded that 'Politics in the North is not politics exploiting religion …. It is more a question of religion inspiring politics than of politics making use of religion'. Bruce, formerly of the Queen's University of Belfast and now Professor at Aberdeen, published *God Save Ulster* in 1985 and *The Edge of the Union* in 1994. He too stresses the religious character, the anti-Catholicism of classical unionism:

> Why be a unionist? To avoid being part of a united Ireland. What is wrong with a united Ireland? It would be a Catholic country. If you do not want to be a Catholic, what

are you? A Protestant. If we understand that sequence, we can understand the political success of Ian Paisley and the role of evangelicalism in the thinking of Ulster Protestants.[7]

The anti-Catholicism of Dr Paisley doesn't hesitate to unchurch the Roman Catholic Church and to include in the hymnbook of his own Church such provocative language as the following:
Our Fathers knew thee, Rome of old,
And evil is thy fame;
Thy fond embrace, the galling chain;
Thy kiss, the blazing flame.

Thy sentence dread is now pronounced,
Soon shalt thou pass away.
O soon shall earth have rest and peace –
Good Lord, haste Thou that day.[8]

Unionist fear of Rome

Northern Ireland unionism, however, does not in general depend on such an extreme form of anti-Catholicism. What is more typical of Northern unionists is a fear that their civil and religious rights and liberties and their economic standard of living would be in danger under Rome Rule, in a State under the domination of the Roman Catholic Church, as they perceive the Republic of Ireland to be. As a distinguished English Methodist who had lived for many years in Belfast put it:
[The Northern Ireland Protestant] is not afraid that if he lives there [in the Republic of Ireland] he would be unable to practise his religion; but he is afraid that he would be obliged to live a great part of his life according to the pattern laid down by someone else's religion …. The philosophy of 'No Surrender', 'not an inch' is kept alive through fear [of Rome]; and I say again, it is religious fear,

which only the Churches can exorcise.... Unfortunately the result of such fear is not only to rule out the reunion of the country; it also produces in the popular mind a less justifiable resistance to any form of shared government in Northern Ireland.[9]

Contrary to what is often believed, this 'religious fear', the anti-Catholicism of Northern Ireland unionism, its fear of Rome, is a middle-class as well as a 'working-class' phenomenon. If this is less obvious it is only because the middle classes everywhere are usually more sophisticated, more inhibited in expressing themselves. It may also be noted *en passant* that two new forms of unionism have just begun to emerge: a) a secular unionism which wants to have little or nothing to do with religion or Church and b) a unionism which is ecumenical in its Protestantism and studiously eschews anti-Romanism. Neither form, however, had acquired much, if any, political influence, until the signing of the Good Friday Agreement.[10]

Partition
The 'new kind of society' for which the Irish Presbyterian delegation 'yearn' in their submission to the Dublin *Forum* tells us all too clearly, if implicitly, how things have been, what kind of society has in the past up to now prevailed in Northern Ireland. Instead of 'togetherness' and 'co-operation', apartheid, politico-religious segregation has been the order of the day: not only separate Churches but separate schools, separate teacher-training colleges, separate hospitals, separate newspapers, separate sporting activities, separate clubs, separate neighbourhoods.

The Northern nationalist Catholic minority deeply resented and resisted the partition of the country and as far as possible withheld co-operation. Only very few, for instance, ever joined the police force, the Royal Ulster Constabulary. Indeed, by equipping themselves with their own social infrastructure they can be said to have formed a kind of 'state within a state'. On the other hand the unionist Protestant majority has been characterised by a curious amalgam of superiority and insecurity. They have tended, in the words of a recent history, to regard the nationalists 'as a hostile "fifth column", deserving only of second-class citizenship'.[11] To retain control they used their power unfairly, especially in the sphere of local government where only ratepayers had a vote, and so brought about the emergence in the late 1960s of the Civil Rights Association to protest against unionist injustices, e.g. discrimination in the allocation of public housing.

The Troubles
Although in the meantime most of the nationalists' grievances have been redressed, it has to be admitted that the violence of the last few decades – what we euphemistically call 'the Troubles' – has in some ways only worsened the apartheid in Northern Ireland and so postponed at least the full achievement of the nationalists' political aspirations. The people are now further apart than before not only psychologically but also geographically. Because of the reversal of their fortunes the unionist/Protestant community has become alienated from Britain; because of the mutual killings, trust and confidence between the communities within Northern Ireland has suffered; because of the resulting fear and, therefore, for reasons of security, mixed neighbourhoods have shown a sharp decrease in number. According to the (Methodist) Superintendent of the Belfast Central Mission, the city is 'more segregated than ever before with up to 80% of people living in segregated areas'.[12] And 'this pattern has been replicated in other towns throughout Northern Ireland, most of which now have clearly defined areas in which the minority population – of Catholics in the east and of Protestants in the west – cluster together for mutual support and a feeling of safety.'[13]

The peace process

This however is far from being the whole truth. A peace process is now taking place. The ceasefires declared in 1994 held almost miraculously for seventeen months. After a quarter of a century there was optimism at last as well as hope. At the time of writing (summer 1997) the IRA has renewed its ceasefire broken in February 1996; there is hope once again, if no longer optimism, that a political settlement will be reached in due course. The present peace process, however fragile and precarious, is, I wish to suggest, an achievement for which the Churches can take much of the credit; instead of being simply part of the problem they have become a significant part of the solution.

If one of the major factors in the sad, tragic history of Northern Ireland has been the coincidence of political and Church affiliation, of Catholics with nationalism and Protestants with unionism, then two events stand out in my memory as particularly significant, heralding the liberation of the Churches from their political captivity and the coming of peace.

Mutual recognition

The first of these events was the installation of Bishop Cahal Daly in Belfast in October 1982 as Bishop of Down and Connor. In the course of his address on this occasion he stated:

> Mutual recognition in each community of the complete legitimacy and legality, the equal dignity and rights, of the other community, with its own self-defined identity, its own sense of loyalty, its own aspiration, so long as these are peacefully held and peacefully promoted is a christian task to which we are all called at this time.[14]

This new vision in which nationalism and unionism are no longer mutually exclusive came to find expression two years later in chapters four and five of the *Report* of the New Ireland Forum established by the Dublin Government in 1983; it is at the present time struggling to become a political reality. Bishop, now Cardinal, Cahal Daly has been outstanding in encouraging the fresh political thinking and the ecumenical initiatives which reconciliation and peace require.

The end of the Churches' captivity

The second event was the demonstration against the Anglo-Irish Agreement which took place at the Belfast City Hall in November 1985. The Anglo-Irish Agreement, signed on 15 November of that year by the British and Irish Governments, established an Inter-Governmental Conference to deal on a regular basis with political matters affecting Northern Ireland. This involvement of 'a foreign power', even if only on a consultative basis, in the administration of Northern Ireland was anathema to unionists for whom Dublin Rule was Rome Rule. In his fury Dr Paisley did not hesitate on the following Sunday to lead his congregation at the Martyrs Memorial Church in the following prayer:

> O God, in wrath take vengeance upon this wicked, treacherous, lying woman [Margaret Thatcher, the British Prime Minister]; take vengeance upon her, Oh Lord, and grant that we shall see a demonstration of thy power.[15]

The protest marches which were organised to object to the Anglo-Irish Agreement and which converged on the City Hall in Belfast on 23 November 1985 drew a huge crowd of over 100,000 people. It was all meant as a reminder of, indeed as a kind of re-enactment of the signing of the Solemn League and Covenant against Home Rule on Ulster Day, 28 September 1912. The November 1985 demonstration was indeed similar in intent, in inspiration and in size to that of September 1912, but with one immensely significant difference. The 1912 signing of the

Covenant in various centres throughout the North was a religious, ecclesiastical, Protestant event: it was preceded by Church services, took place in Church halls and was led by Church ministers. In Belfast the list of signatories was headed by the two great political leaders, Sir Edward Carson and Lord Londonderry, but immediately after them came the Moderator of the Presbyterian General Assembly, the Bishop of Down, Connor and Dromore, the Dean of Belfast, The General Secretary of the Presbyterian Church, the President of the Methodist Conference and the ex-Chairman of the Congregational Union.[16] In 1985, however, the Church of Ireland and the other Protestant leaders, apart of course from Dr Paisley, were conspicuous no longer by their presence but rather by their absence.

'Churches on trial'
How this sea change came about is told by the two well-known and highly-regarded Methodists, Eric Gallagher and Stanley Worrall, in their joint work *Christians in Ulster 1968-1980*, published by the Oxford University Press in 1982. Here they give an honest, sober appraisal of the role of the Churches during the first half of the present 'Troubles'. Their concluding chapter is entitled 'Churches on Trial'. The record of the Churches they find to be 'not wholly a negative one'. On the credit side they emphasise ecumenical developments:

> The main thrust [they write] of the Churches' contribution has taken the form of greatly enhanced ecumenical collaboration at a time of increasing polarisation between the communities at the secular level. In the sixties it seemed for a time as if the suspicion and hostility that divided Catholic and Protestant in the social and political spheres might be subsiding in the light of common interests. The resurgence of violence that followed the demands of the civil rights movement put an end to that, and revived the

antagonism of the past. Nevertheless, during the 1970s the organised Churches achieved considerable innovations and development in their relationships. There have been setbacks and disappointments in the ecumenical field, but they must not be allowed to obscure the fact that there is now more contact, more mutual respect and understanding, between the Churches than at any earlier period of Irish history. How far this will develop is very uncertain at the time of writing.[17]

It was the outbreak of the 'Troubles' which spurred or rather shamed the Churches into official contact for the first time. The groundwork of course had been done, the foundations had been laid in the early 1960s. The Irish Council of Churches does go back as far as 1923 but not until Vatican II did its members, the various Protestant Churches, have much if any contact with the Roman Catholic Church. With Vatican II, however, inter-Church meetings of many sorts had begun to take place which, though not yet official, were mostly held with the knowledge and blessing of Church authorities. When, therefore, the crisis came, official contacts, though still controversial and arousing fierce opposition in some quarters, were sufficiently acceptable to become a practical reality.

The Churches – part of the solution

So a small Joint Group on Social Questions was set up in 1970 and among other things appointed a number of working parties, one of which produced the important report *Violence in Ireland* in 1976. The work of the Joint Group led to the establishment in 1973 of the Ballymascanlon Meetings (so-called after the name of the place where they happened), and these in turn, after some re-organisation, led to the formation of the so-called Irish Inter-Church Meeting (IICM) in 1984. This is composed of representatives of the Irish Episcopal Conference of the Roman Catholic Church and of the member Churches of the Irish Council of Churches and meets approximately every eighteen months. It has set up a Department of Social Issues and a Department of Theological Questions. The former established a Working Party on Sectarianism which produced a very forthright, challenging Report in 1993. The latter prepared a document entitled *Freedom, Justice and Responsibility in Ireland Today*, published in 1997,[18] to which reference has already been made in a previous chapter because of its inclusion of 'ecumenical tithing' among its three specific proposals. Some members had wanted two additional proposals included which would discourage Church-related Orange Marches and encourage greater generosity in allowing eucharistic sharing, but these are merely mentioned, not formally endorsed.[19]

On the debit side Gallagher and Worrall were ready to admit that 'it is in the translation of this general will towards reconciliation, which they have effectively fostered, into practical steps that would be socially and politically effective that the Churches have so far failed'.[20] That, however, was in 1981. It is only since then that much of what they record has come to fruition, that, for example, the Ballymascanlon Meetings have been consolidated and developed into IICM and managed to retain the ecumenically-lukewarm Presbyterian Church in Ireland as a member – but without yet becoming a really dynamic force. Again it is only since 1981 that many other ecumenical initiatives (taking courage from the example of the Corrymeela Community and the Rostrevor Christian Renewal Centre and the Irish School of Ecumenics which already existed) have got under way and, although mostly unofficial, have succeeded in exerting a very considerable influence. These new ventures include, for example, the ECONI (Evangelical Contribution on Northern Ireland) group, the Inter-Church Group on Faith and Politics, the Cornerstone Community, the Columbanus Community of

Reconciliation, Youth Link: NI (Inter-Church Youth Agency), the Armagh Clergy Fellowship and very many others besides. Deserving of special mention is the fact that before the ceasefires a number of individual Church people (notably the Redemptorist priest, Alex Reid, and the Presbyterian minister, Roy Magee) were outstanding in initiating and maintaining contact with paramilitary groups and acting as intermediaries between them and political and government representatives.[21]

The Churches and reconciliation

Not surprisingly, therefore, *The Irish Times* of Dublin, echoing the views of *The Irish News* of Belfast, was able in May 1995 to state that:

> One of the profoundest changes in the political climate in the North in recent years has come from the concerted effort by the Churches, among their members as well as between themselves, to further the cause of reconciliation.[22]

The occasion for this editorial was the Church of Ireland submission to the Forum for Peace and Reconciliation in Dublin and in particular the efforts by its Primate, Archbishop Robin Eames, to encourage more positive thinking among unionists and to remind us all about the fears of each other that still subsist in both communities and which seriously jeopardise our renewed efforts at reconciliation.[23] The new interest in and appreciation of the Churches' ministry of ecumenism and reconciliation is, however, a complex phenomenon. It is not simply that the Churches have become less self-sufficient, more humble, more co-operative, more ecumenical. It is also because recent events in former Yugoslavia and elsewhere have brought in their train the realisation that Northern Ireland is no monstrous anachronism, that religion is indeed more potent – for good and ill – than much secular thinking, especially Marxist, was able previously to recognise.

Togetherness or apartheid?

Although togetherness is the official Northern Ireland policy of both British and Irish Governments at present, it remains the case that togetherness is not the only solution in conflict situations. In their *Northern Ireland: The Choice* Boyle and Hadden have given us the stark reminder that

> [O]ne of the fundamental choices that arises in most conflicts of this kind is between separation or sharing.[24]

And with their eyes on Belgium and Switzerland they devote one of their chapters to 'Structures for Separation'.

If, however, Government policy is to succeed in Northern Ireland, a great deal now depends on the Churches, whose role is still paramount. Indeed a survey by the Centre for the Study of Conflict of the University of Ulster on *The Churches and Inter-Community Relationships* could still conclude, in 1991:

> The Churches in Northern Ireland are the oldest indigenous social institutions in the land and they are communities of people where values are passed on, friends are made, community is experienced and times of supreme personal and societal importance – Baptism, first communion, marriage and burials – are shared. Even for those, mainly Protestant, who no longer maintain any active link to a Church or to belief, the Churches are pervasively present and important. Identity remains most accurately gauged by denomination. Friendship, marriage, residence and school remain stubbornly loyal to religious barriers.[25]

In these circumstances the challenge facing the Churches to overcome segregation and sectarianism and to renew their ministry of reconciliation in accordance with the spirit and suggestions of the IICM reports, *Sectarianism* and *Freedom, Justice and Responsibility in Ireland Today*, is indeed a daunting one. It is, however, a challenge which the initial success of the current peace process seems to be giving the Churches a new confidence to accept.[26] We are still hoping, hoping indeed with the hope that does not disappoint (cf. Romans 5:5), but still hoping against hope, no longer euphorically optimistic.[27] We are encouraged by the signing of the Stormont Multi-Party Agreement on Good Friday 1998, by the fact that the violent events of the summer of 1998 did not succeed in undermining this Agreement and the decisive role played by one particular church minister, the Presbyterian County Armagh Orange chaplain, William Bingham, in saving the situation. In the words of Andy Pollak, writing in *The Irish Times* on 14 July 1998:

> Northern Ireland has seen little courageous leadership from its churches in the past fortnight [1-14 July]; in fact, with a few outstanding exceptions, it has seen little such leadership during the past thirty years. But at times when total mayhem and massacre seem imminent, appeals by ministers of religion to people's basic Christian instincts do appear to have some effect, and they pull back from the brink of Armageddon.

Part III
Ecumenical Initiatives

14
An Ecumenical Lecture Series: Milltown Park Public Lectures 1960-1969

Introduction

The Milltown Park Public Lectures, the subject of this chapter, were an initiative of the Milltown Park Jesuit Faculty of Theology in Dublin. This Faculty, to which I was appointed in 1958, was the predecessor of the present Milltown Institute of Theology and Philosophy. The Lectures were an 'ecumenical initiative' because, in the words of Vatican II, 'Church renewal has notable ecumenical importance'.[1] Some account of the initiative seems particularly appropriate here because it was a Milltown Park Public Lecture on 'The Ecumenical Movement' which began my personal involvement in that movement and so led to the other initiatives which are described in the following chapters.[2] The Milltown Park Public Lectures also form part of the development of theological education and of Church renewal in Ireland and part of the reception process of the insights of Vatican II and as such are of some additional historical interest. Because the records are mislaid if not lost, a list of the topics and speakers of the first decade has been compiled from various sources and is printed here as an Appendix.[3]

Origins

The Milltown Park Public Lectures were inaugurated on 2 March 1960 when Father Patrick Joy SJ, the Faculty's Professor of Moral

Theology, spoke on 'the population explosion'. News of this first session was recorded in *Irish [Jesuit] Province News* (*IPN*) in sober and not very precise language: 'Every lecture was largely attended, and each was followed by a discussion. The series was so successful and so well attended that it has been decided to resume it in October and again during Lent next year.' Speakers and topics were given in this account, but no dates.[4] The language of the House History of the Jesuit Community at Milltown Park (*HD*) was still Latin, but Father Patrick O'Connell, being a classical scholar and a member of staff for whom Latin was still the official medium of teaching, was not intimidated by this: he gave no dates either for this first session but wrote warmly and generously of this 'new academic initiative': *novum inceptum in mundo scholastico*.[5]

A main aim of the Milltown Park Public Lectures was to give a wider audience to the Faculty. As we had no journal of our own to maintain, our audience was confined at that time to the student body which consisted only of ordinands: some fifty Jesuits and some twenty Carmelites (OCarm).[6] A related aim of the Public Lectures was of course to make our contribution to the theological education of the laity. What we would cover in the lectures we expressed in broad terms as 'theological subjects of topical interest' or 'topical subjects of theological interest'. Beginning in spring 1966 questionnaires were distributed each evening asking for suggestions.[7] In general, each session aimed to cover a variety of topics rather than various aspects of a single topic.

Speakers
A main aim of the Public Lectures may have been to give the staff a platform, but an overriding aim was to cover whatever theological subjects were (or ought to be) of topical interest, especially in the context of Vatican II. This broad coverage being beyond the competence of the Milltown Park staff by itself, non-members of the Faculty were regularly invited as visiting lecturers.

A preferential option for Jesuits seems, however, to have operated as a guiding principle in the beginning and non-Jesuits rarely appear on the programme more than once a year. In the opening session this non-Jesuit was none other than the former Jesuit and former President of University College Cork, the redoubtable Reverend Dr Alfred O'Rahilly who had spent most of his life as a well-known and very articulate layman and whose subject was 'the laity in the Church'. Such, however, was the sad state of theological education in the country and/or the low level of trust between clergy and laity that it was not until the twelfth session, half-way through the decade, in the winter of 1965, that a lay person appears for the first time on the programme of the Milltown Park Public Lectures: Professor Neil Porter of University College Dublin, speaking on the topic 'scientist and Christian'.[8] Another two years, however, were to pass, in the course of which four other laymen were given the platform, before a laywoman was invited, and she was a religious (Sr M. Pauline SSL) and her topic 'the religious vocation today'. The first 'real' laywoman to be invited was in fact also the first non-Roman Catholic: Mercy Simms, wife of Archbishop George Otto Simms, Church of Ireland Archbishop of Dublin. In spring 1968 she addressed the topic of 'mothers and careers' and she was followed in the winter session that same year by her husband speaking on the 1968 Lambeth Conference. In the spring 1969 session at the end of the decade, four of the seven speakers were non-Jesuits: one diocesan priest, one laywoman and two laymen, one of whom, Martin Wallace, had a Northern unionist, Protestant background.[9]

Ecumenism

Mercy Simms frequently attended the Public Lectures and indeed made herself conspicuous by standing up to defend the Catholic Archbishop, Dr McQuaid, whenever he was criticised from the floor during 'Question Time' in the second part of the evening –

the two Archbishops had a good personal relationship in private. Other non-Roman Catholics also attended on occasion but the main reason for considering these Public Lectures as an ecumenical initiative is because 'Church renewal has notable ecumenical importance'.[10] It is significant, however, that in February 1969 the related topic of Northern Ireland featured on the programme. The present phase of the 'Troubles' was only just beginning but the inaugural lecture of the spring 1969 session was given by none other than the Deputy Editor of *The Belfast Telegraph*, the unionist/Protestant newspaper which, under the enlightened leadership of Jack Sayers[11] as its editor-in-chief, had distinguished itself in the 1960s by its moderation. The topic of the evening was 'community relations' and a supper party beforehand was attended by the editors of the three Dublin dailies and by the Director-General and Head of News of RTÉ.[12] *The Beadle's Journal (BJ)* records, however, that the attendance was 'poor'. The Battle of the Bogside hadn't yet taken place, nor had the British troops and James Callaghan arrived, nor had Jack Lynch as Taoiseach made his famous television broadcast declaring that 'the Irish government can no longer stand by'.

Attendance
Among those who attended the Milltown Park Public Lectures on several occasions were not only Mrs Simms but also President De Valera, who was sometimes accompanied by his wife.[13] The President attended three times in the winter 1961 session: on 1 November to hear Father Martin D'Arcy on 'drugs, brainwashing and the self', on 29 November to hear Father Aubrey Gwynn on 'the Inquisition',[14] and on 13 December with the Spanish Ambassador and the Director of Dunsink Observatory to hear Father Vives, a Spanish scientist studying theology at Milltown, speak on 'modern science and the origin of the universe'.[15] The following October he attended twice: on the 24th to hear Father

Bernard Leeming, the English Jesuit ecumenist, on 'Christianity in crisis', and again on the 31st to hear his aide-de-camp's brother, Father Martin Brennan SJ, on 'Adam and anthropology'.[16] On 18 November 1964 he attended a lecture by the present writer and in 1966 he again attended twice: on 2 March when Father Patrick Simpson was speaking and on 2 November when Father Michael O'Grady, a personal friend of Bean De Valera, was the lecturer. On 15 February 1967 the President came for a lecture by Father Cecil McGarry SJ, then Rector, on 13 March 1968 for that given by Mercy Simms and on 20 November 1968 for one delivered by Father Philip McShane SJ.

The number of the general public who attended the Milltown Park Public Lectures during the 1960s was remarkably high. *BJ* occasionally records the figures, which the takings at the door made it relatively easy to calculate.[17] At the opening session: 'about 370', 'about 190', 'about 240', 'about 250', 'about 180', 'about 250', 'about 290'. The topic which brought 370 was 'the population explosion'. During the following session attendances were all 'over 300', with the exception of the last evening when the figure was down to 'about 250' but it was 'a very stormy night'. The topic of 'marriage: success or failure?' had brought 'about 470', that of 'evolution: an open question?' brought 'about 600'. Indeed the second session 'drew forth requests from various parts of the country for copies in type or on tape of individual lectures as well as a formal offer from Messrs Gill & Son to consider the whole series for publication – an offer which for a number of reasons it was not possible to accept'.[18]

In the winter 1961 session Father Martin D'Arcy, on the topic of 'drugs, brainwashing and the self' and Father J. Erraught on the topic of 'psychiatry, the moralist and sin', both attracted audiences of 'about 700'. In winter 1962 Father Patrick Joy, speaking on the topic of 'responsible parenthood and fertility control', attracted 'about 650'.[19] The peak was reached on 1 February 1967 when about a thousand people turned up to hear Father Eamon Egan lecture on Teilhard de Chardin.[20] This led to the addition of three further lectures on successive evenings after Easter dealing with aspects of Teilhard de Chardin, for each of which 450 tickets were sold in advance.[21] On 30 October 1968 Father Michael Sweetman, speaking on 'the permissive society', drew an audience of 'about 700'.

In the middle of the decade, however, numbers seem to have sagged: *IPN* records 'relatively small' audiences for the spring 1964 session and 'relatively poor' attendances for the winter 1965 session, but according to *HD* 'the average audience [in winter 1965] was about 200', and in winter 1966 'there was a gratifying return to the crowded halls of earlier years'.[22] In winter 1967 there was a gross attendance of 3,930, giving an average attendance of 437 for each of the nine evenings.[23]

Censorship

In 1963 a form of ecclesiastical censorship was imposed on the Milltown Park Public Lectures and it did, as we shall see, lead to the cancellation of one lecture, but in general it was relatively mild. It applied not to the speakers or their topics, where no restriction was imposed, but only to our press releases. These had to be submitted for prior approval but the censor appointed was the scholarly Mgr Patrick Boylan, former Professor in the Eastern Languages Department of University College Dublin and a former student of Harnack's in Berlin; he was still, however, an ecclesiastic who knew his Archbishop's mind, a Vicar General indeed.

This imposition of censorship, however mild in form, was, to say the least, a considerable inconvenience. It meant advancing the deadline for the receipt of a lecture summary from each speaker, and when this had been turned into a press release, typing it up with as many carbon copies as possible, going by bicycle and bus[24] to deliver one by hand to the censor in Dun Laoghaire, where he was parish priest, and then awaiting a *nihil obstat* by phone or by post before delivering the other carbon copies to the daily papers on the Wednesday afternoon. The days of wordprocessing, fax and e-mail were far ahead in the future, and Milltown Park would not acquire its first community car until late 1969 or early 1970.[25]

With the one exception to be mentioned shortly, nothing more than inconvenience was caused. We learnt our lesson in the winter 1962 session and subsequently were duly cautious. What precipitated the imposition of censorship was the lecture on 31 October 1962 on 'Adam and anthropology' by Father Martin Brennan SJ, lecturer in biology at UCD or, rather, the press reports of the lecture read by Archbishop McQuaid in Rome, if not also reports of these reports sent from Dublin.

The context of course was the First Session of Vatican II (11 October-8 December 1962) and the upset caused especially by the debates on the liturgy and 'the sources of Revelation' among the Bishops, not least among those of a more conservative spirit.[26] Archbishop McQuaid for the most part kept a 'stately silence'[27] during Vatican II. On his return from Rome at its conclusion he was to declare in the Pro-Cathedral: 'You may have been worried by much talk of changes to come. Allow me to reassure you. No change will disturb the tranquillity of your Christian lives.'[28] The Archbishop will doubtless have seen his 1962 imposition of censorship on the press releases of the Milltown Park Public Lectures as, in anticipation, a fulfilment of that promise.

Lecture cancelled

1968 was the year one of our Public Lectures had to be cancelled: a somewhat traumatic experience. Everywhere, of course, 1968 was a turbulent year. It was the year Martin Luther King was shot dead, the year Russian tanks invaded Czechoslovakia, the year violence broke out on the streets of Paris because of student protests and on the streets of Derry because of clashes between Civil Rights marchers and the police. It was also the year of *Humanae vitae*. The cancellation of a Public Lecture cannot, of course, compare with any of those traumas but, in its own way, it was traumatic too. In an essay published in 1994 I recalled the incident as follows:

> One evening in the [Milltown Park Community] refectory after supper, the Rector [Cecil McGarry] made the startling public announcement that the lecture planned and announced to take place that very evening as one of the spring series had been cancelled and would not now take place; that those to act as ushers would, without further explanation, so inform those arriving for the lecture, and the lecturer himself would keep to his room. The lecturer was none other than myself. It was not that I was suddenly ill or indisposed but that higher ecclesiastical authority thought my ideas on original sin, the subject of the lecture, not altogether fit for public consumption.[29]

These ideas had been ventilated in the spring of 1967 in a public lecture at St Paul University, Ottawa, where I was teaching for a term. My Jesuit censors in Canada had passed the text for subsequent publication but their counterparts in England, where the text was to appear in print, had some qualms. These were eased by the insertion of an initial footnote emphasising 'the need for asking questions and proposing tentative solutions if theological science is to make progress' and the text so emended was published in the October 1967 number of the *Clergy Review*. The press release presented in the spring of 1968 to the Dublin diocesan censor was very carefully prepared. It was not, however, considered satisfactory and a Gordian knot solution was imposed: the lecture was cancelled.

In May 1966 Archbishop McQuaid had objected to an article of mine on mixed marriages published in *The Furrow* of that month and had insisted, through my Jesuit Provincial, that I withdraw the permission granted to *The Irish Times* to reprint it.[30]

The Archbishop had indeed expressed his doubts regarding the desirability of my continuing to work in the Archdiocese of Dublin,[31] but the story has a happy ending: eventually in 1970 he acquiesced in the establishment of the Irish School of Ecumenics. The cancellation of the lecture on original sin was passed over in silence in *IPN*. As house historian at the time I did draw attention to it but decided to be economical with the truth and merely added 'owing to unforeseen circumstances'.[32]

The following year, the last of the decade, a lecture in the winter session by Father Jim Healy, entitled 'Perverting the Nation', was not cancelled but it turned out to have unfortunate consequences. Father Healy, Professor of Moral Theology, was one of those who had painfully prepared themselves for a papal response on the birth-control question different from that given in *Humanae vitae* in July 1968. He had been at Bargy Castle, County Wexford, in the autumn with the small group of Irish experts who had acknowledged 'the genuine and widespread crisis of conscience around in Ireland among people of all walks of life, and of every degree of sophistication'.[33] He agonised over this lecture. Afterwards he believed it cast a shadow over his orthodoxy as a teacher of sexual morality and he felt he was under a cloud. As a result he turned instead to questions of justice, rights and hunger strikes. He died on 11 December 1989 at the early age of sixty.

Fundraising
To underline their seriousness it was decided in the beginning to make a charge for the Lectures: ten shillings for all seven in the first session, two shillings for individual lectures. Despite academic practice to the contrary, it was felt that free admission might mislead, might suggest a devotional rather than an intellectual exercise. But if fundraising was not the original aim of the Public Lectures, it became a secondary one. The tragic fire which occurred on 11 February 1949 in the Milltown Park Finlay Wing

(over the present theatre) had considerably reduced the area of the community's living quarters and had necessitated taking over the alcoves of the House Library and of a number of rooms in what was then the Retreat House (now Tabor), with the result that fewer retreatants could be accommodated. A new wing was therefore required and the first stage of the work, begun on 2 July 1951, was completed in July 1953. But as this provided only ten study-bedrooms, a second stage was planned by Father James Corboy, Rector since June 1959, who therefore included the Public Lectures among the various fundraising activities he was sponsoring. As a result we had the help of the Ladies' Committee[34] to collect the entrance charge each evening. The financial contribution of the Public Lectures cannot have been enormous but work on stage two of the new wing began on 16 May 1962 and was completed in July 1963, providing thirty additional study-bedrooms. In April 1962, however, just before the work began, but just after the building fund had by his efforts reached a satisfactory level, Father Corboy was appointed Bishop of Monze in Zambia.[35]

CONCLUSION

From 1969, because of other commitments, I ceased to have any responsibility for the Milltown Park Public Lectures. With the inauguration of the Milltown Institute in 1967, they became the co-operative concern of the Milltown Institute and the Milltown Park Jesuit Community. They ceased in 1981.[36] The Lectures were part of the *aggiornamento* which Pope John XXIII canonised by calling the Second Vatican Council. Religion being good copy in the 1960s, the newspapers gave them very generous coverage and greatly increased their impact. In the first decade they were such a popular success that on occasion, as has been noted above, they attracted audiences of 700 and more. They assisted in the reception process of the new thinking of Vatican II. They helped to satisfy to some extent the appetite for theological education which that Council was whetting. They highlighted the need to provide degree courses in theology for laity as well as ordinands[37] and to provide courses in ecumenics for both. They paved the way for the establishment of the Irish School of Ecumenics in 1970.

15
An Ecumenical Publication: *Irish Anglicanism 1869-1969* [*]

Irish Anglicanism (1869-1969) is the title of a volume of essays which was launched in Dublin with much ceremony and publicity on 15 April 1970 and which the late Bishop Ian Ramsay of Durham kindly referred to (*New Divinity*, November 1970, p. 56) as 'candid and distinguished in its scholarship, outstandingly generous as a gesture'. The launch was hailed at the time as a 'splendid and memorable occasion', 'an historic event'. The enclosed Cistercian nuns in Glencairn, County Waterford, received special permission to watch it on television; how 'moving', 'inspiring' and 'impressive' they and many others found it emerges clearly from a file of personal letters still in my possession, only one of which is anonymous and negative. Now, of course, nearly three decades later, the event is largely forgotten. The purpose of this chapter is to recall it and in this way to encourage readers to be imaginative and courageous in taking their own initiatives in the cause of Christian unity.

The context

As a project *Irish Anglicanism (1869-1969)* was conceived during the summer term of the academic year 1967/8. In a sense Vatican

---
[*] This chapter first appeared in print in *Search: A Church of Ireland Journal* 18/1 (spring 1995), pp. 14-23.

II had only just happened. Renewal and unity were high on the Church's agenda, though still encountering opposition. In the spring term Mercy Simms, wife of the Archbishop of Dublin, had given one of the public lectures at Milltown Park where I was teaching theology: the first Protestant and the second woman to do so. But a lecture on original sin which I was to give myself in that same series had to be cancelled at the request of higher authority.[1] In February a lecture on the Catholic doctrine of Baptism which I gave to the Presbyterian students for the ministry in Belfast led to controversy and a formal debate at General Assembly in June, but happily a motion of censure against the college authorities failed to secure a majority.

It was at this time when, despite lingering opposition, Catholic ecumenism was still in the first flush of its post-Vatican II enthusiasm, that the Church of Ireland announced an official commemoration, from March to September 1970, of the centenary of its disestablishment. Because this had involved loss as well as gain and had been resisted at the time, the centenary was not to be 'celebrated' but 'marked'. But, if ecumenism meant doing everything together as far as conscience permitted, then the centenary should, it seemed to me and others, be jointly marked: the commemoration should be ecumenical, an inter-Church as well as a Church of Ireland event. And the contribution of the non-Anglican Churches, I thought, might appropriately be an academic one: a collection of essays. The editing of such a collection was a task which, in my ecumenical enthusiasm, I was more than willing to undertake.

Preparatory moves
By the end of the summer of 1968, a summer overshadowed by *Humanae Vitae*, Pope Paul VI's negative encyclical letter on birth control, the scope of this volume of essays had become clearer. The essays would be contributed by a group of scholars representing the major non-Anglican Churches and the major

academic institutions in the country; they would attempt 'to survey and assess the role of Anglicanism in Irish life since 1869'. Prefaces would be invited from the President of Ireland, from the Cardinal, from the Methodist President and from the Presbyterian Moderator. Twenty essay subjects had in fact already been identified. Contributors were being approached and a large number had agreed to collaborate, accepting 30 June 1969 as their deadline so that publication could take place in the spring of 1970. In addition Archbishop Simms had given the project his personal approval and invited the historian, Dr Kenneth Milne, then Church of Ireland Education Officer in the Republic, to offer his services as an adviser, an offer which was of course very gratefully accepted. President de Valera had also been approached but declined the invitation to contribute a preface.

When the following academic year began it still remained to finalise the list of twenty contributors, to keep encouraging all of them in their work, to find a publisher and to make arrangements for presenting the volume to the Church of Ireland. I had no idea as yet that a fundraising task also lay ahead. Even so, the prospect was daunting enough, but happily my teaching commitments at Milltown for the first two terms were greatly reduced, leaving me free to devote myself almost entirely to *Irish Anglicanism*. The first item I put on the programme was a general meeting of the contributors. This took place at Milltown Park on 10 October against the background of the Northern Ireland Civil Rights marches which had begun in Derry on the 5th. Dr Milne attended the meeting and present also to help as secretary was one of the theology students: Laurence Murphy SJ, Superior of the Irish Jesuit Province from 1992 to 1998.

Government subsidy

A week later, on 17 October, the search for a publisher started. Collections, I was soon to learn, no matter how scholarly and ecumenical the essays, are not the most tempting of propositions for a publisher. The response was poor. *Irish Anglicanism*, it became clear, was unlikely to be a commercial proposition. If it was to sell at a reasonable price, if it was to appear at all perhaps, it would need to be subsidised. The response, though disappointing, was not, however, entirely negative. One interested party, if not two, had emerged. So the work continued, less optimistically perhaps but not without hope. Encouragement then came in January when Professor John Barkley's completed essay on 'Anglican-Presbyterian Relations' arrived months before it was due. More encouragement came on 7 March when the contributors met together again at Milltown Park and renewed each other's energies to meet the summer deadline. Then just before Easter, on Good Friday, 4 April, a friend who was close to the Taoiseach, Jack Lynch, informed me that, because of the national and ecumenical importance of the project, a government grant was at the very least a distinct possibility.

It was not until the middle of the summer vacation that this exciting news was confirmed and the 'possibility' of government finance became a firm promise. After Easter I was committed to teaching a course in Rome and had to be away. I did before leaving submit a formal request but the follow-up had to await my return. Acting then on the advice of the Taoiseach's private secretary, I had an interview on Friday, 25 July, with an official of the Department of Education, who emphasised all the administrative difficulties involved and the necessity in any case to secure the authorisation of the Minister for Finance. This left me 'more depressed than hopeful' as I took the liberty of putting it in a letter the next day to the Taoiseach's private secretary. Happily, however, I had the opportunity on the following Thursday evening, 31 July, of sharing all my hopes and fears for the project with a governor of the Bank of Ireland who happened to be sitting near me at a private dinner party given by the Taoiseach and Mrs Lynch to say goodbye to Archbishop and Mrs Simms who were

Christian Unity

leaving for Armagh. At the end of the evening the governor suggested I write to him, which of course I did. Subsequently I wrote to the other banks and to the 'top fifty firms', inviting them to be associated with the disestablishment centenary by making a contribution towards the cost of producing and presenting *Irish Anglicanism*; in due course a few of them did. Then, on 15 August, the Department of Education wrote to say that, 'subject to the necessary approval of Dáil Éireann in due course', a grant of £3,000 would be made available. Our financial problems were over.

Northern Ireland
On the other hand the country's political problems were getting steadily worse. That summer of 1969, that August in particular, saw the 'Battle of the Bogside' in Derry, sectarian rioting in Belfast and elsewhere, the politico-religious 'cleansing' of urban neighbourhoods, the erection of barricades, the deployment of British troops and the visit of Home Secretary, James Callaghan. The Taoiseach, too, had made his dramatic broadcast speech saying that 'the Irish government can no longer stand by and see innocent people injured and perhaps worse'. I had no feeling, however, that we were 'fiddling' or just 'standing by' while Northern Ireland burned. *Irish Anglicanism* looked in hope and confidence to a future which would bring peace and reconciliation. Indeed, 'The Future' was the topic and title of my own concluding chapter in the book.[2] The whole project was another venture, however modest, in North-South as well as Catholic-Protestant co-operation and, with the knowledge and approval of the Taoiseach, I was engaged that very summer in trying to associate the Stormont administration with it by way of a financial contribution and a presence at the presentation ceremonies. My intermediary in this was G. B. Newe, the prominent Catholic layman, Secretary of the Northern Ireland

Council of Social Service who later, in October 1971, was appointed by Brian Faulkner, then Prime Minister, as Minister of State in his own department.

On 11 August 'GB' (as everyone affectionately called him) already knew what I was to find out only the following week and, in a letter which provides an interesting sidelight on North-South relations at that critical time, he wrote in his own hand to say that:

> My Government friend tells me that your Ministry of Finance has agreed to give you the whole £3,000. (You see, they maintain close contact.) Stormont now wonders if you really need any more money.
>
> I have urged that you be given a token amount; I mentioned £500, so that it could be said the venture had the support of both Governments. They are going to chew this one over.

The chewing went on for months. In the new year GB was still urging my requests but the 'token amount' never materialised because of 'the usual constitutional and other difficulties' and there was no ministerial presence at the presentation. Only one formal invitation was eventually sent. It went not to the Governor General or Prime Minister or Minister of Community Relations but, at GB's suggestion, to 'our Minister of Development, Mr Brian Faulkner, who is a courageous fellow, with a mind of his own. It is just a chance that he might accept while all the others are dithering.' In fact he sent the usual polite regrets.

The contributors

This, however, is to anticipate. The main work of the summer of 1969 after my return from Rome was to renew and keep contact with the contributors and to encourage them as the deadline approached – and passed. Three of the original group of twenty had excused themselves early on but it had been possible to replace one of these. A fourth eventually had to withdraw because of lack of time to rework his text, but by our extended deadline at the end of August, all the other seventeen contributions were in my hands, edited and ready to be typed up in their final form. The main academic institutions which went unrepresented as a result of the withdrawals were St Patrick's College, Maynooth, Trinity College, Dublin and University College, Cork. (No approach had been made to the New University of Ulster which was just opening.) The late Kevin McNamara, then Professor at Maynooth, later Bishop and subsequently Archbishop, was to have represented Maynooth, but on being appointed Vice-President of the College felt obliged to withdraw because of this added commitment. A more serious gap, however, in the representative character of the group of contributors is the fact that even from the beginning we included no women, only one Methodist, one Presbyterian and one Quaker; and only four from Northern Ireland. Regrettably we were a preponderantly Southern and Roman Catholic team and exclusively male.

The seventeen essays in the book cover a wide range of topics, among them 'Disestablishment: 1800-1869' by Kevin B. Nowlan of UCD, 'Church Renewal: 1869-1877' by Gabriel Daly OSA of the Milltown Institute, 'Education' by Timothy Kelly of St Patrick's College, Drumcondra, 'Political Life: 1870-1921' by Thomas O'Neill of UCG, 'The Irish Language Movement' by David Greene of the Dublin Institute of Advanced Studies, 'Anglo-Irish Literature' by Augustine Martin of UCD, 'Political Life in the South' by J. H. Whyte, then of QUB, 'Demographic Trends' by Thomas Keane of the Central Statistics Office and 'Recent Liturgical Reform' by Vincent Ryan OSB of Glenstal Abbey.

The concluding essay, contributed by myself and entitled 'The Future' [of the Church of Ireland], carries more than one echo of the troubled August of 1969. Two Church of Ireland friends had been good enough to read it and make honest comments. One result was that I expanded my discussion of the Orange Order, adding the phrase 'in its present form' when suggesting that membership of the Order might be incompatible with Christianity. But I continued to maintain that the Church of Ireland, like the rest of us, has no future 'except in a thoroughgoing commitment to ecumenism'. And the hope I dared to express ('neither inspiring nor complimentary', the reviewer in *The Irish Press* subsequently complained) was that out of its experience as a minority Church the Church of Ireland might help the rest of us to prepare for the minority status which was the future facing all Christians everywhere. The tone of that essay surprises me now. I was emboldened, I think, by the forthright editorials of Andy Willis in the *Church of Ireland Gazette*.

The presentation

When on 7 September the whole manuscript had been retyped and was ready to be handed to a publisher, it was to Allen Figgis that I gave it without any hesitation. From early on he had taken a great personal interest in the project and given me much encouragement throughout. I had every confidence that he would, as he did and as I stated in the Preface, make the production of the book 'a labour of love'. It only remained then to arrange for the formal presentation. Some beginning had already been made: Archbishop Simms had agreed to accept the volume as Primate at an ecumenical service in Dublin and 15 April had been fixed as the date. But for most of the first term of the academic year 1969/70, I had to be out of the country, lecturing in the US during October and from then until Christmas in Rome. So it was not until the New Year that work began in earnest to plan the presentation in all its complex detail. One thing that amazes me in retrospect is how I was able to do it, not only without a secretary and without a phone of my own but even without a phone extension in my room. It was fortunate that my only teaching commitment that second term was a course of lectures at Maynooth.

When 15 April came it was in Gonzaga College, the Jesuit secondary school near Milltown Park, that the presentation took place. At an earlier stage Dublin Castle had been proposed as the venue: could the ecumenical service, we enquired, take place in the old Chapel Royal and be followed by a reception in St Patrick's Hall? This grandiose idea did not commend itself to the Taoiseach's Office, which regretted that 'it is not the practice to make the State Apartments available for such functions'. But instead the very generous offer was made that the presentation, if we wished, might take place in the context of a government reception to be hosted by the Minister for Finance, which was to be held in Dublin Castle on 12 May in honour of the Church of Ireland on the occasion of the disestablishment centenary and which would be preceded by a service in St Patrick's Cathedral. The financial advantages of this suggestion became less interesting when a grant had been promised. It would have seriously complicated our tentative plans for an ecumenical service. And the late date was inconvenient. For these reasons the offer was declined and in a letter of 10 September the Minister for Finance, Charles Haughey, who was to host the reception, kindly wrote agreeing that 'indeed it would seem to be the sensible thing to do'.

Ecumenical service

The service in the Gonzaga chapel began at 6.30 p.m. and Sandford Road was closed to traffic from 6.00 p.m. There were 425 guests representing the academic, diplomatic, ecclesiastical, economic, judicial and political life of the country. An admission card indicating an allocated seat had been sent in advance to each person who had accepted the initial invitation. The attendance from Northern Ireland included – besides the contributors and G. B. Newe – John Hume, Maurice Hayes, then Chairman of the

An Ecumenical Publication: Irish Anglicanism 1869-1969

Community Relations Commission, Professor Lelièvre, President of Magee College, representing the Vice-Chancellor of the New University of Ulster, and Professor Faris, Dean of Theology, representing the Vice-Chancellor of QUB. The service was presided over by Cecil McGarry SJ, the Jesuit Provincial, in his capacity as Vice-Chancellor of the Milltown Institute of Theology and Philosophy. Also taking part were Professor J. L. M. Haire, Principal of Assembly's College, Belfast, Chairman of the Irish Council of Churches and Moderator-Designate of General Assembly for the following year with the Rev. Robert A. Nelson, Chairman of the Dublin Methodist District and Secretary of the Dublin Council of Churches. The singing was provided by members of the Methodist choir of the Centenary Church, St Stephen's Green, the Presbyterian choir of Christ Church, Rathgar and the Milltown Park Jesuit choir.

The order of service, non-eucharistic of course, opened with the prayer well known to most Protestants: 'O God ... give us grace seriously to lay to heart the great dangers we are in by our unhappy divisions ...' Archbishop McQuaid insisted, however, that this first petition of the prayer should be altered to read instead: 'seriously to lay to heart the prayer of our divine Saviour that his true followers should be one'. It was the use of incense which worried Principal Haire. The plan was to begin after the opening collect with an enthronement of the Bible which would include incensation. But was this Roman Catholic ritual appropriate in a united service, especially one which was being televised? During Vatican II, however, this enthronement ceremony had taken place each morning in St Peter's and had greatly impressed the Protestant observers and commentators like Paul Blanchard. It was seen as a further sign of Roman Catholic reverence for the Scriptures. On the basis of this experience the use of incense was tolerated at Gonzaga that evening and never regretted.

After the event the Methodist President, the Reverend George Good, who was watching the service on television, wrote to me to say, 'I thought the sermon was magnificent and I would like you to convey my thanks to the Vice-Chancellor for it.' Others who were present in the chapel concurred, but unfortunately no text or recording exists, only the following press reports:

> Father McGarry said that Roman Catholics could well understand the feeling of the Irish Anglican community at the time of the disestablishment because at the same time the Papacy was dispossessed of its states and it, too, found that that was a moment of growth and spiritual strength. (*The Irish Press*, 16 April 1970)

> No country was more Christian than Ireland. But no country was, at the same time, more un-Christian in its divisions. In the Gospel all were reconciled, Jew with Greek, slave with freeman, and the man from the north with the man from the south. (*Church of Ireland Gazette*, 24 April 1970)

> God challenged them to feel the pain and the shame of this [disunity]: to cleanse their hearts of the divisions and bitternesses, of the heavy weight of history that bowed them down in chains of bigotry and prejudice. (*The Irish Independent*, 16 April 1970)

It was towards the end of the service that the actual presentation took place. Handing the Primate a special, handsomely bound copy, the work of Brother John Rogers SJ of the Milltown Park library, I said:

> The book is a token of our appreciation and gratitude. It is a token too of our hope that, as our Anglican brethren were in the past, so they shall ever be 'no petty people'. It is also a prayer for as well as a pledge of forgiveness and love.

Accepting the book the Primate replied:

> It is my hope that the Church to which you have paid this signal honour tonight in the presence of this distinguished

and representative company will continue, thus encouraged, with greater confidence to have among its members, sons and daughters who will not only be faithful servants of our Lord Jesus Christ but also active and caring members of the country in which we live. Christian initiatives are sorely needed here in Ireland as well as in the world at large.

Attendance

The 'distinguished and representative company' to which the Primate referred happily had an Anglican comprehensiveness about it: it included, for instance, the Superintendent of Irish Church Missions, the Reverend Richard Coates. But still the ceremony was very much an establishment affair, as an *Irish Times* editorial complained two days later. Some of the establishment were, however, conspicuous by their absence, notably the Roman Catholic hierarchy, who had arranged to be represented by just one of their number, Bishop Birch of Ossory. And a particular effort had been made to have the youth of the country represented. I made the presentation so I emphasised in my short address:

> … on behalf … above all, of the young people who are here from the four corners of Ireland: from Derry and Armagh, from Galway and Drogheda, from Limerick and Waterford. They are, unfortunately, few in number but they do remind us that our mission is not so much to preserve the present as to ensure and to enrich the Christian faith of the future.

Some student societies were represented, such as the Theological Society of TCD and the Literary and Historical Society of UCD. Delegates from the Girls' Brigade, the Boys' Brigade and the Girls' Friendly Society were also represented. In addition the principals of many schools throughout the country had been most helpful in nominating one of their senior pupils to attend. So it was that the four acolytes in the procession were from

Mungret College, Limerick, Coláiste Iognáid, Galway, The Royal Belfast Academical Institution and Methodist College, Belfast. The latter was represented by the deputy head boy, Keith Jeffery, now Reader in History, University of Ulster at Jordanstown, who wore for the occasion his rowing 'honours' blazer with 'R. C. 1967-8' embroidered on it in silver thread. 'Well, perhaps,' he now reflects, 'I was an honorary RC for an evening, and none the worse for that'. Being an acolyte and carrying a candle in procession were not regular Methodist activities!

The whole service and not only Father McGarry's homily made a great impact. I had been dissatisfied and complained when I learnt that Father Romuald Dodd OP, as producer of the broadcast, was dispensing with any commentary, however discreet, and including only an introduction. This seemed insufficient to me for a broadcast which was going out live at prime time from RTÉ and being transmitted later by BBC Northern Ireland. In the event, however, as the Controller of TV Programmes wrote to me later, 'the programme was very well received by the vast majority of our viewers'. The politico-religious background will of course have helped. It may be remembered that 15 April 1970 was the eve of the Bannside by-election in Northern Ireland, when Ian Paisley unseated Terence O'Neill, heralding a right-wing Protestant backlash against the Chichester Clark reforms. Here in the South concern was mounting and it was just around this time that, unknown to the general public, the events were taking place which would lead in a few weeks to the shock of the Arms Crisis and the Arms Trial. Among those who cancelled at a late stage were Cabinet ministers Jim Gibbons and Charles Haughey.

Reception
After the service a reception was held in the hall adjoining the Gonzaga chapel, the guests being greeted and welcomed by the Vice-Chancellor and the Primate. To end the evening the Vice-

Chancellor later entertained some of the guests to dinner at Milltown Park. In the earlier stages of the planning six of Dublin's leading hotels had been approached and had agreed to host dinner parties for some twenty guests each as their way of associating themselves with the occasion. This, however, was not an ideal arrangement and when our financial worries eased it was decided instead to hold one large dinner party at Milltown Park. For a variety of reasons, however, only about half the guests – 181, in fact, according to the caterers' invoice – could be accommodated. The guests of honour were, of course, all the Church of Ireland bishops and their wives, except Bishop Peacocke of Derry, who unfortunately was unable to travel.

This final part of the presentation ceremonies was less formal, more relaxed, even lighthearted. An imaginative, amusing menu card had been prepared by Allen Figgis and the Jesuit students had arranged a number of concert items to come between the courses: one gave a performance of mime, another sang 'My Lagan Love' and 'Maidin i mBearra', a third entertained us to a cabaret which included a selection of operatic arias, a trio played some Mozart and Beethoven and the choir as a whole sang Rimsky-Korsakov's 'Our Father' and the 'Speed Your Journey' chorus from Verdi's 'Nabucco'. All these items were greatly appreciated and professionally recorded by the Eamonn Andrew Studios, as were the speeches.[3] The toast to the Church of Ireland was proposed by the Taoiseach who, among other things, referred to the enlightenment which its members had shed on the political and cultural scene during the century. Mr J R. Lindsay OBE of Armagh replied. The Primate proposed the toast to the Editor and Father Bruce Bradley SJ, who is now Headmaster of Clongowes Wood College and who, that evening, was singing operatic arias for us, recalls 'the warmth and graciousness of Dr Simms, admiring the "beautiful binding of Brother Rogers" with which the volume *Irish Anglicanism* was adorned and commending Michael Hurley, with whimsical humour and complete sincerity for his Pauline "care of all the Churches".' The mood of the evening allowed me to refer, in my reply, to the anonymous correspondent who had written: 'we all know, of course that Simms has a job lined up for you'! The celebrations went on until well past midnight and, before leaving, Bishop Wyse Jackson of Limerick, well-known composer of limericks, gave me his menu card on which he had written the following:

> For (*sic*) the party laid on by Mike Hurley
> We rose late though we began early
> And the thin and the slim
> Arose from that din
> United, sleek, happy and burly.

Later, on 3 July, as Chairman of the Disestablishment Committee, Bishop Wyse Jackson hosted a small dinner party at the Kildare Street Club and presented me with a piece of silver, in the form of a card tray with gadroon edge and scroll feet, inscribed as follows:

> *Presented*
> *by the*
> *Disestablishment Committee*
> *of the Church of Ireland*
> *to the*
> *Reverend Michael Hurley, SJ*
> *as a token of gratitude for his generous gift of a*
> *Volume of Essays*
> *To mark the centenary of Disestablishment*
> *and further*
> *to thank him and the members of*
> *The Society of Jesus*
> *for their munificent entertainment on*
> *15th April 1970*

16
An Ecumenical Institute: The Origins of The Irish School of Ecumenics*

The Irish School of Ecumenics (ISE) is the sort of academic institution which 'ecumenical tithing' and 'ecumenical formation' (cf. chapter 4) seem to require in order to become a reality.[1] It was formally inaugurated on 9 November 1970 and hence celebrated its Silver Jubilee during the academic year 1995/6, but it can, in a true sense, be said to have begun ten years earlier, on 9 March 1960.

That was the date of a public lecture on 'The Ecumenical Movement' which I gave at Milltown Park. The lecture was one of seven given in the first session of a new initiative which was to continue very successfully twice a year in spring and winter throughout the 1960s and on into the early 1980s.[2] As secretary of the original organising committee I had proposed Christian unity as a topic, presuming that an acknowledged expert, Roman Catholic of course, could be found somewhere in the country to be our speaker. We failed, however, to find one, so on the basis of the very limited knowledge I had acquired during my own theological studies in Louvain and afterwards doing doctoral work in Rome, I made the subject up from books and periodicals and duly delivered the lecture myself.

---

* A somewhat abbreviated version of this chapter apppeared in *One in Christ*, 33/4 (1997), pp. 298-316.

The 1960s: a decade of preparation

That lecture of 9 March 1960 appeared the following January as a pamphlet entitled *Towards Christian Unity*[3] and proved to be the beginning for me of an ecumenical apostolate or ministry which continued to grow and develop all through the rest of the decade. Nothing of all this, however, was foreseen, much less planned. It happened because the winds of change had begun to blow in the Church as well as the world. In particular, Vatican II, with all its perceived ecumenical possibilities, some very real, some quite exaggerated, captured the general imagination and created a brisk demand for talks and articles as well as for discussions on radio and what was then the new medium of television. It was a learning much more than a teaching experience and altogether too interesting, too fascinating for me to hold back and not get involved, insofar as my teaching commitments allowed. It led directly, it now seems clear, to the inauguration of ISE in 1970.

After the lecture and its publication, invitations multiplied. So in January of 1962 I made my first appearance on Irish television: a talk to camera about Unity Week. In May of that year I gave a lecture to the Trinity College branch of the Student Christian Movement, but to satisfy the existing regulations of the Catholic archdiocese, the session had to be held outside College in a hotel.[4] The following August I attended the Central Committee meeting of the World Council of Churches in Paris, not of course as an official observer or visitor but only as an accredited journalist for *The Irish Press*.[5] And in October that same year, on the very weekend Vatican II opened, I was in Belfast lecturing in the Church of Ireland chaplaincy of The Queen's University and preaching at the Catholic chaplaincy Sunday morning Mass in Aquinas Hall, run by the Dominican Sisters until 1994. In his Lenten pastoral the previous year Bishop Mageean of Down and Connor had mentioned my pamphlet, adding 'I cordially commend it to you to read and study'. It was my first ever visit to Northern Ireland and I was made to feel very welcome; it was a foretaste of my later happy years in the Columbanus Community of Reconciliation (CCR) in Belfast, from 1983 to 1993.

During the following years of the 1960s this ecumenical apostolate intensified and expanded. It brought me all around the Dublin Catholic archdiocese, lecturing under the auspices of its then very active Adult Education Committee. It brought me all around the country. In 1964, for example, it took me to Kenmare to address the West Cork Clerical Society of the Church of Ireland, to Cork to address a public meeting organised by Tuairim (a lay organisation with a lively interest in religion which has since become defunct), to Belfast to address the Newman Society at Queen's University and to the Benedictine Abbey in Glenstal, County Limerick for an ecumenical conference which I had helped to organise and which remains an annual event every summer. In 1965 it took me to Newry to address the Catholic clergy of the Dromore diocese; and in 1966 to Downpatrick to address a meeting of the Downe Society and to Drogheda for the first ecumenical conference at the Presentation Convent school in Greenhills.[6] This Greenhills initiative, which I also helped to organise, was suggested by the editor of *The Furrow*, The Reverend J. G. McGarry, and designed to complement Glenstal by taking place in a northern location and in the winter, during Unity Week. It, too, continues as an annual event.

Ecumenism in the 1960s also brought me outside the country to attend meetings: of the World Alliance of Reformed Churches in Frankfurt in 1964[7] (as a journalist still); of the World Methodist Council in London in 1966 (as an 'Accredited Visitor')[8] and of the World Methodist Council-Roman Catholic Church International Commission of which I was appointed a member in 1968 and which met in various places around the world in the following years. Ecumenism in this decade also took me abroad to give short courses of lectures: in Ottawa in 1967 at St Paul University, in Glasgow in 1968 for the Catholic clergy of the archdiocese, in New Orleans in 1969 at the Notre Dame Seminary and also in Rome at the Gregorian University.

All this ecumenical activity was steadily, but as yet quite unknown to me, preparing the way for the foundation of ISE in 1970: it was providing the necessary experience and contacts. The *courses* of lectures which I gave not only abroad but also here at home at St Patrick's College, Maynooth, and elsewhere offered a welcome opportunity to reflect on the experience, to think it all through. The slim volume entitled *Theology of Ecumenism,*[9] which appeared in 1969, shows how I was attempting to analyse and understand the new horizons which were opening up for me. It may have been and was indeed exciting work but it was also disturbing. It created tensions with Church authorities, both Catholic and Protestant. Archbishop McQuaid expressed doubts to my superiors about the desirability of my continuing to work in the Archdiocese of Dublin.[10] The Principal of Assembly's (Presbyterian) College, Belfast was severely criticised for inviting me to lecture his theology students on 'The Catholic Doctrine of Baptism' in February 1968. A motion censuring the College authorities was proposed and debated at the June General Assembly in Church House, with Dr Ian Paisley and his followers protesting angrily outside. Happily the motion was defeated but unhappily the opponents of ecumenism within the Presbyterian Church in Ireland, so far from declining, went on growing in number during the following years.

Irish Anglicanism 1869-1969

The 1960s came to a climax for me on 15 April 1970 with the publication of *Irish Anglicanism 1869-1969*,[11] a volume of essays which I had edited for the centenary of the disestablishment of the Church of Ireland and which was launched and presented to the Primate, Archbishop Simms, during an interdenominational service, televised live by RTÉ, in the chapel of Gonzaga College,

Dublin. It was in the course of this project, which had begun in the summer of 1968, that the ideas which later took shape as ISE and CCR (Columbanus Community of Reconciliation) first emerged and crystallised in my mind. And it was the successful completion of the project (the story of which is told in the preceding chapter[12]) and the widespread appreciation it evoked at a critical moment in Irish history, in North-South relations in particular, which gave me the credibility required to attempt their realisation. But whereas it was to be years, thirteen in fact, before CCR became a reality in 1983,[13] only six weeks were to pass before the opening of ISE was announced at a press conference in Dublin on 28 May 1970 and only six months before it came into operation in October and was formally inaugurated on 9 November. Indeed, the launching of *Irish Anglicanism* in April and the launching of ISE in November were so closely linked (and not only in time) that they became confused. The compiler of 'Some Notable Events in the Catholic Life of Ireland in 1970' for the 1971 *Irish Catholic Directory* conflated the two. There is no entry for 9 November but that for 15 April reads misleadingly as follows:

> An Ecumenical Service was held in Gonzaga College, Dublin, today to launch the new school of Ecumenics ...
>
> A specially bound volume of essays, edited by Father Hurley, commemorating the disestablishment of the Church of Ireland was presented to the Church of Ireland Archbishop of Armagh, Most Reverend Dr Simms.[14]

1969/70 proved to be a very full, very busy academic year. As soon as the typescript of *Irish Anglicanism* was in the hands of the publisher in early September 1969, my first move with regard to what was eventually to become ISE was to share the idea with my Jesuit superiors and try to persuade them to support it, to own it. It could have no future, I knew, certainly no long-term future as a mere personal initiative of my own. Providentially, my Provincial then (1968-75) was Cecil McGarry.[15] He was not only a former Rector and former student of mine at Milltown Park but also a former lecturer in ecclesiology who, for his doctorate in Rome, had made a special study of modern Anglican ecclesiology, and read a paper on the subject at the 1965 Glenstal Ecumenical Conference. Significantly, too, at this very time he was preparing a special Province Delegate Meeting to take place in early January 1970 to discuss the future of Irish Jesuit ministry and was inviting submissions. A letter of his to me dated 4 November shows that I had already made such a submission about ISE (no copy, however, survives), but in his view not in sufficient detail: 'I would fear for the ideas [he wrote] unless they are developed: they may be taken to be impractical hopes or dreams, whereas they could be made attractive needs.'

Ecumenics: what and why?

For most of that first term I had teaching commitments outside the country and this letter reached me at the Gregorian University in Rome. The result was the paper 'Ecumenics: What and Why?' which attempted to meet the Provincial's request for more detail and which I finished on 7 December 1969. The first part of the paper outlined in some detail a two-year programme for those who had already completed their basic theological studies. It envisaged courses in Comparative Christianity, the History of the Ecumenical Movement, the Methodology of Ecumenism, the Sociology of Religion, in Pastoral Ecumenical Problems, and Inter-Church Conversations. Not surprisingly, granted my 1960s' background of learning by experience, it also emphasised field education, very ambitiously suggesting both term-time work and a vacation project either in the USA or in Geneva/Rome. But it concentrated exclusively on 'Inter-Church Relations'; there is no mention of 'Inter-faith Relations' or of

'Peace Studies'.[16] In other words the present tripartite syllabus of ISE developed only by degrees.

My answer to the question 'Why?' in this paper provides an echo of the debate which had begun in the mid-1960s as to whether ecumenism in religious and theological education should be a dimension or a discipline: a dimension of all disciplines or a special discipline by itself. In June of the following year, 1970, the Vatican Secretariat for Promoting Christian Unity published its views on the question in Part II of its Directory and declared that 'Even though all theological training has an ecumenical aspect, courses on ecumenism are not therefore superfluous.'[17] It was not until 1993 that the Vatican made such courses obligatory instead of optional for BD students. My view in 1969, as a result of my experience during the previous years, was that the special discipline was necessary for the sake of the dimension and that an institute such as ISE was necessary for the sake of both. It would meet 'the present need for ecumenically competent personnel'; it would educate and train those who would teach the discipline and who by so doing would help to create the dimension. Like the Johann-Adam-Möhler-Institut für Ökumenik at Paderborn and the Institute for Ecumenical Research at Strasbourg,[18] ISE would be 'a centre of research which houses a community of scholars' but unlike them it was to have its own systematic teaching programme and would not merely sponsor occasional seminars or simply engage in service teaching for other institutes.

This paper was subsequently published in the following July number of *The Furrow*. More significantly, however, at least in the immediate instance, it arrived in good time for the Irish Jesuit Delegate meeting held at Manresa House, Dublin, from 5-7 January 1970 and was approved by this meeting as 'very reasonable':

> It involves only one man [manpower was a crucial criterion of the delegates], who has had the freedom to establish himself as a world-wide expert in this field, recognised formally by the Bishops [at the previous October meeting of

the Irish Bishops I had been appointed a member of their Advisory Committee on Ecumenism], with the contacts among all the Christian denominations which offer the opportunity of financial and staff support, and may make an Institute possible.[19]

Financial and Church support

This approval was not only 'very reasonable' but very generous because the paper, although addressing fairly thoroughly the questions 'What?' and 'Why?' and in an appendix the question 'Who [will teach]?', failed to address the question 'How?', i.e. the crucial problems of structure and finance and recruitment of students. These, along with the immediate preparations for the launch of *Irish Anglicanism* on 15 April, came to absorb my attention from the New Year on. During these months of 1970 I sometimes referred to ISE as 'in process of formation'[20] – a phrase borrowed, of course, from the history of the World Council of Churches.

Strange as it may seem to those who know something of the subsequent history of ISE, finance was the least of our problems in the beginning: the Irish Flour Millers' Association (IFMA) seemed happy to be our benefactors. Their energetic Public Relations Officer, Dan Mullane, had taken a professional interest in both ecumenical projects (*Irish Anglicanism* and ISE). He saw them as having 'considerable national importance'[21] and succeeded in persuading Peter Desmond Odlum to give them not only his own support but that also of the Association in which the Odlum Group of companies played a prominent part. At Mr Mullane's suggestion I wrote formally to Peter Odlum about the two projects on 1 October 1969 and, on my return to Ireland, had an encouraging meeting with him in his office on the afternoon of 28 January 1970.

Feeling assured of financial support, my next priority was to meet with the Provincial's solicitor and on an informal, unofficial basis with members of the other Churches to inform them about the proposed initiative and to seek their advice, support and patronage. Scribbles in my diary remind me that I discussed it with some Church of Ireland friends on 20 January on the occasion of a meeting to launch an appeal for the rebuilding of Damer Court which took place at the Four Courts Hotel in Dublin; with the Principal of Edgehill (the Methodist Theological) College, Belfast on 23 February; with the Dublin Council of Churches on 24 February and with the Secretary of the Irish Council of Churches on 13 May. There will, of course, have been other meetings, but contact with the Roman Catholic authorities and in particular with Archbishop McQuaid was reserved to the Provincial. Without the permission or at least the acquiescence of the Catholic Archbishop in whose jurisdiction the School was to be based it would have been impossible for the Provincial to go ahead with ISE.

Archbishop McQuaid had already acquiesced in the arrangements for an ecumenical service on 15 April on the occasion of the launch of *Irish Anglicanism*. Would he acquiesce again? On the margins of a meeting of provincials and bishops on 23 April Father McGarry raised the question with him and wrote to me as follows from Limerick the day after:

> We finished so late that I only saw the A. B. [Archbishop] for a moment. He is not at the moment sympathetic to things ecumenical. He does not want you to read a lesson at St Patrick's [Dublin, on 12 May, at the special service for the centenary of Disestablishment]; of course there is no problem about presence. Seeing the way things were and the lateness of the hour, I just said to him that I would be coming to see him on my return to Dublin about the School of Ecumenics, 'when he would, I hoped, be feeling more ecumenically benign'. I don't know what will happen, but it is too important to prejudice in any way while there is any hope of acquiescence on his part. Keep smiling, hoping and praying.

Eventually the attitude of the Archbishop became less negative and more sympathetic. Just a month later, on 22 May, the Provincial felt able to write to the President of the Episcopal Conference, Cardinal Conway, and to the Secretary of the Episcopal Commission on Ecumenism, Bishop Ahern of Cloyne, informing them about 'the proposed opening of a small school of ecumenical studies in Dublin'. In his letter to the Secretary he added: 'Approval of the School and its commendation by your Episcopal Commission would be something I would greatly appreciate.' A week later, on 28 May 1970, a press conference organised largely by Dan Mullane was held in a Dublin hotel.

Public announcement
The press statement issued for this conference puts the proposed school in the context of the frustration which even then was becoming increasingly widespread in ecumenical circles:

> Ireland is not alone today in having an acute ecumenical problem. All over the world there is a growing suspicion if not conviction that ecumenism has reached a dead-end.... The scandal of disunity has become the scandal of ecumenism.
>
> Education in ecumenism has unfortunately not kept pace with progress in ecumenism. Ecumenics is the subject which teaches ecumenism but ecumenics scarcely exists in religious education or theology programmes at any level in any country. If there are no teachers of ecumenics the reason is that there are no Schools of Ecumenics. The Irish School of Ecumenics proposes, among other things, to fill this gap and so to help to remedy, at its real source, the present worldwide ecumenical malaise.

The press statement went on to make quite clear what 'Ecumenics: What and Why' had left unclear: ISE would be an independent, unofficial, interdenominational institute, 'confident that its courses will be immediately recognised by other theological institutions as fulfilling certain requirements for degrees conferred by them'. It would not be associated with the Milltown Institute, a possibility originally envisaged,[22] which would have placed it under Roman Catholic auspices. As an interdenominational initiative ISE would be unlike the ecumenical institute at Paderborn which is under the auspices of the Roman Catholic archdiocese and unlike the ecumenical institute at Strasbourg which is under the auspices of the Lutheran World Federation.[23] It would be more like the World Council of Churches' institute at Bossey near Geneva, except that Bossey is official and non-Roman Catholic and less systematic in its whole approach, and more like the Tantur Ecumenical Institute for Theological Studies in Jerusalem which, when it opened the following year, would be governed by an ecumenical board – its members serving only in a personal capacity – but remain Vatican property.[24]

The Irish School of Ecumenics – it was stated – is not an official institution of the Irish Churches but its authentic interdenominational ecumenical character is guaranteed by its five patrons and by its teaching staff as well as by its students who in principle will be half Roman Catholic, half non-Roman Catholic.

The five patrons were named in alphabetical order: Bishop John W. Armstrong (Church of Ireland), Reverend Professor John M. Barkley (Presbyterian), Very Reverend Cecil McGarry SJ (Roman Catholic), Reverend Robert A. Nelson (Methodist) and Mr Peter Odlum.[25] The latter was not denominationally or otherwise identified in the press statement which had been typed in the offices of the IFMA. Although a member of the Church of Ireland and of Quaker background, it was not on behalf of either of these connections but rather on behalf of the IFMA that he saw himself acting as ISE patron. When, through unforeseen circumstances, he found himself unable to be present at the press conference he arranged for his place to be taken by Norman Odlum, a brother and business associate. The other four patrons were all present in person. The various teachers were also named in the press release. Representing the different Christian traditions, they were very generously taking time off from their ordinary duties, academic or pastoral, to offer short courses at ISE in the areas of their competence. These courses, it was announced, would be taught in a classroom made available by the College of Industrial Relations which was very conveniently situated near Milltown Park in Dublin and was then under Jesuit auspices.

The weeks following the 28 May press conference were spent making the existence of ISE more generally known and preparing for its opening and formal inauguration. A letter of mine to Peter Desmond Odlum of 10 August summarises the results of all this activity: so far, apart from one crisis,[26] all had gone well and I had 'solid expectations for at least eight' students for the first academic year. A four-page prospectus was printed (no copy seems to have survived) and widely distributed: the July issues of *The Furrow* and *Theology* carried it as an insert. Contact was made with some of the people prominent in the theological world of Scotland, England and the USA with a view to recruiting students. In the course of a two-week visit across the water in late June I visited Edinburgh where I met Professor Tom Torrance; Birmingham where I met Principal John Habgood of Queen's College (a joint Anglican-Methodist initiative) – he was later to be Archbishop of York – and London where I met Professor G. R. Dunstan of King's College. All were very encouraging and so, in a letter, was Dr Walter Wagoner, Director of the Boston Institute of Theology (a federation of seven theological schools), who wrote of his 'enthusiasm for your Ecumenical Institute and its related programs .... There is nothing quite as comprehensive and thorough – your plan differs from Bossey.'

The Rector of Milltown Park was also approached about the possibility of a site in the grounds for an ISE building. With the approval of the Jesuit Provincial such a site was allocated (that now occupied by Cherryfield Lodge), meetings were held with Andy Devane of the architectural firm, Robinson, Keefe & Devane, and with officers of the Planning Department of Dublin Corporation, and sketch plans were drawn up not only for a permanent building but also for a temporary prefabricated structure which would be ready by the end of September. The cost of this building, approximately £16,000, and the running expenses of the School for the first year, approximately £14,000, would be underwritten by the IFMA. A formal letter to this effect was sent to the Provincial on 10 September.

The World Council of Churches

Contact was also made with the World Council of Churches (WCC) in the hope that the General Secretary, the Reverend Dr Eugene Carson Blake, would accept an invitation to give the inaugural lecture; the arrangements for this were finalised on 24 July when I passed through Geneva on my way to Rome on other business. Granted my own background, a Protestant seemed necessary to inaugurate the School in order to emphasise its inter-Church character, and nobody seemed more appropriate than the General Secretary of the leading non-Roman Catholic ecumenical body. This invitation, however, turned out to be controversial. In the mid-1970s, in the aftermath of the School's International Consultation on Mixed Marriage, it would be adduced by Roman Catholic critics, who included Archbishop Dermot Ryan of Dublin, as an argument to suggest that ISE was more Protestant than Catholic in its ecumenical sympathies and theological thinking. At the time a number of Northern Presbyterians considered the invitation inopportune, insensitive to the depth of anti-ecumenical feeling which was growing among Northern Protestants and the main target of which was the WCC. There was a suggestion that the invitation be withdrawn.

Mutual ignorance continues to characterise relations in Ireland between North and South, with the additional features of indifference in the South and antipathy in the North. It was, of course, more prevalent in 1970 than it is now, but even then many of us did know from experience something of the depth of Protestant anti-ecumenical feeling in the North. One of the leaders of the anti-ecumenical wing of Irish Protestantism at that time was the Minister of Agnes Street Presbyterian Church in Belfast, the Reverend Donald Gillies. His *Unity in the Dark* had appeared in 1964, arguing that the ecumenical movement 'bids to become the greatest menace to the truth of the Gospel since the time of the Reformation'.[27] In late November 1965 Donald Gillies and I had appeared together on a BBC Northern Ireland television programme as members of a panel to discuss a recently published book entitled *Rome: Opponent or Partner?* During that programme Mr Gillies had not hesitated to make clear that because of my Roman Catholicism, his evangelical convictions and conscience would not allow him to consider me to be a Christian.[28]

Until the end of the decade the main argument of the opponents of ecumenism and of the WCC in particular was theological: its 'Romeward trend', its unfaithfulness to 'the historic evangelical Protestant faith' which prescribed scripture alone, grace alone, faith alone. In the 1970s, however, an additional argument began to surface: the WCC was allegedly supporting terrorists in Africa and, if in Africa, perhaps also in Northern Ireland.

> Grants from the Special Fund of the WCC's Programme to Combat Racism were causing misgivings in many countries. Naturally the misgiving was even greater in a country subjected to terrorism by the Provisional IRA. This greatly strengthened an opposition already growing on theological grounds.[29]

This was the situation which some Northern Presbyterians saw developing in the summer of 1970. Their Church's membership of the World Council was at risk and they wanted above all to protect this. There was every reason therefore why an official such as the Moderator of General Assembly should absent himself from the General Secretary's lecture. The current Moderator was none other than Principal J. L. M. Haire who had hosted my lecture on Baptism two years previously, had taken a prominent part in the ecumenical service for the presentation of *Irish Anglicanism* on 15 April and, two months previously, had invited me as one of his special guests to his installation as Moderator. The situation now, however, was so serious that Principal Haire did decide to absent himself. It is a well-known fact that the constraints of office often oblige authorities, both civil and religious, to follow the prevailing rather than their personal views.

On the other hand there seemed to be no compelling reason why the School should withdraw the invitation. On the contrary there seemed to be every reason for leaving it stand. Many felt that 'we cannot have another Ripon case on our conscience'. In retrospect the cancellation of the Bishop of Ripon's lecture in Belfast was seen to have been unwise: it had only served to strengthen the hands of the anti-ecumenical extremists.[30]

So the invitation to Dr Eugene Carson Blake was not withdrawn. It led the following year to an ill-fated if not ill-advised intervention in Northern Ireland on the part of Sodepax (Joint Committee on Society, Development and Peace), itself a short-lived ecumenical experiment between the Vatican and the WCC.[31] Otherwise the visit was highly successful. It helped that the General Secretary was himself a Presbyterian and that he was accompanied on his visit by a Northern Irish Methodist, the Reverend Wilbert Forker, who was then on the WCC staff in Geneva.

The negative repercussions of the visit affected ISE in the first instance; they were mainly financial and the financial crisis they caused was to erupt in September. Whether there were negative repercussions for the Presbyterian Church in Ireland is arguable. It did terminate its membership of the WCC in 1980, but the part played in this by the ISE invitation of 1970 was negligible and, once freed the following year from the constraints of the Moderatorial office, Principal Haire resumed his ecumenical activities. For the rest of his life he was a faithful supporter of ISE which now sponsors a Memorial Lecture in his honour every two years with the help of an endowment fund set up by his family and friends for this purpose.

Northern Ireland conflict analysis

Another of my concerns during that July and August of 1970 was, as I told Peter Desmond Odlum in my letter, a project due to begin in the early autumn under the joint auspices of ISE and the Centre for the Analysis of Conflict (CAC) in London. It was to be a 'controlled communication' involving representatives of the opposing traditions in Northern Ireland. This project was, in fact, carried out: a first session at least took place. Because it was an early attempt – though of a particular kind – at the cross-community exercises which have since become common, because it was the first academic exercise to take place under the auspices of ISE, because it introduced to Northern Ireland the influential Australian expert in conflict resolution, Dr John Burton, and because it anticipated in a way the place which Peace Studies has since come to acquire in ISE,[32] this 'controlled communication' deserves some mention here. After twenty-five years, however, it is not easy to reconstruct what happened and how it came to happen.[33]

It was Professor G. R. Dunstan[34] who introduced ISE and the CAC to each other. He spoke of the Centre's work when he gave me lunch at King's College, London on Thursday, 2 July, and duly reported my positive reactions to his friend Tony de Reuck, an associate of the Centre, who lost no time in passing them on to the Director, Dr John Burton, at University College, London. He in turn wrote to me without further delay the following Wednesday, 8 July, offering to sponsor an initial session in London and explaining the nature of the exercise: 'a face-to-face situation presided over by a group of social and political scientists who would contribute their knowledge about the nature of conflict and help the parties to a conflict to make accurate assessments of the motivations of each other'.

CAC's interest in opportunities for research but also an urgency deriving from the deteriorating political situation will explain the speed of these reactions. Spurred on by this I immediately contacted Mr G. B. Newe of the Northern Ireland Council of Social Service and Mr Maurice Hayes of the Community Relations Commission, both of whom were encouraging and helpful. I met them in Belfast on 15 July and again on 7 August, and with the co-operation of Mr Billy Blease, Northern Ireland Officer of the Irish Congress of Trades Unions, arrangements were in place by mid-August for a group of six shop stewards to participate in a 'controlled communication', to take place in London from 13 to 19 September, all expenses to be borne by CAC. Tony de Reuck's letter to me (14 August) begins effusively:

> We owe you our delighted congratulations and warmest thanks – your proposed group for the Northern Ireland controlled communication is as good as could have been hoped for, most appropriate and acceptable.

In the event nothing went wrong; everything went smoothly. Two of the shop stewards who had participated and whom I have succeeded in identifying and meeting were quite positive in their recollections, one of them saying that it was 'a truly wonderful experience'. Also participating was Dr Maurice Hayes, who finds space for a mention of the event in his published memoirs[35] and who, in a lengthy conversation, referred to it as 'an exciting thing and influential'. All six shop stewards, he felt, would have had Northern Ireland Labour

Party links and been anti-sectarian in outlook. Though divided politically and religiously they were more united on socio-economic issues – and also 'in vilification of the referee' at a soccer match they attended together!

Dr Hayes gave me to understand that what made this 'controlled communication' particularly influential in his view, was the fact that it introduced Dr Burton to Northern Ireland. His background and his approach impressed Dr Hayes. He had been head of the Australian Department of Foreign Affairs before becoming an academic, researching conflict in various parts of the world, including Cyprus. And his approach as well as his experience was impressive: it was gradualist – 'foothills before heights':

> He had developed a model of conflict resolution that encouraged people to work together on functional matters in which they had a common interest, until they built up enough trust to deal with the more divisive issues.[36]

Further sessions of the 'controlled communication' had been envisaged and tentative arrangements been made for a preparatory visit to Belfast by Dr Burton and Mr de Reuck sometime between 20 September and 17 October. These further sessions did not take place but Dr Burton and two of his assistants[37] did become involved in Northern Ireland affairs and prepared a report for the Community Relations Commission in 1971. An investigation and assessment of all these activities would seem to be a worthwhile project remaining to be undertaken.

Financial crisis

A decision by the IFMA to withdraw support from ISE because of its links with the WCC was the financial crisis which hit the School in September. Hard on the heels of the Association's letter of 10 September undertaking to fund ISE, which the Provincial had acknowledged on the 11th, thanking them 'for the munificence of their gesture', the following arrived on his desk:

> Dear Father Provincial,
> In connection with the setting up of an Irish School of Ecumenics, my Committee have given this matter further consideration, and I am to ask that no action be taken on foot of the contents of our letter of even date, pending a Meeting on the subject between my Committee, yourself and Fr Hurley.

I had already the previous day received a telephone warning about this development from the Public Relations Officer and wrote to him as follows on the 10th:

> I feel it may be helpful, especially to avoid misunderstanding, to put on paper what I take to be the meaning and result of our telephone conversations yesterday. Since your Association's letter to the Provincial dated 10 September the circumstances have changed: the World Council of Churches has taken an action which your Association cannot approve of or be associated with and which in the Association's judgement, would make it impossible to obtain funds from other sources to ensure the future of the Irish School of Ecumenics. In these changed circumstances your Association could make financial assistance available only to a School of Ecumenics which concerned itself exclusively *with Ireland*: with the promotion of better relations between Catholics and Protestants, between North and South, in Ireland, and which – to accomplish this – did not involve any non-Irish personnel either as students or teachers. Because the Irish School of Ecumenics does at present include non-Irish students and teachers, your Association has no choice but to withdraw its letter of 10 September to the Jesuit Provincial, in order that it may be

seen to have no connection whatever with the World Council of Churches.

The reference is, of course, once again to the WCC's Programme to Combat Racism and its alleged support for 'terrorist' organisations. My letter went on to explain away ISE's links with the WCC and concluded: 'If, as you said, today's decision [by the IFMA Executive Committee] is bound to be negative I shall make an effort to enlist financial support from others. I must at least try.' I had just returned from a meeting of the Methodist-Roman Catholic International Commission at Lake Junaluska in the USA and was due to attend a *Concilium* congress in Brussels from 12 to 17 September. I cancelled my attendance at this latter, staying at home instead to write begging letters and make begging telephone calls – with some encouraging results, notably a cheque for £1,000 from the Carmelite Provincial at Whitefriars Street, Father J. Linus Ryan, OCarm. The immediate crisis was averted and, everything else being in readiness – teachers, students, a library (courtesy of Milltown Park) and a classroom (courtesy of the College of Industrial Relations) – the ecumenical feast, like the marriage feast of Cana, went on. Building plans had to be abandoned and the name of Peter Desmond Odlum had to disappear from the list of patrons, but the academic year opened as intended on 19 October. ISE's basic financial situation has, however, remained precarious ever since.

The official meeting envisaged in the second letter of 10 September from the IFMA was delayed because of the Provincial's absence from the country. When it took place on 30 November the position as conveyed to me by the Public Relations Officer remained unchanged. The following day, however, the President, Secretary and another member of the Executive[38] called on the Provincial to present ISE with a £5,000 cheque which was to receive 'no publicity or public acknowledgement' and to express their 'extreme embarrassment' at the situation which had arisen but also their interest in and hopes for ISE. In his letter of acknowledgement to the President the Provincial wrote:

> I would ask you to thank your Association for me, for their generosity in this matter, and to tell them that I appreciate very much the complications which arose in this very difficult situation. I regret any embarrassment which they may have felt and hope that they will be able to allow all of this to fade into the past.

In preparing this memoir on 'The Beginnings of ISE' it seemed appropriate to try to renew contact with IFMA. What I found was that the Association itself had gone out of existence in 1989 and that those most immediately involved in 1970 were either deceased or too ill to be interviewed.[39] I did, however, have the good fortune of a long informative meeting on 25 October 1994 with A. W. Dickson Spence (Dickie Spence), a well-known cricketer and umpire who was on the staff of IFMA in 1970, and who was its last Secretary. (He died suddenly in May 1996.) As a result of this meeting and of other contacts, I have come to see that in 1970 the flour-milling industry was already in steep decline owing to the removal of tariff restrictions and a decline in consumption, that on economic grounds alone the generous offer of support for ISE coming mainly from Peter Desmond Odlum, a former President, and from the Public Relations Officer, Mr Dan Mullane, would have been difficult to sell to the shareholders in the first instance or to maintain subsequently. I now understand and accept that the decision to withdraw support was, therefore, a business one, that the WCC angle was an excuse rather than the real reason. The discovery that IFMA was a twenty-six county organisation and hence less vulnerable to anti-ecumenical attitudes, has made this new understanding of what happened in 1970 all the more credible. Some puzzlement must remain but in retrospect it is difficult not to feel relief as well as gratitude: gratitude for the invaluable encouragement which ISE 'in process of formation' received in its early stages, but relief also that it was saved at birth from becoming dependent on a failing financial resource.

University recognition

When ISE's first academic year opened on 19 October, there were seven, not eight students. They came from a wide variety of backgrounds: from England, Malta, South Africa, Scotland and the USA, as well as two from Ireland. They were all Roman Catholic except for two Anglican priests, one of whom, when the year was over, was to become Assistant Secretary of the Board for Mission and Unity of the Church of England. None of these first students obtained a degree at the end. The hope expressed at the May Press Conference that the School's courses 'will be immediately recognised by other theological institutions as fulfilling certain requirements for degrees conferred by them'[40] was premature and indeed naive insofar as it failed to realise that academic institutions are just as slow to move as the Churches. But before the academic year even began, during the summer of 1970, sure and firm grounds for our hope of university recognition emerged in the person of the Reverend Professor Anthony Hanson of Hull University who, when he visited me during the holidays, offered any help he could as Head of the Hull Department of Theology. Before the year had ended that hope had in fact been realised.

But first of all an approach was made locally, to Trinity College Dublin (TCD). The interdenominational character of ISE and my own Roman Catholic background seemed to suggest that a link with a Protestant or non-denominational department of theology would be more appropriate than with a Catholic one, such as St Patrick's College, Maynooth. TCD, I found, would be happy to equiparate ISE students with those from the Institute for Advanced Studies and thus allow them, if suitably qualified academically, to register for an MLitt or PhD degree. But it could not see its way to granting a postgraduate award for the successful completion of ISE's own course. Because of Hull's readiness to help, no serious effort was made at this time to overcome TCD's reservations, expressed in meetings with the Deans of Graduate Studies and Arts.[41] So I travelled to Hull in early January and again in late February. Professor Hanson himself visited ISE in late March and satisfied himself that the syllabus provided adequate material for a one-year postgraduate course such as Hull's own B Phil. On his return, therefore, he proposed ISE's affiliation with the University and steered a proposal to this effect through Department, Faculty and Senate with consummate skill and characteristic speed.

In his submission Professor Hanson had added one non-academic consideration: 'If we can accommodate this course within our B Phil arrangement, we shall be making a very practical contribution to the improvement of the embittered situation in Ireland.' There is an added significance, therefore, in the fact – however coincidental – that the Vice-Chancellor of Hull, Sir Brynmor Jones, chose the week of 12 July to come to Dublin and hold a press conference to announce the good news. The following month, August 1971, was to see the introduction of internment without trial. Just six months later, on 30 January 1972, came Bloody Sunday. The need for what ISE was offering was becoming ever more glaring.[42] It may also be noted that ISE's affiliation with Hull is the clearest sign of the link already suggested between *Irish Anglicanism* and ISE. Anthony Hanson's twin brother Richard was then Bishop of Clogher and was present at the 15 April ceremonies. It was he who must have commended ISE to Anthony. They both became ardent supporters of ISE and in 1987 dedicated their joint work, *The Identity of the Church,* to me.[43]

Floreat ut pereat

According to the only surviving account, that in the *Irish Christian Advocate*,[44] I had, in my speech at the press conference on 16 July, thanked the University of Hull 'for bringing it [ISE] closer to the death demanded by its motto: "may it flourish in order to perish" '. This motto in its Latin original, *floreat ut pereat*, had occurred to me one morning during the early summer. It gives lapidary expression to the insight I had expressed in 'Ecumenics: What and Why?'

> In conclusion it must be noted that schools of ecumenics, like all the institutions of the ecumenical movement, are not only born to die but are born to put themselves to death, to commit suicide; that they live to die as soon as ever possible, as soon as the task is completed of reconciling the Churches in the unity which is God's will for his people.[45]

This motto and the eucharistic nature of the Church suggested to Mr Gerard Slevin who was then the Chief Herald that an ear of wheat would be an appropriate emblem for ISE: the ear of wheat which in the Fourth Gospel dies to yield a rich harvest and which in the eucharist becomes for us the Body of Christ. The logo combining emblem and motto was designed by Myra Maguire of the National College of Art, who was a member of the Presbyterian Church in Ireland.

The idea of dying and rising was also emphasised during that summer of 1970 by the gift of a crucifix, especially as the gift came from an unusual, unexpected source. Protestants prefer crosses to crucifixes but this crucifix had belonged to the Very Reverend Andrew Gibson, MC, DD, a former Moderator of the General Assembly of the Presbyterian Church in Ireland. As a chaplain in World War I he had found it in the mud and rubble of an unidentified French village and, having failed to find the owner, brought it back to Ireland and gave it a place of honour in the study of his Cork Manse for twenty-one years. The crucifix was presented to the School by Dr Gibson's son and the minister of Rathgar Presbyterian Church, The Very Reverend T. A. B. Smyth. The Dublin sculptor Mr Garry Trimble was commissioned to carve a new cross of Irish oak for the figure and to design and execute an accompanying commemorative plaque cast in bronze. Both were ready for the School's inauguration in November and in my concluding address I referred to the crucifix as the School's 'most cherished possession'.

CONCLUSION

On the occasion of the inauguration (of which there is a rather full account in the pages of the *Irish [Jesuit] Province News*[46]) the General Secretary of WCC, Reverend Dr Carson Blake, spent two days in Dublin during which he was entertained to lunch at the Shelbourne Hotel by the Minister for Education, received by the President at Áras an Uachtaráin, dined in Commons at Trinity College as the guest of the Provost, preached at St Patrick's Cathedral, gave a live studio interview on television and a lengthy press conference in the Library of Abbey Presbyterian Church just before returning to Geneva. The inauguration itself, which was not a public occasion but by invitation only, was attended by some 350 guests, representing the academic and ecclesiastical worlds in particular. This augured well for the future of the School, especially as the guests included three Roman Catholic bishops, which was highly significant for the contrast with 15 April when only one Catholic bishop attended.

It remained to obtain administrative assistance (a part-time secretary, Ruth Moran, began work in early January 1971) and to mount a fundraising campaign, which was launched with simultaneous press conferences in Belfast and Dublin on 15

January 1971. The School also needed to acquire a premises of its own with residential accommodation. Thanks to a bequest made to a Jesuit friend, Father John Mulligan, this latter was acquired in the summer of 1971 and named Bea House after the Jesuit Cardinal who as President of the Secretariat for Promoting Christian Unity had done so much at Vatican II to launch the Roman Catholic Church into the ecumenical movement. Bea House was in operation by the beginning of the second academic year, in October 1971. The appointment of permanent academic staff had to wait until the academic year 1972/3.[47] Regular courses in Northern Ireland, as distinct from occasional lectures, in particular the Certificate Adult Eduction course, had to wait until the academic year 1979/80. It was time then, as the end of the first decade approached, to hand over to another. The Irish Presbyterian theologian, the Reverend Dr R. H. S. Boyd took office in the autumn of 1980 as ISE's second Director.[48]

The end of the second Christian millennium is in sight as I conclude this memoir on the beginnings of ISE. The hopes for an 'ecumenical second spring' now being expressed by Pope John Paul II and the other leaders of the world Church are encouraging as well as sobering. They are sobering because they remind us of our lack of success hitherto: Church unity has not taken place in our generation: it will not take place in 2000 as it did not, despite the Nottingham 1964 resolution of the First British Conference on Faith and Order, take place on Easter Day 1980. But these hopes for the new millennium are also encouraging because, among other reasons, the means by which they can be realised now exist. The forging and refining of these instruments for ecumenical progress has been one of the achievements – and not the least – of the post-Vatican II years. ISE is one of these instruments and its relevance was never more fully and formally and explicitly recognised than in the 1993 document on *Ecumenical Formation* issued by the Joint Working Group of the Roman Catholic Church and the WCC, and in the chapter on 'Ecumenical Formation' in the *Directory On Ecumenism* published that same year by the Pontifical Council for Christian Unity.[49] So, with a play on the ISE motto, I end, not too presumptuously I hope, by expressing the wish: *floreat [ISE] ne pereat [ecumenismus]*: May the Irish School of Ecumenics flourish lest the Ecumenical Movement perish![50]

17
An Ecumenical Sabbatical: Mount Athos and China

INTRODUCTION

The sabbatical year which I enjoyed from 1980 to 1981 had as a main aim to help me to break new ground, territorially and religiously, and so I visited such places as Mount Athos and Addis Ababa, Jerusalem and Johannesburg, Kinshasa and Katmandu, Zanzibar and Varanasi, and also got to the end of the medieval silk route at Xian and further on to Beijing and walked on the Great Wall of China. The January Unity Week that year was particularly memorable because it found me for the first time in Africa and in India where the basic ecumenical insight (that unity is for mission so that the world may believe) was originally born. On the opening Sunday I was in Dar-es-Salaam – 'harbour of peace' – preaching at the English Mass in the interdenominational chapel at the university. Later in the week I was visiting Agra and Fatehpur Sikri where, in the sixteenth century, as H. G. Wells put it, 'while Christians in Europe were killing each other, Akbar [the Mogul Emperor] was busy synthesising cultures and religions'. My visits to Mount Athos and to China were, with the Sitagarha long retreat mentioned in chapter 18 *infra* on the Columbanus Community, the highlights of this sabbatical.

MOUNT ATHOS

The following diary account of a 1980 visit to the independent monastic republic of Mount Athos reveals something of the ancient antipathy between Catholics and Orthodox which an earlier chapter has shown not to have abated but rather intensified as the millennium draws to a close. It therefore raises doubts as well as hopes that the new millennium will in fact inspire fresh initiatives in the cause of Christian unity and lead to an ecumenical second spring. Because, however, there is an ecumenical faith that moves mountains, it leaves us hoping – but hoping against hope.

Salonica: Tuesday

An advertisement for Hugh Leonard's play, *Da*, is one of the first things I notice in Aristotle Square on my arrival here this evening (30 September). I'm simply passing through Salonica, coming from the Meteora monasteries of Thessaly and going on tomorrow to the Orthodox monasteries of Mount Athos, the most eastern of the three peninsulas jutting out from the coast of Macedonia in northern Greece.

Ouranoupolis: Wednesday

At midday I had an appointment to see Metropolitan Rodopoulos at the University, where he is Professor of Canon Law. He speaks excellent English and entertained me most hospitably to lunch afterwards on the balcony of his apartment overlooking the bay. He is a very sympathetic supporter of the ecumenical movement and served as a member of the Academic Council of the Irish School of Ecumenics in its early years, but he doesn't think progress in the new Orthodox-Roman Catholic dialogue will be dramatic. If I understood him right, he also seems to think that the monks on Mount Athos will not allow me to join them, not only for the Eucharist but for any of their services. I find this incredible even for Mount Athos.

With all our talk, it is 4.30 p.m. before we realise it and the Metropolitan very kindly drives me to the 5.30 p.m. bus for

Ouranoupolis: this is a seaside village at the top of the south side of the Mount Athos peninsula and it is from here you take the boat to the port of entry. The road to Ouranoupolis takes us over the mountains, past wayside shrines and beehives and through the village of Stagira, birthplace of Aristotle, but it is dark by then. About 8.00 p.m. as we near our destination and most of the other passengers have got off, a friendly young man engages me in conversation. He wonders – in broken German – if I also am going to visit the Holy Mountain. He is a Greek – his name is Rallis – and when we arrive I have no difficulty with his help in getting lodgings for the night.

Our fellow-lodgers include two Orthodox priests and a young German named Tom, who is also going to Mount Athos. When we have settled into our rooms, Rallis, Tom and I go out to share a bottle of wine. Rallis lives near Salonica and has just finished his studies as a mechanical engineer. He has friends on Mount Athos and will stay a week or ten days. Greeks don't need special permits as we do, nor are they limited to the ordinary four-day stay. His family is very religious; he himself does not keep the regular Friday fast but he does keep the Lenten fast. Tom is from Hamburg and begins university in the autumn. His family background is Protestant, but he has been an atheist and is now becoming an Orthodox Christian in the Russian Church in Exile. Tom is a very serious young man.

Dafni and Karies: Thursday

The boat for Dafni, which is the name of the port of entry to Mount Athos, isn't due to depart until 9.45 a.m. Before that Rallis, Tom and I explore the little seaside village of Ouranoupolis, have morning coffee and buy ourselves provisions for the lean days ahead, cheese and chocolate and fruit.

Examining the map when we get on board I see that the port of Dafni where we are heading is over half-way down the southern coast and that the whole peninsula is about twenty-five miles long and seven miles wide. Looking around at my fellow passengers, I see that one of the monks with his different headgear is quite obviously Russian and I approach him. He speaks English but better French and is quite willing to talk. He belongs to the Russian Church in Exile and lives in a monastery in the south of France. He has previously spent a year here on Mount Athos but found the regime too hard and is now going back to visit friends.

There are twenty monasteries, he explains, and they have parcelled out the whole peninsula between them. No new monasteries can be established, only *sketes* or dependent monastic institutions.

We pass the monastery of Panteleimon and he speaks of the Russian influence on Mount Athos before the Revolution, when this monastery numbered some two thousand monks. It still is, he says, a Russian monastery, but has only a handful of monks. There are two other non-Greek monasteries: one Serbian and the other Bulgarian.

About midday we all disembark at Dafni and climb aboard a bus which takes us slowly and dangerously up the steep, narrow dirt road to the village of Karies. This is the 'administrative capital' of Mount Athos, and the Roman Catholic Church had a small school here from 1636-41. All of us non-Greeks have now to present ourselves at the police station, but it is closed for lunch. There is a restaurant of sorts where we repair for a bite to eat, and afterwards I buy a useful map giving the location of all the monasteries and the distance in kilometres and walking hours, between them. By then the police station is open; it is staffed for the monks by the Greek police.

Here my permit from the Ministry of Foreign Affairs in Athens is scrutinised and exchanged for another document. This I bring along to the monastic GHQ, where I receive my *diamoneterion*, the visa which everyone needs and which calls on the individual monasteries to give me hospitality for the five days I have requested. Rallis, Tom and I now say goodbye because we are going to different monasteries and I set out on my own path to Stavronikita.

Stavronikita: Thursday

It was Metropolitan Rodopoulos who suggested Stavronikita; the Abbot had studied at Paris and would be good to meet. This monastery is situated on the northern coast of the peninsula, so the walk there has to be downhill and, according to the map, I should make it in an hour and a half. The prospect therefore is not too daunting – some journeys on Mount Athos take four hours and more – but I'm carrying too much in my shoulder bag and the afternoon sun is beating down fiercely and the signposting is not too clear and being alone I begin to be anxious. Am I really going in the right direction on the right path? If I've taken a wrong turn and am going astray and don't arrive before sunset when the monasteries close up, what on earth am I going to do for the night? Eventually, to my great relief, I see below a tower which must be Stavronikita.

The guestmaster greets me silently, motions me to take a seat and disappears for a moment to return with a square of Turkish delight and a glass of water. Then he asks for my *diamoneterion* and enters all the details in the guestbook. Shortly afterwards two young Greeks arrive and he does likewise but then he goes off, bringing the Greeks with him, and I am left on my own in the waiting room wondering what's going on.

Since my arrival, however, the *simantron*, the wooden sounding-board which summons the monks to prayer is being struck, and so I am forced very reluctantly to the conclusion that vespers are on and that Metropolitan Rodopoulos was right: as a non-Orthodox I am barred. The conclusion is only too true. Forty-five minutes later the guestmaster returns and invites me with him to the church, where now the lights are being extinguished and the departing worshippers are venerating the icons. I stand in silent prayer, but I do not join in the veneration; my resentment doesn't allow me. Later I shall very much regret this.

It is now 5.00 p.m. and supper follows with the monks, a privilege which, as I shall discover, not every monastery on Mount Athos grants to its guests. The meal is excellent, and from the glances I can manage around the refectory as we eat in silence, I gather that there are sixteen monks present; but, very puzzlingly, there is not one old man among them. After supper the guestmaster shows the two Greeks and myself to our room which is three flights up, overlooking the sea and with five beds. He tells me that the Abbot is away but that another monk who speaks English will see me tomorrow morning after lunch about 9.30 a.m. (*sic*). There is still light and the doors are not closed so I wander outside to calm my troubled spirits in the cool of the evening. At 6.30 p.m. I am back in the house. Oil lamps are now lighting in the corridors. I light the one in our dormitory and sit and try to think and write but I am still upset when I go to bed some time later.

Stavronikita: Friday
We were called at 2.45 this morning but I had to presume the call was only for my Orthodox companions who could join the monks for the office. When I emerge about 7.00 a.m. the church is locked. Later I find out that all the monastery churches on Mount Athos are closed between offices for security reasons; icons have been stolen.

At my request the guestmaster now opens the church but remains inside with me and when I go to sit down, he indicates that we should be leaving. He then offers the two Greeks and myself a coffee in his waiting room and we get into conversation. One of the Greeks is a mathematics teacher, the other an artist of some sort; both are from Athens. They speak English fairly well and try to explain to me in friendly fashion why I cannot join in prayer with the monks: the Orthodox have the truth and Catholics are in error. When I suggest that in this matter of ecumenism Mount Athos may be out of step with the rest of the Orthodox world, one of them says that he believes Demetrios, the Patriarch of Constantinople, to be in the pay of the Freemasons.

From 8.00 a.m. I sit quietly at the open window of our dormitory, looking out to sea, listening to the waves breaking gently on the rocks below, preparing questions for my session later with the English-speaking monk and reviewing my plans for the day. To my left I can see the monastery of Pantokratoros, but I decide now to visit Iviron instead. This is out of sight to my right. It is the second-oldest monastery on Mount Athos, celebrating this year its foundation in Georgia just a millennium ago, in 980. Last summer I had a memorable few days in Tbilisi and a most interesting audience with the Orthodox Patriarch there. I decide to go to Iviron in order to pray for the Church in Georgia.

The meal at 9.30 a.m., which we are allowed again to take with the monks, is definitely lunch and a very good lunch, but one of the servers admonished me for sitting with my legs crossed under the table. Afterwards I sit outside and chat with the English-speaking monk, a Greek whose name is Father Simeon and who came here from Athens in 1974.

According to my watch it is 10.45 a.m. on 3 October but for him it is 4.45 p.m. on 20 September. They still follow the Julian calendar (as do all the monasteries except one) and for them sunset is midnight. This means that the monks retired last night at 12.30 a.m. (6.30 p.m. by me), got up at 7.00 a.m. (1.00 a.m. by me), had lunch at 3.30 p.m. (9.30 a.m. by me) and, were this not Friday, would have supper this evening at 11.00 p.m. (5 p.m. by me). On Mondays, Wednesdays and Fridays they take only one meal in the day.

At present, I gather from Father Simeon, there are twenty monks in the monastery, four of them priests. There are no elderly monks because the monastery had been closed and reopened only in 1968 to begin a new chapter in its history; it changed from being ideorrhythmic to being coenobitic. The coenobitic style of monastic life is stricter, with greater emphasis on community; the ideorrhythmic monks live a more independent, individualistic life. Fifteen of the monasteries are now coenobitic and the total monastic population numbers between 1,400 to 1,500.

They do not allow other non-Orthodox Christians to be in church with them during the offices, because we would be mere spectators and because 'the Holy Fathers' forbid it; we may, however, stay in the porch. Before taking my leave of Father Simeon and thanking him, I tell him that I also am a monk, a religious. 'But where,' he asks, 'is your habit?' An Orthodox monk, no matter what work he is at, never seems to leave aside his habit.

Iviron: Friday

It's already about midday by my watch when I say goodbye to Stavronikita and set out on the path along the cliffs towards Iviron which, according to the map, I should reach in less than an hour. Unfortunately, I lose my way and spend an anxious quarter of an hour moving blindly through thick vegetation in what I hope is the right direction. At last I arrive safely and have the added pleasure of a brief meeting with Rallis who is about to leave, but the guesthouse, I find, is closed until 4.00 p.m. Meantime the water is tempting and a swim would be very welcome but the monks, I gather, are forbidden to go in so I refrain and instead look around and take a rest in the shade.

Iviron seems at first sight to be a much bigger establishment than Stavronikita but less well maintained. You come up from the pier through an entrance gate which has the date – 1867 – painted overhead into a large quadrangle. In the centre of this there are three churches to the left and buildings to the right, which later I am able to identify as the library and a former refectory. All around there are stairways which presumably lead to the private apartments of the monks – this is an idiorrhythmic monastery. On the north side is the guesthouse. Although somewhat dilapidated in appearance, Iviron is certainly an impressive place.

By the time the *simantron* sounds for vespers I am fully rested and recovered from my walk along the cliffs and I decide to go into the church and see if I shall be allowed to stay for the office. There is no difficulty discovering which of the three churches is to be used. I join the monks there and happily none of them objects to my presence. At the end I join with them in venerating the icons. Afterwards the guesthouse opens and other visitors arrive. The guestmaster offers us an ouzo with turkish delight and water; doesn't ask for our *diamoneterion* but invites us very casually to enter the details ourselves in the guestbook, and then shows us to the dormitories. The toilet facilities are very primitive indeed.

Supper is at 5.00 p.m. and when all the visitors gather together we turn out to be a very motley group: a Greek Orthodox priest (who has spent eight years in Melbourne but speaks only very broken English) with a few of his parishioners, three Germans, two Austrians and an American from Cleveland who is Orthodox and can speak Greek. We are eating on our own in the guesthouse and not with the monks, presumably because in idiorrhythmic monasteries the monks do not eat together in a common refectory. The fare is barely tolerable, even with the glass of retsina which we have to wash it down, and I shall later have to dip into the provisions bought at Ouranoupolis. After supper I ask to be called at 5.00 a.m. in order to attend the later part of the morning office, and wander around outside again, chatting with some of the other guests. Before too long, however, I retire upstairs to the dormitory. There I read by lamplight and go over in memory the happy events of my visit last year to Georgia. And last thing before going to bed I review my plans for tomorrow. Dionisiou, which I am visiting next, is on the south side of the peninsula. To get there from Iviron which in on the north side I have to walk up to

Karies, the 'administrative capital', in time to catch the bus from Dafni where I can get a boat for Dionisiou. This means an early start tomorrow.

Iviron: Saturday

The church is all dark when I come down this morning but with the help of my torch I discover the Greeks and the American at the back and I sit with them until the chanting of the office is over. Neither they nor the monks resent my presence but I begin to wonder if this tolerance is due to conviction or to indifference. At 6.30 coffee is served in the guesthouse and we learn that later in the morning, because it is Saturday, there will be a bus to Karies. This is great news if it can be relied on; it saves me a two-hour uphill walk and it also gives me more time here at Iviron. I decide to risk it and wait for the bus and in the meantime to look around some more.

Four monks are in evidence around the guesthouse, two of them on the younger side, and while I wait I manage to engage one of these in conversation. He speaks English quite well, having spent five years in New York. Until fairly recently he has been a monk at Grigoriou but left it to come here because he found it too strict. In all, he tells me, there are fifteen monks at Iviron and 1867 – the date over the gate – is the date the monastery was rebuilt after one of the fires which seem to have destroyed almost every monastery on Mount Athos at one time or another. While I wait I also succeed in getting into the library. A monk carrying books appears in the quadrangle and allows me to accompany him. The library is well kept and includes among its treasures some relics of the Patriarch of Constantinople, Gregory V, who was hanged by the Turks in 1821. I also catch a glimpse of the monastery making its wine: a young monk in wellington boots stands in a barrel treading the grapes and keeping his balance by means of a rope hanging from a bar above. He is, of course, wearing his habit!

Dionisiou: Saturday

When the bus for Karies arrives about 10.30 I find that Tom is one of the passengers and, like long-lost friends, we exchange all our news. He is coming from the monastery of Philotheou and feels somewhat deflated. Not only was he not allowed to join the monks at prayer in the church but he couldn't join them for meals in the refectory either. Being an Orthodox aspirant he took this very hard, but for the monks he was still a heretic. Philotheou, he says, has only become coenobitic in recent years and is very strict. The number of monks rose from nine to ninety and has now dropped to forty but only because many have gone to strengthen other monasteries. Tom leaves the bus at Karies but I continue on down to the port of Dafni where I had arrived on Thursday. Here, with a number of other visitors, I take a small boat for Dionisiou which is further on along the coast in the opposite direction from Ouranoupolis. On the way we pass Grigoriou where I plan to stay tomorrow night.

The monastery of Dionisiou rises sheer out of the sea on top of a steep rock and makes a most impressive sight from the boat. It is only a short walk up from the harbour and, when we arrive, we are greeted by the guestmaster with a glass of ouzo as well as the usual turkish delight and water. He is careful, however, to ask us for our *diamoneterion* and to take down all our particulars before showing us to the dormitories. His English is quite good and I gather from him that there are some forty-five monks, that vespers will be at 9.00 p.m. (it is now 7.15 p.m. by the monastery time though only 1.15 p.m. by my watch) and that my presence would be tolerated in the porch of the church.

While waiting for vespers I stand out over the sea on one of the many balconies which project from the monastery walls and admire the splendid view. Then I go to the church. The resentment I had felt at Stavronikita has now given way to sadness and the sobering realisation that the Roman Catholic Church has much to regret and repent of in its relations with the Orthodox Church. I assist therefore at the office from the porch in a spirit of penance which a passing monk gauchely tries to improve by admonishing me for sitting with my legs crossed. Supper follows immediately but only for the monks. The guests eat separately and later. This seems to me perfectly logical because community meals in monasteries include prayer and spiritual reading. I do not therefore take it as hard as Tom did but it is pushing the policy of apartheid to an extreme. Supper when it comes is excellent and very welcome because I haven't really had a proper meal since lunch yesterday at 9.30 a.m. at Stavronikita. After supper I page through some of the English-language periodicals provided in the guesthouse. To my horror I read that ecumenism is 'a spiritual disease' ... 'totally alien to Orthodoxy', and that Patriarch Demetrious of Constantinople 'speaks the language of the ideology of freemasonry'. I go to bed with a heavy heart. The plan for tomorrow is to leave early to get the boat for Grigoriou.

Dionisiou: Saturday
The church is open and empty when I come down this morning at 6.00 a.m. Sitting in the porch in calmer mood I think further about the alienation which exists between Eastern and Western Christians; how appropriate it is that Roman Catholics do penance for our misdeeds, especially during the Crusades, and how inappropriate it would be for an Irishman to reproach the Orthodox for their long memories. As far as the monks of Mount Athos are concerned, it is quite disconcerting that their anti-ecumenism should be a feature not of a decadent but of a flourishing monasticism. Isolationism would appear to be one important factor. In any case, experience has shown that ecumenical prejudices anywhere can be softened only by contact with other Christians. But has the Roman Catholic Church in Greece the requisite resources? Promising myself to discuss this question with friends in Athens in the next few days, I hurry off down to the harbour to catch the boat which is due at 8.00 a.m.

Grigoriou: Sunday

It is only a short, twenty-minute run to the monastery of Grigoriou which is further back the coast in the direction of Dafni. On the way I remember the young Iviron monk who told me he had found it too strict here, but it can't, I tell myself, be any grimmer, ecumenically, than Dionisiou was. When we arrive at 8.45 a.m. we climb up the steps from the harbour, pass under a vine trellis in the monastery courtyard and find that the monks are just finishing lunch. Straightaway we are invited to 'second table' and while we eat, the refectory is being set for supper to the accompaniment of chanted prayers.

There is a long interval now between lunch and vespers but it gives me ample opportunity for looking around, for chatting with some of the guests and perhaps some of the monks and for quiet reflection. Besides, I have asked for an appointment with the Abbot to whom I bring greetings from Metropolitan Rodopoulos; it was he who recommended me to visit both Dionisiou and Grigoriou.

Later in the morning as I wander around I manage to engage one of the monks in conversation. As it happens he is an ex-Roman Catholic from Latin America who came in contact with Orthodoxy in Paris. He is adamant that Christian unity can be achieved only by repentance and a return to the common faith of the first millennium, i.e. only in the Orthodox Church. He considers joint prayer, even the recitation of the Our Father, to be impossible because our classical differences in trinitarian theology mean that our notion of God the Father is quite different. He thinks that Western Christianity has been corrupted by rationalism and materialism.

In the course of the afternoon I reflect that Mount Athos, although a very beautiful and interesting place, is only for the robust – physically, spiritually and ecumenically. The monks are concerned to keep mere tourists out and I share their concern. Despite their precautions, however, too many visitors seem to have too little real interest in religion. As a result Christianity and monasticism suffer from their association here with religious intolerance – and with primitive plumbing. I share this reflection with one of my fellow-visitors and Dominique agrees with me. He is a university student, French and Roman Catholic. He regrets in particular that the monasteries of Mount Athos, unlike Taizé and other places in Europe, do so little to help the faith of their visitors.

After vespers, during which I sit in the porch of the church, the Abbot receives me. He is very hospitable – I am offered a fig and a coffee – but also very firm. He is happy with the development of monasticism on Mount Athos and thinks that the few remaining idiorrhythmic monasteries will have become coenobitic in five or six years' time. He is less than happy about the development of ecumenism in the Orthodox Church. He emphasises that he is not opposed to all dialogue but only to that form of dialogue which encourages common prayer and the kiss of peace. What is needed in his view is that Roman Catholics – and other Western Christians – repent of their errors, be baptised (*sic*) and so restored to the unity of the Church.

Supper follows immediately on this sobering, chilling conversation and the Abbot conducts me very graciously to the refectory where we guests are allowed to eat at the same time as the monks. Afterwards I retire at once to the dormitory. Today's conversations have done no more than put in words what was otherwise conveyed at Dionisiou and also at Stavronikita. But the words none the less have had a shattering effect, all the worse because of the Abbot's exquisite courtesy and because he is quite obviously a deeply religious man.

Grigoriou: Monday

Before taking the boat this morning, my last on Mount Athos, I spend some time again in the porch of the Grigoriou church reflecting on the experiences of the last few days. For myself I am happy and grateful to have had these experiences, however painful and penitential. But Pope John Paul's visit to Constantinople last

December comes to mind and the hope he expressed there and then that the end of the second and the beginning of the third millennium would bring unity between Catholics and Orthodox.

How, I ask myself, can Christian unity ever become a reality by the year 2000 if Orthodox attitudes are as negative as I have been finding them here on Mount Athos? This, I see, is another question I must discuss tomorrow in Salonica. It is time now to take my departure so I venerate the icons – regretting once again my failure to do so at Stavronikita – and walk down to the harbour to catch the boat, first for Dafni and then for Ouranoupolis.

Salonica: Monday
For some strange reason there is the formality of a customs check at Dafni before you leave the Holy Mountain but I am carrying no stolen icons or anything else of an incriminating nature. In conversation on board with other passengers it emerges that not all the monasteries are rigid in the matter of joint worship. The pattern in idiorrhythmic monasteries, in particular in the three non-Greek monasteries, seems to be more relaxed and much as I had experienced it myself at Iviron, but whether from conviction or indifference remains unclear. One of the passengers with whom I chat has left his car at Ouranoupolis and he very kindly offers me a lift to Salonica, which I gladly accept. Hugh Leonard's *Da* is no longer playing but I stroll along the seafront from Aristotle Square to the White Tower and watch the sun go down, and the thought suddenly strikes me that monks of course, engaging in dialogue on the subject of monasticism, would be the most appropriate to improve relations with Mount Athos.

Athens: Tuesday
Before leaving Salonica today I have appointments at the University with Metropolitan Rodopoulos and Professor Kalogirou of the Theology Department. They both assure me that Greek Orthodox

attitudes in general are not as negative as those of Mount Athos. On the other hand I also gather that they would not consider 'unity by 2000' to be a very realistic objective. My Roman Catholic friends in Athens with whom I discuss the matter this evening show me the text of a special statement on 'Dialogue with Roman Catholics' issued last April by the Abbots of Mount Athos. It is more outspoken, perhaps, than was Abbot Grigoriou in conversation, but otherwise no different. They admit that people in general are not as extremist in their attitudes as the monks of Mount Athos are, but they insist that anti-ecumenical and anti-Roman Catholic prejudice is widespread and deeply ingrained and must be taken very seriously. They agree that such prejudice can be overcome only by contact and co-operation, by what Pope John Paul at Constantinople called 'the dialogue of charity'. They also agree that, as far as Mount Athos is concerned, Latin Rite religious and monks would be the most appropriate partners in the dialogue of charity. They very much doubt, however, that the Roman Catholic Church in Greece has by itself the resources to cope at any level with this challenge. The prospect may not be very encouraging but, as I prepare to leave Greece tomorrow, the phrase in the gospels about 'the faith that can move mountains' keeps coming to my mind. This gives me renewed hope. If there is a Christian faith that can move mountains, there is also an ecumenical faith that can move even the Holy Mountain of Mount Athos, especially on the eve of the third Christian millennium.[1]

CHINA

There is continuing anxiety about the divisions within the Catholic Church in China between, on the one hand, the bishops recognised by Rome but not by the Government – 'the underground Church' – and on the other hand those who, accepting State registration, are recognised by the Government but not by Rome – 'the official Church'.[2] There is a new fear that these divisions may spread to Hong Kong as a result of its return to the jurisdiction of Beijing. This anxiety and this fear give an added interest to the following account of the religious impressions left by a 1981 visit to China. But what I wrote then seems only all the more true now:

> The 'great new fact' which I experienced is that, after a cruel winter of hardship and suffering, spring is quite definitely in the air again for Christianity in China.[3]

Pre-Vatican II Liturgy

On each of my three mornings in Beijing I went out by myself to early Mass at the Nan Tang, the seventeenth-century Jesuit church, the Cathedral of the Immaculate Conception, which has been open again since 1971. On the first morning, 18 March, I found to my great surprise that a solemn Requiem Mass in Latin, according to the Tridentine Rite, was taking place with a congregation of about five hundred for Bishop Francis X. Zhao SJ of Xianxian who had died in prison in 1968, having consecrated six other bishops. The celebrant was Bishop Joseph Zong Huaide of Jinan, president of the Chinese Catholic Patriotic Association. The absolution at the catafalque was given by Bishop Michael Fu Tieshan of Beijing.

On the second morning, the feast of St Joseph, there was a congregation of about two hundred who recited prayers in Chinese, according to local custom, all during the Mass which of course was again celebrated in Latin and according to the Tridentine Rite. The third morning was not a special occasion and the numbers were down to about eighty. On this, as on the previous day, Mass was celebrated successively at the high altar from 5.30 to 7.00 a.m. and there were also some Masses at one of the side altars.

These three early morning Masses were a pure pre-Vatican II experience. It was very moving to hear once again the chants of the Requiem, to see the altar-servers go up at the elevation and hold the corners of the celebrant's chasuble, and to end Mass with 'the last gospel', the reading of the Prologue from St John. I was impressed by the fact that a good half of the congregation each morning were men of all ages and that the leader of the prayers was also a man, but young people in their teens were conspicuous by their absence. I was told later in Hong Kong that a government regulation prohibits preaching and the administration of baptism to those under eighteen.

Tomb of Matteo Ricci

While in Beijing I also succeeded in visiting the tomb of the famous Jesuit missionary, Matteo Ricci, the fourth centenary of whose arrival in China would take place the following year. The property in which the tomb is located formerly belonged to the Jesuits and then to the Vincentians. It is now in the hands of the Beijing municipality which uses it to run a school for cadres, or party leaders. A visit to the tomb therefore requires a special permit which the Irish ambassador kindly obtained for me. To the right of Ricci is Ferdinand Verbiest, to his left is Adam Schall, both companions of his. In front of each is a large impressive stele with an inscription in Latin and Chinese. All three are enclosed in a small plot surrounded by a railing and there is now no sign of any other grave. The first blossoms I saw in China were in these grounds, near this little cemetery. I prayed that a second spring was beginning for the Chinese Christianity which these great missionaries had done so much to promote.

Apart from these visits, my stay in Beijing was spent sightseeing – the Forbidden City, The Temple of Heaven, the Great Wall and the tombs of the Ming Dynasty. By a happy coincidence the Ming tomb which we were brought to visit was that of Wan Li (1573-1619), the emperor who had welcomed Ricci. I did not manage to visit the Dong Tang (St Joseph's), the second Catholic church which was then open in Beijing.

Xian
From Beijing our group flew about 550 miles south-west to Xian and stayed there three nights. Xian is one of China's ancient capitals and is associated specially with the Tang dynasty (618-906 CE), considered to be one of the greatest periods in Chinese history. Its achievements include not only the first newspaper and the first true porcelain, exclusively white, but also the creation of the examination system as a means of entering the imperial civil service. Xian is perhaps best known today as the place where Chiang Kai Shek was kidnapped in 1946 and for the archaeological finds of the 1950s and 1970s – a six-thousand-year-old neolithic village and the thousands of clay figures of soldiers and horses found in the tomb of the first emperor of a unified China (246-210 BCE). In the days of the Tang dynasty, Xian was the beginning – or end – of the silk route, and China at that time, it is said, was more open than in the following thousand years. In 1981 foreigners in Xian were an unusual sight, and we attracted enormous attention, but according to the local tourist literature 'thousands of foreign diplomatic envoys, students, clergymen and merchants' lived there under the Tang. These of course included Christians.

Nestorian stele
The coming of Christianity to China in 635 and the welcome it received is recorded on a famous stele carved in 781 which can be seen today in the Shaanxi Historical Museum at Xian.[4] Unfortunately this Nestorian Christianity for which there is today a new sympathy[5] was suppressed by imperial edict in 845 but did not altogether disappear. According to Latourette the

marvel is that it survived so long, for two centuries and a half, in what was then 'the mightiest empire on earth', with 'Buddhism at the acme of its vigour'.[6] It is salutary to stand by the nine-foot monument of black limestone and to reflect that Christianity, although, like Buddhism, foreign in origin, has never succeeded in becoming a popular religion in China as Buddhism did.

I was told in Beijing that a Catholic church was open in Xian. On my return to Hong Kong I was able to confirm this information; the cathedral, I gathered, had been open since the previous Christmas with three priests serving it, one of whom is not a member of the Patriotic Association. During my stay in Xian, however, to my great disappointment I was unable to locate this church. The only reward I had for my efforts was an invitation to his home for an evening meal from a friendly young student who tried to help me. The fact that he and his family felt free to welcome me in this way seemed to be a good indication of the new relaxed atmosphere in China today.

China's Muslims

Our stay in Xian ended with a visit to the Great Mosque which dates from 742. There are fourteen mosques in Xian for some sixty thousand Muslims. In the country as a whole the number of Muslims is estimated to be between ten and fifty million. They belong to ten different national minorities and are concentrated in western areas: Qinghai, Ningxia, Gansu. During the cultural revolution the Great Mosque in Xian was closed for a year. Muslims in China appear to many to be receiving especially favourable treatment.

From Xian we went due east on a seven-and-a-half-hour train journey to Loyang, another ancient capital and now a centre of heavy industry. During a short stay we spent a whole morning visiting some of the Lungmen Grottoes which are of great artistic and religious interest. In all there are over a thousand grottoes and some hundred thousand statues of the Buddha, ranging in size from over one inch to fifty-seven feet. They belong to the four-hundred-year period from AD 494 to the end of the Tang dynasty during which the notorious Empress Wu was a great supporter of Buddhism.

Shanghai and Canton
From Luoyang another train journey of over fourteen hours took us to Shanghai which, in the old pre-World War II days, was such an important colonial and Christian centre. Today the concessions belonging to the Western powers have disappeared and Christianity is emerging from the catacombs. During our few days I saw crucifixes and statues of Madonna and Child on sale at the railway station and I attended Mass one morning early in the cathedral at Xujiahui. As in Beijing there was a succession of Masses from 5.30 to 7.00 a.m., with a congregation of about eighty who seemed, however, to be more elderly and female than the Beijing congregation. It was an ordinary weekday, of course. I gathered that about a thousand go to Mass on Sundays, that seventeen young people were baptised the previous Christmas and that a Catholic church outside Shanghai reopened at the end of 1980. I also gathered that there were five Protestant churches open, and that these held eleven services at weekends attended by some fifteen thousand worshippers, about a quarter of whom were young people.

Our twelve-day trip to China ended with a one-night stay in Canton, whose Catholic bishop Dominic Tang Yee-ming (Deng Yiming) SJ, released from prison a short time previously, but not a member of the Patriotic Association, was very much in the news at the time. Unfortunately, I was able to admire the magnificent cathedral only from the outside because we were leaving early and it did not open until 7.00 a.m. My taxi driver, however, smiled, said 'Amen' and blessed himself.

The Patriotic Association
While in China I had lengthy conversations – in English, French and Latin – with five Catholic priests, two of whom were not members of the Patriotic Association. I had a formal interview with the help of an interpreter with the general secretary and deputy general secretary of the Patriotic Association. I also met officials of the Protestant Three-Self Movement. While in Hong Kong I had numerous conversations about China with people of quite different background, competence and viewpoint.

For their part, members of the Patriotic Association make the following points:
1. They state that no change of doctrine has taken place in the Catholic Church in China.
2. They stress that responsibility for the present estrangement between Rome and themselves lies with Rome: by refusing to approve their episcopal consecrations since 1958 the Vatican showed no understanding of their extreme situation; by forbidding them to co-operate in any way with their government, the Vatican forbade them, in effect, to love their country.
3. They are happy that the Vatican has now changed its mind and allows Catholics to be patriotic. They go on to add, however, that these words must now be followed by appropriate deeds.
4. They look forward to the normalisation of relations between themselves and the Pope and between the Vatican and their government. They resent the Vatican's present diplomatic relations with Taiwan, stressing that the Vatican is now the only state in Europe to recognise Taiwan.
5. They also resent the circulation in China of a Vatican document listing in Latin and Chinese various permissions granted by Rome to priests and faithful in China. They see this as divisive, as calling on the priests and people who are not

members of the Patriotic Association to worship apart and in secret.

6. They are emphatic that the Catholic Church in China is not under government control. They explain that the Church is ruled by the Episcopal Conference and the Church Affairs Committee; that the role of the Patriotic Association, membership of which is voluntary, is to act as a bridge between Church and State; helping Catholics to be patriotic and to promote the four modernisations (agriculture, industry, defence, science and technology) and helping the government to know and understand the Church's viewpoint.

Attitudes towards the Patriotic Association
Among those who are not members of the Patriotic Association a more sympathetic and nuanced attitude towards the Association and its members is now emerging. The following points in particular struck me:

1. There is a new willingness to admit that in the past the Church was too closely associated with the colonial powers and that (in the words of the late Bishop Francis Hsu of Hong Kong, which someone quoted for me from an address given in 1968) 'the Church failed to make its message intelligible and obviously relevant', that it was 'a powerless, helpless spectator' in the 'phase of soul-searching agony' which China went through 'between the surge of rational, national renewal in 1919, and the Communist conquest of power in 1949'.

2. There is a new openness, a new readiness to listen to and to learn from the members of the Association. The mood is one, not of condemnation as before, but of understanding. As Pope John Paul II put it at Manila in February 1981:

> For many years we have not been able to have contact with each other .... But in those long years you have undoubtedly lived through other experiences which are still unknown, and at times you will have wondered in your

consciences what was the right thing for you to do. For those who have never had such experiences it is difficult to appreciate fully such situations.[7]

3. There is a new willingness to admit that, for all the Association's ambiguities, many of its members are good Catholics who have also suffered for the faith and who continue to believe at heart in the importance of communion with the Pope.

4. Whereas it was quite usual previously to refer to the Patriotic priests and people as 'the Patriotic Church' and to pray, at Benediction for instance, 'for those who have joined the Patriotic Church but who now repent and seek the way back to the fold', there is now a new sensitivity to the implications of this terminology as promoting schismatic attitudes and actions and a new determination to avoid it altogether.

5. There is a more sophisticated theology of the papacy and a new realisation that ecclesiastical 'self-government, self-support, self-propagation' ('independence, autonomy and self-rule') is not incompatible with papal primacy and full communion with the Holy See.

CONCLUSION

It only remains to add that those who are beginning to be more open in their attitude to the Patriotic Association and its members are growing in number, though they still have questions especially about the government's role in Church affairs and about the Association's analysis and interpretation of events. Pope John Paul, in a special message on 3 December 1996 to the Bishops of China, addressed them according to Vatican II terminology as 'vicars and ambassadors of Christ', thereby reminding the Chinese political authorities that the bishops were not the Pope's 'vicars and ambassadors'. The Pope urged the bishops to recognise that they 'are called today, in a particular way, to express and promote full reconciliation between all the faithful' and to make this their special contribution for the celebration of the year 2000.[8] Already more than half of the so-called 'official' bishops have secretly been reconciled to the Pope and the new Coadjutor Bishop of Hong Kong, who knows the religious situation on the mainland very well, has not hesitated to state: 'I am optimistic about the future of the Church in Hong Kong and in China.'[9]

Many, however, still remain hesitant and negative, all the more so in some cases because of the Pope's creation of a third category of Catholic Bishop: those recognised both by Rome and by the government. The new thinking is resented and resisted, the new political and religious situation arouses fears and anxieties, especially but very understandably among those who suffered in Communist China and fled and now fear a repetition of the persecution in Hong Kong. A Roman Catholic ecumenist cannot help recalling that the situation was somewhat the same when Catholics began to be more sympathetic in their attitude to Protestantism and to Protestants. Ecumenism is basically a methodology which, *mutatis mutandis,* can be applied in any case of estrangement. Its relevance to China today is perhaps what strikes me most forcibly. More 'contact, conversation and cooperation' are required between the underground and the official bishops of the Catholic Church if the new millennium is indeed to usher in a second spring.[10]

18
An Ecumenical Community: The Origins of the Columbanus Community of Reconciliation

The ecumenical movement owes a considerable debt to those communities which have reconciliation in religion and society as their special purpose and which are associated with, among other places, Taizé in France, Iona in Scotland and Corrymeela in Ireland. Columbanus in Belfast is a fairly recent addition to the family of these communities of reconciliation and this chapter tells the story of its origins.

India 1981
Where and when did the idea of the Columbanus Community first come to mind? The place was in India but had Irish links: the little village of Sitagarha near Hazaribag where the Church of Ireland's Dublin University Mission to Chota Nagpur had once been at work, leaving behind such monuments as St Columba's Hospital and St Columba's College. The date was Tuesday, 18 February 1981, in the middle of a thirty-day retreat which was part of the sabbatical I was enjoying at the end of my ten years as Director of the Irish School of Ecumenics.[1]

But was this the first time the idea came to mind? I thought so for over a year, until April 1982. During a visit to Germany early that month it was brought to my attention by Br Matthias of the Jesus-Bruderschaft (a religious community of the German Evangelical Church) at Gnadenthal near Frankfurt, that in the last chapter and last paragraph of *Irish Anglicanism* I had *already* looked forward to the establishment of 'a religious community adapted to the needs of our day and country: an interdenominational brotherhood of reconciliation in the spirit if not in the form of the well-known foundation at Taizé'. That piece had been written in the summer of 1969 during the final stages of the editing of the volume of essays I was preparing for the centenary of the disestablishment of the Church of Ireland in April 1970.[2] In a letter of 4 May 1982 to Archbishop Armstrong, Church of Ireland Primate, I referred to the 1969 paragraph as 'a staggering discovery',[3] which it truly was. Twelve years later, as my retreat notes show, I was still thinking of an Irish Taizé; what was new was the precise location: 'in NI', in Northern Ireland. Meantime, however, the idea had gone completely out of my mind, suppressed presumably in the storm and stress of the founding and first decade of the School of Ecumenics.

I sometimes ask myself what brought the idea to the surface again. The peace of the long retreat when I ceased to be 'careful and troubled about many things' and was trying to concentrate on the one thing necessary will have helped. Perhaps my visit just before the retreat to the celibate Anglican community, the Brotherhood of the Ascended Christ, of the Cambridge Mission to Delhi, and my subsequent visit to the similar community of the Oxford Mission to Calcutta will also have helped. I had always felt that religious congregations had a special responsibility to be promoters of Christian unity, and in an article in *Doctrine and Life* for January 1980,[4] I was happy to be able to quote Pope John Paul to that effect. Addressing 'a group of Superiors General of non-Catholic religious orders of men and women' he had stated:

> Who more than religious should experience in prayer the urgency, not only of manifesting unity but also of living it in the fullness of truth and charity?... Are religious not called in a special way to give expression to the yearning of Christians that the ecumenical dialogue – which by its

nature is temporary – should be brought to term in that full ecclesial fellowship which is 'with the Father and with his Son Jesus Christ' (1 Jn 1:3)? Should religious not be the first to pledge the fullness of their generosity before God's salvific plan, each one repeating with St Paul: 'What am I to do, Lord?' (Ac 22: 10).

If that is so and if one of the basic insights of the ecumenical movement is that the Churches should do everything together as far as conscience permits, then an attempt by a religious to start some sort of an interdenominational residential community can only seem entirely logical and no way surprising.

Initial moves

As soon as my long retreat was over, on 9 March 1981, I wrote for advice to a number of Jesuit friends as follows:

> The favour I'm asking is your advice. During this year, as you know, I've been exploring job opportunities and as a result I now have a proposal for the Provincial which basically suggests that I start teaching in Africa from next January.
>
> At the last moment, however, a complication has arisen in the shape of a completely new idea which leaves me confused. At times I think I could carry it off; at other times I have grave doubts. The idea is this: that I try to establish in Northern Ireland a sort of Irish Taizé: an interdenominational religious community of men devoted to the promotion of peace and unity but with the whole wide world as their parish. The community would be a cross between a Benedictine monastery and a Jesuit house. As at Taizé, prayer and liturgical prayer would be very important but the community (mostly graduates? mostly non-ordained?) would disperse for apostolic work of the type which the School of Ecumenics thinks its graduates should do.

So my question is: can I now (having talked to you about it) safely put this idea out of my head as a distraction and temptation? Or might there be something in it really so that I ought to explore it further? If so, what sort of further exploration would you suggest?

Some of the replies to this letter were quite negative: 'Africa has greater needs than Ireland'; 'your field is academic'. And when I came back to Ireland in June I did so not just with a general suggestion that I teach theology in Africa but with a definite invitation to join the staff of the new Catholic Institute of West Africa in Port Harcourt, which was to open in October and where I had visited and been interviewed on my way home. On the other hand the idea of an Irish Taizé had grown on me, and I also came back with a more definite wish to get involved in starting such a venture – and with a clearer outline of what shape it might take and how it might become a reality. This I had elaborated in fifteen points during Holy Week in Nairobi. The projected community had a title: 'Brothers of Unity and Peace' (BUP). It was to be

> an interdenominational male religious community, based in Northern Ireland, devoted to prayer and work for unity and peace. It would be sponsored by the Jesuit Order in collaboration with (a) the Taizé Brothers, and (b) an Anglican religious order of men. A fourth, Orthodox, sponsor [I noted – remembering, no doubt, my visit to Mount Athos the previous 5 September[5]] would be ideal but seems impractical. The initial core group of ten to twelve members will be sought among the three sponsoring agencies. What precise forms of work for unity and peace (in addition to prayer) BUP undertakes will depend on the competence of the members and on the needs of the situation and the moment. BUP, although fully integrated in NI, will have the whole wide world as its parish. A trust

will be set up to support the work of BUP, the terms of the trust and the appointment of trustees to be agreed by the sponsors; the BUP community will live on alms and earnings.

What I proposed then to my Provincial, Father Joseph Dargan SJ, when I met him on Wednesday, 8 July 1981, was at least to postpone taking up the Port Harcourt post and to undertake a feasibility study about my Northern Ireland dream. He agreed and asked for a report by Easter 1982.

Soundings

What happened next was a series of interviews which can be summed up as follows: twenty-four interviews with Anglican bishops, religious communities and agencies in Canada, England, Ireland and Scotland; four with communities and leaders in the German Evangelical Church; four with individuals and clergy groups of English and Irish Methodists; fifteen interviews with Presbyterian leaders and groups in France, Ireland and Scotland (including Taizé, Corrymeela and Iona); and thirty-five with Roman Catholic bishops, groups, communities and official bodies, directly in England, Ireland and Rome, and by correspondence with religious in Canada, the USA, Germany and Holland. There was also time spent with an *ad hoc* inter-Church group of clergy in Belfast on three occasions in the spring of 1982.

This list is certainly impressive; in retrospect I can only admire and envy the zeal and energy it demonstrates. During those six months, from autumn 1981 to Easter 1982, I was living in the Jesuit community at Milltown Park. I was also a member of a small Jesuit group with a particular interest in Northern Ireland affairs, whose encouragement and advice was of crucial importance and to whom I reported regularly. In addition I had the help in Belfast of a devoted Church of Ireland friend, Doreen

Freer, who acted as my PA, so to speak, and as Honorary Secretary to the project. Her home and time and phone and car were at my entire disposal. She arranged Belfast appointments for me, met me at Central Station, drove me round, gave me overnight accommodation, and when a small bequest came her way, she insisted on sending a cheque for £1,000, the very first financial contribution which the project received. My aim in these months was to meet people of influence and authority in all the Irish Churches, to share my vision with them and to listen to their reactions; in particular to make contact with the religious communities in the Anglican, Lutheran and Reformed/Presbyterian traditions, to visit as many of them as possible and to enlist their support. The fact that I had been deeply involved in ecumenical work all during the previous two decades quite clearly made an immense difference during this period. I already had many friends and acquaintances in all the Churches and not only in Ireland, and the Roman Catholic bishops no longer seemed as uneasy about me as they had been in the years after the 1973 International Consultation on Mixed Marriage. The general reaction in fact was, to my surprise, quite positive, so much so that I became concerned and would often ask myself: 'Are they being honest with me or just being nice to me?' But the sympathy and support was quite sincere, owing much to the heightened sense of need which the worsening situation in Northern Ireland was arousing.

When Easter came my report to the Provincial was low-key. It began by stating that 'the study is inconclusive – for lack of sufficient time', but went on to list four positive results: (a) the climate of tolerance and prayerful support for the venture has emerged as reasonably satisfactory; in particular the Church of Ireland House of Bishops has written to say it would have their 'sympathetic encouragement'; (b) the shape of the proposed community has become clearer; (c) three men (2 RC religious; 1 Presbyterian layman) and three women (2 RC laywomen; 1 C of E religious) have come forward and shown interest in membership; (d) a gift of £1,000 has been received from a Belfast widow. Feasibility, however, the report continued, 'stands or falls on the emergence, after appropriate assessment, of suitable candidates. On this test the study, with its given deadline, is negative.' The report ended by recommending that the study be continued until Christmas and the Provincial accepted this. The study had so far cost him £2,300, not including my living expenses.

Emerging shape
In what ways had 'the shape of the proposed community' become clearer during the preceding six months? A number of significant changes had taken place. It had ceased to be an all-male community and this I attribute to the influence of Sr Benvenuta OP (Sr Margaret MacCurtain) with whom I had talked in August. Membership had become temporary, and the seed for this change was sown by Reverend Dr Robin Boyd, who had succeeded me as Director of the School of Ecumenics and who had pointed out that temporary celibacy had often been undertaken by Protestants for the sake of their evangelistic and missionary work. Temporary membership, I could also see, would facilitate Catholics as well as Protestants. I remembered an article in *Doctrine and Life* by Father Joe Dunn, regretting that it was impossible, in principle, to join a religious congregation for a limited number of years. Thirdly, membership was now open to married couples and this change was owing to the advice of Reverend Dr Eric Gallagher. In a letter of 18 October, after a meeting of Methodists at which this point had been raised, he wrote:

> I could envisage such folk playing a most useful and meaningful role. *Inter alia* they could bring an element of life-experience that might otherwise be absent. In addition they might well be able to make a financial commitment younger members could not manage.

Fourthly, the triple sponsorship of the Nairobi Holy Week document has disappeared: Taizé could not see its way to being involved, and among Anglican religious the women were showing more interest than the men. Fifthly and finally, justice had joined unity and peace as an aim to be promoted by the new community, an emphasis owing to my Jesuit brethren. One change, however, that was mooted without success was to locate the community not in Northern Ireland but in Glencree, County Wicklow: the vision of 1981, unlike that of 1969, was firmly earthed in Northern Ireland.

Between Easter and summer of 1982 my main concern was how to publicise the proposed community in order to see if there were or would be vocations. I had already prepared a short article for publication but my Jesuit brethren thought it too vigorous and forthright. In its place I then proceeded to prepare a leaflet. The files contain a Draft I (13 March), a Draft IA (no date), a Draft II (no date), a Draft III (3 May), a Draft IV (no date) and the final printed version which was available in the early summer. Each draft was submitted to a number of individual friends and to an inter-Church group which met in Belfast on 10 and 26 March and on 29 April. This consisted of Reverend Dr Eric Gallagher (Methodist), Very Reverend Tom Patterson (Presbyterian), Reverend Canon Edgar Turner (Church of Ireland) and myself. The process was a lengthy one and Doreen Freer was getting impatient. On 7 May she wrote to say that 'It's time, I would hold, to move on to the next stage; otherwise you could go on revising for ever'. And on 16 May she wrote: 'You will have to be "bloody, bold and resolute" with all amenders of Draft IV, or draft-making is going to become an end in itself.' But good will and support were evident, and progress, I found myself writing on 4 May to Archbishop Armstrong, 'is surprisingly – and frighteningly – good'.

What changes were made? A question-and-answer format was adopted at the suggestion of Dr Eric Gallagher. The sub-title, which was at first 'A Northern Ireland Proposal', became in Draft III 'An Irish Inter-Church Proposal'. Columbanus, described in the earlier drafts as a 'monk', becomes a 'missionary' in the final version. 'Prayer and work for unity, justice and peace' becomes eventually 'prayer and work for unity in the Church, justice in society and peace on earth', in order to avoid any possible political misinterpretation. And 'alms' in Draft I became 'gifts' in Draft IA. In addition the length of a member's stay in the community changes from 'at least three to five years' in the first drafts to 'at least three years' in the fourth version. The patrons under whose auspices the Community would exist began as 'four individuals' unofficially representing the main Churches, but ended up in the final version as simply 'a number of such individuals'; it was eventually agreed that there should be six: three Roman Catholic, three non-Roman Catholic.

Name

Naming the Community after Columbanus was a suggestion of my own. Columbanus was the sixth-century Irish missionary, younger contemporary of Columba of Derry and Iona, who set sail from his monastery at Bangor (County Down) and established religious communities in Luxeuil (France) and Bobbio (Italy). The name doesn't occur in the article mentioned above but Draft I of the leaflet is entitled 'The Columban Community of Reconciliation'. This led to much discussion. Was one form of the name, Columban, more Catholic and the other, Columbanus, more Protestant in usage? It emerged that the Church of Ireland did have a St Columbanus parish in the diocese of Down, but the Sisters of Mercy also had a St Columbanus Home in Helen's Bay. And there could be no doubt that the Knights of Columbanus were Roman Catholic. On the other hand, Columban was the form consistently used by the Church of Scotland editor of the saint's works.[6] But the Roman Catholic missionaries who had taken his name also called themselves Columban Fathers and Columban Sisters. There was the added difficulty that Columban was the adjectival form of Columba of Derry and that the Iona Community in Scotland was forming 'Columban Houses' in Glasgow and elsewhere in his memory. And what would the Columban Fathers, the Missionary Society of St Columban, think? Perhaps, it was suggested, they might be offended if we took the name Columban. When consulted, they did feel there might be confusion between them and us if we too used the form Columban. So it was that we eventually opted for Columbanus.

But from whom was the proposal for this Columbanus Community coming? Where and to whom should an interested person write? Corrymeela and its Leader at the time, Reverend Dr John Morrow, who had already shown a positive interest and invited me to share my vision at the Community Members' weekend in April, readily agreed that we might use their Upper Crescent address in Belfast. Two names, it was suggested, should be given from each of the four main Churches. So it was that, in the final version of the leaflet, Reverend David Lapsley appeared with Dr Patterson, Canon Leckey with Canon Turner, Reverend Dr Norman Taggart with Reverend Dr Eric Gallagher, and Father George Wadding CSsR with myself as 'sponsors' of the proposal. These eight individuals were clearly not 'sponsors' in the sense of my Nairobi document. Their principal role was to facilitate the establishment of the Community. Draft I of the leaflet describes them as 'the members of an unofficial inter-Church committee interested in promoting the venture'. In discussion, a preference was expressed for the word 'group' instead of 'committee'. Subsequent drafts relegated their names to the end of the leaflet in answer to the question: 'To whom should those interested in this proposal write?' In the fourth version their names appear early on in answer to the question: 'Who are sponsoring the proposal?' The question in the final version is just the one word 'Sponsors?' No ongoing role for the Sponsors was explicitly envisaged. But, if their vocation was somewhat like that of John the Baptist, happily they did not, like him, 'decrease', much less disappear. The Sponsors still exist as advisers who meet regularly, three times a year, with the whole Community and who provide an invaluable ministry of encouragement, support and ideas.

Publicity
The aim of the leaflet which was available by June was to publicise the proposal in order to discover by Christmas how many, if any, might be interested in joining. Some friends, however, felt quite hesitant about such publicity as involving 'a considerable risk that the notion will attract hostile comment from the extreme right in Catholic and Protestant Churches'. But Bishop Brendan Comiskey was more positive. In a letter of 31 March he wrote:

> With regard to the media, it is difficult to know whether to let them find out for themselves or whether to take the initiative and let them know what you intend. Somehow or other, in a venture of this nature, I would enlist their good will and support by choosing when and where you or some of the other people involved might be interviewed.

Following this advice – and remembering what St Paul says in Romans 10:14 – an approach was made to Trevor Williams (now Leader of the Corrymeela Community) of the BBC radio programme *Sunday Sequence*. He agreed to broadcast an interview with me about the proposal on 26 September. A press release embargoed for that date was then prepared and in due course distributed to the media, and every opportunity was taken during the summer months to circulate the leaflet as widely as possible. One of the friends to whom I sent it was Archbishop Little of Melbourne. When replying on 23 July he wrote:

> I shall ask the Editor of our Catholic journal, *The Advocate*, to publish something about the Columbanus Community

of Reconciliation. I am sure that there is a vocation somewhere in this city. It would be wonderful if we could have someone from Australia in the foundation community.

The Archbishop was right. There was someone in Melbourne who had a vocation and he was a diocesan priest. When Malcolm Crawford read the *Advocate* piece he got in touch and came on a preliminary visit in April. But this is to anticipate.

Between September and Christmas there were about twenty-six pieces of coverage of the project on radio, television and in various newspapers, secular and religious, mainly in Ireland, but also in some English newspapers and on Vatican Radio. A letter to Cardinal Ó Fiaich gives a first analysis of the results as follows:

> There has been a fair amount of publicity since late September. As a result we have had 64 enquiries and no negative reactions. Of the 64, 32 were men, 32 women; 37 RC, 20 Anglican, 6 Presbyterian and 1 Methodist; 26 from the North, 20 from the South, 18 from elsewhere (mostly England but one from a young Irishman in Thailand).
>
> Of these 64, 14 at least are possible candidates: 4 men, 10 women; 9 RC, 3 Anglicans, 2 Presbyterians – I say 'at least' because 11 new contacts (included in my '64') turned up at Corrymeela House on 7 December as a result of our advertisement in the *Belfast Telegraph,* but we don't know yet how these 11 will develop. I am hoping that assessment of candidates can begin in the New Year and interviewing take place in the week beginning 6 February.

There had been both an afternoon and an evening meeting at Corrymeela House on 7 December. These meetings were planned as a sort of climax to the publicity efforts of the previous months. A poster with the same text as the *Belfast Telegraph* advertisement of 3 December had been circulated. It began with the question: 'Is reconciliation a priority for you?' and continued:

> Would you join a residential community of Roman Catholics and Protestants committed to prayer, reflection and work for reconciliation?

If the reader reacted positively to this, he or she was then invited to come and meet the Sponsors of the Columbanus Community on 7 December at Corrymeela House in Belfast. People aged between twenty-five and forty-five were especially welcomed. Granted the precise nature of the invitation, the response was more gratifying than disappointing and in the event one of these eleven was to become a founding member. I was unable to be present myself because of a cold but most of the other Sponsors were in attendance with the faithful Honorary Secretary who drew up a detailed report for me written in her own hand.

Membership

Events did not subsequently move as quickly as I had hoped in my letter to Cardinal Ó Fiaich. Some of the 'possibles' I already knew quite well, but it took more time than I anticipated to make contact with all the 'possibles' to see if they were ready to accept the application form which we had devised. Twelve emerged from this process as 'probables'. It remained then to arrange interviews for them with the Sponsors and with Dr Mary Darby, a consultant psychiatrist who had kindly agreed to help. The interviewing, with Dr Patterson as Chairman, took place eventually in two sessions: the first in Dublin at Milltown Park on Monday, 28 February 1983, the second in Belfast at Doreen Freer's home on Saturday, 3 March. As a result of the interviews it was reluctantly but unanimously agreed that it would be best to advise three of the 'probables' to withdraw and not to proceed any further. Eight were accepted as 'novices' so to speak, to begin a six-month period of spiritual preparation. In April a ninth, Malcolm Crawford, was accepted. He had been interviewed during his preliminary visit which lasted from 13 to 26 April.

The period of spiritual preparation consisted chiefly of four meetings. The first, attended by all nine novices, was a long residential weekend at Milltown Park, from Thursday 21 April to Monday 25 April, with Father Myles O'Reilly SJ as director and facilitator. It was not a retreat in any conventional sense. It did, of course, include time for prayer together and in private but the emphasis was on exercises designed to help us to get to know each other in some depth. This did reveal a serious incompatibility between two of us and afterwards the expert advice of our consultant psychiatrist was of great practical help; only one of the two eventually became a founder member. This residential weekend was followed by two one-day meetings: the first in Belfast at the Anglican Franciscan Friary on Saturday, 14 May, the other in Dublin on Wednesday, 8 June (during the General Assembly of the Presbyterian Church) at Milltown Park. The fourth meeting was again residential: at the Benedictine Abbey, Glenstal, County Limerick. Here we attended the annual ecumenical conference from 28 to 30 June (which, being the twentieth, was something of a special occasion), and then stayed on as a group for an extra twenty-four hours as guests of Abbot Celestine who, from the beginning, had taken a great interest in the proposed community.

During the May and June meetings we had focused our attention on three topics: our prayer life, obedience and authority, poverty and work. On each of these we had been invited to submit a short memo, copies of which survive in the files. The aim was not so much to reach conclusions about particular aspects of the life. It was, however, generally accepted at this stage that our house should have a prayer room or chapel but no reservation of the Eucharist; that some form of prayer together should be obligatory morning and evening at least; that meetings for prayer and community business would begin with the lighting of a candle and the invocation 'in your light, Lord, may we see light'; that each member would make a financial contribution to cover the cost of personal upkeep; that the community's lifestyle be simple and that the leader be chosen by the members for a year in the first instance. The main aim of these four meetings, of this period of spiritual preparation, was to discern if we had in fact a vocation to the Columbanus Community: could we commit ourselves to its purpose as this had emerged, could we commit ourselves to its members as these had emerged, and, if so, who would be our choice as Community Leader for the first year? Dr Patterson wanted a letter from each of us giving a response to these questions. 'There are two aspects of their response' (he wrote to me on 10 June): 'First of all, it calls for each candidate's personal response and commitment to the purpose of the Community in light of all that they have learnt and experienced over the past months and secondly, their willingness to commit themselves to the Community which will be the people they have been meeting with over this period. The first will have a decisive effect on the second as it is this which will be the "holding point" for them in any stress or strain that may arise. So I would suggest two questions: 1) Have you now come to the point where you can make a personal commitment to membership of the Community if called upon to do so? 2) After four group meetings with the other eight candidates for membership of the Columbanus Community, how do you feel about becoming a founder member with them in the Community?'

Dr Patterson saw these responses as formal applications for membership. When the Sponsors met in Belfast on 13 July we learnt that six such applications had been received and that a seventh was on its way. All were granted except for one. Of the other two 'probables' one was simply postponing, hoping, as indeed happened, to join the Community in the New Year, the other was hesitating and would eventually decide not to apply. So the founding members would be seven: six in the beginning with the seventh following later on. Their choice of leader fell on me and the beginning, it was decided, would be on 15 September 1983. The six members were: Annette Eisenmann (a German RC, graduate student in philosophy at Queen's University, Belfast), Sr Monica Cavanagh (a RC Presentation Sister), Sr Eileen Mary Lyddon, S. L. G. (Anglican Sisters of the Love of God, Oxford), Mrs Clare O'Mahony (RC widow, Limerick), Margaret Wilkinson (Presbyterian, formerly a missionary in India) and myself. The seventh was Father Malcolm Crawford who arrived in January 1984.

Location

My Easter 1982 report to Father Dargan, the Jesuit Provincial, had stated that feasibility 'stands or falls on the emergence, after appropriate assessment, of suitable candidates'. But it depended on much else besides. From Christmas 1982 on, as vocations began to be forthcoming, as progress was being made on the personnel fronts, the story of the marriage feast in Matthew 22 kept coming to mind more and more. As I put it in a letter to Cardinal Ó Fiaich on 2 April 1983: '*Omnia sunt parata* [everything is ready, Mt 22:4] except of course that it's not wedding guests who are missing, but a house in which to hold the feast.'

Feasibility involved not only vocations but also the acquisition of a house in which to live, and this in its turn involved a decision about location. The printed leaflet openly asked the question 'where?' but the reader had to be content at that stage with the following uncertain answer:

> Somewhere in Northern Ireland but where exactly has not yet been decided. The search, it is felt, must first be for people and only then for a place and premises. The location would preferably be in some place fairly accessible and fairly quiet.

From the beginning, however, it had seemed clear to everyone that Belfast was the appropriate place. Why then the hesitation? The reason was that we wanted a prior assurance that the local Church authorities would welcome us. We didn't want to proceed without their blessing. To be an authentic inter-Church community we knew we needed their blessing. At that particular moment, however, this was a very delicate matter, in particular as far as the Roman Catholic Church was concerned. The feasibility study happened, unfortunately, to coincide with the most difficult and tense years in the whole tempestuous history of the Jesuits. Relations between the Society of Jesus and the Papacy reached an all-time low in 1981 when the Pope intervened in the normal procedures of Jesuit government and nominated a delegate of his own to govern the Society. Reactions varied: there was much support and sympathy, but also much embarrassment and confusion as well as indignation and anger. Happily, before too long communication and confidence was restored and the storm blew over, but while it lasted it was hardly the most propitious moment for Jesuits to get involved in, much less take a leading part in, a new and novel ecumenical initiative.

Patrons
Despite the general nervousness of the times, my superiors, so far from discouraging me or in an excess of caution suggesting that I postpone the venture for the moment, gave me their full support, insisting only that I proceed with the utmost care and correctness. So it was that early on in the feasibility study I sought and secured interviews with Cardinal Ó Fiaich (12 August 1981), with two members of the Episcopal Commission on Ecumenism (Bishop Cahal Daly, then in Longford, on 15 September, and Bishop Kevin McNamara, then in Kerry, on 12 October), with the President of the Vatican Unity Secretariat, Cardinal Willebrands,

on 19 October and with the Vice-President, Bishop Torrella, on 21 October. The reaction of all five was quite positive but understandably guarded and cautionary on the matter of eucharistic sharing. This was a good beginning. Then, as the nature of the proposed community and the role of Patrons became more clear, the question naturally arose: would one of the Roman Catholic bishops consent to be a Patron? Would it be appropriate and advisable to issue such an invitation? Opinion was divided on this. In the early summer of 1982 the Rev Ernest Gallagher, Principal of Edgehill College and former President of the Methodist Church in Ireland, and the Very Reverend Professor J. L. M. Haire, former Principal of Union Theological College and former Moderator of the Presbyterian Church in Ireland, had both agreed to be Patrons. It was decided to make an approach to Cardinal Ó Fiaich only when encouraged to do so by his Auxiliary, the late Bishop James Lennon of Drogheda, to whom I wrote on 27 June 1982:

> Following your advice I saw His Eminence on Friday [25 June]. He would not rule out the possibility of becoming a Patron/Visitor himself if Archbishop Armstrong would also act. This is very good news. I do hope Archbishop Armstrong feels free: he will be consulting his brother Bishops in September.

In any circumstances this 'very good news' would have been given a hundred thousand welcomes. In the particular circumstances of the moment when relations were strained between the Vatican and the Jesuits it brought enormous relief and immense joy. On the part of the Cardinal it was a characteristically bold and generous step and not taken lightly, as he stressed in his formal letter of acceptance of 8 November:

> I always weigh very carefully any invitation I receive to become a Patron, and this is particularly so in the case of the Columbanus Community. I have given your invitation a

lot of thought and on balance I have decided in favour of accepting.

Belfast

Armagh, however, was not where we wanted to be. The Church of Ireland, Methodist and Presbyterian authorities in Belfast were aware of our wish to get established there and were placing no obstacle in our way. This was particularly true of Bishop McCappin of Connor and of Bishop Eames of Down and Dromore. But the Roman Catholic Bishop in Belfast was Dr Philbin. He, it was presumed and feared, would have definite reservations because he had been unhappy with the activities in his diocese of some individual Jesuits, including myself, and the Cardinal's good will might not be enough to reassure him. Dr Philbin, however, it was being said, was due to retire before too long. And so it happened. On 8 September 1982 the announcement came that the Pope had accepted his resignation and that Bishop Cahal Daly of Ardagh and Clonmacnois would succeed him. Dr Daly was duly installed as Bishop of Down and Connor on 17 October and included in his installation address the now widely accepted but then still quite novel view that:

> Mutual recognition in each community of the complete legitimacy and legality, the equal dignity and rights, of the other community, with its own self-defined identity, its own sense of loyalty, its own aspirations, so long as these are peacefully held and peacefully promoted, is a Christian task to which we are all called at this time.

Bishop Cahal Daly's translation from Longford to Belfast was widely and warmly welcomed and not least by all of us involved in the proposed Community. As a member of the Episcopal Commission on Ecumenism he had known about our hopes since 15 September 1981, and a year later on 20 August 1982 I had been back in Longford to keep him informed about developments, in particular about the publicity campaign planned to begin at the end of September. A month after his installation and a few days after receiving the Cardinal's letter of 8 November, I wrote to him as follows:

> You will be interested and pleased to know that His Eminence the Cardinal has agreed to be one of the Patrons of the Columbanus Community of Reconciliation.
>
> Up to this time we have deliberately refrained from saying anything about a location for the Community; we wished to have some assurance beforehand of a *nihil obstat* or welcome from the local Church authorities. But it would greatly help our present efforts to get 'vocations' if we could say where the Community would be situated in the beginning.
>
> Almost all the advice we have so far received points to the Greater Belfast area as the most appropriate location. The Sponsors and Patrons would be grateful therefore to know how Your Lordship would feel about the presence in your Diocese of Down and Connor of the Columbanus Community of Reconciliation, should it come into existence. From being an 'Inter-Church Proposal', it would then be an 'Inter-Church Experiment'.

Two weeks later, on 29 November, the Diocesan Secretary, Father Edward O'Donnell, wrote acknowledging my letter and adding: 'Bishop Daly is consulting with the Diocesan Chapter, Ecumenical Committee and others in Down and Connor concerning the matter you raise. After this he shall write to you himself.'

It was not until the end of March 1983 that Bishop Daly gave an assurance that the Columbanus Community would be welcome in his diocese. The delay, we gathered, was not unusual but it was nonetheless disconcerting and it set back any moves to go house-hunting in Belfast. Otherwise, however, everything went ahead according to plan: the search for prospective members by means of publicity, the assessment of the candidates who emerged and also fundraising efforts, including two visits to Germany for that purpose in January and March. Eventually, on 3 March 1983, the Ballymascanlon inter-Church meeting gave me an opportunity for an informal meeting with Bishop Daly. We featured in a photograph the following morning on the front page of the *Irish News*. More importantly, I was invited to phone for an appointment. This, arranged first for Thursday, 24 March, had then to be postponed until Saturday the 26th. At this meeting any fears I had were allayed: Bishop Daly was still positive about the proposal; he assured me that the Columbanus Community would be welcome in Down and Connor and, on 30 March, which was Wednesday in Holy Week, he signed and had sent to me the following clear statement of approval and support:

To Those Whom It May Concern
I have at various times discussed with Father Michael Hurley SJ the proposal for the establishment in Northern Ireland of a residential community of Catholics and Protestants, committed, as the brochure announcing the proposal puts it, 'to pray and work for unity in the Church, justice in society and peace on earth'. Our discussions occurred at different stages of the evolution of this proposal; and from the outset I have felt that the proposal is opportune and that it should be encouraged.

That a group of Catholics and Protestants should together commit themselves to form a community of prayer and reflection would make a significant contribution to the advance of ecumenism and to the promotion of reconciliation between the religious traditions in Northern Ireland. Anything which would contribute to these ends is to be welcomed by Christians in all denominations. Since becoming Bishop of Down and Connor, I am more conscious than ever of the urgency of working for mutual understanding, respect and acceptance between the Churches. Nothing can contribute more powerfully to this end than prayer; and prayer shared by men and women of the different traditions has a special efficacy.

Hence I welcome the proposal to establish the said community in Belfast, under the title of the 'Columbanus Community of Reconciliation'. I am confident that Catholics will give the proposed community their prayers and their support.

Finance
But the acquisition of a house required not only a decision about location and a welcome to that place by the various Church authorities but also the wherewithal to buy or to rent. The printed leaflet had a paragraph entitled 'Finance?', and gave the following answer: 'In due course the community should be self-supporting but for funds to obtain premises and get itself established it would be dependent on gifts from benefactors.'

From January 1983 onwards financial considerations loomed ever larger. Benefactors were sought both at home and abroad. At home I concentrated on the religious orders, and abroad on the German Churches. These were known to be very generous, but no German money, it soon emerged, would be forthcoming unless it came from both Catholic and Protestant sources: neither Church would give unless both gave and unless their Joint Working Group on Northern Ireland approved. And neither would any German money be forthcoming unless there was Irish money to match it and an Irish recommendation from ecclesiastical authorities. Fundraising, as usual, proved to be a complex operation requiring much patience and perseverance and co-ordination. Already I had been on three visits to Germany (in October 1981, in March-April 1982 and in November 1982), but mainly to make contact with the Lutheran religious communities. In 1983 I paid two more visits, in late January and late March, for fundraising purposes, visiting a variety of Church officials in Bonn, Freiburg, Stuttgart and Würzburg. It was on these visits to Germany that I fell in love with the triptych in Cologne Cathedral, 'The Adoration of the Magi', by Stephen Lockner, a copy of which I acquired for my room. Fundraising is hard work but in our case it was greatly facilitated by the immense good will of Cardinal Ó Fiaich who supplied me with a letter of introduction and wrote letters of appeal on our behalf to Cardinal Höffner of the German Episcopal Conference and to Archbishop Lemaître of *Kirche in Not* (Aid to the Church in Need). Sizeable contributions were eventually forthcoming from both these sources and also from the German Evangelical Church through its *Diakonisches Werk*. On the home front the Presbyterian Association Foundation and the Provincials of various religious congregations gave generously, and the Irish Ecumenical Church Loan Fund provided a low-interest loan. In the period up to 15 September 1983 donations from benefactors amounted to almost £100,000, just over half coming from Irish sources, just under half from German and other sources.

Beginning

The day on which the members were due to foregather in Belfast was 15 September. Naturally we were hoping that by then we would have a house to move into in a mixed area of the city. From Easter on we were taking a practical interest in properties coming on the market, especially in North Belfast, but it wasn't until mid-July that 683 Antrim Road was brought to our notice. After the Sponsors' meeting on 13 July Dr Gallagher and myself visited the house and felt it was right. Dr Gallagher had the structure examined by one of his friends in the building industry, who, as it happened, was an Orangeman. The report was positive but because of the holidays and because of our agent's wish to move slowly and the owner's wish not to vacate until towards the end of the year, it soon became clear that we wouldn't get possession by 15 September; the actual date was 11 November. Some such delay, however, had been anticipated since early summer. We had decided to come to Belfast in any case and to live as a dispersed community until 683 Antrim Road became ours. Each of us would find hospitality with friends, preferably in North Belfast, and we would meet together in some place each day to pray and share. So it happened. As planned, six members met on Thursday, 15 September at 2.30 p.m. at Grosvenor Hall, the Belfast Central Mission, where Dr Taggart, our host, led us in a short service at which Dr Patterson gave an address and Father George Wadding was also present. The Columbanus Community of Reconciliation had begun. The feasibility study was over.

POSTSCRIPT

Some fifteen years have now gone by and the Columbanus Community of Reconciliation still continues. Its homeless beginning was not without symbolism, foreshadowing the precarious existence which has always been its lot. Formally inaugurated on 23 November 1983, the Feast of St Columbanus, the Community owes everything to the encouragement of countless friends to whom it contributes in return the encouragement of its life and work as one 'practical example of what a more united Church, a more just society and a more peaceful world could be like'. Since 1991 leadership of the Community is in the able hands of Sr Róisín Hannaway SSL.[7]

Appendix

Milltown Park Public Lectures 1960-1969: topics, speakers, dates

1960

SPRING

The Population Explosion	Rev. P. Joy SJ	(2 March)
The Ecumenical Movement	Rev. M. Hurley SJ [1]	(9 March)
Separated Christians of The East	Rev. P. O'Connell SJ	(16 March)
Salvation for the non-Christian	Rev. M. O'Grady SJ	(25 March)
The Laity in the Church	Rev. Dr. A. O'Rahilly	(30 March)
Responsibility for Crime	Rev. M. Sweetman SJ	(6 April)
Understanding the Mass	Rev. D. O'Sullivan SJ	(13 April)

1960

WINTER [2]

Dissident Churches of the East	Rev. J. Gill SJ	(12 October)
Marriage: Success or Failure	Rev. M. Moloney SJ	(19 October)
Brainwashing	Rev. P. Joy SJ	(26 October)
An Approach to Teilhard de Chardin	Rev. C. Reilly SJ	(2 November)
Evolution: An Open Question?	Rev. J. Moore SJ	(9 November)
The Old Testament	Rev. P. Simpson SJ	(16 November)
The Christian and Literature	Rev. J. C. Kelly SJ	(23 November)
Christian Disunity in Africa	Rev. J. FitzGerald SJ	(30 November)

1961

SPRING

The Early Irish Church and the Papacy	Rev. J. Ryan SJ	(15 February)

Christian Unity

Adolescents and their Parents	Rev. M. Moloney SJ	(22 February)
Creation and Fall of Adam and Eve	Rev. P. Simpson SJ	(1 March)
The Primacy of Rome and the Orthodox Church	Rev. P. O'Connell SJ	(8 March)
The Dead Sea Scrolls and Christianity	Rev. K. Smyth SJ	(15 March)
Personal Religion	Rev. J. O'Mara SJ	(22 March)
Rescuing the Faith in Latin America	Rev. Timothy Connolly (Superior General of the Columban Fathers)	(29 March)

1961

WINTER

Drugs, Brainwashing and the Self	Rev. M. C. D'Arcy SJ	(1 November)
The Significance of the New Social Encyclical	Rev. L. McKenna SJ	(8 November)
The World Council of Churches and its Forthcoming Assembly	Rev. M. Hurley SJ[3]	(15 November)
Psychiatry, the Moralist and Sin	Rev. J. Erraught SJ	(22 November)
The Inquisition	Rev. A. Gwynn SJ	(29 November)
The Gospel Before the Gospels	Rev. K. Smyth SJ	(6 December)
Modern Science and the Origin of the Universe	Rev. T. Vives SJ	(13 December)

1962

SPRING

The Church in the Congo Faces the Future	Rev. S. Kachama-Nkoy SJ	(7 March)
The Truth About Patriotism	Rev. T. Hamilton SJ	(14 March)
Old Testament Sacrifice	Rev. P. Simpson SJ	(21 March)
Martin Luther: A Reappraisal	Rev. A. Gwynn SJ	(28 March)
The Gospels: Historical Fact and Inspired Truth	Rev. K. Smyth SJ	(4 April)
The Christian and Work	Rev. M. Connolly SJ	(11 April)
The Changing Image of the Passion	Rev. C. Barrett SJ	(18 April)

Appendix

1962

WINTER

Christianity in Crisis	Rev. B. Leeming SJ	(24 October)
Adam and Anthropology	Rev. M. Brennan SJ	(31 October)
Responsible Parenthood and Fertility Control	Rev. P. Joy SJ	(7 November)
Protestantism and Our Lady	Rev. M. Hurley SJ [4]	(14 November)
Holy Writ or Holy Church?	Rev. P. Simpson SJ	(21 November)
The Layman in the Church	Rev. E. McDonagh (Maynooth)	(28 November)
Papal Primacy in Scripture and the Early Church	Rev. K. Smyth SJ	(5 December)

1963

SPRING

The Council's Debate on the Bible	Rev. K. Smyth SJ	(27 February)
The Evolution of the Earth	Rev. R. Ingram SJ	(6 March)
Art and Religion	Rev. D. O'Sullivan SJ	(13 March)
The Spirituality of the Early Irish Church	Rev. F. Shaw SJ	(20 March)
Chastity and Charity	Rev. D. Reid SJ	(27 March)
Interpreting the Sermon on the Mount	Rev. P. Simpson SJ	(3 April)
The Mass – a Sacrifice	Rev. M. O'Grady SJ	(10 April)

1963

WINTER

God in History	Rev. M. C. D'Arcy SJ	(23 October)
What is Gospel Truth?	Rev. K. Smyth SJ	(30 October)
Catholic Reform and Christian Unity	Rev. M. Hurley SJ	(6 November)
Ireland Tomorrow	Rev. R. Burke-Savage SJ	(13 November)
Freedom, Responsibility and Guilt	Rev. E. F. O'Doherty (UCD)	(20 November)
The Ten Commandments and Biblical Research	Rev. P. Simpson SJ	(27 November)
Trent in Retrospect	Rev. P. J. Corish (Maynooth)	(4 December)

Christian Unity

1964

SPRING

The Schools and Christian Responsibility	Rev. J. Veale SJ	(5 February)
Covenant and Grace	Rev. P. Simpson SJ	(12 February)
Modern Technology and Traditional Faith	Rev. T. Burke OCarm	(19 February)
Faith as Dialogue	Rev. E. FitzGerald SJ	(26 February)
Psychological Understanding of Children	Rev. D. Casey SJ	(4 March)
Ecumenism and Conversion	Rev. M. Hurley SJ [5]	(11 March)
The Christian Conscience in a World of Want	Rev. P. Joy SJ	(18 March)

1964

WINTER

Unity and Authority	Rev. P. O'Connell SJ	(21 October)
Evolution and Olduvai	Rev. J. Moore SJ	(28 October)
Christianity and Sexuality	Rev. J. M. Nolan (UCD)	(4 November)
Liturgy and Devotion	Rev. E. FitzGerald SJ	(11 November)
Confession and Conversion	Rev. M. Hurley SJ	(18 November)
What is Matter?	Rev. P. Heelan SJ	(25 November)
Resurrection: Faith and Fact	Rev. P. Simpson SJ	(2 December)

1965

SPRING

The Mystery of the Church	Rev. R. Murray, SJ	(17 February)
The People of God	Rev. K. Condon CM	(24 February)
The Pilgrim Church	Rev. P. Simpson SJ	(3 March)
Ecumenism	Rev. M. Hurley SJ [6]	(10 March)
Collegiality	Rev. C. McGarry SJ	(24 March)
Laity	Rev. J. O'Mara SJ	(31 March)
The Eastern Churches	Rev. P. O'Connell SJ	(7 April)

1965

WINTER

Church and World	Rev. M. Hurley SJ [7]	(20 October)
A Just Society	Rev. J. Healy SJ	(27 October)
Scientist and Christian	Professor Neil Porter (UCD)	(3 November)

Appendix

Wisdom Not of This World	Rev. P. Simpson SJ	(17 November)
The Church and Our Lady	Rev. D. Flanagan (Maynooth)	(17 November)
Art and Morality	Rev. C. Barrett SJ	(24 November)
Sacrament as Encounter	Rev. M. O'Connell SJ	(1 December)

1966

SPRING

Pope and Patriarch	Rev. P. O'Connell SJ	(16 February)
Trade Unionist and Christian	Mr Charles McCarthy	(23 February)
Vatican II and Revelation	Rev. P. Simpson SJ	(2 March)
Why Investment in Education?	Rev. S. Ó Catháin, SJ	(9 March)
New Missionary Perspective	Rev. M. Pelly, SJ	(16 March)
Religious Liberty	Rev. E. McDonagh (Maynooth)	(23 March)
Manager and Christian	Rev. L. McKenna SJ	(30 March)

1966

WINTER

Schools after Vatican II	Rev. J. Veale SJ	(26 October)
How Doctrine Changes	Rev. M. O'Grady SJ	(2 November)
Priest and People	Rev. L. Breen CC	(9 November)
Prosperity and the Christian	Rev. J. Healy SJ	(16 November)
Woman in St Paul	Rev. W. Harrington OP	(23 November)
Christ and Divorce	Rev. M. Hurley SJ [8]	(30 November)
Conscience and Authority	Rev. C. Barrett SJ	(7 December)

1967

SPRING

Teilhard de Chardin	Rev. E. Egan SJ	(1 February)
Education: Rights and Responsibilities	Mr Denis Buckley	(8 February)
What is the Church?	Rev. C. McGarry SJ	(15 February)
Choosing a Career	Rev. P. Andrews SJ	(22 February)
Suffering and Providence	Rev. J. O'Mara SJ	(1 March)
Marxism and Christianity	Dr Patrick Masterson (UCD)	(8 March)
Youth and Sex	Rev. M. Sweetman SJ	(15 March)
Teilhard's Spirituality	Rev. J. O'Mara SJ	(5 April)

Christian Unity

Teilhard's Evolutionary Thought	Rev. M. Brennan SJ	(6 April)
Teilhard's Philosophy and Theology	Rev. E. Egan SJ	(7 April)

1967

WINTER

Christianity on the Screen	Rev. J. C. Kelly SJ	(18 October)
Science and the Christian	Rev. C. Reilly SJ	(25 October)
Clerical Celibacy	Rev. P. O'Connell SJ	(1 November)
The Challenge of Alcoholism	Member of AA and Rev. J. Healy SJ	(8 November)
Moral Precept and Gospel Spirit	Rev. P. Simpson SJ	(15 November)
The Religious Vocation Today	Sr M. Pauline SSL	(22 November)
Growth into Adult Faith	Rev. J. M. Nolan (UCD)	(29 November)
Marriage Relationship	Rev. P. A. Baggot SJ	(6 December)
Relevance for Ireland of the recent Laity Congress in Rome	Mr Vincent Grogan	(13 December)

1968

SPRING

Changing the Constitution	Rev. L. Ryan DD (Carlow)	(21 February)
The Problem of God	Rev. E. Egan, SJ	(28 February)
Human Values in Literature Today	Rev. M. P. Gallagher SJ	(6 March)
Mothers and Careers	Mrs G. O. Simms	(13 March)
Hippie Culture	Rev. C. Barrett SJ	(20 March)
The Challenge of Humanism	Rev. F. Cull SJ	(27 March)
Understanding Original Sin	Rev. M. Hurley SJ [9]	(3 April)

1968

WINTER

Lambeth and After	Most Rev. G. O. Simms[10]	(23 October)
The Permissive Society	Rev. M. Sweetman SJ	(30 October)
Prayer	Rev. Eltin Griffin OCarm	(6 November)
Prejudice and Discrimination	Rev. M. MacGreil SJ	(13 November)
The Understanding of God	Rev. P. McShane SJ	(20 November)
Formation of Conscience	Rev. P. Corcoran SM	(27 November)
The Dutch Catechism	Rev. P. O'Connell SJ	(4 December)

Appendix

1969

SPRING

Community Relations	Mr Martin Wallace	(12 February)
The New Laity	Mr John Horgan	(19 February)
The Church and Secondary Education	Rev. S. O'Connor SJ	(26 February)
Freedom and Responsibility	Rev. C. Barrett SJ	(5 March)
Is the Mass a Meal?	Rev. R. Moloney SJ	(12 March)
Students and Religion	Ms K. O'Doherty	(19 March)
Christian Marriage Today	Rev. Enda McDonagh (Maynooth)	(26 March)

1969

WINTER[11]

Philosophy and Revolution	Rev. E. Egan SJ
Perverting the Nation	Rev. J. Healy SJ
Change in Understanding the Bible	Rev. A. Ryan OCarm
Does Faith Change?	Rev. G. Daly OSA
Change and Church Authority	Rev. P. O'Connell SJ
Change and the Priesthood	Rev. D. N. Power OMI
Understanding Change	Rev. C. O'Donovan SJ

Notes

(Numbers in italics opposite the running heads indicate the pages in the present text to which the notes refer.)

Introduction

1. Quoted *The Irish Times*, 30 November 1964, p. 6.
2. *La Documentation Catholique*, 20 mars 1983, p. 325; *Ecumenical Trends*, April 1983, p. 54.
3. John C. Murray, 'Ecumenism: The Next Steps', *One in Christ*, 25/2 (April 1989), p. 163.
4. Bruno Delorme, *Lumière et Vie*, 45/5 (December 1996), pp. 75-80. The balance is redressed in a note entitled 'L'Oecuménisme: Impossibilité ou Réalité?' contributed by a Dominican, Bruno Carra de Vaux, ibid. pp. 81-83.
5. Martin Van Elderen, 'Common Understanding and Vision: A Survey of the Discussion in the WCC', *The Ecumenical Review*, 49/1 (January 1997), p. 6. The author is Publications Editor for the WCC.
6. Ibid. p. 5
7. Todor Sabev, *The Orthodox Churches in the World Council of Churches: Towards the Future* (Geneva: WCC Publications, 1996), p. 19.
8. 'WCC Consultation with its Orthodox Member Churches', The *Ecumenical Review*, 48/2 (April 1996), p. 190; Ion Bria, 'Time to unfold the Orthodox Tradition', ibid. pp. 205, 210. This and other articles in the same issue form part of the proceedings of a WCC Consultation with its Orthodox Member Churches in June 1995.
9. Cf. G. R. Evans, *Method in Ecumenical Theology* (Cambridge: CUP, 1996), pp. 1-18; cf. also Paul A. Crow Jr, 'Ecumenism, Spirituality and the Dark Night of the Soul', *One in Christ*, 29/2 (April 1993), pp. 100-112.
10. Christians in Asia sound a more hopeful note. Cf. *Asian Movement for Christian Unity*, A Joint Project of the Christian Conference of Asia (CCA) and of the Federation of Asian Bishops' Conferences (FABC). *FABC Papers*, 77 (Hong Kong); *CTC Bulletin*, Vol 14, no. 2, October 1996.
11. Konrad Raiser, 'WCC Central Committee September 1996 – Report

of the General Secretary', *The Ecumenical Review*, 49/1 (January 1997), p. 91.
12. §96 (p. 107).
13. Words of the Archbishop of Canterbury when greeting Pope John Paul at the Vatican on 3 December 1996.
14. Cf. chapter 2, n. 69, p. 354 *infra*.
15. *Feeling our Way* is the title Archbishop Fisher of Canterbury gave to a collection of ecumenical sermons he preached in 1960 when visiting the Patriarchs of Jerusalem and Constantinople and, on his way back home, visiting Pope John XXIII and greeting him with the words 'Your Holiness, we are making history'. It was the first visit of an Archbishop of Canterbury to the Vatican since 1397; cf. Bernard and Margaret Pawley, *Rome and Canterbury Through Four Centuries* (London: Mowbrays, 1974), pp. 334-5.
16. A Church of England Report in 1918 had stated: 'In the region of moral and social questions we desire all Christians to begin at once to act together as if they were one body, in one visible fellowship'; cf. Ronald C. D. Jasper, *George Bell Bishop of Chichester* (Oxford: OUP, 1967), p. 25.
17. I have used this phrase on at least two occasions when in optimistic if not euphoric mood: in a comment on the Decree on Ecumenism in *The Irish Times*, 30 November 1964, p. 6; and in an article on 'Reconciliation and the Churches in Northern Ireland' (cf. chapter 13) written during the summer of 1995 while the ceasefires still held.
18. Quoted by Ian Ker, *John Henry Newman – A Biography* (Oxford: OUP, 1990), p. 382.
19. *Lund Report,* pp. 15-16.
20. Decree on Ecumenism §12, *Vatican II*, ed. A. Flannery OP (Dublin: Dominican Publications, 1992), p. 462.
21. *The Tablet*, 22 March 1997, p. 386.
22. *The Tablet*, 23 March 1996, p. 409.
23. The opening paragraph of my paper 'Christian Unity by 2000?', delivered at Tantur near Jerusalem in 1980, seems worth quoting:

> To concentrate on the unity of all Christians in a place so hallowed by other great religious traditions as well as the Christian could appear to be downright unecumenical and indeed grossly insensitive. I should like, therefore, at the outset to declare my conviction that inter-faith dialogue, i.e. between the different religions, also belongs to the ecumenical enterprise and has an increasingly important role to play in inter-Church dialogue itself; that the search for peace and unity among

Christians is but a means to an end, as one of the conditions of the possibility of effective mission towards non-believers and of effective dialogue with believers of all religions (*One in Christ* 19/1 (1983), p. 2.).

Chapter 1: Hoping against Hope

1. Carroll Stuhlmueller CP, *The Jerome Bible Commentary* (London: Geoffrey Chapman, 1969), p. 116.
2. *Sectarianism: A Discussion Document* (Belfast: Irish Inter-Church Meeting, 1993), p. 115.
3. Cf. *infra*, chapter 18.
4. ECONI (Evangelical Contribution on Northern Ireland), Holywood, County Down.
5. This text appeared in print in *Doctrine and Life*, 44/2 (February 1994), pp. 106-109, under the title 'We Had Hoped'. A second version was made for a sermon on 'Hope' in Coventry Cathedral on 25 September 1994 and another for a sermon in King's College Chapel, Cambridge, on 28 April 1996 which was printed in *The Month*, June 1996, pp. 238-241, under the title 'Hope and Forgiveness'.

Chapter 2: Christian Unity by 2000?

1. *One in Christ* 16 (1980), pp. 44-46. Cf. *One in Christ? Towards Catholic-Orthodox Unity*, ed. Paul McPartlan (Slough: St Paul's, 1993).
2. The Pontifical Council for Christian Unity (PCPCU), *Information Service*, 86 (1994/II-III), pp. 104-105. In *Tertio millennio adveniente* he refers in paragraph 18 to 'that new springtime of Christian life which will be revealed by the Great Jubilee, if Christians are docile to the action of the Holy Spirit' (London: CTS), p. 26.
3. §§23, 34 (London: CTS, 1994), pp. 31, 43-5.
4. PCPCU, *Information Service*, 90 (1995/IV), p. 122.
5. *Orientale Lumen* (London: CTS, 1995); *Ut Unum Sint*, §§103, 3, 79 (London: CTS, 1995), pp. 115, 6, 90.
6. Kenneth Scott Latourette, 'Ecumenical Bearings of the Missionary Movement and the International Missionary Council', *A History of the Ecumenical Movement 1517-1948*, ed. Ruth Rouse and Stephen Charles Neill (London, 1954), p. 353.
7. R. E. David and D. L. Edwards (eds.), *Unity Begins at Home*: A Report from the First British Conference on Faith and Order (London: SCM, 1964), p. 43. For what follows cf. ibid. pp. 43-48.

8. Frederick C. Copleston SJ, *Memoirs of a Philosopher* (London: Sheed & Ward, 1993), p. 35
9. Bernard and Margaret Pawley, *Rome and Canterbury Through Four Centuries* (London: Mowbrays, 1974), pp. 307-8.
10. Tim Pat Coogan, *De Valera: Long Fellow, Long Shadow* (London: Hutchinson, 1993), p. 500.
11. Victor Griffin, *Mark of Protest, An Autobiography* (Dublin: Gill & Macmillan, 1993), p. 29.
12. John C. Heenan, *A Crown of Thorns, An Autobiography 1951-1963* (London: Hodder & Stoughton, 1974), pp. 326-327.
13. *Ut Unum Sint,* op.cit. §§3, 20, pp. 5, 26.
14. §6 (London: CTS, 1993), p. 8.
15. Bryan R. Wilson, *Religion in Secular Society: A Sociological Comment*, London, 1966, pp. 128, 33, 224. Paul Johnson writes in similar cynical terms: 'ecumenism starts to creep in only when faith grows feeble', *The Spectator,* 1 September 1996.
16. *The Tablet,* 9 November 1996, p. 1492.
17. Martin Wroe, 'Profit in Unity', *The Observer,* 28 May 1995.
18. Ibid.
19. *Ecumenical News International (ENI) Bulletin,* 29 April 1996, pp. 17-18; for membership of the Commission cf. ibid. pp. 313-318.
20. Father John Hotchkin, 'The Ecumenical Movement's Third Stage', *Origins,* 25/21 (9 November 1995), p. 361.
21. Cf. e.g. Romans; 1 and 2 Corinthians.
22. Günther Gassmann, 'Montreal 1963-Santiago De Compostella 1993: Report of the Director', *On The Way to Fuller Koinonia (FK)* Official Report of the Fifth World Conference on Faith and Order (Faith and Order Paper no. 166), pp. 14, 13.
23. PCPCU, *Information Service,* 89(1995/II-III), pp. 97-9; ibid. 90 (1995/IV), pp. 140-141.
24. *Journal of Ecumenical Studies,* 1978, p. 225
25. Quoted by William Purdy, *The Search for Unity. Relations between the Anglican and Roman Catholic Churches from the 1950s to the 1970s* (London: Geoffrey Chapman, 1996), p. 213.
26. PCPCU, *Information Service,* 69 (1989/1), p. 8; cf. also Francis A. Sullivan SJ, 'Lessons We Have Learned from the Participation of Rome in Ecumenism' *Milltown Studies,* 34 (1994), p. 17, and Aidan Nichols OP, *Rome and the Eastern Churches* (Edinburgh: T&T Clark, 1992), pp. 55-102.
27. Cf. Aidan Nichols, op. cit. (n. 26 *supra*), pp. 27-52.

28. PCPCU, *Information Service*, 88 (1995/1), p. 2. According to René Laurentin this term [*theotokos*] 'est le centre et, en quelque sorte, le tout de la doctrine orientale sur la Mère du Christ'... It is 'un raccourci audacieux' of the mystery of the Incarnation: *Catholicisme,* Tome 14, (Paris: Letouzey et Ané, 1996), p. 1127.
29. Cf. Francis A. Sullivan, loc. cit. (n. 26 *supra*), pp. 18-22, quoting Bishop Walter Kasper. Rome has always had a preferential option for the East. Nichols (op. cit. p. 331) suggests that Rome 'not only desires but *needs* reunion with the Orthodox East. In the face of her own numerous theological liberals ... Catholicism's grasp of the historic Christian tradition can only be strengthened by the accession of Orthodoxy to communion with Rome.'
30. William Purdy, op. cit (n. 25 *supra*), pp. 111-114, 121-122.
31. Jan Grootaers, 'An Unfinished Agenda: The Question of Roman Catholic Membership of the World Council of Churches, 1968-1975', *The Ecumenical Review*, 49/3 (July 1997), pp. 305-347.
32. PCPCU *Information Service*, 83 (1993/11) pp. 86-87.
33. *One in Christ,* 19/1 (1983), p. 5.
34. Thomas F. Best and Günther Gassmann (eds.), *FK* (n. 22 *supra*), pp. xiv, 12.
35. *The Ecumenical Review* 49/1 (January 1997), pp. 13-33, esp. pp. 26-27.
36. Art. cit. (cf. n. 20 *supra*), p. 356.
37. Gerard O'Connell, 'An Ecumenical Spring', *The Tablet,* 27 April 1996, p. 543.
38. *FK* (n. 22, *supra*), pp. xiv, 12.
39. Cf. Anne Murphy, 'The Lenses of Gender', *The Way,* October 1996, pp. 323-329.
40. §15 *Vatican Council II* (Dublin: Dominican Publications, 1992), p. 465.
41. §3 op.cit. p. 6.
42. Ibid. §1, p. 4; *Ut Unum Sint,* §54 (London: CTS), p.662. According to Aidan Nichols 'a secondary strand [in the Pope's 'ecclesial-strategy'] may be to draw in the Churches of the East so as to redress the effects of theological liberalism, and of neo-Protestantism, in the Latin Church since the Second Vatican Council'. *Rome and the Eastern Churches,* op. cit. (n. 26 *supra*) pp. 102, 331.
43. §27. *In Orientale Lumen,* §19, p. 40 ibid., Pope John Paul speaks strangely of 'our reciprocal [*sic*] exclusion from the Eucharist'.
44. Cf. chapter 17 *infra*, pp. 292-316
45. *The Tablet*, 15 June 1996, p. 802. And the number has probably increased since then.

46. Ibid. Cf. for subsequent developments, Michel Bourdeaux, 'Religious Freedom Russian Style', *The Tablet*, 27 September 1997, pp. 1216-1218.
47. *The Eastern Schism* (Oxford: OUP, 1955).
48. *Orientale Lumen*, §19, p. 38.
49. *One in Christ*, 30/1 (1994), pp. 75-82; *Eastern Churches Journal* 1/1 (winter 1993/94), pp. 17-25.
50. Art. cit. (n. 26 *supra*), *Milltown Studies* 34 (1994), p. 21.
51. Serge Keleher, 'Comments on Balamand', *Eastern Churches Journal* 1/1 (winter 1993/94), p. 43.
52. For this and the following quotations cf. *One in Christ* 32/2 (1996), pp. 179-181. *The Information Service* of the PCPCU did not carry the text because 'the Patriarch had made it clear to us that it was not for publication'.
53. *The Tablet,* 3 August 1996, p. 1031, 22 June 1996, p. 832.
54. *The Tablet*, 18 June 1997, p. 842; 5 July 1997, p. 879. Representatives did attend in 1998: ibid. 4 July 1998, p. 887.
55. Some Orthodox commentators are now more open to eucharistic sharing as a means of growing together. Cf. Ion Bria, 'Time to Unfold the Orthodox Tradition', *The Ecumenical Review,* 48/2 (April 1996), p. 209: 'The position according to which it is a sort of dogmatic-constitutional principle that only full unity of faith allows sacramental and eucharistic communion should be more nuanced'.
56. There is of course much truth in the remark of Steven Runciman (op. cit. p. 79): 'There are idealists who fondly believe that if only the people of the world could get to know each other there would be peace and good will for ever. This is a tragic delusion.' Mere contact is of course insufficient: some sympathy is also required and a willingness to learn – and unlearn.
57. §§22-7, pp. 45-51.
58. *One in Christ*, 19/1 (1983), pp. 10-11.
59. *One in Christ*, 4/2 (1968), pp. cf. ibid. 5/1 (1969), pp. 64-105; *Beyond Tolerance: The Challenge of Mixed Marriage,* ed. Michael Hurley SJ (London: Geoffrey Chapman, 1975); John F. Hotchkin, '*Familiaris Consortio* – New Light on Mixed Marriages', *One in Christ*, 22/1 (1986), pp. 73-79; George Kilcourse, *Double Belonging: Inter-Church Families and Christian Unity* (New York/Mahwah, NJ: Paulist Press, 1992), p. 115; *One in Christ*, 30/1 (1994), pp. 83-92. The Association of Inter-Church Families held its ninth biennial international conference at Virginia Wesleyan College in July 1996.
60. *Directory,* §145, quoting *Familiaris consortio,* §78 (London: CTS), p. 68.

61. §129, p. 64.
62. §46, p. 53.
63. Ruth Reardon, 'A Source of Joy: *Ut Unum Sint* and Inter-Church Families', *One in Christ*, 31/3, pp. 280-286; Eoin de Bhaldraithe, 'Joy of Intercommunion', *The Tablet*, 29 June 1996, p. 856; Bill Cosgrave, 'Intercommunion: A Change in the Requirements', *Ferns Diocesan Bulletin*, No. 51, September 1996, p. 4; Ladislas Örsy, 'Inter-Church Marriages and Reception of the Eucharist', *America*, 12 October 1996, pp. 18-19. Reardon and Örsy argue that inter-Church marriages can in themselves be regarded as 'particular cases'.
64. *One in Christ*, 19/1 (1983), p. 11.
65. So also Cardinal Cassidy, cf. Gerard O'Connell, 'Dialogue must go on', *The Tablet*, 20 April 1996, p. 506.
66. §13, Cf. Bishop Moorman, Vatican Observed (London: Darton, Longman & Todd, 1967), p. 189.
67. Cf. *The Tablet*, 30 April 1994, p. 542; 20 April 1996, p. 513.
68. Gerard O'Connell, *The Tablet*, 20 April 1996, p. 507.
69. It was to have been declared in July 1997 at the Lutheran World Federation Assembly in Hong Kong, but because of revisions required by the Lutheran Church in Finland and the LWF member Churches in Germany, the date has been postponed to 1998, cf. *Ecumenical News International* (ENI), 9 October 1996, p. 30. A key sentence in the consensus document states: 'By grace alone, in faith in Christ's saving work, and not because of any merit on our part, we are accepted by God and receive the Holy Spirit, who renews our hearts while equipping and calling us to good works', ibid., p. 32. For the background cf. Günther Gassmann, 'Lutheran-Catholic Agreement on Justification (I): A Historical Breakthrough', *Ecumenical Trends*, 25/6 (June 1996), pp. 1-5; 'Lutheran-Catholic Agreement on Justification (II): The Ecclesiological Dimension', ibid. 25/7 (July-August 1996), pp. 1-7; John Hotchkin, art. cit. (note 20, *supra*), pp. 360-361. In June 1998 the Catholic Church presented its official response to the Joint Declaration of the Doctrine of Justification. Cardinal Cassidy concluded: 'the consensus reached on the doctrine of justification, despite its limitations, virtually resolves the long-disputed question at the close of the twentieth century'. *The Tablet*, 4 July 1998, p. 886.
70. '*Apostolicae Curae*: Past and Future Processes', *The Month*, November 1996, p. 434.
71. PCPCU, *Information Service*, 90 (1995/IV), p. 128.

72. The Lund principle recalled recently by Cardinal Cassidy in his interviews with *The Tablet,* 27 April 1996, p. 543.
73. Mícheál Mac Gréil, *Prejudice in Ireland Revisited* (Maynooth: 1996), pp. 190-195, 436-7.
74. Cardinal Franz König, 'That they may all be one: the call of the year 2000', *The Tablet,* 21 October 1995, pp. 1340, 1341.
75. The Pope's own words early in his Pontificate about our involvement in the ecumenical movement as quoted in PCPCU, *Information Service,* 40 (1979/III), p. 8.
76. The original version of this chapter was prepared for delivery as a public lecture at the Tantur Institute for Theological Studies near Jerusalem on 16 October 1980 – the second anniversary, as it happened, of John Paul II's election as Pope. It was printed in the *Tantur Yearbook 1980-1981,* pp. 53-68, and in *One in Christ,* 19/1 (1983), pp. 2-13. The present version was prepared for delivery as two lectures in the Catholic Chaplaincy of the University of Salford on 26 and 27 November 1996, and subsequently as a single 'Colmcille Lecture' for the Letterkenny Theology Project in County Donegal on 15 April 1997. An abbreviated version of this chapter appeared in *Doctrine and Life,* 48/1 & 2 (1998, January & February), pp. 18-30, 82-93.

Chapter 3: Reconciliation and Forgiveness
1. Cf. *Reconciliation: The Continuing Agenda,* ed. Robert J. Kennedy (Collegeville: The Liturgical Press, 1987), *passim.*
2. Cf. *Reconciling Memories,* ed. Alan D. Falconer (Dublin: The Columba Press; new, enlarged edition, 1998); G. Gassmann & H. Meyer, *The Unity of the Church: Requirements and Structure* (Geneva: Lutheran World Federation, 1983); Ulrich Duchrow, *Conflict over the Ecumenical Movement* (Geneva: World Council of Churches, 1981).
3. For help in providing me with relevant materials I am grateful to the Education Secretary of the Justice and Peace Department of the Southern African Catholic Bishops' Conference (SACBC) in Pretoria; to the Information Officer of the South African High Commission in London; and to Seán Ó Ruairc of the Newsroom of Radio Telefís Éireann in Dublin for the tape of an April 1995 interview with Father Sean O'Leary of the Justice and Peace Department of SACBC.
4. The Secretariat of the Forum is based at Dublin Castle, Dublin 2. The inaugural meeting took place on 28 October 1994. Proceedings were

suspended when the IRA broke their ceasefire in early February 1996 and did not subsequently resume.

5. Stella P. Hughes and Anne L. Schneider, 'Victim-Offender Mediation: a Survey of Program Characteristics and Perceptions of Effectiveness', *Crime and Delinquency*, 35/2 (April 1989), pp. 217-233. For this reference and other relevant materials I am indebted to the US Embassy in Dublin and the US Information Agency, Washington DC.
6. *The Kairos Document: A Theological Comment on the political crisis in South Africa*, 2nd revised edition (London: Catholic Institute for International Relations/British Council of Churches, 1986) pp. 9-16.
7. Mike Ritchie, 'Looking for Justice: Liberation Theology in the Irish Setting,' *Irish Reporter*, 18 (Belfast, 1995), p. 21.
8. Cf. Brian Lennon SJ, *After the Ceasefires: Catholics and the Future of Northern Ireland* (Dublin: The Columba Press, 1995) pp. 112, 128, *passim*.
9. *Il Concilio Vaticano II* (Bologna: Edizioni Dehoniane, 1966); J. Deretz-A. Nocent, OSB, *Synopse des Textes Conciliaires* (Paris: Editions Universitaires, 1966), pp. 1107-1108; id. *Dictionary of the Council* (London: Geoffrey Chapman, 1968), p. 362. The English edition omits the reference to the Liturgy Constitution.
10. J. Alberigo, *Indices Verborum et Locutionum Decretorum Concilii Vaticani II,* 10 vols, all prepared by the Istituto per le Scienze Religiose, Bologna, and seven of them published by it, the three others published by Vallechi Editore, Florence, 1968-86. The *Indices* cover only twelve of the sixteen documents.
11. *Reconciliation in Religion and Society*, ed. Michael Hurley SJ (Belfast: Institute of Irish Studies, 1994), pp. 1-5.
12. §§1, 2, 3 (London: CTS, 1984), pp. 4-7.
13. The Great Jubilee of 2000 will, it is hoped, see this begin to happen on a large scale as, in response to the Debt and Development Coalition, the rich lending nations cancel the backlog of unpayable debts crushing the most impoverished nations.
14. Cf. Alain Blancy, 'Can the Churches Convert? Should the Churches Convert?,' *The Ecumenical Review,* 44 (1992), pp. 419-428; L. Orsy SJ, 'Kenosis: The Door to Christian Unity,' *Origins* 23/3 (1993), pp. 38-41.
15. Op. cit. p. 10.
16. Op. cit. §§23, 31, 26 loc. cit. pp. 81, 119, 95-6. The emphasis here is, however, more personal than social. Cf. James Dallen, 'Recent Documents on Penance and Reconciliation', *Reconciliation: The Continuing Agenda* (n. 1 *supra*), pp. 95-113.

17. Gérard Gilleman SJ, *The Primacy of Charity in Moral Theology* (London: Burns & Oates, 1959), p. 333.
18. John Paul II, *Dives in Misericordia*, §12 (Boston: St Paul Editions, 1980), p. 37.
19. Ibid., §14, loc. cit. pp. 44-45.
20. According to Donald W Shriver Jr in *Forgiveness and Politics* (London: New World Publications, 1987), 20, forgiveness has four dimensions: its judgment against a wrong perpetrated, its empathy for the humanity of the wrongdoers, its refusal to exact a penalty from the wrongdoers in exact proportion to the wrong, and its ultimate aim of restoring the community relationship of all parties to this transaction. Id., *An Ethic for Enemies: Forgiveness in Politics* (New York: OUP, 1995).
21. An Inter-Church Group on Faith and Politics, 'Forgiveness and the Northern Ireland Conflict', *Intercom* (Dublin: Veritas) 25/2 (March 1995), p. 10.
22. Joseph Liechty, 'Repentance and Hope for Peace in Ireland', *Doctrine and Life* (Dublin: Dominican Publications), 44/2 (February 1994), p. 69.
23. Op. cit. Explanatory Note 12, loc. cit. p. 34.
24. Donald W. Shriver Jr also distinguishes between 'readiness to forgive' on the one hand and 'actual forgiveness' or 'consummated forgiveness' which includes the repentance of the offender on the other. Because of this distinction Shriver can state that 'actual forgiveness, in the absence of actual repentance, is questionable – is really a contradiction in terms …. The Bible knows of no consummated forgiveness in the absence of repentance.' Cf. 'Theological Reflections' in Brian Frost, *The Politics of Peace* (London: Darton, Longman and Todd, 1991), p. 195. This 'actual, consummated forgiveness' of Schriver seems to be the equivalent of reconciliation. A somewhat similar distinction is to be found in William Temple who writes: 'For real forgiveness the action of two wills is needed; it cannot be complete till the wrongdoer changes his attitude or, in other words, repents. But he may be led to do this by the love shown in his victim's readiness to forgive.' Cf. *Christus Veritas* (London: Macmillan and Co., 1949), p. 268. It is quite clear, however, in these pages that for Temple 'real forgiveness' or 'true forgiveness' is precisely the restoration of 'fellowship', p.m. reconciliation.
25. Oliver P. Rafferty, *Catholicism in Ulster 1603-1983* (Dublin: Gill & Macmillan, 1994), p. 7.
26. Antonia Fraser, *King Charles II* (London: Weidenfeld and Nicolson, 1979), p. 190. Cf. Donald W. Shriver Jr, loc. cit. (n. 24 *supra*) pp. 191-194.

27. Patrick O'Connell SJ, 'On the Way to Reconciliation: The Events at Rome and Istanbul of December 7th 1965', *The Heythrop Journal* 7/2 (spring 1966), pp. 183-187.
28. Cf. n. 3 *supra*.
29. *The Times* (London), 26 January 1995; *The Guardian*, 28 April 1995.
30. (Chicago: Loyola University Press, 1989), as quoted in the 'Editorial Comment', *The Month*, 28/1 (January 1995), pp. 3-4.
31. 'Reconciliation in Judaism', *Reconciliation in Religion and Society*, op. cit. (n. 11 *supra*), p. 185.
32. Cf. Michael Hurley SJ, 'Chronicle: Ecumenism', *The Furrow* (Maynooth), 16/8 (August 1965), pp. 493-495.
33. *The Irish Times*, 27 October 1994.
34. Ibid., 19 November 1994.
35. Ibid., 22 January 1995.
36. Cf. John Waters, ibid., 14 February 1995.
37. John Waters, ibid., 14 March 1995.
38. Willie Walsh, 'Ecumenism: A Journey Halted?', *The Furrow*, 48/5 (May 1997), p. 270.
39. 17 May 1997, p. 4.
40. 15 May 1997. Mary Kenny and Mgr Gerard Sheehy were the authors of these sharply critical articles. Martin Browne replied to them in the issue of 19 June.
41. So Joseph Liechty, loc. cit. (n. 22 *supra*), p. 69.
42. Cf. Wilhelm Niesel, *Reformed Symbolics* (Edinburgh and London: Oliver and Boyd, 1962), pp. 201-210.
43. Exodus 34:6.
44. 31:20.
45. Cf., e.g., Jean-Claude Djereke, 'Peace and reconciliation in Rwanda today: what can the Church do?', *The Month*, 28/6 (June 1995), pp. 228-231.
46. *The Tablet*, 27 May 1995.
47. Cf. David Stevens, 'Bearing the Cross: Martin Luther King Jr and the Southern Christian Leadership Conference', *Studies*, 78 (summer 1989) pp. 206-208; Brian Lennon SJ, *After the Ceasefires* (n. 8 *supra*), pp. 22-23.
48. Donald W. Shriver Jr, *Forgiveness and Politics* (note 20 *supra*); 'A Struggle for Justice and Reconciliation: Forgiveness in the Politics of the American Black Civil Rights Movement, 1955-68', *Studies*, 78 (1989), pp. 136-150.
49. Op. cit. (n. 8 *supra*), pp. 23, 26, 98.
50. Some historians and sociologists tend to be negative, cf. Bryan Wilson

reviewing David Martin's *Reflections on Sociology and Theology*, *The Tablet*, 5 July 1997, p. 869: 'Forgiveness – even were it forthcoming – would make no sense, and make no difference'. Cf. also footnotes 39 and 40 *supra*.
51. Loc. cit. (n. 22 *supra*), pp. 68-69.
52. An Inter-Church Group on Faith and Politics, *The Things that Make for Peace* (Belfast: Faith and Politics Group, 1995), p. 14.
53. §33 (London: CTS, 1994), p. 43.
54. Catholic Press and Information Office, Dublin, p. 2.
55. *The Report of the Working Party on Sectarianism* (Belfast: Irish Inter-Church Meeting, 1993), p. 42.
56. Gabriel Daly, 'Forgiveness and Community', *Reconciling Memories* (n. 2 *supra*), p. 213.
57. Ibid.
58. Ibid. pp. 209, 208.
59. Ibid. p. 198.
60. 'Ceasefire' in *The Great Orchid* (London: Jonathan Cape, 1995), p. 39.
61. Mary Holland, *The Irish Times*, 1 June 1995.
62. *Ecumenical News International Bulletin*, 9 (14 May 1997), p. 24.

Chapter 4: Ecumenical Tithing
1. Above 'Unity by 2000?' chapter 2, p. 51.
2. London: CTS, 1993.
3. *The Ecumenical Review* 45/4 (1993) pp. 490-494; PCPCU, *Information Service*, 84 (1993/III-IV), pp. 176-180.
4. 'The New Catholic Ecumenical Directory: A Protestant Reading', *The Ecumenical Review* 47/4 (1995), pp. 419-425.
5. Cf. chapter 8 *infra*, pp. 132-145.
6. Cf. Róisín Hannaway, 'Eucharist and Reconciliation', *Reconciliation in Religion and Society*, ed. Michael Hurley SJ, Belfast, 1994, pp. 189-193.
7. The 1967 *Ecumenical Directory* stated (§47) that Roman Catholics could fulfil their Sunday or holyday obligation at the Orthodox Divine Liturgy. The 1983 Code of Canon Law makes no mention of this exception, simply stating (canon 1248 §1) that the Sunday obligation is fulfilled 'anywhere in a Catholic rite'. The 1993 *Directory on Ecumenism* does not renew the exception. According to an article in *The Jurist* 'It could be argued that the favor of satisfying the Sunday and holy day obligation at an Eastern non-Catholic Eucharist was suppressed by the 1983 code …. More likely, I believe, the code's

silence left the favor intact in keeping with the principle of c. 21 and the rule that favors are to be multiplied': cf. John M Huels OSM, 'The 1993 Ecumenical Directory: Theological Values and Juridical Norms', *The Jurist*, 56/1 (1996), n. 48, p. 416.
8. 'Decree on Ecumenism', §22, *Vatican Council II*, ed. Austin Flannery OP (Dublin: Dominican Publications, 1992), p. 469.
9. *The Canon Law Digest VI* (New York, 1969), pp. 675-8, 684-5.
10. The original version of this chapter was part of a paper prepared for delivery at the Glenstal Ecumenical Conference in June 1983 (cf. *Doctrine and Life*, September 1983, pp. 406-414).

Chapter 5: George Otto Simms: Ecumenical Exemplar
1. George Otto Simms, Anglican priest, born 4 July 1910, ordained deacon 1935, priest 1936, Curate Assistant St Bartholomew's, Dublin 1935-1938, Chaplain Lincoln Theological College 1938-39, Dean of Residence Trinity College, Dublin, 1939-52, Chaplain-Secretary Church of Ireland Training College 1943-52, Dean of Cork 1952, Bishop of Cork, Cloyne and Ross 1952-56, Archbishop of Dublin and Primate of Ireland 1956-69, MRIA 1957, Archbishop of Armagh and Primate of All Ireland 1969-80; publications include *The Book of Kells: a short description*, 1950, *The Book of Kells* (a facsimile edition, jointly edited with E. H. Alton and P. Meyer), 1951, *The Bible in Perspective*, 1953, *Christ Within Me*, 1975, *Irish Illuminated Manuscripts*, 1980; married 1941 Mercy Gwynn (three sons, two daughters), died 15 November 1991.
2. George was curate at St Bartholomew's when Father Colquohoun of St John's had his licence removed for six months. According to the *Magazine of the Church of St John the Evangelist* (December 1991, p. 4), 'against the advice of his friends and colleagues Father George cycled over to St John's to celebrate the daily Mass during the period of Father Colquohoun's ban'.
3. The Most Reverend G. O. Simms, *Addresses and Papers of Michael Lloyd Ferrar 1909-1960* (London: 1962), p. 32. Cf. also a talk given by the Archbishop at the Anglican Congress in Toronto 1963 (*Proceedings*, p. 233), and an article entitled 'On Irish Spirituality' which he contributed to the Disestablishment issue of *Theology* (May 1970, p. 197). The Reverend Michael Ferrar was Warden of the Divinity Hostel in Dublin from 1939 to 1960.
4. Before retiring Raymond Jenkins had served the Church of Ireland in

many capacities: as Dean of Residence at TCD, Warden of the Divinity Hostel, Vicar of All Saints, Grangegorman, Archdeacon of Dublin and Honorary Secretary of the General Synod. His name occurs frequently in the pages of Lesley Whiteside's *George Otto Simms, A Biography* (Gerrards Cross, 1990) as that of 'a very influential friend' (p. 45). He died on 16 January 1998. *The Daily Telegraph* carried an obituary on 31 January 1998.

5. The Dean of St Patrick's, The Very Reverend J. W. Armstrong (later to be Primate), was the Church of Ireland sponsor and organiser of the proposed conference at Greenhills. The reaction from Archbishop McCann was negative: so the Dean himself once told me and so Archdeacon Jenkins later confirmed. Both consulted Archbishop Simms about the problem. After a further approach from the Dean the Primate withdrew his objections and the conference went ahead. It is possible, indeed likely, that Archbishop Simms intervened.

6. When the membership was announced on 3 November 1966 it was criticised by the *Church of Ireland Gazette* in an editorial of 11 November on the grounds that no Irish Anglican was included. I also did a critique in *The Furrow* (December 1966, pp. 781-6) in an article entitled '*Non Anglicani sed Angli?*'. This was reprinted in the *Church of Ireland Gazette* the following month and brought me a letter from Lambeth Palace expressing displeasure. Archdeacon Jenkins later informed me that while in Rome at the Anglican Centre in October 1966 he was told by Bishop Moorman that the membership of the forthcoming Preparatory Commission would include an Irish Anglican, The Bishop of Ossory, The Right Reverend H. R. McAdoo. The omission of the latter's name from the initial list was not therefore the fault of Lambeth Palace and can only be explained by an intervention of the Church of Ireland Primate, Archbishop McCann. Happily, Bishop McAdoo joined the Preparatory Commission after its first meeting and subsequently became a member – and indeed Anglican Co-Chairman – of the Anglican-Roman Catholic International Commission which succeeded the Preparatory Commission and which met for the first time in January 1970.

7. *Addresses and Papers of Michael Lloyd Ferrar,* op. cit. (n. 3 *supra*), pp. 20, 21.
8. 'On Irish Spirituality', *Theology,* May 1970, pp. 198, 194.
9. *Anglican Congress 1963: Report of Proceedings* (Toronto, 1963), p. 235.
10. *Theology,* May 1970, p. 197.

11. *Proceedings*, p. 235.
12. Cheltenham College, which seems to have some unidentified Irish connection. Bishop Richard and Professor Anthony Hanson (Church of Ireland) were also at school there, as was Bishop Donald Kennedy (Presbyterian Church in Ireland, Church of North India), who told me there was a Boyne House there in his day.
13. *Theology,* May 1970, p. 195.
14. Anglican Congress 1963: Report of Proceedings, op.cit. p. 234.
15. W. B. Stanford, *A Recognised Church* (Dublin: APCK, 1944); *Faith and Faction in Ireland Now*, Dublin 1946.
16. *Christ, Youth and The Conflict of Life* (Dublin: APCK, 1943), p. 18.
17. *Everyman, An Annual Religio-Cultural Review*, Servite Priory, Benburb, 2 (1969), pp. 121-3.
18. Cf. Lesley Whiteside, op. cit. pp. 26, 47.
19. *The Irish Times,* 25 November 1991, p. 13; *Church of Ireland Gazette*, 29 November 1991; *Church Times*, 29 November 1991.
20. *Anglican-Roman Catholic Marriage*. The Report of the Anglican-Roman Catholic International Commission on the Theology of Marriage and its Application to Mixed Marriages (London: 1975), pp. 2, 31.
21. This passage is taken from the manuscript of a lecture given in Canada and printed here with the permission of Mercy Simms who died on 1 June 1998. *The Irish Times* carried an appreciation on 25 June 1998.
22. *Journal of the General Synod*, 1980, p. 83.
23. Eric Gallagher and Stanley Worrall, *Christians in Ulster 1968-1980* (Oxford: OUP, 1982), p. 211.
24. Ibid., p. 133.
25. Ibid.
26. Very Reverend John Arnold, 'How the Spring comes in Siberia', *Independent,* 16 November 1991.
27. Gallagher and Worrall, op. cit. p. 151.
28. *Journal of the General Synod*, 1974, p. XIV.
29. Ibid. 1980, p. XII.
30. Cf. chapter 15 *infra*.
31. These are the words inscribed on a silver salver presented to me later by the Disestablishment Committee.
32. 'Thoughts after Lambeth', *Studies,* winter 1968, pp. 345-60.
33. A much abbreviated version of this chapter appeared in *Studies,* summer 1992, pp. 212-216.

Chapter 6: Ecumenism, Ecumenical Theology and Ecumenics

1. Cf. above chapter 2, pp. 38-39.
2. 'Decree on Ecumenism', §1, *Vatican Council II*, ed. Austin Flannery OP (Dublin: Dominican Publications, 1992), p. 452.
3. On the missionary dimension of ecumenism, cf. Michael Hurley SJ, *Theology of Ecumenism* (Cork: Mercier Press, 1969), pp. 20-28.
4. *Final Statement and Recommendations of the First Asian Congress of Jesuit Ecumenists,* Manila, 18-23 June 1975.
5. Cf. 'Introduction', p. 10 *supra.*
6. Drawn up by the WCC in 1950 to clarify what inter-Church relations involved for its member Churches.
7. According to a plaque in the entrance hall: *Orientis uni Ecclesiae conciliandi voto ... motus.*
8. K. Rahner, *Theological Investigations*, XI, p. 26.
9. As recalled in the following pages, the Faith and Order Conference at Lund in 1952 underlined the disadvantages of comparative Christianity in the search for Christian unity; cf. also Michael Hurley SJ, *Theology of Ecumenism*, op.cit. pp. 77-85.
10. Oliver Tomkins, *One Lord, One Baptism* (London: 1960), p. 5.
11. A phrase from the Decree on the Church's Missionary Activity, *Vatican II*, op. cit. p. 820: 'The division of Christians is injurious to the holy work of preaching the Gospel to every creature, and deprives many people of access to the faith.'
12. Decree on Ecumenism, 4, ibid. p. 458.
13. Cf. Michael Hurley SJ, 'Ecumenics: What and Why?', *The Furrow*, 21/7 (July 1970), pp. 416-27.
14. Pp. 77-79.
15. Irish Episcopal Conference, *Directory on Ecumenism in Ireland*, Dublin 1976, §§44-49, pp. 24-26.
16. J. K. S. Reid, 'Theological Education – The Challenge of Ecumenism', *Biblical Theology* 17/2 (May 1967), p. 10. Professor Reid would of course today happily add 'and women'.
17. The original version of this chapter was prepared as a paper read on 5 November 1976 to a meeting of the Irish Theological Association in Dublin; on 17 January 1977 to a meeting of the academic staff of the United Theological Seminary in St Paul, Minneapolis, and on 20 January 1977 to a meeting of the fellows of the Ecumenical Institute, St John's Abbey, Collegeville, Minnesota. The text was printed in the *Irish Theological Quarterly,* 45/2 (1978), pp. 132-139.

Chapter 7: Baptism in Ecumenical Perspective
1. *One in Christ*, 22/3 (summer 1986), p. 266.
2. *Baptism Today and Tomorrow* (London: 1966), pp. 136, 162, 164.
3. Stephen F. Winward, *The Dedication Service* (London: 1960), p. 13.
4. Ibid. p. 14.
5. A. Gilmore, *Baptism and Christian Unity* (London: 1966), p. 96.
6. Ibid. p. 101.
7. *Baptism Today and Tomorrow*, op.cit. pp. 102, 136, 152, 137.
8. Ibid. p. 169.
9. Martin Reardon, *Christian Initiation: A Policy for the Church of England*, London, 1991, p. 1.
10. 'The Schedule Presented by Three Members of the Canterbury Joint Committee and entitled by them "Baptism, Confirmation and Communion (Christian Initiation Today)"', pp. 29-31, printed with separate pagination in *Baptism and Confirmation Today* (London: SPCK, 1955).
11. *Crisis for Baptism:* The Report of the 1965 Ecumenical Conference Sponsored by the Parish and People Movement, ed. Basil S. Moss (London: 1965), p. 24.
12. *Christian Initiation. Birth and Growth in the Christian Society*, The Report of the Commission on Christian Initiation (London: General Synod of the Church of England, 1971), §105, p. 39.
13. Ibid. §102, p. 38.
14. This Report is incorporated with separate pagination in *Christian Initiation*. This appendix is at p.14.
15. *Christian Initiation*, §93, p. 36.
16. Ibid. §§119-29, pp. 42-43.
17. Ibid. §96, p. 36.
18. Ibid. §104, p. 39.
19. Ibid. §97, p. 37.
20. A 1995 statement by the Bishop of Lincoln quoted by James Beyrens in *Confirmation, Sacrament of Grace* (Leominster: Gracewing, 1995), p. 47.
21. Quoted by Martin Reardon, op. cit. (n. 9 *supra*), p. 36. Canon Reardon stresses (pp. 35-8) the educational changes that the establishment of a catechumenate would entail. The revised initiation services which General Synod 1997 referred to the House of Bishops (*Church Times*, 18 July 1997, p. 4) did not include this service of Thanksgiving.
22. 'The Constitution on the Sacred Liturgy' §64, 'Dogmatic Constitution on the Church' §14, 'Decree on the Church's Missionary Activity' §14, *Vatican II,* ed. Austin Flannery OP (Dublin: Dominican Publications, 1992), pp. 21, 366, 828-9.

23. Aidan Kavanagh, 'Christian Initiation in post-Conciliar Roman Catholicism: A Brief Report', unpublished paper delivered to Societas Liturgica, 1977, p. 10. Cf. the same author's 'Initiation: Baptism and Confirmation', *Worship 46* (1972), pp. 262-76; Roger Béraudy PSS, 'Le Nouveau Rituel du Baptême des Adultes', *La Maison Dieu*, 121, 1975, pp. 122-42; Adrien Nocent OSB *et al.*, 'L'Ordo Initiationis Christianae Adultorum', *Ephemerides Liturgicae*, 88 (1974), pp. 163-270.
24. *Rite of Christian Initiation of Adults*, Provisional Text (Washington DC: United States Catholic Conference, 1974), §§10, 15, pp. 3, 4.
25. Ibid. §15, p. 4.
26. Ibid. §18, p. 4.
27. Ibid. §19, p. 5.
28. Ibid. §36, p. 8.
29. Ibid. §39, p. 8.
30. *Baptism and Church Membership*. A report of a working party to Churches Together in England, London, 1997, p. 33.
31. 'Dogmatic Constitution on The Church', §8; *Vatican Council II,* op.cit. p. 357; 'Decree on Ecumenism', §3, ibid. p. 455.
32. 'The conciliar teaching does not have to be read in an exclusive sense to mean that the one Church subsists *only* in the Catholic Church; it also may subsist in other Christian traditions, perhaps fully in some and in varying degrees in others.' So John M. Huels OSM, 'The 1993 Ecumenical Directory: Theological Values and Juridical Norms', *The Jurist*, 56/1 (1996), p. 405.
33. Flannery, op. cit. p. 510.
34. *One in Christ,* 11/4 (1975), pp. 374-5.
35. Ibid. p. 374. Cf. Enda McDonagh, *Between Chaos and New Creation* (Dublin: Gill & Macmillan, 1986), pp. 83-86.
36. 'Final Report of the dialogue between the Secretariat for Promoting Christian Unity of the Roman Catholic Church and leaders of some Pentecostal Churches and participants in the Charismatic movement within Protestant and Anglican Churches, 1972-1976', *One in Christ*, 12/4 (1976), p. 314. Cf. also 'The Pentecostal/Catholic Dialogue', PCPCU, *Information Service,* 91 (summer 1996/1-11), pp. 42-44. Cecil M. Robeck Jr, in an article on 'Evangelicals and Catholics Together', refers to 'the surprising convergence reached on the subject of Baptism': cf. *One in Christ,* 33/2 (1997), p. 152.
37. John F. Matthews, *Baptism: a Baptist View* (London: 1976), p. 28.
38. Neville Clark, 'The Theology of Baptism', *Christian Baptism,* ed. A.

Gilmore (London: 1959), pp. 325-6. But cf. Martin Reardon, op. cit. (n. 9 *supra*), pp. 44-6.
39. In so doing I am changing my mind. My answer was negative in a paper on 'The Problem of Baptism' written in 1966 and published in *Ecumenical Studies: Baptism & Marriage*, ed. Michael Hurley SJ (Dublin: Gill & Son, 1968), pp. 23-60. Cf. in particular pp. 45-46.
40. John F. Matthews, *Baptism: A Baptist View,* op.cit. p. 25.
41. 'Faith and Order of the Church: The Doctrines of the Church', Clause 5.
42. *One Baptism, One Eucharist and a Mutually Recognized Ministry,* Faith and Order Paper No. 73, Geneva, 1975.
43. *The New Delhi Report* (London: SCM, 1961), p. 117.
44. 'Pastoral Constitution on the Church in the Modern World', §22, *Vatican Council II,* ed. A. Flannery OP, op.cit. p. 924.
45. Donald Pridge and David Phypers (Illinois: Inter-Varsity Press, 1977).
46. Decree on Ecumenism, §22, *Vatican II,* ed. A. Flannery OP, op.cit. p. 469.
47. The original text of this chapter was prepared for a seminar on Christian initiation held in Rome under the auspices of the Friars of the Atonement in October 1977 during the Synod of Bishops. It was subsequently published in *One in Christ,* 14/2 (April 1978), pp. 106-123 and in *Foundations. A Baptist Journal of Theology and History* 22 (1979), pp. 218-232

Chapter 8: Eucharist: Means and Expression of Unity
1. The view adopted is basically that which I put forward in 'The Sacrament of Unity: Intercommunion and some Forgotten Truths', *The Way,* 9/2 (April 1969), pp. 107-117, but the approach is somewhat different.
2. *Documents on Christian Unity: A Selection from the First and Second Series 1920/30,* ed. G. K. A. Bell (London: 1955), p. 198.
3. For John Wesley the Eucharist was a 'converting ordinance': cf. *Journal,* 28 June 1740, ed. Telford, II, p. 361; *Standard Sermons* II, p. 60.
4. Cf. chapter 9 *infra*.
5. Denzinger-Schönmetzer, *Enchiridion Symbolorum,* no. 1638.
6. Ibid. no. 1743.
7. Cf. Jean-Marie Tillard, 'The Bread and the Cup of Reconciliation', *Concilium,* 7/1 (1971), pp. 38-54; John Quinn, 'The Lord's Supper

and Forgiveness of Sin', *Living Bread, Saving Cup*, ed. R. Kevin Seasoltz OSB (Collegeville: Liturgical Press, 1987), pp. 231-241. I am grateful to Father Finbarr Clancy SJ for these two references.
8. Cf. Michael Hurley SJ, 'Penance: Sacrament of Reconciliation', *Sin and Repentance*, ed. Denis O'Callaghan (Dublin and Sydney: Gill & Son, 1967), pp. 109-126.
9. 'Instruction [of 1 June 1972] concerning cases when other Christians may be admitted to eucharistic communion in the Catholic Church', *One in Christ*, 8/4 (October 1972), p. 395.
10. Anglican/Roman Catholic 'Agreed Statement on Eucharistic Doctrine', *One in Christ*, 8/1 (January 1972), p. 71. *One Baptism, One Eucharist and a Mutually Recognized Ministry (BEM)*, §§5-13, ibid. 18/4 (1982), pp. 358-360.
11. G. Diekmann, 'Worship', *Theology of Renewal* (Montreal 1968), II, p. 93.
12. 'Decree on the Church's Missionary Activity', §2, *Vatican Council II*, ed. Austin Flannery OP (Dublin: Dominican Publications, 1992), p. 814.
13. Loc. cit. (n. 10), p. 70.
14. §§20-26 *One in Christ*, 18/4 (1982), pp. 362-364.
15. Cf. Sr Róisín Hannaway SSL, 'Eucharist and Reconciliation', *Reconciliation in Religion and Society*, ed. Michael Hurley SJ (Belfast: Institute of Irish Studies, 1994), pp. 189-193; Michael Hurley SJ 'An Ecumenical Mass', *The Furrow*, 47/3 (March 1996), pp. 155-156; Jean-Marie Tillard OP, *The Tablet*, 6 January 1996, p. 29.
16. Cf. chapter 2 *supra*, p. 28. The original version of this chapter was prepared as a paper for delivery to an ecumenical conference on 'Eucharist, Ecumenism, Community' held at Monash University, Clayton, Melbourne, 13-16 February 1973, in connection with the fortieth International Eucharistic Congress. It appeared in *One in Christ* 9 (1973), pp. 270-283.

Chapter 9: Catholicity: The Witness of Calvin's *Institutes*
1. Oekumenische Rundschau, 'Use the Days of Grace! The Ecumenical Movement on the Way to the Third Millennium', *The Ecumenical Review*, 48/1 (1996), p. 94.
2. A. Harnack, *What is Christianity?* (London: Williams and Norgate, 1901), pp. 262, 276.
3. *Catholicity* (Westminster: 1947), p. 43.

4. The phrase used in his influential Cambridge sermon of 1946 by Archbishop Fisher of Canterbury in relation to the Free Churches, inviting them to 'take episcopacy into their system'.
5. Martin Van Elderen, Common Understanding and Vision; A Survey of the Discussion in the WCC, *The Ecumenical Review,* 49/1 (January 1997), p. 5.
6. Gordon Rupp, 'Calvin, Prophet of Christian Order', *The Times,* 27 May 1964, p. 11.
7. Cf. n. 20 *infra.*
8. *The History and Character of Calvinism* (New York: OUP, 1962), p. 119.
9. Art. cit. (note 6).
10. *Institutio christianae religionis,* 1559, ediderunt Petrus Barth, Gulielmus Niesel (Joannis Calvini Opera Selecta, III-V), München 1957, 1959, 1962. *Calvin: Institutes of the Christian Religion* (The Library of Christian Classics, XX, XXI), ed. J. T. McNeill, tr. F. L. Battles, 2 vols with continuous pagination, London, 1961. Unless otherwise indicated all references in the rest of this chapter are to Calvin's *Institutes.* Each of the four books is divided into chapters and these into sections; a colon will be used to distinguish chapters and sections. References will be added in parenthesis to the volume and page of the Barth-Niesel edition and to the page of the McNeill edition; and these references will be separated by a semi-colon. E.g. IV, 3:1-2 (V, 42-4; 1053-5). In quoting I give Battles' translation with only occasional modifications.
11. P. 1011, n. 1.
12. III, II:10 (IV, 191; 737).
13. III, 2:33-7 (IV 44-7; 580-4).
14. III, 2:29 (IV, 39; 575).
15. III, 3 (IV, 55-84; 592-621).
16. IV, 10:1 (V, 165; 1180).
17. The *Institutes* was in fact referred to as a *summa pietatis* in the very title of the first (1536) edition: 'Containing almost the Whole Sum of Piety and Whatever It is Necessary to Know in the Doctrine of Salvation. A Work Very Well Worth Reading by All Persons Zealous for Piety', McNeill's edition, xxxiii. In his introduction to the final (1559) edition Calvin wrote as follows: 'It has been my purpose in this labour to prepare and instruct candidates in sacred theology for the reading of the divine Word, in order that they may be able both to have easy access to it and to advance in it without stumbling.' This statement throws some interesting light on Calvin's conception of the Church and its relationship to Scripture.

18. Cf. J. Guitton, *The Church and the Gospel* (E. tr.), (London: 1961), p. 203.
19. J. Thompson and J. L. M. Haire, 'The Reformation Today', *Biblical Theology,* 15/2 (July 1965), pp. 15-16.
20. That there was a mystical strain in Calvin is recognised by, e.g., James Quinn SJ in his 'Calvinism', *A Catholic Dictionary of Theology,* I (London: Thomas Nelson & Sons Ltd, 1961), 314-315: 'Calvin's approach to theology is entirely different from that of the systematic theologian. For him theology is not the study of ideas about God. Its object is God himself. In this sense he is much more a mystical theologian – or an Old Testament Prophet – than a scholastic …. The whole object of Calvin's theology is not to tell us about God but to allow God to reveal himself to the individual soul …. This strain of mysticism is the real key to Calvinism.'
21. IV, 2:11-12 (V, 40-2; 1051-3).
22. Calvin treats of *pietas* in I, 2:1 (III, 35; 41). In the chapter title referred to above and elsewhere Battles translates *pii* as 'godly', but here at least Calvin's own French translation (given by A. Ganoczy, *Calvin theologien de l'Eglise et du ministére,* Paris, 1964, p. 212) is *'fidèles'*, which has more ecclesial connotations.
23. IV, 1:1, 4 (V. 1-2, 7; 1012, 1016).
24. F. J. Paul, *Romanism and Evangelical Christianity* (London: 1940), p. 111.
25. IV, 8:1 (V, 133; 1149); IV, 12:1 (V, 212; 1229).
26. IV, 15:20-2 (V, 300-303; 1320-3). 'It is also pertinent here to know that it is wrong *perperam fieri* for private individuals to assume the administration of Baptism; for this as well as the serving of the Supper *coenae dispensatio* is a function of the ecclesiastical ministry *pars Ecclesiastici ministerii*. For Christ did not command women, or men of every sort, to baptize, but gave this command to those whom he had appointed apostles.' *A Manual of Church Doctrine According to the Church of Scotland* (by H. J. Wotherspoon and J. M. Kirkpatrick, 2nd ed., revised and enlarged by T. F. Torrance and R. S. Wright, London: 1965), p. 27, has the following statement: 'The prohibition by the Church of Scotland of Baptism by others than ordained ministers may be considered disciplinary rather than a doctrinal requirement, and to be intended to emphasize the fact of this irregularity.' In the Presbyterian Church in Ireland a stricter view which would consider lay Baptism invalid has in the past, I gather, generally been held and still is widely held but not so generally as formerly. Cf. *infra*, n. 70.

27. IV, I:II (V,15; 1025).
28. IV, 3:6 (V, 48; 1058).
29. IV, 1:4, 5, II (V, 7, 8, 9, 15; 1016, 1017, 1018, 1025).
30. IV, 1:10(V, 14; 1024).
31. IV, I :12 (V, 16; 1025).
32. IV, 1:13, 19 (V, 18, 23; 1028, 1033).
33. IV, 2 (V, 30-2; 1041-53).
34. IV, 1:2 (V, 4; 1014).
35. IV, 3:1 (V, 42; 1053); IV, 4:1 (V, 57; 1068).
36. IV, 3:2-3 (V, 44-5; 1055-6). Calvin's Catholic reverence for the ministry is shown above all in the fact that, despite his rejection of 'the five other ceremonies, falsely termed sacraments' (IV, 19), he came eventually to accept ordination and especially the imposition of hands as a true sacrament though not in the case of Roman ordinations: cf. IV, 19:28, 31 (V, 463, 465; 1476, 1479). 'Surely, they are utterly wicked when they dare designate this rite with the title of sacrament. As far as the true office of presbyter is concerned, which is commended to us by Christ's lips, I willingly accord that place to it' (*libenter eo loco habeo;* cf. *'Quant est de l'imposition des mains, qui se fait pour introduire les vrais Prestres et Ministres de l'Eglise en leur estat: il ne repugne point que on ne la receoyve pour Sacrament'* – quoted from the French edition by Barth Niesel *ad loc.*) 'There remains the laying on of hands. As I concede that it is a sacrament in true and lawful ordinations, so I deny that it has place in this farce...' (Roman ordination ceremony). *'Superest impositio manuum, quam ut in veris legitimisque ordinationibus Sacramentum esse concedo, ita nego locum habere in hac fabula...'* Cf. A. Ganoczy, op. cit. (note 23), pp. 318-27.
37. IV, 8:1 (V, 134. 1150). So Battles translates '*Est igitur Ecclesiastica potestas non maligne quidem ornanda, sed tamen includenda certis finibus.*'
38. IV, 12:1 (V, 212; 1230).
39. Cf. A. Ganoczy, op. cit. (note 22), pp. 192 ff; F. Wendel, *Calvin: The Origins and Development of his Religious Thought* (tr. P. Mairet) London, 1963, p. 142. Both adduce evidence to show that the change is also owing to the influence of the Strasbourg reformer, Martin Bucer.
40. IV, 6:5 (V, 93-4; 1106-7).
41. IV, 6:8 (V, 96; 1109).
42. IV, 6:4 (V, 92; 1105).
43. Ibid. (V, 93; 1106). Battles here translates 'impersonating unity itself'!
44. Cf. Ganoczy, op. cit. (n. 22 *supra*), pp. 396-400.

45. IV, 7:12 (V, 116; 1131).
46. IV, 4:2 (V, 58-9; 1069-70). *'Politiae tantum et pacis conservandae gratia.'* The 'merely' is omitted by Battles.
47. IV, 11:6 (V, 201; 1218).
48. IV, 3:15 (V, 56; 1066).
49. IV, 3:8 (V, so; 1061). Cf. n. 60 *infra*.
50. IV, 1:10 (V, 14-5; 1024-5). Cf. IV, 1:16, 19 (V, 20, 23; 1031, 1033).
51. IV, 14:9, 17 (V, 266, 274; 1284, 1285, 1292).
52. IV, 14:14 (V, 271; 1289).
53. IV, 3:1 (V, 42; 1053).
54. Cf. K. Delahaye, *Ecclesia Mater* [*Unam Sanctam* 46], Paris, 1964, pp. 170-95.
55. IV, 3:3 (V, 45; 1056).
56. IV, 1:1, 5 (V, 1, 8, 9 ; 1012, 1017, 1018); IV, 3:3 (V, 45; 1055).
57. IV, 15:14 (V, 295; 1314): *'Neque tantum nudo spectaculo pascit oculos: sed in rem praesentem nos adducit, et quod figurat, efficaciter simul implet'*.
58. IV, 12:4 (V, 214-15; 1232).
59. IV 12:7 (V, 218; 1235).
60. It is so easy to consider collegiality at any level of Church government as merely the acceptance of modern democratic trends that the following observation by Professor J. K. S. Reid (*Presbyterians and Unity*, London 1962, p. 90) deserves to be quoted: 'Democracy had scarcely been thought of when the form of Presbyterian polity was worked out. Indeed, so far from democratic ideas giving rise to Presbyterianism, it is historically rather Presbyterianism that played a great part in promoting and determining the rise of democracy. For another, democracy comes out of a quite different order of ideas. It is, in the well-known words, the government of the people by the people for the people. But in the Church government is of the people of God, by the Spirit of God, for the glory of God. Two such different ideas cannot be assimilated without the greatest confusion.' Cf. also T. F. Torrance, 'The Corporate Episcopate', *Royal Priesthood* [Scottish Journal of Theology: Occasional Papers 3] (Edinburgh-London: 1955), pp. 88-108; A. Ganoczy, 'Le structure collégiale de l'Église chez Calvin et au IIe Concile du Vatican', *Irénikon*, 38 (1965), pp. 6-32; C. McGarry, 'Collegiality and Catholicity', *Irish Theological Quarterly*, 32 (1965), p. 189.
61. IV, 6:9-10, 17 (V, 96-8, 103-4; 1110-1111, 1117-18).
62. IV, 1:1, 5 (V 1, 9; 1011, 1018) IV, 3:1 (V, 43; 1054).
63. IV, 14:3 (V, 260; 1278).

64. IV, 3:1 (V, 42; 1053); IV, 6:9 (V, 97. 1111).
65. IV, 14:17 (V, 275. 1293).
66. IV, 3:2 (V, 44; 1055): *'Seque adeo ipsum praesentem quodammodo exhibet, Spiritus sui virtutem in sua hac institutione exercendo, ne inanis sit vel otiosa.'* Battles has 'He shows himself as though present', but *quodommodo* modifies rather the verb and it seems desirable to retain *'exhibet'* in its English form. The term seems characteristic of Calvin's sacramentology and it is a familiar one in Calvinist theology. Cf. IV, 14:26 (V, 284; 1303): *'In utrisque* [Old and New Testament sacraments] *Christi exhibitio: sed in his uberior ac plenior'*. Cf. *A Manual of Church Doctrine*, p. 18: A Sacrament '"exhibits": a word which, as used in theological documents, has the same meaning as "applies", that is to say, it actually conveys and confers its spiritual part. What a Sacrament signifies, seals and applies is ... *Christ* who is full of grace and truth'. Cf. G. MacGregor, *Corpus Christi*, p. 179, n. 1. The idea of 'efficacy', however, though certainly present (the glorified Christ is Lord) should surely not be allowed to obscure what seems (in Calvin and in sacramentology generally) to be the more basic idea of 'visibilisation'.
67. The above comparison is not explicitly made by Calvin himself in the *Institutes* but it is implied in his 'maternal approach' to the mystery of the Church (as it is implied in the New Testament, by St Luke, e.g. when he represents the Holy Spirit coming on Mary and on the apostles at the beginning of his gospel and of Acts). Max Thurian in his *Mary, Mother of the Lord, Figure of the Church* (E. tr., London: The Faith Press, 1963) is able to quote texts which show that Luther considered Mary as type of Mother Church but significantly gives no such quotations from Calvin who, unlike Luther, nowhere apparently refers to Mary as our mother. This does not mean, however, that Calvin was unaware of Mary as figure of the Church. His awareness of this relationship seems clear in his sermons which emphasise that she is our model, that we ought to take her as our schoolmistress, become her schoolchildren and learn from her how to have faith and obedience and trust in God. Cf. W. Tappolet, A. Ebneter, *Das Marienlob der Reformatoren*, Tübingen, 1962, pp. 161-218. Calvin's theology of the Church lays particular emphasis on its ministerial role of teaching, instructing, educating: cf. IV 1:5 (V 7-10; 1016-20); IV, 3 (V 42-57; 1053-68). It is within this category of ideas, therefore (rather than that of motherhood), that Calvin makes the 'exchange of idioms' which indicates an awareness of an essential 'typical' relationship between Mary and the Church.

p. 165

68. Cf. C. McGarry, 'The Eucharistic Celebration as the Manifestation of the Church', *Irish Theological Quarterly*, 32 (1965), p. 325.
69. IV, 1:7 (V, 12; 1021); IV, 15:1, 12 (V, 285, 294; 1303, 1313); IV, 16:30 (V 335; 1352); IV, 17:1 (V 342; 1360); IV, 18:19 (V, 433; 1446). Calvin holds that justification is possible without the sacrament of Baptism but that this non-baptismal justification comes through the preaching of the Church. Cf. IV, 14:14 (V, 272; 1290): 'We know that justification is lodged in Christ alone, and that it is communicated to us no less by the preaching of the gospel than by the seal of the sacrament, and without the latter can stand unimpaired (*in solidum posse constare*).' Calvin also holds that the unbaptised infants of believers are not necessarily damned. He emphasises this in arguing against lay Baptism. It is in this context (of the possibility of salvation for unbaptised infants of believers) that Calvin gives us his exposition of the 'obsignatory view' of Baptism; cf. IV, 15:20, 22 (V, 301, 303; 1321, 1323). On the basis of the foregoing it is stated (Calvin: *Institutes*, ed. McNeill, 1321, n. 39) that 'Calvin does not teach with the Augsburg Confession, art. ix, that "Baptism is necessary to salvation".' But what Calvin wrote was: 'Few realise how much injury the dogma that Baptism is necessary for salvation, badly expounded, has entailed.' '*Quantum damni invexerit dogma illud male expositum, Baptisma esse de necessitate salutis, pauci animadvertunt*': cf. IV, 15:20 (V 301; 1321) where '*male expositum*' seems the operative phrase. Cf. also IV, 16:26 (V, 331; 1349): 'It merely suffices to prove that Baptism is not so necessary that one from whom the capacity to obtain it has been taken away should straightaway be counted as lost'. '*Tantum evincere sufficit, non esse adeo necessarium, ut periisse protinus existimetur cui eius obtinendi adempta fuerit facultas*'. '*Adeo*' is the operative word here. These two statements are in no way at variance with but on the contrary fully in harmony with the truth that 'Baptism is necessary for salvation' understood in its traditional, Catholic sense. Calvin is here simply emphasising the distinctions and refinements contained in the dogma itself. Catholic theology increasingly admits that unbaptised infants need not and ought not 'straightaway be counted as lost', as deprived of the beatific vision. According to the Second Vatican Council (The Church in the Modern World, §22, *Vatican Council II*, ed. A. Flannery OP, op. cit. p. 924), the universality of redemption must mean a real possibility of salvation for all.
70. IV, 15:19 (V, 300; 1319).
71. IV, 1:5 (V 10; 1019).

72. IV, 17:44 (V, 410; 1422).
73. IV, 17:43, 46 (V, 409, 412; 1421, 1424); IV, 18:8 (V, 424; 1437).
74. When an earlier version of this chapter was read as a paper at the Maynooth Union Summer School in the summer of 1965, spontaneous applause from the largely clerical audience greeted this quotation: concelebration of the Eucharist was then relatively if not entirely new.
75. IV, 18:8 (V, 424; 1437).
76. IV, 1:5 (V, 9; 1018); IV,17:43 (V, 409; 1421).
77. IV, 17:40, 43 '(V, 405, 409; 1418, 1421).
78. Quoted from a letter of Calvin by McNeill in his edition of the *Institutes*, 1232, n. 8. Emphasising its eucharistic finality Niesel (op. cit. p. 198) states: 'Thus Church discipline does not exist in order to promote moral conduct in the Church or in order to attain purity of Church life.' Wendel (op. cit. 300) disagrees with this statement but the difference seems to be one of emphasis merely and Wendel may be thinking more of Genevan practice, Niesel of Calvin's theological principles; cf. IV, 12:5 (V, 215; 1232). The following passage from 'Articles concerning the Organization of the Church and of Worship at Geneva' is worth quoting as given by McNeill, *The History and Character of Calvinism*, p. 138, who says 'it is likely that Calvin was its principal author': 'Most honoured lords: it is certain that a Church cannot be called well ordered and regulated unless in it the holy Supper of Our Lord is often celebrated, and attended – and this with such good discipline that none dare to present himself at it save holily and with singular reverence. And for this reason the discipline of excommunication, by which those who, unwilling to govern themselves lovingly, and in obedience to the Holy Word of God, may be corrected, is necessary in order to maintain the Church in its integrity.'
79. IV, 17:11 (V, 354; 1372): *'Dico igitur, in Coenae mysterio per symbola panis et vini, Christum vere nobis exhiberi, adeoque corpus et sanguinem eius, in quibus omnem obedientiam pro comparanda nobis iustitia adimplevit: quo scilicet primum in unum corpus cum ipso coalescamus: deinde participes substantiae eius facti, in bonorum omnium communicatione virtutem quoque sentianus.'*
80. IV, 17:38 (V, 402; 1414-1415).
81. This is frequently affirmed; e.g. IV, 17:10 (V, 351; 1370): 'Even though it seems unbelievable that Christ's flesh, separated from us by such great distance, penetrates to us, so that it becomes our food, let us remember how far the secret power of the Holy Spirit towers above all our senses, and how foolish it is to wish to measure its immeasurableness by our

measure. What, then, our mind does not comprehend, let faith conceive: that the Spirit truly unites things separated in space.'
82. IV, 17:7 (V, 348; 1367).
83. IV, 17:9 (V, 351; 1369, 1370).
84. IV 18 (V, 417-35; l429-48). Cf. Heribert Schutzeichel, 'Calvins Urteil über die Messe und das Messopferdekret des Trienter Konzils', *Catholica,* 4/1997, pp. 264-299.
85. IV, 17:30 (V, 388; 1402): *'quorum tolerabilior, vel saltem magis verecunda est doctrina'.* In Calvin's view the Lutheran doctrine, because it involves the ubiquity of Christ's glorified body, means a denial of the real humanity of the glorified Christ. For this reason chiefly he finds it intolerable. Cf. IV, 17:7 (V, 349; 1367): 'The extravagant doctors, who, while in the grossness of their minds they devise an absurd fashion of eating and drinking, also transfigure Christ, stripped of his own flesh, into a phantasm.'
86. Cf: IV, 17:7 (V, 3-9, I 367): '…if one may reduce to words so great a mystery, which I see that I do not even sufficiently comprehend with my mind. I therefore freely admit that no man should measure its sublimity by the little measure of my childishness *(infantiae meae modulo).* Rather, I urge my readers not to confine their mental interest within these too narrow limits, but to strive to rise much higher than I can lead them. For, whenever this matter is discussed, when I have tried to say all, I feel that I have as yet said little in proportion to its worth. And although my mind can think beyond what my tongue can utter, yet even my mind is conquered and overwhelmed by the greatness of the thing. Therefore, nothing remains but to break forth in wonder at this mystery, which plainly neither the mind is able to conceive nor the tongue to express. Nevertheless, I shall in one way or another sum up my views; for, as I do not doubt them to be true, I am confident that they will be approved in godly hearts.'
87. J. T. McNeill, op. cit. p. 1011, n. 1.
88. Ed. Max Thurian, Vols I-VI, *Faith and Order Papers,* 129, 132, 135, 137, 143, 144, Geneva, 1986-1988.
89. The original version of this chapter was prepared as a paper on 'The Church in Protestant Theology: Some Reflections on the Fourth Book of Calvin's *Institutes',* for delivery to the Maynooth Union Summer School in 1965 and was printed in the published proceedings of the School, *The Meaning of the Church,* ed. Donal Flanagan (Dublin: Gill & Son, 1966), pp. 110-143.

Chapter 10: Wesley Today and Evangelisation Today

1. Cf. *A History of the Methodist Church*, Vol I, eds. Rupert Davies & Gordon Rupp, London, 1965, *passim; John Wesley's Letter to a Roman Catholic*, ed. Michael Hurley SJ, 'Introduction', London/Belfast 1968, pp. 22-47; Dennis Cooke, 'Evangelicalism and Reconciliation', *Reconciliation in Religion and Society*, ed. Michael Hurley SJ (Belfast: Institute of Irish Studies, 1994), pp. 131-132.
2. *Mission and Evangelism: An Ecumenical Affirmation* §34, WCC Mission Series, Geneva 1983, p. 58. Cf. Roman Catholic Synod of Bishops 1971, *Justice in the World*: 'Action on behalf of justice and participation in the transformation of the world fully appear to us as a constitutive dimension of the preaching of the Gospel, or, in other words, of the Church's mission for the redemption of the human race and its liberation from every oppressive situation' (Boston: St Paul Editions, 1971), p. 4.
3. Cf. Emilio Castro, 'The Missionary Challenge to the Church at the End of the 20th Century', *Reconciliation,* ed. Oliver Rafferty SJ (Dublin: Columba Press, 1993), pp. 130-139; John D'Arcy May, 'Is Interfaith Dialogue undermining Inter-Church Dialogue?', ibid. pp. 159-175; Robin Boyd, 'The Meeting House: The End of Interfaith Dialogue', ibid. pp. 176-200; *Mission and Evangelism: An Ecumenical Affirmation* (Geneva: WCC Publications, 1983), §§41-44, pp. 71-75.
4. Cf. J. Weldon Smith III, 'Some Notes on John Wesley's Doctrine of Prevenient Grace', *Religion in Life*, 34 (1964-5), pp. 68-80; E. Anker Nielsen, 'Prevenient Grace', *The London Quarterly & Holborn Review*, 184 (1959), pp. 188-94; Colin W. Williams, *John Wesley's Theology Today*, London 1960, pp. 41-6; Mark S. Masa, 'The Catholic Wesley: A Revisionist Prolegomenon', *Methodist History*, 22/1 (October 1983), pp. 38-53; Eamon Duffy, 'Wesley and the Counter-Reformation', *Revival and Religion since 1700*, eds. Jane Garnett and Colin Matthew, London 1993, pp. 1-19.
5. John Wesley to Thomas Whitehead(?), 10 February, 1748, *Letters*, ed. Telford (London: Epworth Press, 1960), reprint, II, pp. 117-118 .
6. Cf. Donal Dorr SSP, 'Wesleyan Total Corruption', *Irish Theological Quarterly,* 31 (1964), pp. 303-21.
7. 'The Righteousness of Faith', 1742, *Standard Sermons*, fifth edition, ed. Sugden (London: Epworth Press, 1961), I, p 141 .
8. 'The Spirit of Bondage and Adoption', 1743, *Standard Sermons*, I, p. 187.

9. 'The Doctrine of Original Sin', 1756, *Works*, London, 1860, IX, p 268.
10. 'On Working Out Our Own Salvation', *Works*, London, 1860, VI, p. 512.
11. 'Declaration on the Relationship of the Church to Non-Christian Religions', *Vatican Council II,* ed. A. Flannery OP (Dublin: Dominican Publications, 1992), p. 739.
12. 'On Working Out Our Own Salvation', *Works*, London 1860, VI, p. 509.
13. 'The Scripture Way of Salvation', 1765, *Standard Sermons*, II, p. 445.
14. Edward H. Sugden, ed. *Standard Sermons*, I, p. 304, n. 1.
15. 'The Great Privilege of Those That Are Born of God', *Standard Sermons,* I, pp. 304, 312.
16. 'Minutes of the Conference' 25 June 1744, *John Wesley,* ed. Albert Outler (New York: OUP, 1964), p. 137.
17. 'The Way to the Kingdom', *Standard Sermons*, I, p. 160.
18. 'The Witness of the Spirit', *Standard Sermons*, II, pp. 358-359.
19. John Wesley to Thomas Whitehead(?), 10 February, 1748, *Letters*, ed. Telford, II, 118.
20. 'On Faith', *Works*, VII, London, 1860 p. 197. I owe this and the following reference to the kindness of the Reverend Professor Geoffrey Wainwright.
21. *Journal,* 11 October 1745, ed. Curnock (London: Epworth Press, 1961), reprint, III, p. 215.
22. John Wesley to John Mason, 21 November 1776, *Letters*, ed. Telford, VI, p. 239.
23. 'Minutes of the Conference', 13 May, 1746, *John Wesley,* ed. Albert Outler op. cit. (n. 16 *supra*), p. 157.
24. 'Minutes of the Conference', 16 June, 1747, ibid. p. 167.
25. 'On Working Out Our Own Salvation', *Works,* VI, p. 512.
26. 'Upon Our Lord's Sermon on the Mount, Discourse XI', *Standard Sermons,* I, p. 541.
27. John Wesley to Dr Burton, 10 October 1735, *Letters*, ed. Telford, I, p. 188.
28. Journal, 2 December 1737, ed. Curnock, I, p. 409.
29. 'Upon Our Lord's Sermon on the Mount, Discourse I', *Standard Sermons,* I, p. 329.
30. 'Minutes of Several Conversations between the Reverend Mr Wesley and others, 1744-1789' (The Large Minutes), *Works,* VIII, p. 338.
31. John Wesley to Dr Burton, 10 October 1735, *Letters*, ed. Telford, I, p. 188.

32. *Journal*, 28 June 1740, ed. Telford, II, p. 361; 'The Means of Grace', *Standard Sermons*, I, p. 251; chapter 8 *supra*, p. 131.
33. 'The Law Established Through Faith, Discourse I', *Standard Sermons*, II, p. 60.
34. 'The Origin, Nature, Property, and Use of the Law', *Standard Sermons*, II, p. 53.
35. Ibid. p. 52.
36. 'Sermon Preached Before the Society for the Reformation of Manners', 1763, *Standard Sermons*, II, p. 482.
37. 'The Way to the Kingdom', *Standard Sermons*, I, p. 149.
38. Cf. n. 11 *supra*.
39. 'A Caution Against Bigotry', *Standard Sermons*, II, pp. 122, 124; 'Catholic Spirit', *Standard Sermons*, II, p. 141.
40. The original version of this chapter was prepared for presentation to a meeting of the Methodist/Roman Catholic International Commission in Venice in early October 1974. An expanded version was presented later that month to a Consultation held at Drew University, in Madison, New Jersey, to celebrate the publication by Oxford's Clarendon Press of a new critical edition of Wesley's works. This fuller version of the paper was published in the proceedings of the Drew Consultation, *The Place of Wesley in the Christian Tradition*, ed. Kenneth E. Rowe (Metuchen: The Scarecrow Press Inc., 1976), pp. 94-116.

Chapter 11: The Church of Ireland: Challenges for the Future

1. Quoted by David L. Edwards, '101 Years of the Lambeth Conference', *The Church Quarterly*, 1/1 (July 1968), p. 32. Cf. also David M. Paton, *Anglicans and Unity* (London: 1962), pp. 17-37.
2. *Church of Ireland, Gazette* 13 May 1966, p. 3.
3. Cf. Michael Hurley SJ, 'Ecumenism: time for the breakthrough', *The Month*, April 1985, pp. 126-128.
4. Cf. chapter 2 *supra*, pp. 38-39.
5. A. T. Hanson and R. P. C. Hanson, *Reasonable Belief* (London: OUP, 1980), reprinted 1987, p. 265.
6. Paul Avis, 'Keeping Faith with Anglicanism', *The Future of Anglicanism*, ed. Robert Hannaford (Leominster: Gracewing, 1996), p. 2.
7. Ibid. p. 4.
8. H. R. McAdoo, *Anglican Heritage: Theology and Spirituality*, Norwich 1991, p. 86. The essay by Paul Avis referred to in the two previous

footnotes finds the Stephen Bayne statement 'rather disturbing' (p. 2), and that of Archbishop Runcie 'not only mistaken, but positively unhelpful' (p. 5). The author insists both on the 'true provisionality' of each and every Church (p. 6) and on 'the abiding value of Anglicanism' (p. 5). Another essay in the volume *The Future of Anglicanism* hopes it has no future, seeing its disappearance as an opportunity to 'get down to the business of recovering the Anglican way of being a reformed catholic Christian': Samuel L. Edwards, 'A Light at Nightfall: The Dissolution of Christendom as an Opportunity for Anglican Renewal', ibid. pp. 146-147.

9. Ibid. 'Postscript from the Present', pp. 86-107 *passim*.
10. Quoted by David L. Edwards, loc. cit. (n. 1 *supra*), p. 32.
11. The Most Reverend Richard Clarke, *The Irish Times,* 29 July 1997, p. 5.
12. Gallagher & Worrall, op. cit. p. 195. The following quotations are also taken from this source (pp. 197, 195).
13. According to Eric Gallagher and Stanley Worrall, 'The unfortunate Dean Cuthbert Peacocke, later Bishop of Derry and Raphoe, was subjected to abuse, pressure, and threats of damage to his cathedral. Massive separate demonstrations were planned by the Orange Order and by Ian Paisley and others. Evangelical Protestantism was enraged. With no support apparently forthcoming from any level, ecclesiastical or secular, the Dean was in an impossible position. He withdrew permission for the Bishop's visit.' *Christians in Ulster 1968-1980* (Oxford: OUP, 1982), p. 36.
14. *Orange and Green.* A Quaker Study of Community Relations in Northern Ireland, published by Northern Friends Peace Board, 1969, p. 36.
15. Cf. chapter 13 *infra*.
16. The Working Party – of which I was a member – first met in February 1991 and its Report was published in the summer of 1993: *Sectarianism: A Discussion Document* (Belfast: Irish Inter-Church Meeting, 1993).
17. So, according to *The Church of Ireland Gazette* (23 May 1997, p. 8), Archdeacon Gregor McCamley of the Diocese of Down, in seconding the motion on sectarianism passed by General Synod and quoted below, p. 190.
18. *The Irish Times,* 6 August 1996.
19. Notably in connection with the Loyalist protests outside Harryville Roman Catholic Church near Ballymena which took place on Saturday evenings at Masstime during the past year.

20. Michael Hurley SJ, *Northern Ireland – A Challenge to Theology* (Edinburgh: University of Edinburgh Centre for Theology and Public Issues [Occasional Paper no. 12], 1987), p. 21.
21. *The Irish Times,* 27 June 1997. In the summer of 1986 the present Archbishop of Dublin (then Bishop of Meath and Kildare), Most Reverend Walton Empey, had called on the Church of Ireland 'to review its connection with the Orange Order'(*The Irish Times,* 28 July 1986).
22. *Church of Ireland Gazette,* 23 May 1997, pp. 2-5.
23. Ibid. pp. 7-8. An interim report was presented to General Synod in May 1998.
24. So it was described by the chief Ireland correspondent of *The Times,* Nicholas Watt, on 11 July.
25. As he himself recalled on his retirement from politics some years ago he had his primary education for reasons of convenience in the local Roman Catholic school and has altogether happy memories of those years; during religious knowledge class he sat at the back of the room.
26. E.g. Gregg Ryan, Ireland correspondent, *The Church Times,* 16 May 1997, p. 1.
27. In 1969, so I was given to understand, one of the Church of Ireland bench of Bishops was still a member of the Order.
28. So Gregg Ryan, loc. cit. (n. 26 *supra*), p. 1.
29. It published a Report in 1986 entitled *The Evangelical-Roman Catholic Dialogue on Mission 1977-1984: A Report,* edited by Basil Meeking and the well-known Church of England clergyman, Reverend John Stott (Grand Rapids, MI: William B. Eerdmans Publishing Company). Cf. Thomas P. Rausch SJ, 'Catholic-Evangelical Relations: Signs of Progress', *One in Christ,* 32/1 (1996), pp. 40-52; Cecil M. Robeck Jr, 'Catholics and Evangelicals Together', ibid. 33/2 (1997), pp. 138-160.
30. Based at 12 Wellington Place, Belfast BT1 6GE.
31. *The Primitive Faith and Roman Catholic Developments* (Dublin: 1957), p. 101.
32. Quoted by William Purdy, *The Search for Unity* (London: Geoffrey Chapman, 1996), p. 141.
33. The original version of this chapter appeared in *Irish Anglicanism 1869-1969,* the volume of essays which I edited in 1970 for the centenary of the Disestablishment of the Church of Ireland and which is the subject of a later chapter in this book.

Chapter 12: Jesuits and Protestants Today

1. This text, of obscure origin, resurfaces regularly: it was printed in *The Portadown Times* on 27 June 1997, p. 26, and in a leaflet distributed in Portadown on the occasion of the Orange march on 6 July 1997. Cf. Robert Wright, 'Two Shades of Orange', *The Tablet*, 19 July 1997, p. 918.
2. Ian R. K. Paisley, *The Jesuits: Their Start, Sign, System, Secrecy, Strategy*, Belfast, no date.
3. For what follows cf. Michael Hurley SJ, *Theology of Ecumenism* (Cork: Mercier Press, 1969), pp. 45-56.
4. For much of what follows, cf. F. J. Crehan SJ, 'The Bible in the Roman Catholic Church', *The Cambridge History of the Bible*, ed. S. L. Greenslade (Cambridge: CUP, 1963), pp. 199-237, and Eric Fenn, 'The Bible and the Missionary', ibid. pp. 383-407.
5. Paul Blanchard, *Paul Blanchard on Vatican II* (London: 1967), pp. 186-7.
6. For much of what follows I am greatly indebted to the UBS archivist, Miss Kathleen Cann, who was most helpful with information and photocopies of documents. When the UBS General Office and its files were being transferred from Stuttgart to Reading in 1988, 'one lorry-load of files caught fire and was totally destroyed. I am sorry to say that this included the section on co-operation with the Catholic Church – some twenty files. What I have here are the files of the UBS World Service Office in London, which contain a certain amount of the same material, but only half-a-dozen files' (letter of 6 September 1990).
7. Address of Dr Laton E. Holmgren, Secretariat for Promoting Christian Unity, *Information Service*, 1967/1, p. 10.
8. Secretariat for Promoting Christian Unity, *Information Service*, 7, May 1969, pp. 10-12.
9. 'The Shape of the Common Bible', *A Commentary On Guiding Principles, Information Service*, Secretariat for Promoting Christian Unity, 5 (June 1968), pp. 16-17.
10. *Guidelines for Interconfessional Cooperation in Translating the Bible*, Rome, 1987, pp. 9-10.
11. *Religious Freedom 1965-1975*, ed. Walter J. Burghardt (New York: Paulist Press, 1976), p. 2.
12. *Theological Studies*, 40 (1979), pp. 705-6.
13. Paul Blanchard, *Paul Blanchard on Vatican II*, pp. 339, 89.
14. *Religious Freedom 1965-1975*, p. 52.
15. Patrick Riordan, 'Does the Church Teach?', *Doctrine and Life*, 37/1 (January 1987), pp. 19-27. The constitutional ban on divorce was lifted in 1996.

16. Stanley Worrall, 'The Role of the Churches in British-Irish Relationships', *Anglo-Irish Encounter Conference on the Role of the Churches in British-Irish Relationships*, 26-27 November 1985, p. 37.
17. This is the text of a public lecture, delivered at Queen's University, Belfast on 6 December 1990, in commemoration of the 450th anniversary of the founding of the Jesuits in 1540 and of the 500th anniversary of the birth of the founder, Ignatius of Loyola, in 1491; an abbreviated version appeared in *Studies,* summer 1992, pp. 203-211.

Chapter 13: The Churches and Reconciliation in Northern Ireland
1. Meetings were suspended on the breakdown of the IRA ceasefire in February 1996 and have not been resumed.
2. *The Irish News,* 24 March 1995.
3. For what follows cf. *inter alia* Jonathan Bardon, *A History of Ulster,* (Belfast: Blackstaff Press, 1992), Oliver P. Rafferty, *Catholicism in Ulster 1603-1983* (Dublin: Gill & Macmillan, 1994).
4. According to Kevin Boyle and Tom Hadden in *Northern Ireland The Choice* (London: Penguin Books, 1994), p. 31, 'it is clear that the proportion of Catholics in Northern Ireland has increased from a figure of at least 33 per cent in 1971 (31.4 per cent stated + some unstated) to a figure of at least 40 per cent in 1991 (38.4 per cent stated + some unstated)'. This rate of increase, however, is unlikely to be maintained in the next decades. According to the demographer Paul Compton, writing in 1985, 'the likelihood of an eventual Roman Catholic majority, despite superficial appearances to the contrary, is now receding and is more remote than seemed possible a decade or so ago'. Cf. 'An Evaluation of the Changing Religious Composition of the Population of Northern Ireland', *The Economic and Social Review,* 16/3 (1985), pp. 201-224. There is still a perception among some that Catholics may well outnumber Protestants in the foreseeable future and this aggravates Unionist/Protestant fears: cf. *A Citizens' Enquiry: The Opsahl Report on Northern Ireland,* ed. Andy Pollak (Dublin: The Lilliput Press, 1993), pp. 38-43. Paul Compton once again rejects this prognosis in his recent *Demographic Review Northern Ireland 1995* (Belfast: Northern Ireland Economic Council, 1995), considering it to be 'a gross exaggeration of the real speed of change' (p. 241). He concludes his summary of the projection scenarios as follows:

> What we can be certain of, however, is that the numerical gap between ODs [other denominations] and Catholics will continue to

narrow, possibly eventually *(sic)* leading to [a] situation of rough numerical equivalence with neither group in a decisive majority (p. 227).

Extrapolating [he wrote at p. 226] current birth and death rates by denomination (but excluding other factors such as migration) produces a Catholic majority in or around the year 2030.

Cf. Garret FitzGerald, 'Vision of NI Catholics outbreeding Protestants is a Dangerous Myth', *The Irish Times,* 26 July 1997, p. 10.

5. *The Tablet,* 18 March 1995.
6. Dublin 1984, pp. 122, 167.
7. *The Edge of the Union* (Oxford: OUP, 1994), p. 29.
8. Dennis Cooke, 'Evangelicalism and Reconciliation', *Reconciliation in Religion and Society,* ed. Michael Hurley SJ, Belfast 1994, p. 136. Principal Cooke is author of *Persecuting Zeal: A Portrait of Ian Paisley,* (Dingle: Brandon, 1996), an analysis of Dr Paisley's theology.
9. Stanley Worrall, 'The Role of the Churches in British-Irish Relationships', *Anglo-Irish Encounter,* Dublin, 1986, pp. 36-37.
10. I associate the former with Dr Christopher McGimpsey who stated at the New Ireland Forum in 1984 that unionism is 'a particular political ideology', adding 'I would like to see that ideology not exclusive but general so that anyone of any religious persuasion could join it'. The latter I associate with ECONI (Evangelical Contribution to Northern Ireland, c/o 12 Wellington Place, Belfast BT1 6GE), who have published *For God and His Glory Alone* (1992), and other materials.
11. Eamon Phoenix, *Northern Nationalism* (Belfast: Ulster Historical Foundation, 1994), p. 399; cf. also Oliver P. Rafferty, *Catholicism in Ulster 1603-1983,* Dublin, 1994, p. 221.
12. Quoted, in *The Irish News,* 24 March 1995.
13. Boyle and Hadden, op. cit. (n. 4 *supra*) p. 7.
14. A 'Commemorative Publication' published after the installation by *The Irish News,* p. 10.
15. Quoted by Paul Bew and Gordon Gillespie, *Northern Ireland: A Chronology of the Troubles 1968-1993,* Dublin, 1993, p. 189; cf. Dennis Cooke, op. cit. (n. 8) pp. 1-2, 197-8.
16. *The Ulster Covenant, A Pictorial History of the 1912 Home Rule Crisis,* ed. Gordon Lucy (Banbridge: The Ulster Society, 1989), p. 29.
17. Op. cit. pp. 207, 211. Dr Stanley Worrall, who has died, was an English Methodist layman who lived for many years in Northern Ireland, working mainly in the field of education as Principal of Methodist College, Belfast. Reverend Dr Eric Gallagher is a former

President of the Methodist Church in Ireland in whose honour a book of essays was published by The Methodist College, Belfast in 1994 with the title *Esteem*, edited by T. W. Mulryne and W. J. McAllister.
18. Dublin, 1997.
19. *Freedom, Justice & Responsibility in Ireland Today* (Dublin: Veritas Publications, 1997), p. 93. Cf. Gerry O'Hanlon, 'The Churches in Ireland Today', *The Furrow*, 48/7-8 (July/August 1997), pp. 399-405.
20. Op. cit. p. 198.
21. Cf. John McMaster, *An Inter-Church Directory for Northern Ireland*, Belfast 1994; Andy Pollak, 'Let us Praise Unknown Priests', *Intercom* (Dublin, December-January 1995, pp. 26-7); John Hume, 'In Praise of Peace Priests', *Link-Up* (Dublin, December, 1994), pp. 18-20.
22. *The Irish Times*, 15 May 1995.
23. In his presidential address to the General Synod of the Church of Ireland on 16 May, Archbishop Eames stated: 'Let us be frank about it. Fear of each other lies at the root of our problems. We have failed to trust each other' (*The Belfast Telegraph*, 16 May 1995).
24. Op. cit. p. 2.
25. Op. cit. p. 111. The survey was conducted by Duncan Morrow.
26. Some of the evidence for this confidence I find in the publication during 1995 of three books: the first (in order of appearance) by the Roman Catholic, Reverend Brian Lennon SJ, is entitled *After the Ceasefires: Catholics and the future of Northern Ireland* and was published in Dublin by the Columba Press; the second by the Anglican (Church of Ireland), Reverend Timothy Kinahan, under the same imprint, is entitled *Where do we go from here? Protestants and the Future of Northern Ireland*; the third, which was published in Belfast by the Blackstaff Press, is by the Presbyterian former Moderator, Very Reverend John Dunlop and entitled *A Precarious Belonging: Presbyterians and the Conflict in Ireland.* All three books are full of encouragement. My own emphasis continues to be on the neglected, as I see it, role of forgiveness in the Churches' understanding and practice of their ministry of reconciliation. Cf. the earlier chapter on this subject, pp. 54-77 *supra*.
27. The original version of this chapter was prepared in the summer of 1995 during the ceasefires, for publication in *The Reconciliation of Peoples: Challenge to the Churches*, ed. Gregory Baum and Harold Wells, Geneva and Maryknoll, 1997, pp. 118-128. It was revised and rewritten after the renewal of the IRA ceasefire in the summer of 1997, and some slight modifications and additions were made in July 1998, when this book was going through press.

Chapter 14: An Ecumenical Lecture Series: Milltown Park Public Lectures 1960-1969

1. 'Decree on Ecumenism', §6, *Vatican Council II*, ed. Austin Flannery OP (Dublin: Dominican Publications, 1992), p. 459.
2. Cf. chapters 15ff.
3. The three main sources consulted were 1) *Irish Province News* (*IPN*), the in-house newsletter of the Irish Jesuits printed four times a year until 1994; 2) *The Milltown Park Historia Domus (HD)*, the house history of the Jesuit Community of Milltown Park; and 3) the *Beadle's Journal (BJ)*, a daily journal formerly kept by the 'Beadle', the Jesuit student ('scholastic') who was the official liaison officer between his confrères and the authorities, especially the Rector. I am grateful to Father Michael J. Kelly SJ of the University of Zambia for drawing my attention to the existence of this third source which lapsed in late 1974 and is now altogether forgotten, and also to Father Frank Sammon SJ, currently Rector of the Jesuit Community at Milltown Park, for giving me access to *BJ* in the House Archives. The daily newspapers are a fourth source of information but have not been consulted in preparing this chapter.
4. 10/3 (July 1960), p. 70.
5. P. 19. In this chapter references to *HD* are to the current volume, beginning from 1957. The language of *HD* continued to be Latin until 1965.
6. And in September 1962 the Carmelites were to start their own theologate at Gort Muire in Dundrum.
7. *IPN*, 12/1 (January 1967), p. 16.
8. Having been a subject treated in the opening session of spring 1960 by the Reverend Dr Alfred O'Rahilly, the role of the laity was twice more considered between then and winter 1965, but by clerics: by Professor Enda McDonagh, to whom the unfortunate title 'Layman [*sic*] in the Church' was given, during the winter 1962 session and by Father Joseph O'Mara SJ in the spring 1965 session.
9. In a conversation on 23 October 1997, Barry White of the *Belfast Telegraph* confirmed to me that this was the personal background of Martin Wallace.
10. Cf. n. 1 *supra*.
11. He was a devout Methodist. The Deputy Editor's name was Martin Wallace.
12. *HD*, p. 73.
13. The following details are mostly from *HD*.

14. *IPN*, 10/9 (January 1962), p. 308.
15. *IPN*, 10/10 (April 1962), p. 342.
16. *IPN*, 10/13 (January 1963), p. 469.
17. Cf. paragraph on 'Fundraising', pp. 247-248.
18. 10/6 (April 1961), p. 212. The onerous task of managing the Public Lectures devolved on the resident Jesuit students: one with overall responsibility who came to be called the Manager, others to help in various ways, distributing programmes to bookshops and churches, securing advertising space in some of the city centre cinemas, arranging the seating, stewarding in the car park and ushering in the hall. Much depended on the interest and energy of the Manager and his team and the outstanding Manager of the decade was the sociologist, Father Mícheál Mac Gréil, then studying theology at Milltown Park. Cf. *IPN*, 12/1 (January 1967), p. 16.
19. This figure is given in *HD*, p. 35. All the other figures in this paragraph from *BJ*.
20. According to *BJ* 'about 1,000,000 [*sic*] turned up', causing 'absolute chaos'.
21. The second session on 2 November 1960 had included a lecture on Teilhard de Chardin which attracted an audience of '330'.
22. From 1965 to 1970 the present writer was himself the house historian. *BJ* records the numbers for the winter 1966 session as follows: 430, 270, 300, 300, 270, 330, 400.
23. *HD*, pp. 51, 59, 66. Where were these large audiences accommodated? In the present hall (theatre) and, as required, in adjoining rooms (now the Institute Staff Room and Conference Room), and sometimes in a classroom downstairs. From the second session on the lecture was relayed to these rooms. From spring 1967 the lecturer could sometimes be seen as well as heard by means of closed circuit TV, courtesy of Kevin Street College of Technology. Early in 1963 two hundred chairs upholstered in red were acquired but until then, until the seventh session in spring 1963, chairs had to be borrowed from our neighbours, Gonzaga College, and transported from there and back each week with the help of the farm hands and their tractor.
24. By bicycle to Merrion Road church and then by bus the rest of the way.
25. While a member of the Milltown Park Community (1969-71) Father Sean McCarron won a car in a lottery in England and brought back its cash value in lieu. The Rector at the time (Father Jack Brennan [1968-1971]) used the money to acquire a car: so Father Jack Brennan in a

conversation on 3 October 1997. The acquisition of the car is not mentioned in the pages of *IPN*. But *BJ* on 30 October 1969 reports the win in England and *HD* (p. 77) reports the acquisition in its account of events in the year ending 31 July 1970.

26. Xavier Rynne, *Letters from Vatican City* (New York: Farrar, Strauss & Company, 1963).
27. John Feeney, *John Charles McQuaid* (Dublin: Mercier Press, 1974), pp. 44-47. Archbishop McQuaid did, however, speak in the First Session during the Liturgy debate on 24 and 31 October but gave up his right to speak on 7 November. Cf. Rynne, op. cit. pp. 131, 133, 137.
28. Ibid. pp. 54-5.
29. 'Triple Vocation', *Call and Response*, ed. Frances Makower (London: Hodder & Stoughton, 1994), p. 142. In a letter at Christmas 1997 Father Cecil McGarry confirmed this version. A different version is to be found in *BJ* stating that a first announcement of the cancellation had in fact been made on the preceding Wednesday at the end of the previous Lecture. The keeper of the Journal, the Beadle, adds: 'no reason given'. In his Christmas 1997 letter Father McGarry recalls that the Archbishop had wished to have me removed from the archdiocese, but that in an interview on the very afternoon of the proposed lecture he had yielded on this wish, not, however, on his wish to have my public lecture on original sin cancelled.
30. This led to a second leader in *The Irish Times* of 19 May 1966 entitled 'Silent Dialogue'. The previous Saturday the paper had announced the forthcoming reprint. The leader 'deplored the fact' that I had been instructed to request that the article not be reprinted.
31. Cf. n. 29 *supra*. This I had gathered in previous conversations with Father Cecil McGarry who was Rector of Milltown Park from 1965 to 1968 and Provincial from 1968 to 1975.
32. *HD*, p. 66.
33. Cf. *The Furrow*, 19/11 (November 1968), p. 657.
34. The names of Mrs Evelyn Kiely and of Mrs Irene Griffith deserve to be recorded.
35. *IPN, passim*, e.g. 10/12 (July 1962), p. 380.
36. A vibrant Saturday theology programme under the direction of Father Brendan Lawler SJ had been in existence since 1965. It was brought to an end in 1989; so I gathered in conversation (19 November 1997) with Peter and Maura Taylor, who helped Father Lawler as tutors from 1969 to 1989. The present Milltown Institute Adult Education Programme began in 1990.

37. A need subsequently met by the Milltown Institute and by the Divinity School at Trinity College, Dublin, but not yet by the Colleges of the National University of Ireland.

Chapter 15: An Ecumenical Publication: *Irish Anglicanism 1869-1969*
1. Cf. Michael Hurley SJ, 'Triple Vocation', *Call and Response*, ed. Frances Makower (London: Hodder & Stoughton, 1994), p. 142; chapter 14, pp. 247-248 *supra*.
2. A greatly revised version is printed in chapter 11, pp. 182-196 *supra*.
3. These tapes and most of my papers dealing with *Irish Anglicanism* were deposited in the Representative Church Body Library on 11 December 1989 and graciously accepted by the Primate, Archbishop Eames, at a luncheon party which he kindly hosted in Church House.

Chapter 16: An Ecumenical Institute: The Origins of the Irish School of Ecumenics
1. ISE includes in its research and teaching not only inter-Church relations but also inter-faith relations and Peace Studies. It operates mainly in Dublin but also in Belfast and other centres in Northern Ireland.
2. The thirty-ninth and last session seems to have been held in the spring of 1981 – according to the *Milltown Park Historia Domus 1957* (Milltown Park Jesuit Community History), p. 123.
3. Catholic Truth Society of Ireland, Dublin.
4. 'The Vatican Council and the Ecumenical Situation Today', *The Irish Ecclesiastical Record*, 98 (1962), pp. 28-42. This periodical and the hotel where the lecture was delivered (The Cumberland Hotel, Westland Row) have both since disappeared.
5. 'The World Council of Churches' Recent Paris Meeting', *The Irish Press*, 3 and 4 September 1962.
6. I edited the proceedings of the early conferences in Glenstal and Greenhills for Gill and Son Dublin: *Church and Eucharist*, 1966 and *Ecumenical Studies: Baptism and Marriage*, 1968.
7. 'Presbyterians in Council': The Reformed Churches Four Hundred Years After', *Studies* 53 (1964), pp. 286-304; *Biblical Theology*, 15 (March 1965), pp. 1-14.
8. It was as a result of this meeting that I prepared an edition of *John Wesley's Letter to a Roman Catholic* with Prefaces by Bishop Odd Hagen, then President of the World Methodist Council, and Cardinal

Augustine Bea, then President of the Vatican Secretariat for Christian Unity, which was published jointly by Geoffrey Chapman, London, and Epworth House, Belfast (and in the USA by Abingdon Press), but only in 1968 because of difficulties in obtaining a satisfactory text from the Unity Secretariat and in overcoming the ecumenical hesitations of Epworth House. A Swedish translation appeared simultaneously in Stockholm.

9. *Theology Today,* Series no. 9, Mercier Press, Cork. Italian, French and Spanish translations appeared subsequently. I am hoping to prepare a new edition in the near future.
10. So I have gathered in recent conversations with Father McGarry who was Jesuit Provincial from 1968-1975 and who succeeded in reassuring the Archbishop. Cf. chapter 14 *supra*, n. 29.
11. Subtitled *Essays on the Role of Anglicanism in Irish life presented to the Church of Ireland on the occasion of the centenary of its Disestablishment by a group of Methodist, Presbyterian, Quaker and Roman Catholic scholars,* published by Allen Figgis, Dublin.
12. Cf. chapter 15 *supra*, pp. 250-264.
13. Cf. 'The Beginnings of the Columbanus Community of Reconciliation', chapter 18, pp. 317-340 *infra*.
14. P. 731. Chronicling the year's events the house historian of the Milltown Park Jesuit community also saw correctly that *Irish Anglicanism* and ISE were linked but concluded less correctly that this was intentional, that the former was deliberately preparing the way for the latter; cf. *Milltown Park Historia Domus 1957,* p. 76.
15. Now based in Nairobi where, until recently, he was principal of Hekima College, the Jesuit School of Theology.
16. The inclusion of Inter-Faith Relations in the ISE programme can be traced to the 1974 International Consultation on Mixed Marriage which, at the suggestion of Seán McBride, Nobel Peace Prize winner and then a member of the ISE Executive Board, included consideration of Inter-faith marriage, cf. *Unity,* n. 36 (May 1988), p. 6. A letter of 4 June 1970 from Reverend John Collins OML, however, shows that I had envisaged a course on comparative religion as part of the original programme. Father Collins wrote declining an invitation to give such a course because of commitments at the School for African and Oriental Studies in London.

What became the third part of the ISE programme originated firstly in a recognition of the importance of the non-theological factors in ecumenism and secondly in the basic ecumenical conviction that the unity of the Church is for the sake of the unity of humankind, that the aim of ecumenism is 'so that the world may believe and be at peace'. In 1978 these insights found expression in the School's International Consultation on Human Rights. But already in the very first year there was co-operation with the Centre for the Analysis of Conflict in London in organising a 'controlled communication' for Northern Ireland shop stewards (cf. pp. 280-282 *infra*), and courses on 'Sociology of Religion' and on 'Prejudice and Discrimination' were part of ISE's own programme. 'Religion and Society' was the title of this third part of the School's syllabus until 1982 when it became Peace Studies; cf. *Unity*, 19 (summer-autumn 1982), p. 4; ibid. 26 (spring 1985), p. 6, n. 47 *infra*.

17. 'Ecumenism in Higher Education', chapter 2, §6, *Information Service*, 10, p. 6
18. The Paderborn Institute was founded in 1957, adding 'für Ökumenik' to its title after Vatican II. The Strasbourg Institute was inaugurated on 1 February 1965.
19. Irish Jesuit Province Archives. Minutes of Discussions on 6 January, p. 14.
20. E.g. in a February memo in my files. The inauguration of the World Council was planned for 1938 but the plans were delayed by World War II and it was formally inaugurated only in 1948. In the intervening years it was referred to as 'in process of formation'.
21. A phrase prompted by Mr Dan Mullane which I used in my letter of 1 October 1969 to Peter Desmond Odlum.
22. E.g. in the Provincial's letter of 4 November 1969.
23. The decision to establish the Strasbourg 'Institute for Ecumenical Research' was made by the Helsinki Assembly of the Lutheran World Federation in 1963.
24. Tantur was not to open until 1971.
25. All now (August 1998) deceased except Father McGarry.
26. That arising from the invitation to the General Secretary of the WCC, cf. following pages.
27. Published by the Banner of Truth Trust, London, p. 16.
28. That was perhaps an unpromising beginning but it was a real one. Subsequently, after an exchange of Christmas cards, we met frequently but discreetly and became friends. Believing as a good Presbyterian that light can come 'from any quarter' Donald had the courage to modify his views on ecumenism and on Rome and, in the 1970s, to support the Presbyterian Church's continuing membership of the WCC. He died in the early months of 1996.

29. Eric Gallagher & Stanley Worrall, *Christians in Ulster 1968-1980* (Oxford: OUP, 1982), p. 143.
30. Ibid. pp. 35-36. Cf. chapter 11 *supra,* p. 189.
31. King's Pawn, The Memoirs of George H. Dunne SJ (Chicago: Loyola University Press, 1990) gives an account (pp. 355-364) of this intervention in which the author was himself the main actor; the account is less than accurate in some details (e.g. Cardinal Conway's 'acting secretary' was not a Jesuit) and hence may not be altogether reliable on the whole.
32. And also, perhaps, because I have tended to play down the role of the Northern Ireland conflict in the origins of ISE; cf. *The Irish Press,* 28 December 1979, p. 7.
33. Most of the original correspondence is preserved in the ISE files. I am grateful to Professor Dunstan for his letter of 12 February 1996 refreshing my memory of events in July 1970; to the Assistant Director of External Affairs and to Professor Cedric Smith of University College, London for helping me to discover the present location of CAC (at Rutherford College, University of Kent) and to identify its present Director, Professor John Groom; to the latter and Professor Smith for the present address of Dr John Burton (in Canberra); to Dr Burton for his letter of 2 November 1994 and the introduction to Mr J. Camplisson of Belfast, a former colleague of his who now works at conflict resolution at home and abroad and who gave me an interview on 14 February 1996 and showed me a file about Dr Burton's Northern Ireland activities given him by Dr Burton in 1988 at Fort Mason University, USA, but who was not involved in the 'controlled communication' of September 1970; and to the two former shop stewards who had participated in this exercise and who very kindly met me in Belfast on 13 December 1995. Above all my gratitude is due to Dr Maurice Hayes who shared his memories of the 'controlled communication' with me on 27 October 1994.
34. F. D. Maurice, Professor of Moral and Social Theology at King's College, editor of *Theology.* A member of the Anglican/Roman Catholic Commission on the Theology of Marriage and Mixed Marriages, he contributed a paper entitled 'Respecting the Unity: A Plea for Church Restraint' to ISE's International Consultation on Mixed Marriage in 1974 (*Beyond Tolerance:* London: Geoffrey Chapman, 1975, pp. 59-72). Professor Dunstan was largely instrumental in getting ISE's annual London Lecture hosted by King's (cf. *Unity,* 14, summer 1980 p. 3). This lecture, inaugurated on 21 March 1977 by Professor Enda

McDonagh, took place for many years at some convenient date near St Patrick's Day, 17 March.
35. *Minority Verdict: Experiences of a Catholic Public Servant* (Belfast: Blackstaff Press, 1995), p. 97. Dr Hayes had some knowledge of Dr Burton's work and been in touch with him before 1970 – hence the reason for mistakingly pre-dating the London 'controlled communication' to 1969. In an undated letter of February 1996 he writes: 'However, the basic truth remains that it was my experience of your workshop which encouraged me to involve him further.'
36. Ibid.
37. They are named by Dr Hayes (op. cit. p. 97): John Bayley and Ron Wiener. Father George Dunne (op. cit. p. 360) also refers to them as involved in his Sodepax initiative: 'I retained the services of two experts in conflict resolution.'
38. The President was W. Hastings Brown, a County Wexford Presbyterian, the Secretary was D. P. Maguire, a Catholic with a brother who was a Jesuit priest, the third was also a Catholic.
39. Mr Hastings Brown conveyed his regrets to me through a mutual friend, the Reverend Frank Forbes, a Church of Ireland Rector in County Wexford. Mr Dan Mullane, the Public Relations Officer, died as a result of an accident in 1988. Mr D. P. Maguire has also died. According to the late Dickie Spence, when I spoke to him in October 1994, the records of the Association went at the dissolution in 1989 to Odlums, the last remaining mill, which – he gave me to understand – has since been taken over by Greencore.
40. Cf. p. 277 *supra*.
41. The reservations, I gather from Dr T. B. H. McMurry, who was then Dean of Graduate Studies, related to financing and academic standards. 'It was felt' [he recalls in a private communication] that the College might be left with a considerable financial burden if the School failed. The College Officers were worried about the academic standards of an untried institution, and were cautious about allying the College with it.' 'The request' 'was not referred at any stage to the College Board.' At the end of the decade conversations resumed between ISE and TCD. As a result the Council of the University decided on 2 July 1980 to appoint a committee to explore the possibilities of a formal agreement and beginning from the academic year 1982/3, suitably qualified ISE students became eligible for TCD's M Phil degree. With hindsight it has been noted that a TCD link in the early 1970s would have been less than ideal because the TCD Divinity School was still mainly if not

exclusively Church of Ireland; it was not re-organised to become denominationally open until the late 1970s.

42. Cf. *Violence in Ireland. A Report to the Churches*, Belfast-Dublin, 1976, pp. 67-89, on 'The Task of the Churches', which ends with this forthright statement: 'We conclude by reiterating the futility of calling for reconciliation and peace in the community in the absence of full reconciliation between the Churches themselves.' ISE is not mentioned by name in this Report which comes from an official inter-Church working party and this silence probably reflects the negative reactions of the Catholic hierarchy to ISE's International Consultation on Mixed Marriage held in September 1974.

43. A. T. Hanson and R. P. C. Hanson. *The Identity of the Church* (London: SCM Press, 1987).

44. 5 August 1971, p. 2. No other record of this address seems to exist. *The Irish Christian Advocate* is the organ of the Methodist Church in Ireland. The Vice-Chancellor's statement was, however, reported in all the Irish dailies and also in *The Times* of London. It was the subject of editorials in the *Irish Independent* and *The Irish Times*.

45. *The Furrow*, 21/7 (July 1970), p. 427.

46. *Irish Province News* (*IPN*) is a quarterly newsletter of Irish Jesuit communities and their works. Until it ceased publication in 1992 each issue contained a short account of ISE's current activities. The first issue of *Unity: News and Views of the Irish School of Ecumenics* came out at Whit 1974. For the early years of ISE, *IPN* is the only *printed* source of information.

47. A Research Lecturer in Systematic Theology (for some years entitled the JKL Lectureship after the famous ecumenical pioneer, James Doyle, Bishop of Kildare and Leighlin) was appointed in December 1972; a Research Lecturer in the Sociology of Religion in May 1973, and the following month, a Research Lecturer in Social Ethics, but only for a year to help with the preparations for the International Consultation on Mixed Marriage which was held in September 1974. In 1979 the Research Lectureship in the Sociology of Religion was allowed to lapse. Instead the Research Lectureship in Social Ethics was revived as the William Temple Lectureship, and came in time to focus on Peace Studies in particular, cf. n. 16 *supra*.

48. Cf. *Unity*, 15 (autumn 1980).

49. Cf. chapter 4 *supra* on 'Ecumenical Tithing'.

Chapter 17: An Ecumenical Sabbatical: Mount Athos and China

1. An abbreviated version of this part of the chapter appeared in *The Irish Times*, January 1981.
2. Cf. China Forum of the Council of Churches for Britain and Ireland, *A Future and a Hope: China – the country, her people and their Church*, London, 1996.
3. *The Tablet*, 23 May 1981, p. 495.
4. This monument was first discovered, unearthed from the ground, in 1623 and two years later, in 1625, a Latin translation of the inscription was done by a Jesuit missionary, Nicholas Trigault. In the last century it was sometimes dismissed as a Jesuit forgery: cf. Kenneth Scott Latourette, *A History of Christian Missions in China*, New York, 1932, pp. 51-60; P. Y. Saeki, *The Nestorian Monument in China*, London, 1916, pp. 26, 33.
5. Cf. chapter 2 *supra*, pp. 33-34 and William Dalrymple, *From the Holy Mountain* (London: HarperCollins, 1997), pp. 140-141.
6. Latourette, op. cit. p. 54.
7. *Acta Apostolicae Sedis*, 73 (1981), p. 348.
8. *L'Osservatore Romano*, Weekly Edition in English, 11 December 1996, p. 3
9. *China Church News*, May 1997, p. 9.
10. An abbreviated version of this part of the chapter appeared in *The Tablet*, 23 May 1981, pp. 493-495. I wish to express my thanks to Reverend J. Shields SJ, lecturer in the Religion Department of the Chinese University of Hong Kong for his help, especially in correcting my spelling of Chinese names.

Chapter 18: An Ecumenical Community: The Origins of the Columbanus Community of Reconciliation

1. Cf. previous chapter for an account of other events in this ecumenical sabbatical.
2. Cf. chapter 15 *supra*.
3. This and the other letters and papers quoted in what follows are preserved in the archives of the Columbanus Community.
4. 'A Decade of Ecumenism', p. 27.
5. Cf. previous chapter.
6. G. S. M. Walker (ed.), *Sancti Columbani Opera* (Dublin: The Dublin Institute of Advanced Studies, 1957).
7. The text of this chapter first appeared in print, but without the postscript, in *One in Christ*, 30/1 (1994), pp. 61-74.

Appendix: Milltown Park Public Lectures 1960-1969

1. Published by Veritas in 1961 as a pamphlet entitled *Towards Christian Unity: An Introduction to the Ecumenical Movement*.
2. The compilation of this winter 1960 list was possible only with the help of all three sources named in footnote 3 of chapter 14. *IPN* merely gives the names of the three speakers who were members of the Milltown Park Community (Fathers Joy, Reilly and Simpson). *HD* gives names and topics but for seven evenings only, omitting Father Simpson. *BJ* has all eight names, topics, dates and numbers attending.
3. *Studies* 50 (1961), pp. 327-42.
4. *The Furrow* 14 (1963), pp. 212-24; 349-60.
5. *Irish Theological Quarterly* 31 (1964), pp. 132-49.
6. 'The Ecumenism Decree: Facts and Reflections', *Irish Ecclesiastical Record*, 105 (1966), pp. 12-126.
7. *The Capuchin Annual*, 35 (1968), pp. 107-20.
8. *Irish Theological Quarterly*, 35 (1968), pp. 58-72.
9. *The Clergy Review*, 52 (1967), pp. 770-86. This lecture was cancelled, cf. pp. 245-247 *supra*.
10. 'Thoughts after Lambeth', *Studies*, winter 1968, pp. 345-360.
11. The three sources consulted for this appendix do not make it possible to give precise dates for this session but these could doubtless be supplied from the daily newspapers.

Index

A
Abbott, Walter, SJ 203, 206, 207-208, 210
Acts of Oblivion, examples 62
Addis Ababa (UBS Assembly 1972) 208
The Adoration of the Magi (triptych) 339
Adult Education Committee (Dublin) 266
Africa, Catholic Institute of West Africa 320
After the Ceasefires: Catholics and the Future of Northern Ireland (1995) 356
Ahern, John, Bishop of Cloyne 274
Alexis, Patriarch, Russian Orthodox 44
The Alternative Prayer Book 93
America (Jesuit magazine) 208
America, Latin 218
America, United States of 30, 51
   American Bible Society 207
   Black and Irish Churches 70-71
   Boston Institute of Theology 276
   Church of Christ Uniting 38-39
   and religious liberty 211-212, 213-214, 216
Anglican Church (*see also* Church of Ireland; Protestant Churches)
   1918 Report on unity 349
   baptism 117-121
      rebaptism 128, 130
   Ceylon, church union and 35
   communities in India 318
   Congress, 1963, and anti-ritualism 93
   ecumenical initiatives 30
   Franciscan Friary 330
   marriages, mixed 45-47
   religious, and Columbanus Community of Reconciliation 324
   and the Roman Catholic Church 32, 45-46
      Eucharistic sharing 49-51, 132
   Tithe War 83
   unity, early commitment to 90
   Vatican II, response to 50
Anglican-Roman Catholic International Commission 15, 184
   Agreed Statement on the Eucharist 110, 143
   Final Report 2, 9, 186
   Joint Preparatory Commission 92, 36, 361
   marriage, mixed 96
   methodology of dialogue 33
Anglo-Irish Agreement (1985) 223
   unionist protest 229-230

Anointing of the Sick 49
anti-Roman Catholicism 151-152, 224-226, 188-189, 194, 205
Aquinas, Thomas, Saint 149
Arlow, William, Rev 192
Armagh Clergy Fellowship 233
Armstrong, John W., Bishop 275, 318, 232, 334, 361
Asia 348
Asian Congress of Jesuit Ecumenists 106
Assyrian Church of the East 32, 34, 352
Athenagoras I of Constantinople (1965) 40
Athos, Mount (*see also* Hurley Michael, SJ, Mount Athos (1980-81)) 41, 45
Atonement 171-172, 176
Augustine of Hippo, Saint 153, 158
Aurelius, Marcus 176
Australia
　Archbishop Little of Melbourne 327-328
　Crawford, Malcolm 328, 332
　Uniting Church 35

B
Balamand Statement 42-45, 353
Ballymascanlon Meetings 98, 231, 232, 337
Bangkok 208
Bank of Ireland 253-254
Bannside by-election (1970) 262
baptism 48, 153, 369, 165
　1968 Belfast lecture controversy 251
　Anglican 117-121, 127, 130
　Baptist Church and 116-117, 122, 126-127, 128
　of children 116, 121-122
　inter-church infants 123-125, 126
　Church of North India and 128-129
　and Church union 127
　Faith and Order Commission (Lima) 115
　post-baptismal sin 136
　postponement and original sin 130
　rebaptism 125-129, 165
　Roman Catholic Church and 121-122, 127, 129-130
　Vatican II 121, 123, 130, 131
Baptism, Thanksgiving and Blessing 119
Baptism Today and Tomorrow 364
Baptist Church (*see also* Protestant Churches) 116-117, 122, 126-127, 128
Bargy Castle, County Wexford 247
Barkley, John M., Rev 253, 275
Bartholomew I of Constantinople 23
　on the Balamand Statement 44
Battle of the Bogside, Derry 254
Battle of the Boyne (1996 commemoration) 191
Bayne, Stephen 182, 183, 379
BBC (Northern Ireland) 262, 278
　radio, *Sunday Sequence* 327
Bea, Augustin, Cardinal 200, 202-203, 290, 389
The Beadle's Journal 242, 387
Beasley-Murray, G R, Dr 116, 117
Beguin, Oliver, Dr 207
Belfast (*see also* Northern Ireland) 222
　1969 unrest 98
　Anglo-Irish Agreement (protest)

229-230
Belfast Central Mission 227, 340
Columbanus Community of Reconciliation 19, 318, 324-325, 333, 335-338
Daly, Cahal, Bishop 66-67, 68, 69, 228-229,
Edgehill 171
Lord Mayor's chain of office 20
Sandy Row 187
Shankill 187
St Anne's Cathedral 188
The Belfast Telegraph 242
Belgium 234
BEM Report (Baptism, Eucharist and Ministry) 115
baptism 129
Catholic influence on 38
sacramental doctrine of 167
the Eucharist 143
Benedictine Abbey, Glenstal 267, 330
Between Chaos and the New Creation 365
The Bible
on forgiveness 68-70, 72, 357
Protestants and 203, 204
the Roman Catholic Church and the United Bible Societies 206-210
pre-Vatican II 203-205
post-Vatican II 205
Biblical references
encouragement 18
Eucharist 141
forgiveness 72
getting the message across 327
gifts of the Spirit 17
God's forgiveness 69
hope 15, 16, 235
obedience and humility 31
prevenient grace 172-173, 174
proselytism 202
readiness 332
religious manifesting unity 319
this-worldly hope 18
tithing 83
unity 23
Bill for the Promotion of National Unity and Reconciliation (South Africa) 63
Bingham, William 235
Birch, Bishop of Ossory 261
birth control 247
Humanae Vitae 245, 251
Blake, Eugene Carson, Rev 277, 279, 289
Blanchard, Paul 205, 259, 381
Blease, Billy 281
Book of Kells 89, 94, 360
Boston Institute of Theology 276
Boyd, R. H. S., Rev Dr 290, 323
Boylan, Patrick, Rev 244
Boyle, Kevin 234, 382
Boys' Brigade 261
Bradley, Bruce SJ 263
Brennan, Jack, Father 387
Brennan, Martin, Father 243
British Council of Churches 24
British Government 98, 222-223, 234
Brown, Hastings 392
Bruce, Steve (sociologist) 224
Buddhism 311
Burton, John, Dr 280-281, 282, 392
Byrne, Archbishop of Dublin (1939) 27
Byzantine Rite Catholic Church 41, 44

C

Caird, Donald, Archbishop 96
Calvin, John (*see also The Institutes of the Christian Religion*) 68, 369, 372
   his Catholicity 147-148
   and the Eucharist 134
Callaghan, James 98
Canterbury, Archbishops of
   Carey, George L. (1991-) 66, 68, 69
   Fisher, Geoffrey F. (1945-1961) 349
   Lang, Cosmo Gordon (1928-1942) 26
Carmelites 240, 284, 385
Carpentier, René 58
Carson, Edward, Sir 230
Cassidy, Cardinal 2, 37, 39, 51, 354
catechumenate, the 115-116, 118-122, 130
Catholic Church *see* Roman Catholic Church
Catholic Emancipation Act (1829) 197
The Catholic Herald (London) 67
Catholic Institute of West Africa 320
Catholic-Protestant Working Group (France) 124
Catholic Spirit 180
A Caution against Bigotry 180
Cavanagh, Monica, Sr 332
Ceasefire (poem) 76
Celestine, Abbot 330
Centre for the Analysis of Conflict (London 1970) 280-281, 391 (1991) 234
Ceylon 35
Chillingworth, *Commentaries on the New Testament* (1597) 203
China (*see also* Hurley, Michael, SJ: China 1980-81))
   Assyrian Church of the East, mission 34
   divisions in the Catholic Church 307-308, 315-316
   The Patriotic Assocation 313-315
Christ
   Ascension 164
   sacrifice 31
   and social gospel 170
   sole teacher 150
   this-worldly hopes 19
   two natures of 33
   as unifier 25
Christian Order 197
'Christian Unity by 2000?' 349-350
Christianity and Crisis 217
Christians in Ulster 1968-1980 187, 230
Church of England *see* Anglican Church
Church of Ireland (*see also* Anglican Church; Protestant Churches) 93, 94-96, 98, 182
   across political borders 223-224
   and Columbanus Community of Reconciliation 318, 324, 334-335
   commemoration of disestablishement 251- 254, 257, 258
   Disestablishment Committee 264
   Dublin University Mission (India) 317
   and Forum for Peace and Reconciliation 233

and the Orange Order 186-196
and reform 184-186
Simms, George Otto,
    Archbishop 89-100
West Cork Clerical Society 267
Church of Ireland Gazette 91, 188, 257, 260, 361
Church of North India 128-129
The Church Times 67, 201
The Churches and Inter-Community Relationships 234
churches of Ireland *see* Ireland, churches of
Churches Respond to BEM 167
Churches Together in England 122
Cistercians 250
Civil Rights Association 227
Clarke, Richard, Bishop of Meath and Kildare 185, 379
Clement XI (Giovanni Francesco Albani) 204
Clement XIV (Lorenzo Ganganelli) 197
Clergy Review 246
Combined Loyalist Military Command 222
Coates, Richard, Rev 261
Code of Canon Law, Sunday obligation 85-86, 359
Code of Canons of the Eastern Churches 43, 353
Coláiste Iognáid, Galway 261
Coleman, John A 214
collegiality 154, 156, 158-160, 163, 186, 371
Collins, John, Rev 389
Colquohoun, Father 360
Columbanus Community of Reconciliation
    (*see also* Hurley, Michael, SJ,
Columbanus Community of Reconciliation) 19, 232, 269
Columbanus, Saint 325
Comiskey, Brendan, Bishop 327
Commentaries on the New Testament 203
Common Christological Declarations 33, 34
communism, effect of fall 41-42
common worship *see* Eucharist, the
Community Relations Commission 281, 282
comparative Christianity 108-109, 363
Congregation for the Doctrine of Faith 36, 80
conscience 8-9, 105
    as prevenient grace 171-175
Consensus Statement on the Doctrine of Justification 5
Constitution of the Church of North India 128
Constitution on Divine Revelation 206
Constitution on Fast and Abstinence 86
Constitution on the Sacred Liturgy 143
conversion 137-139, 204
Copleston, Frederick, SJ (1925) 26
Copts 32, 33
Corboy, James, Father 248
Cork, University College 256
Cornerstone Community 19, 232
corporate repentance 73-74
Corrymeela Community 19, 232, 326, 327, 328, 329
Council of Chalcedon (451), two natures of Christ 33
Council of Churches for Great

Britian and Ireland 221
Council of Ephesus 33
Council of Florence (15th century) 36, 41, 51, 105
Council of Trent 136, 204
Crawford, Malcolm 328, 332
Crisis for Baptism 364
Cunningham, Margaret 95
Cyprian, Bishop of Carthage 153, 159, 163
Czechoslovakia 245

D

D'Arcy, Martin, Father 242, 243
Daly, Cahal B., Cardinal 67
   and Columbanus Community of Reconciliation 333, 335-337
   and Irish conflict 66-67, 68, 69, 228-229
Daly, Gabriel, Father 75
Darby, Mary (psychiatrist) 329
Dargan, Joseph, SJ 321, 332
Declaration on the Relationship of the Church to Non-Christian Religions 173
Decree on Ecumenism (1964) 1
   ecumenism, importance of 104
   Eucharistic sharing 46, 49, 50-51
   on forgiveness and repentance 70
   hope 28
   inter-faith relations 8
   Orthodox Church 40
   proselytism 201-202
   reconciliation through stages 36-37
   theology 111
Decree on the Church's Missionary Activity 363, 367
Dei Verbum 206
Demetrios, Patriarch of Constantinople 298, 303
Derry 245, 254
Department of Theological Questions (IICM) 78, 232
De Valera, Eamon (1883-1975) 242
Devane, Andy (architect) 277
Dialogue with Roman Catholics (statement of Mount Athos Abbots) 307
Directory for the Application of Principles and Norms of Ecumenism 28
   baptism 125
   ecumenical formation 80-82, 290
   education 114
   Eucharist 48-49, 359-360
   marriages, mixed 48
Directory on Ecumenism in Ireland 113
Disciples of Christ, Church of 32
disunity (*see also* sectarianism) 1, 104, 182-183, 274
divine quality of the Church 146, 152-154, 160-161, 162-165
divorce (1986 Irish referendum) 217
Doctrine and Life 318, 323
Dodd, Romuald, Father 262
Dominican Sisters 266
Downe Society, Downpatrick 267
Dromore, Newry 267
Drumcree (1996) 191-192; (1997) 194; (1998) 196
Dublin (*see also* Ireland)
   1969 unrest 97
   Adult Education Committee 266
   Archbishop Connell 206
   Castle 258
   Christ Church Cathedral 15, 66

Divinity Hostel 360
Industrial Relations, College of 276
Irish Council of Churches 273
Lord Mayor's chain of office 20
Sandymount 89
social problems 16
Trinity College 91, 256, 261, 286-287, 392-393
University College 241
Dun Laoghaire 244
Dunlop, John, Rev 220
Dunn, Joe, Father 323
Dunstan, G R 276, 280, 391, 392

E

Eames, Robin, Archbishop, Church of Ireland Primate 190, 193-194, 233, 335, 384
ECONI (Evangelical Contribution on Northern Ireland) 232
Ecumenical Collaboration at the Regional, National and Local Levels 36
Ecumenical Directory (1967) 125
Ecumenical Formation: Ecumenical Reflections and Suggestions 80, 290
ecumenics 112-114
Ecumenics: What and Why? 270-271
ecumenism (*see also* unity)
  action, need for 1-2, 25-26
  action according to conscience 8-9
  crisis as inspiration 28-31
  discipline or dimension? 271-272
  early years of 90
  and the Eucharist 138-145
    as reconciliation? 137-140
  and evangelicalism 79, 199-203

fear 6, 32
forces against 2-4
  pre-1962 26-27
hope of 'second spring' 4
  signs of 18-20, 30
Michael Hurley's early commitment 265-267
inter-faith dialogue 106
John Paul II's commitment to 22-23; 28
marginal nature of 82
mixed marriages, opportunities of 46-48
Northern Ireland, reconciliation 231-233
and proselytism 199-203
'reconciled diversity' 183-185
reform of Churches 185-186
scepticism 52
sociological view 29
spirit of 78-82
and theology (general) 107-108
and theology (specific) 108-111
tithing 83-88
vision for the future, realistic 7-8, 9
ecumenists
  aims 105 -106
  and the Eucharist 139-140
  characteristics of 103-105
The Edge of the Union 224
education 33, 113-114, 169, 274
  importance of 81
  Milltown Park 248-249
Egan, Eamon, Father 243
Eisenmann, Annette 332
Ely Report, baptism 118-120, 121
Erraught, J., Father 243
Eucharist, the
  Agreed Statements 110, 143

Calvin and 134, 165-167, 374-375
as converting ordinance 179
and ecumenical tithing 84-87, 359-360
as missionary power 143-144
non-polemical view 140-142, 367
and Penance 135-137
as proclamation of salvation 142-143
before reconciliation? 137-140
and reconciliation with Church 133-134
sharing of 46, 48-49, 143-145, 232
   Catholic and Orthodox 41, 353
   Catholic and Anglican 49-51, 132
sociological view 145
and unity, as means or expression of? 132-133
European Ecumenical Institutes (1976) 107
Evangelical Roman Catholic Dialogue 194
Evangelicals and Catholics Together 365
Evangelicalism (*see also* Wesley, John) and Catholicism 146-148
and ecumenism 79, 199-203
mission through the Eucharist 143-144
Protestants and the Bible 204
excommunicated, reconciliation 133-137

F
Faith and Order Commission (*see also* WCC)
BEM document 115
and divine nature of the Church 147
Lund Conference 39, 109
Lund Report (1952) 8, 355
Nottingham Conference, 1980
unity target date 24-25
and Roman Catholic Church 37-38
theological debate 32
Familiaris consortio 48, 49
Faris, Professor 259
Faulkner, Brian (1969) 255
Ferrar, Michael Lloyd, Rev 89, 92, 360
Figgis, Allen 257, 263
Fisher, Geoffrey Francis, Archbishop of Canterbury (1960) 349
FitzGerald, Garret 223
For God and His Glory Alone 19
Forgiveness and Community 359
forgiveness
Acts of Oblivion, examples 62
Biblical references 68-70, 72
Shriver, Donald W., on 357
Church ministry, its part in 70-77
through forgetting? 62-63
justice and love 58-59
Lutheran/Calvinist dichotomy 68
of offender more than offence 57, 59
pessimism 358
towards reconciliation 7, 56-58, 60-62, 357
and repentance 58, 64-68, 70, 357
secular approach and

responsibility 73-77
Forker, Wilbert, Rev 279
Forum for Peace and Reconciliation 54, 220, 226, 355-356, 382
   Church of Ireland (1995 submission) 233
France
   Catholic-Protestant Working Group 124-125
   Taizé 54, 324
Francis X. Azhao, Bishop 308
Free Church Federal Council (1940) 26
Freedom, Justice and Responsibility in Ireland Today (1997) 232, 234
Freer, Doreen 322, 324, 329
The Furrow 246, 267, 271

G

Gallagher, Eric, Rev Dr 187, 230, 232, 323, 324, 339-340, 379, 384
Gallagher, Ernest, Rev 334
Gassmann, Günther 351, 354
Gazzada, Italy (1967) 90
Germany 51, 354
churches and fund-raising for
   Columbanus Community of Reconciliation 338-339
   Jesus-Bruderschaft (Evangelical) 317
Ghana 208
Gibbons, Jim 262
Gibson, Andrew, Rev 288
Gilleman, Gérard, SJ 58
Gillies, Donald, Rev 278, 390
Girls' Brigade 261
Girls' Friendly Society 261
Glencairn, County Waterford 250

God Save Ulster 224
Gonzaga College, presentation service, *Irish Anglicanism 1869-1969* 258-263
Good Friday Agreement (1998) 223, 235
Good, George, Rev 259
Goodall, Norman, Dr 25
Gort Muire (Dundrum) 385
grace, prevenient 171-178
Great Schism 1, 42
Greece (*see also* Hurley, Michael, SJ: Mount Athos (1980-81)
   Mount Athos 41, 45
   Russian Church in Exile 295
Greenhills 92, 267, 361
Gregg, Archbishop 94, 195
Gregory I (The Great) 158-159
Group des Dombes 57
Guiding Principles for Interconfessional Cooperation in Translating the Bible 208
Gwynn, Aubrey, Father, 99, 242

H

Habgood, John 276
Hadden, Tom 234, 382
Hagen, Odd, Bishop 389
Haire, J. L. M., 259, 334
   and ISE inauguration 279-280
Halifax, Lord 90
Hannaway, Róisín, Sr 340
Hanson, Anthony 184, 286-287
Hanson, Richard, Bishop 184, 287
Harryville Roman Catholic Church 178
Haughey, Charles 258, 262
Hayes, Maurice 258
   'controlled communication' 281-282, 392

Healy, Jim, Father 247
Heenan, John Carmel, Archbishop (1962) 27-28, 201
Hibernian Bible Society 207
Hickey, John (sociologist) 224
Hinduism 170
Hinsley, Cardinal (1940) 26
Höffner, Cardinal 339
Home Rule Bill (1913) 222
hope 4-5
   crisis as inspiration 28-31
   Decree on Ecumenism 28
   initiatives, present day 30
   John Paul II's expressions of 22-23
   other-worldly or this wordly? 16-17
   progress since 1925 26-27
   renewed interest in ecumenism 35-36
   theological dialogue, progress 31-35
   transcending optimism 18-19
Hotchkin, John, Father 38-39
Hsu, Francis, Bishop of Hong Kong (1968) 314
Hull University, recognition for ISE 286-287
Humanae vitae 245, 247
Hume, John 258
Hurley, Michael, SJ: China (1980-81) Beijing:
   Requiem Mass for Bishop Francis X. Azhao SJ 308; government regulations 308-309; Matteo Ricci tomb and sightseeing 309
   Canton:
     news of Dominic Tang Yee-ming 312; The Patriotic Association 313-315
   Loyan:
     Buddhism 311-312
   Shanghai:
     emerging Christianity 312
   Xian:
     the early Christians 310-311, 394; a Catholic cathedral, local hospitality and visit to the Great Mosque 311
Hurley, Michael, SJ: Columbanus Community of Reconciliation in 1998 340
   Eucharistic sharing 334
   financing 322, 338-339
   Germany, visit to 339
   inauguration (1983) 340
   inspiration for 317-321, 323-324
   Jesuit/Roman Catholic Church relationship (1981) 333, 334, 335
   location, search for 332-333, 336, 339-340
   media coverage 327, 328-329
   members
     search for 327-329
     preparation of 330-332
   name, choice of 325-326
   Patrons 325, 334-336
   publicity, drafts and leaflet 324-325, 327
   soundings 321-323
   Sponsors 326-327
Hurley, Michael, SJ, and ISE
   Blake, E. C., Rev Dr, invitation controversy 277
   'controlled communication' 280-282
   denominational independence 274-275

discipline or dimension? 271-272
early commitment 265-267, 269-270
ecumenical apostolate (1964-70) 267
Ecumenics: What and Why? 270-271
first years 289-290
floreat ut pereat 288
funding 272, 277, 282-287
gift of a crucifix 288-289
inauguration 277-280, 287, 289
Irish Anglicanism 1869-1969 269, 287, 389
universities' recognition 286-287
Hurley, Michael, SJ: Mount Athos (1980-81)
   Athens:
      talks with Metropolitan Rodopoulos and Professor Kalogirou (on Unity 2000); talk of anti-ecumenism and anti-Catholicism 306-307
   Dafni and Karies:
      conversation with monk of Russian Church in Exile, journey to Karies 295-296
   Dionisiou monastery:
      hears of anti-ecumenism at Philotheou and feels sadness at Roman Catholic/Orthodox relationship;
      contemplates penance; shocked by anti-ecumenism literature 302-303; contemplates isolationism in relation to anti-ecumenism 303
   Grigoriou monastery:
      conversation with a ex-Roman Catholic monk – more anti-ecumenism 304;
      contemplates effect of intolerance on Christianity 304-305;
      conversation with Abbot – more anti-ecumenism 305;
      reflects upon Orthodox negativity 306
   Iviron monastery:
      anxiety upon way 299; joins in Vespers and meets fellow travellers 300-301;
      talks with monk, sees library and wine-making 301
   Ouranoupolis:
      Metropolitan Rodopoulos on Orthodox antipathy; journey through Stagira; fellow travellers 293-294
   Salonica:
      idea of improved ecumenic relationship through other monks 306
   Stavronikita monastery:
      anxiety upon way and arrival 297;
      Vespers, discovers he is debarred 297-298; supper with monks 297; church locked 297; conversation with Greek visitors about anti-ecumenism 297-298; conversation with Father Simeon 298-299
Humanae Vitae 245, 251
Hyde, Douglas (1939) 27

I

The Identity of the Church 287
Ignatius Loyola, Saint (1491?-1556) 203-204
IICM *see* Irish Inter-Church

Meeting
India 317, 318
   Church of South India,
    formation 35
   Church of North India 128-129
L'Impossible Oecuménisme 2
Industrial Relations, College of
   (Dublin) 276
Institute for Ecumenical Research
   see
    Tantur Institute for
    Theological Studies
*The Institutes of the Christian
Religion* (see also Calvin, John)
   Ascension 164
   Catholicity 151-152
   the Church and the Bible 368-369
   collegiality 154, 156, 158-160, 163, 371
   discipline 154-158, 163, 166
   divine nature of the Church 152-154, 160-161, 162-165
   the Eucharist 165-167, 374-375
   the excommunicated 154-155
   God's forgiveness 153
   piety 167, 375
   sacraments 161, 164, 370, 372
   salvation and sanctification 149-151, 160
   schism 155-156, 160-161
Inter-Church Families, Association
   of 48
Inter-Church Group on Faith and
   Politics 73, 232
inter-Church marriage *see* marriage,
   mixed inter-Church relations
   8, 16, 349-350
   baptism 123-131
   'rebaptism' 125-127

Inter-Church Youth Agency (Youth
   Link) 233
inter-faith
   dialogue 106
   Inter-Faith Relations and ISE 389
IRA (Irish Republican Army) 222
Ireland (*see also* Dublin; nationalists;
   Northern Ireland)
   Anglo-Irish Agreement (1985) 223, 230-231
   Bank of 253-254
   divorce, 1986 referendum on 217
   Forum for Peace and
    Reconciliation 54, 220, 226, 355-356, 382
   Government (1939) 27
   justice and forgiveness 71
   mixed marriages 47
   partition 226-228
   reconciliation, role of Churches 232-235
   'the Troubles', root of 221-223
   and the World Catholic
    Federation
     (of Biblical associations) 208
Ireland Tomorrow (1969) 95
Ireland, Churches of
   and Columbanus Community of
    Reconciliation 326
   commemorating 1869
   disestablishment 251-254
   overcoming sectarianism 234
   Report on sectarianism (1993) 19
Irish Anglicanism (1869-1969)
   contributors and titles 255-257
   Columbanus Community of
    Reconciliation, looking
    forward 318

Gonzaga service, order of 259-262
guests 258-259
reception 262-263
and the ISE 269, 287, 389
and the political situation 1969 254-255
publication of 250-254, 257
The Irish Catholic (Dublin) 67
Irish Catholic Directory (1971) 269
Irish Congress of Trades Unions 281
Irish Council of Churches 232, 273
Irish Flour Millers' Association 272, 282-287
The Irish Independent 260
Irish Inter-Church Meeting(s) 78, 231-232
  Department of Theological Questions 78, 232
  Freedom, Justice and Reponsibility in Ireland Today 232, 234
  Sectarianism 232, 234, 359
Irish Jesuit Delegate meeting (1970) 271
The Irish News 220, 221, 223, 233, 337
Irish Presbyterian General Assembly (1965) 65, 72
The Irish Press 257, 266, 260, 261
Irish Province News 239-240
Irish School of Ecumenics (*see also* Hurley, Michael, and ISE) 56, 99, 184, 247, 388
  early years 293
  inter-religious dialogue 10
  inter-faith relations 389
  patrons 275-276, 284
  students (1970) 286
The Irish Times 233, 235, 246, 387
ISE *see* Irish School of Ecumenics

Islam 170
Israel 275

J

Jackson, Wyse, Bishop 264
January Unity Week (1981) 292
Jeffery, Keith 262
Jenkins, Raymond, Archdeacon 91, 361
Jesuits (Society of Jesus) (*see also* Milltown Park Jesuit Community) 218
  Asian Congress of Jesuit Ecumenists 106
  and The Bible 203-210
  Irish Jesuit Delegate meeting (1970) 271
  proselytism 200-203
  and Protestants 197-200
  religious liberty 211-217
  students 263, 386
  Thirty-first General Congregation (1965-66) 198
Johann-Adam-Mohler-Institut für Ökumenik (Paderborn) 271, 275
John Paul II (Karol Wojtyla)
  Anglican and Protestant Churches, hopes 45-46
  Anglican/Roman Catholic International Commission 33
  and Bartholomew I of Constantinople 23
  and Bohemia and Moravia 70
  and China 315-316
  Christian East, Apostolic Letter (1995) 23
  at Constantinople (1979) 21, 307
  corporate repentance 74
  Dives in misericordia (On the Mercy

of God) 58
ecumenical 'spring', Riga (1993) 5, 22
ecumenism, commitment to 21-23, 52
Familiaris consortio 48
justice and love 58-59
Manila (1981) 314-315
on mixed marriage 48
and Orthodox Church 40, 352, 42
Pannanhalma, cancellation 44
Reconciliatio et Paenitentia 56, 58, 60
Redemptor hominis 21
religious communities and unity 318-319
repentance and forgiveness 60
on Russia 42
Tertio millennio adveniente 74
'two natures' of Christ 33-35
Ut Unum Sint (On Commitment to Ecumenism) 5, 23, 28, 49
Year 2000, Apostolic Letter 5, 7, 22, 46, 52-53
John XXIII (Angelo Guiseppe Roncalli) and Archbishop Fisher 349
on theological dialogue 33
Joint Declaration of the Doctrine of Justification 354
Joint Working Group (JWG) 80, 290
Jones, Brynmor, Sir 287
Joy, Patrick, Father 239, 243
Judaism 56, 62, 224
The Jurist 359-360
justice
added aim of Columbanus Community of Reconciliation 324
and forgiveness 63, 71
love, importance of 58-59
and reconciliation 55-56
justification, doctrine of 51, 354

K

Kairos (1985) 55, 58, 60-61
Kalogirou, Professor 306
Katholisch-Oekumenisches Institut of Münster 107
Kelly, Michael J., SJ 385
Kennaway, Brian, Rev 192
Kennedy, Donald, Bishop 362
Kessler, Diane C., 80
Kilcourse, George 353
King, Martin Luther 245
Kondruisiewicz, Tadeusz, Archbishop 42
Konfessionskündliches Institut (Lutheran) 107
König, Franz Cardinal 52, 355

L

laity 241, 243, 246, 385
Tuairim, Cork 267
Lambeth Conference (1998) 5
Lang, Cosmo Gordon, Archbishop 26
Lapsey, David, Rev 326-327
Latin Rite Catholic Church 45
Latourette, Kenneth Scott 310
Lecky, Canon 326-327
Leeming, Bernard, Father 242
Lelièvre, Professor (Magee College) 258
Lemaître, Archbishop 339
Lennon, Brian 71, 356, 384
Lennon, James, Bishop 334
Leo I 33

Leo XIII (Gioacchino Vincenzo Pecci) 204
Letter to a Roman Catholic 389
Letterkenny Theology Project (1997) 355
liberality, Christian (19th century) 204
liberty, religious 211-219
Liechty, Joseph, Dr 73
Lima (1982) 115
Lindbeck, George 216
Lindsay, J. R. 263
Little, Archbishop of Melbourne 327
Lockner, Stephen (artist) 339
Londonderry, Lord 230
Longley, Michael (poet) 76
Looking for Justice: Liberation Theology in the Irish Setting 356
Lund
  Faith and Order Conference 39
  and ecumenical theology 109
  Lund Report 8, 355
Luther, Martin
  and the Eucharist 167, 372, 375
  and repentance 68
Lutheran Church
  doctrine of justification 51, 354
  religious liberty 216
  Riga (1993) 5
  and Roman Catholic Church 38
  theological dialogue 32
  World Federation Assembly (1997 Hong Kong) 354
Lyddon, Eileen Mary, Sr 332
Lynch, Jack
  in 1969 242
  and Irish Anglicanism 253

M
MacBride, Sean 389
Mac Gréil, Mícheál 386
MacCurtain, Margaret, Sr 323
McAdoo, H. R., Bishop 92, 361, 184-185, 186
McCann, Archbishop 92, 182
McCappin, Bishop 335
McCarron, Sean, Father 387
McDonagh, Enda 385
McGarry, Cecil, SJ 243, 244, 246, 259, 260, 387,
  and Irish School of Ecumenics 270, 273; 275
McGarry, J. G., Rev 267
McGimpsey, Christopher, Dr 192, 383
McGuinness, Catherine, Judge 191
McNamara, Kevin, Archbishop 256, 333
McNeill, J. T. 147
McQuaid, Archbishop 100, 241, 245-246, 259, 268, 273-274, 387
McShane, Philip, Father 243
Magee, Roy 233
Mageean, Bishop of Down and Connor 266
Maguire, D. P. 392
Maguire, Myra (National College of Art) 288
Malines Conversations (1921-26) 90
The Malta Report (1968) 36
marriage, mixed 45, 46-48, 49, 67, 96-97
  ecclesiastical censorship of article (1966) 246
  ISE's International Consulation controversy 277, 322, 389,

391-392
  and infant baptism 123-127
  Marxism 233
Mary Holland (journalist) 76
Mary, Blessed Virgin 34, 372
Maynooth College 257, 257
Maynooth Union 374, 375
Mehaffey, Bishop (1994) 66
Mercier, Cardinal 90
Methodist Church (*see also*
  Protestant Churches; Wesley,
  John) 9, 35, 223, 384, 386
  Belfast Central Mission 227, 340
  and Columbanus Community of
    Reconciliation 334, 335
  ecumenical initiatives 30
  Edgehill 273
  and *Irish Anglicanism 1869-1969*
    256, 259, 262
  reconciliation and Eucharist 134,
    366
  theological dialogue 32
  World Methodist Council-
    Roman Catholic Church
    International Commission 9,
    267
Metropolitan Rodopoulos 293-294,
  306
Milltown Institute of Theology and
  Philosophy 217, 239, 259, 275,
Milltown Park Jesuit Community
  (*see also* Jesuits) 11, 99, 100, 330
  fire of 1949 247-248
  site for ISE 276-277
Milltown Park Public Lectures
  (1960-69)
  accommodation 386
  censorship, ecclesiastical 244-247
  Church renewal 242
  dates 341-347

  funding 247-248
  Northern Ireland 'Troubles' 242
  origins 239-240
  speakers 240-241, 242-244, 341-347
  topics 242-244, 341-347
Milne, Kenneth, Dr 252
ministry (*see also The Institutes of the
  Christian Religion*) 70-77
mission *see* Evangelicalism
Molyneaux, James 194
Moorman, Bishop 361
Moravian Church 169
Morrow, John, Rev 326
mortal sin 135
Mulligan, John, Father 290
Mullane, Dan 272, 274, 392
Multi-Party Agreement (on
  Northern Ireland 1998) 223, 235
Mungret College, Limerick 262
Murphy, Laurence, SJ 252
Murray, John Courtney, Father 211-
  212, 213-214, 217
Muslims 311

N

National Council of Churches
  (1993 Hong Kong) 37
nationalists (*see also* Ireland)
  peace process 228
  politics 221-223
  religious dimensions 71, 223-
    224, 275, 382-383
Ne temere 90
Nelson, Robert A., Rev 259, 275
Nestorius 34
*The New Catholic Ecumenical
  Directory: A Protestant Reading*
  80-82, 359
A New Framework for Agreement; A

Shared Understanding between the British and Irish Governments 223
New Ireland Forum 383
  Report (1983) 229
The New York Times (obituary, John Courtney Murray) 211
Newbigin, Leslie, Bishop 25
Newe, G. B. 254, 281
Newman Society 267
Newman, John Henry, Cardinal (1852) 7
non-Christian faiths
  salvific role? 170, 178-179
  salvation through prevenient grace? 176-178
non-members of Church, reconciliation 138-140
The Norms for Priestly Training in Ireland 113
Northern Ireland (*see also* Ireland; Belfast)
After the Ceasefires: Catholics and the Future of Northern Ireland 356
  Bloody Sunday 287
  Community Relations Council 54
  'controlled communication' (1970) 280-282
corporate repentance and forgiveness 73-77
  Cultural Relations Committee 54
  Derry (1968) 245
  Battle of the Bogside 254
  Drumcree (1996) 191-192;
    (1997) 194;
    (1998) 196
  hope, signs of 20
  Judaism 224
  mixed marriages 47
  the Orange Order 186-196
  peace process 228
  political reconciliation, role of Churches 231–235
  Portglenone Cistercian Abbey 27
  Presbyterian Church 220-221
  Protestant attitudes 217
  'the Troubles'
    (1969) 97, 254
    (1993) 15-16
    roots of 221-222
    religious aspects of 221, 223-227
  Ulster Unionist Party 192
  Northern Ireland The Choice 234, 382
Nottingham (1964) *see* Faith and Order Commission

O

Ó Fiaich, Tomás, Cardinal 334, 339
O'Connell, Patrick, Father 240
O'Donnell, Edward, Father 336
O'Grady, Michael 243
O'Mahony, Clare 332
O'Rahilly, Alfred, Rev Dr 241
O'Reilly, Myles, SJ 330
Odlum, Norman 278
Odlum, Peter Desmond 272, 275-276, 283-284, 285
On Commitment to Ecumenism 5, 23, 28, 49
On Working Out Our Own Salvation 172, 173-174
One in Christ 48
Orange Order, the 232, 235, 257, 340, 186-196, 379, 380
Ordo Initiationis Christianae Adultorum 121
Oriental Institute 107

Orientale lumen 5, 40, 44, 45
Orthodox Church (*see also* Hurley, Michael, SJ: Mount Athos (1980-81)) 105
  anti-ecumenical mood of 3-4
  and Catholic Church 4-5, 21-22, 40-45, 105, 292-293, 352
  Divine Liturgy 85, 359
  internal divisions 43-44
  Mount Athos as exception 309-310
  theological dialogue 32, 33-34
Orthodox/Catholic Joint International Commission (1990) 42-43
Ostkirchliches Institut of Würzburg 107
Ottawa, St Paul University 246
Oulton, J. E. L., Professor 91

P

Paisley, Ian, Dr 200, 220, 225, 229, 262, 268, 379, 383
Patriotic Association, the (China) 313-315
Patterson, Carlisle, Rev 66
Patterson, Tom, Very Rev 324, 326-327, 331, 340
Paul Blanchard on Vatican II 381
Paul VI (Giovanni Battista Montini)
  and the Anglican Church 195
  Apostolic letter on Mixed Marriages 124
  Constitution on Fast and Abstinence 86
  Humanae Vitae 245, 251
  and the Orthodox Church 40
Pauline, M., Sr 241
Penance, sacrament of 49, 135-136, 137

Pentecostal Church
  baptism 126
  theological dialogue 32
Philbin, Bishop 335
Pius XI (Achille Ambrogio Damiano Ratti) 107, 133
politics and reconciliation 73-77
The Politics of Peace 357
Pollak, Andy 235
Pontifical Council for Promoting Christian Unity (see also Secretariat for Promoting Christian Unity) 37, 350
Portadown Times 381
Porter, Neil 241
Portglenone Cistercian Abbey 27
Presbyterian Church (*see also* Protestant Churches) 35, 232
  and Columbanus Community of Reconcilation 334, 335, 339
  and early years of ecumenism 268
  and Ireland 220, 223-224, 226
  and *Irish Anglicanism 1869-1969* 256
  and ISE's inauguration 277, 278-280
  theological dialogue 32
press releases, censorship (1962) 244-247
The Primacy of Charity in Moral Theology 58
Profit in Unity (1995) 29-30
The Programme of Priestly Formation 113
proselytism 42-43, 199-203
Protestant Churches (*see also* individual denominations) 45-46, 259

anti-ecumenicism (1970s) 278
and BEM 167
baptism 122, 127, 130
Catholic-Protestant Working
    Group (France) 124-125
and the Bible 203, 204
in China 312, 313
and Declaration on Religious
    Freedom 216
and divine nature of the Church
    146-147, 150
early years of ecumenism 268
ecumenical work 19
Eucharist 132, 141
sharing 46, 49, 50-51
and Jesuits 197-200, 202-203
and Latin America 218
mixed marriages 45-47
*The New Catholic Ecumenical
Directory – A Protestant
Reading* 359
in Northern Ireland 187, 218
reconciliation and Eucharist 132,
    134, 138
and Unionists 224-225
United Bible Society 206-208
unity, schemes of 35
Providentissimus Deus 204
publications commemorating 1869
disestablishment 251-254
Purdy, Bill, Canon 9

Q
Quakers 169, 171, 190
and *Irish Anglicanism 1869-1969*
    256

R
Rahner, Karl 32
Ramsey, Ian, Bishop 250

Reardon, Martin, Canon 364
Reardon, Ruth 354
reconciled diversity 38-39, 54, 104,
    183-185
Reconciliatio et paenitentia 56, 58,
    60
reconciliation (*see also* unity) 155
    Christian attitude 54-55
    through communities 35-36
    corporate responsibility 73-77
    of excommunicated 133–137
    forgiveness, importance of 70-73
    individual responsibility 57, 67
    at the expense of justice? 55-56,
        58
    of non-members of Church 138-
        140
    Northern Ireland, role of
        Churches 231-328
political approach and responsibility
    73-77
'reconciled diversity' 38-39, 54,
    104, 183-185
Scriptural 68-70
through stages 35-37
through repentance and
    forgiveness 7, 56-58, 60-68,
    357
terminology, problems of 55-56
Reconciliation in Religion and Society
    356
Redemptorist Congregation 233
Reflections on Sociology and Theology
    358
Reformation 1
Reid, Alex 233
Reid, J. K. S. 371
*Religion and the Northern Ireland
Problem* 224
renewal, Church 115-123, 242

repentance
  of Christian west 41, 42
  corporate 73-77
  and forgiveness 64-68, 70, 357
  Pope John Paul II's Jubilee letter 22-23
  Scriptural 68-70
  towards reconciliation 7, 56-58, 60-68, 357
  and salvation through prevenient grace 171-178
Reuck, Tony de 280, 281, 282
Richie, Mike 356
Riga (1993) 5, 22, 46
Riordan, Patrick, Father 217
Ripon, Bishop of (1967) 188, 279
Rogers, John, SJ 260
The Role of the Churches in British-Irish Relationships 383
Roman Catholic Bishops of Ireland, on corporate repentance 74
Roman Catholic Church across political borders in Ireland 223-224
  and the Anglican Church 32, 45-46, 50-51
  baptism 121-122, 129-130
  rebaptism 127, 129-130, 366
  Catholic-Protestant Working Group (France) 124-125
  and the Bible 203-205
  Bishops' Committee for Christian Unity (Heythrop 1962) 27
  and Calvinist Evangelicalism 146-152
  in China 307-308, 312
    and Patriotic Association 314
  ecclesiastical censorship 244-247
  ecumenism, early years 268
  Eucharistic sharing 49-51, 84-86, 132, 359
  in Greece 303, 307
  and *Irish Anglicanism 1869-1969* 261
  Irish Episcopal Conference 232
  and Jesuits 333, 334, 335
  Joint Working Group 80, 290
  justification, doctrine of 354
  and Lutheran Church 38
  and the Methodist Church 9, 267
  and Orthodox Church 4-5, 21-22, 40–45, 105, 292-293, 352
  Penance and Eucharist 132-137
  and Protestants 198
  reconciliation through stages, commitment to 36-37
  religious liberty 212-216
  theological dialogue 31-35
  and the United Bible Society 206-210
  and WCC 37-38
Roman Catholic Synod of Bishops (1971) 376
Roman Catholic-Pentecostal Dialogue 126
Rostrevor Christian Renewal Centre 232
Royal Belfast Academical Institution 262
RTÉ 242, 262
Runci, Archbishop 184, 379
Runciman, Steven 42
Rupp, Gordon 148
Russia
  and Constantinople 43
  foreign missions in 41
  Roman Catholic presence 42
Russian Church in Exile (Greece)

295
Ryan, Dermot, Archbishop 277
Ryan, J. Linus, Father 284

S

sacraments 161, 164, 370, 372
Sacred Congregation of the Council 87
Salford University, Catholic Chaplaincy 355
Salmeron, Alphonso, SJ 203
Salonica 293
salvation 160
    through prevenient grace 171-178
    and sanctification 149-151
Sandymount (Dublin) 89
Sayers, Jack 242, 386
schism 155-156, 160-161
Scottish Churches Initiative for Union 30
Scriptures, The *see* The Bible
Second Eucharistic Prayer for Reconciliation 54
Secretariat for Promoting Christian Unity (*see also* Pontifical Council for Promoting Christain Unity) 1, 36, 200, 208
    ecumenical training 271
    Roman Catholic-Pentecostal Dialogue 126
Sectarianism (1993 IICM report) 234
sectarianism (*see also* disunity)
    Northern Ireland 186-196, 220-227
    through ecumenical inertia 79
secularity, religious potency 233, 234
The Septuagint 208

Shenouda III (1988) 33
Shriver, Donald W. Jr 70, 357
Simeon, Father (Stavronikita) 298-299
Simms, George Otto, Archbishop (1910-1991) 360
    The Alternative Prayer Book 93
    Armagh (1969-1980) 97-99
    birth 90
    and the Church of Ireland 92-94
    ecumenism, commitment to 89, 90-92
    and *Irish Anglicanism* 1869-1969 252, 257
    as an Irishman 94
    visits to Milltown Park 99-100
    on mixed marriages 97-98, 100
    social message 95-96
Simms, Mercy 99, 100, 241, 243, 251
Simpson, Patrick, Father 243
Slevin, Gerard 288
Smyth, T. A. B., Very Rev 289
Sodepax 279, 392
Solemn League and Covenant against Home Rule 229
South Africa, Republic of
    forgiveness 63
    Kairos and repentance 60-61
    reconciliation at expense of justice? 55, 58
    Truth and Reconciliation Commission 54, 355
Spain, Santiago de Compostela (1993) 38
Spence, A. W., Dickson (Dickie Spence) 285
Statement on Baptism, Eucharist and Ministry *see* BEM

Stormont
   and *Irish Anglicanism 1869-1969* 254-255
   Multi-Party (Good Friday) Agreement (1998) 223, 235
Student Christian Movement 266
Student Volunteer Movement for Foreign Missions 24
Sullivan, Frank, Father 43
Sunday obligation 85-87
Sweetman, Michael, Father 244
Switzerland 208, 234
Sword of the Spirit 26
Synods
   Church of Ireland 98, 99, 384
   Anglican 120

T

The Tablet 39, 51, 67
Taggart, Norman, Dr 326-327, 340
Taizé, France 54
   and Columbanus Community of Reconciliation 324
Tang Yee-ming, Dominic, SJ 312
Tantur Institute for Theological Studies 271, 275, 355, 390
Taoiseach, the
   and *Irish Anglicanism 1869-1969* 253, 258, 263
   1969 broadcast 254
Temple, William, Archbishop 26, 357
That they may all be one: the call of the year 2000 355
Theological Education – the Challenge of Ecumenism 363
Theological Studies 213
theology
   denominational 111-112
   ecclesiastical censorship of

Milltown Lectures (1963) 244-247
   and ecumenism 104-105, 107-108
   ecumenism's own 108-111
   education 113-114
   limitations of 44-45
non-polemical character of 141-142
The Theology of Baptism 366
The Theology of Christian Initiation 118
Theology of Ecumenism 268
The Things that Make for Peace 359
Third World debts 356
Tithe War 83
tithing, ecumenical 83-88
Tomkins, Oliver, Bishop 185
Torella, Bishop 334
Torrance, Tom 276
Towards Christian Unity 266
Tridentine Decree on Justification 174, 176
Tridentine Rite 308
Trimble, Garry (sculptor) 289
Trinity College (Dublin) 91, 256, 261
   recognition for ISE 286-287; 392
Triple Vocation, Call and Response 388
Truth and Reconciliation Commission 54
Turner, Edgar, Canon 324, 326-327

U

UBS *see* United Bible Society
Ulster Unionist Party 192
unionists
   Anglo-Irish Agreement, protest 229-230

Milltown Park Public Lectures 241, 242
and partition 226-228
and the peace process 228
politics 221-223
and reconciliation 233
religious dimension to 220-221, 223, 228, 382-383
sociological view of 224-225
Unitatis redintegratio see Decree on Ecumenism
United Bible Society 206-210, 291, 381
unity (*see also* ecumenism, reconciliation)
1980 target date 24-25
by year 2000? 5, 7, 22, 46, 52-53
in Christ 25
through local activity (by stages) 51, 52
religious communities, importance of 318-319
through the Eucharist? 132-137
Unity in the Dark 278
University College, Cork 256
University College Dublin 241, 244, 245
Uppsala (1968), Sweden 6, 145
USA *see* America, United States of
Ut unum sint see On commitment to Ecumenism

V

Valera, De, Eamon (1883-1975) 242
Vatican II 15, 240
Anglican Church response to 50
on baptism 121, 123, 130, 131
The Bible, enthronement 259
Church renewal 239
Declaration on Religious Liberty 216
documents, Dehoniane Latin-Italian edition 55
ecumenical spirit 266
the Eucharist 143
and Evangelicalism 147
First Session, theological upset 245
and Irish Church Council 232
and Jesuits 198
Milltown Park Public Lectures and 248
and non-Christian religions 173
on Orthodox Church 40
penance in relation to reconciliation 54
reconciliation 54, 57
religious liberty 212-213
theological education 114
Victim Offender Reconciliation Programme 54
Vatican Secretariat for Promoting Christian Unity *see* Secretariat for Promoting Christian Unity
violence 71, 222
Violence in Ireland 231
Vives, Father 242

W

Wadding, George, Father 326-327, 340
Wagoner, Walter, Dr 276
Wales, ecumenical projects 30
Walker, G. S. M. 392
Wallace, Martin 241
Walsh, Bishop 67, 68
Ways to Community 38
WCC (*see also* BEM; Faith and Order Commission) 104

Index

Aarhus (1964) 1
Amsterdam Declaration on Religious Liberty 212
Bossey Institute 275
Central Committee Meeting (Paris) 266
on Church disunity 104
ecumenical apathy 2-3
Ecumenical Formation: Ecumenical Reflections and Suggestions 80
Evangelical spirit 147, 368
and Irish School of Ecumenics 278-279
Joint Working Group, with Roman Catholic Church 80, 290
mission and evangelism 170, 376
New Delhi Assembly 105
and Statement 185
and Orthodox Church 3-4
and Presbyterian Church 220
Programme to Combat Racism 278, 284, 285
religious liberty 213
and Roman Catholic Church 37-38
theological debate, multilateral 31-32
Towards a Common Understanding and Vision of the WCC 5
Uppsala (1968) 6
Wells, H G 292
Wesley, Charles 170
Wesley, John (*see also* Methodist Church; Evangelicalism)
Catholic Spirit 180
A Caution Against Bigotry 180
Letter to a Roman Catholic 271, 275
non-Christian salvation 176-178
original sin 171-172
other religions 179-181
prevenient grace 171-177, 176
response of sinners 175
social gospel 169-170
West Cork Clerical Society 267
Western Latin Rite monks 45
Westminster Government *see* British Government
Wilkinson, Margaret 332
Willebrands, Cardinal 1-2, 333
William III, of Orange 20
Williams, Trevor 327
Willis, Andy 257
Wilson, Bryan (sociologist) 29, 30, 145
women
increasing influence of 39-40
and *Irish Anglicanism 1869-1969* 256
ordination of 32, 50, 186
patristic idea of motherhood 161-162
World Alliance of Reformed Churches 267
World Catholic Federation (of Biblical associations) 208
World Council of Churches *see* WCC
World Methodist Council-Roman Catholic Church International Commission 267
Worrall, Stanley 187, 217, 230, 232, 379, 383-384
Wright, Frank 187

Y
Yarnold, Edward, Father 9, 51, 355
York, Archbishop of (1940) 26
Youth Link (Inter-Church Youth Agency) 233
Yugoslavia 233

Z
Zambia 385